DOSTOEVSKY

DOSTOEVSKY

The Making of
a Novelist

BY

ERNEST J. SIMMONS

Vintage Books

A DIVISION OF RANDOM HOUSE

New York

"Stagnation! O, Nature! Men are alone on earth—that is the misfortune! 'Is there a living man in the field?' cries the Russian hero. I cry the same, though not a hero, and no one answers my cry. They say the sun gives life to the universe. The sun rises and—look at it, indeed, is it not dead? Everything is dead, and everywhere there are the dead. Only men, and silence round them—this is the earth! 'Men love one another'—who said that? Whose command is that?" Mine. (Bitteret)

DOSTOEVSKY, *A Gentle Creature*

Preface

The present book—a study of the works of Dostoevsky—is an attempt to throw some light on
those factors that influenced his creative process
and his religious, political, and social thought.
Biographical material is used only when it seems
to contribute to this general purpose. Quotations
from Dostoevsky's fiction have been based on the
admirable translations of Constance Garnett, but
in every instance these have been compared with
the originals, and, when it seemed advisable,
changes have been made. All quotations from
Dostoevsky's non-fictional works—letters, notes,
and articles—have been translated, with very few
exceptions, from the Russian. Italicized words in
the quotations, unless otherwise indicated, are
in the originals. I am much indebted to my friend,
Mr. John Webster Spargo, for his careful reading
of the manuscript.

E. J. S.

Contents

Introduction

Nowadays it is considered critical heresy to accept any part of the doctrine Tolstoy expounded in *What Is Art?* It is none the less interesting to observe that he applied the fundamental proposition of this aggravating treatise—i.e. that art consists in the communication of feelings, as opposed to thoughts—to the works of his great literary rival Dostoevsky. On the basis of this absolute dichotomy Tolstoy concluded that the best art communicated the best feelings, and the best feelings, he believed, depended upon the religious perception of the age.

Tolstoy was not always generous in his judgment of Dostoevsky, but he did include his novels among "the best works of art of our time," because they communicated "religious feelings urging towards the union and brotherhood of man." And it is a curious fact that most of the critics of Dostoevsky ever since have been largely concerned with his religious feelings, with his constant search for God and world harmony.

Now art is not a temple of pleasure, but neither is it a church, and this emphasis upon Dostoevsky's religious thinking at the expense of his purely artistic accomplishments is unfortunate. Tolstoy was scornful of the inability of the educated public to differentiate between a true work of art, which does communicate feelings, and a false one, which communicates nothing at all. One sometimes loses patience with the critics of Dostoevsky for their persistence in failing to discriminate between the novelist and the religious philosopher.

To be sure, Dostoevsky has meant all things to all
peoples, and the number of things he has meant to
foreigners already comprises a literature that is perhaps greater in quantity, if not in quality, than any
that has been written about a modern author, with the
possible exception of Tolstoy. Dostoevsky is one of the
most original novelists in world literature, and this very
originality often makes it difficult to grasp the full significance of his major productions. A reading of his
best novels may leave one a bit bewildered or uncon-
vinced, but one always comes away from them with a
feeling of having undergone a deep and abiding experience, of having come in contact with transcripts
of life which have made one think.

America and nearly every country in Europe has
contributed to this vast literature about Dostoevsky
and his works. As one might expect, the Germans have
led all the rest. One German critic has gone so far as
to say that since Luther's time there has been no
greater spiritual influence on Germany than Dostoevsky. These are strong sentiments, and of course they
refer to Germany before the advent of Hitlerism. The
surprising fact is that the Nazis, with their uncanny
ingenuity in propaganda, have not exploited the obvious possibilities of torturing certain aspects of Dostoevsky's beliefs into a prophecy of their own declared
future world supremacy.

Since the Great War most of the Western European
critics of Dostoevsky have been chiefly concerned with
establishing his fame as a prophet. They regard him as
a complex of ethical, cultural, religious, and political
ideas in which they perceive a prophecy of a new life.
The symbol of a coming struggle against individualism,
he stands forth as the champion of a kind of spiritual
universalism. In easy generalizations they tag him as
the "great human heart," the "religion of the future,"
a "mysteriously mystical soul," and finally a "reservoir
of Christian love." Of course, the invariable solution
for the more difficult abstract problems created by

these critical metaphysicians is that handy epithet "Russian soul." Perhaps Dostoevsky set his future expositors a bad example by his own frequent and loose use of this phrase. We are all familiar, however, with the assured manner of non-Russian writers who employ the "Russian soul" to explain nearly anything good or bad that has come out of that country. Although enthusiasts may find more anthropological or religious justification for the existence of a Russian soul than an English or an Eskimo soul, it is safe to say that, if the phrase ever did mean anything originally, that meaning has long since vanished through persistent misuse.

A consequence of all this literature has been the creation of a kind of legend, which has served to obscure the fundamental direction of Dostoevsky's thought and to minimize the significant artistic achievement of his fiction. For instead of being disinterested endeavours to study his works, the efforts of many of these postwar investigators to make a prophet of him are merely subjective cultural wish-fulfilments. They saw in Dostoevsky a great creator of new cultural, religious, philosophical, and mystical beliefs, which would take the place of those destroyed by the Great War. They lost their own faith and ideals, and in Dostoevsky they found a panacea in his doctrine of love, in his belief in the goodness of the masses, and in the essential religiosity of the Eastern Orthodox Church as opposed to the decadent Roman Catholic Church. In their eyes Dostoevsky became the prophetic inspiration of their other idols—Tagore, Gandhi, and Spengler—who preached the decline of the West and the new life-force and wisdom of the East. These post-war critics did not share the fear of certain thinkers today who identify Dostoevsky's prophetic, messianic, and millennial exaltation with Lenin's famous phrase: "Let us turn towards Asia; we shall overcome the West by way of the East."

Russian criticism of Dostoevsky before the Soviet

Revolution was more varied in its approach and perhaps less tendentious in its aims. On the whole, the Russians never evinced the boundless devotion to him which has characterized his Western European critics. They were not particularly subject to the mesmerizing influence of the "Russian soul." From the very beginning, their deeper knowledge of the Russian character and of the social and political conditions that form the background of his novels lent a convincing authenticity to their studies. There exists the customary misconception among foreigners that Dostoevsky was not appreciated by his countrymen during his lifetime. The tradition of the "unappreciated author," whose great genius is not discovered until after his death, is an agreeable fallacy which we like to indulge in perhaps because it flatters our conviction of the perverseness of literary critics. No doubt the unhappy life of Dostoevsky, the long and bitter struggle he had with poverty, lends a greater enchantment to the posthumous success-story.

Actually, Dostoevsky achieved wide popularity during his lifetime. No young author of his future fame ever knocked his head so violently against the stars of success with a first production as Dostoevsky did with *Poor Folk*. The supreme literary critic and dictator of the day, Belinsky, went into ecstasies over *Poor Folk*, and he hailed Dostoevsky as even greater than Gogol, who was already among the immortals. Although Dostoevsky's fortune varied considerably after this first production, the great novels that followed, with one or two exceptions, were well received. Upon his death the tremendous public funeral accorded him was simply a fitting climax to a life of nationally recognized fame. This popularity was pretty generally reflected in the native critical appreciations of his novels during his lifetime.

For a short time after his death in 1881, Dostoevsky's fame suffered a partial eclipse. It was soon revived in the discussions of such critics as A. Volynsky, V.

Rozanov, and D. Merezhkovsky. More so than the Western critics, the Russians devoted their efforts primarily to Dostoevsky's own works. Closely reasoned studies of the novels and of the author's creative process were produced. Nor were the significant questions of politics, religion, ethics, and philosophy neglected, though the native critics did not study these matters in a vacuum, as it were; they investigated them against the background of actual conditions in Dostoevsky's lifetime. Despite many strictures, pre-revolutionary Russian criticism accorded Dostoevsky a secure place among the great novelists.

It has become a commonplace now to observe that the Soviet Revolution brought about a complete upheaval of values in things literary as well as in nearly everything else in Russia. During the period immediately following the Revolution, the tendency was to scorn anything that had to do with the old bourgeois art. Russia's great writers of the past were rejected, and the demand was for a new and vital literature that would embody socialist realism and serve the needs of the ruling masses.

All this, of course, was simply the destructive revolutionary fury of youth. The Soviets soon realized the value of their precious literary heritage and the need of learning from it and of building their new socialist culture upon it. And they found support for this stand in their hallowed texts of Marx and Lenin, for these leaders had been thoroughly aware of the value of the cultural past in constructing a revolutionary future. The new departure did not mean that socialist values in literature would be eschewed; the old would be preserved and whatever necessary would be appropriated, but the new literature would mirror the ideology of the Soviet State.

One by one the old Russian classics have been admitted to the Soviet hall of literary fame. To be sure, they must first undergo the purging fire of Marxian criticism, and in some cases the authors have been subjected to a course of posthumous political and social rehabilitation. For various reasons Dostoevsky does not lend himself easily to the Soviet methods of literary canonization. Lenin could not discover in him, as he did in Tolstoy, a "mirror of the Russian revolution." Gorky extolled his genius and compared him to Shakespeare, but on the other hand he condemned him as a "petty-bourgeois and defeatist," guilty of the unpardonable sin in Soviet morality of selfish individualism, which is as certain, Gorky characteristically concluded, "as there are no goats without a smell." In a foreword to the excellent Soviet edition of Dostoevsky's letters, a commentator remarks: 'An edition of Dostoevsky's letters in our day, intended for dissemination among broad circles of readers, may invoke a whole series of objections. And the first of these would concern the very need or even the possibility of a sale of Dostoevsky in Soviet lands in a period of cultural revolution and bitter struggle against mysticism, idealism, and decadence." Further on, however, this apologist reassures his conscience and his readers by declaring: "It would be absurd to force Dostoevsky upon the masses, but to know him is both useful and necessary among very broad strata of our intelligentsia, occupied as they are in the struggle with the class enemy on the ideological front."

There is more truth than apology in this last statement, for Dostoevsky has profoundly influenced several prominent Soviet novelists. His works are still widely read, and on occasions he has received official recognition from the State. Perhaps surer indications that he is still a living force in Russia are the new editions of his works, and the large number of popular and scholarly investigations of his life, novels, and journalistic writings. Since the war, however, the several works on Dostoevsky which have recently appeared in the Soviet Union have been harshly treated by the critics.

The chief difficulty that Soviet critics have to face

is how to reconcile the apparent reactionary nature of Dostoevsky with their own socialist ideology. Whatever he may have been in his youth, when he was sent to Siberia for radical activities, by the end of his life he was generally regarded as a reactionary, an admirer of the tsar, and a professed believer in the Russian Orthodox faith. This would seem to be sufficient to justify the least biased Soviet critic in leaving Dostoevsky undisturbed and safe in his pre-revolutionary immortality.

The character of Dostoevsky's mind, however, his manysidedness, the large comprehension he had of contemporary problems, and the curious, often double-edged nature of his conclusions easily lead some Soviet critics to doubt that he was an incorrigible reactionary. There is reason to believe that he profoundly understood the psychological elements of revolution, however much he may have misunderstood their actual manifestations in his own day. Revolt had a fascination for him, and despite his cruel attacks on the underground Russia of his time, one is surprised at the implied sympathy in his works for this underground plotting. Certain Soviet critics prefer to regard him as neither a reactionary nor a revolutionist, but both one and the other at the same time. This may seem paradoxical and irrational, yet a profound dualism, a struggle of opposing tendencies, was the special characteristic of his emotional, mental, and spiritual nature. This same quality appears in the heroes of his novels, whose strong will to rebellion is often pregnant with an equally strong inclination to reaction. What he condemns utterly is the liberal and petty-bourgeois revolutionist, a fact that Soviet critics have seized upon as an indication of his correct tendencies and as proof of the importance of his works as social and political documents of the age.

One conclusion, at least, is self-evident. The majority of critics have steadily persisted in regarding Dostoevsky as a prophet, a philosopher, a psychologist, or a social thinker, and not primarily as a novelist. Although this emphasis is easy enough to explain in the circumstances, it is well to remember the obvious fact that if Dostoevsky had regarded himself as a philosopher he would most likely have written philosophical books and tracts. Of course, he regarded himself as a novelist, and he should be criticized and appraised as a creative artist. When a loose critic like Middleton Murry says that the novels of Dostoevsky are not novels at all, and are considered such only by those incompetent to tell the difference, then one must come to the bewildering conclusion that all his life Dostoevsky thought he was writing novels when he was really not writing novels— much as M. Jourdain never realized that he had been talking prose all his life.

Now it is impossible to consider Dostoevsky as a literary artist entirely apart from the profound and original thinking he expressed through the medium of his creative works. An artist, however, creates life and not systems of thought, and hence it is a mistake to tag his thinking with any formal designation, for a wrong emphasis is bound to be the penalty. Thus, if the end of humanism is the perfecting of the individual, then it would be possible to call Dostoevsky one of the great humanists of the world. I hasten to add, before those pale critical ghosts of the recent past begin their gibbering, that he had nothing else of the humanist in him. It would perhaps be wiser to call him a humanitarian, a term which the modern humanists liked to reserve for those presumptuous fellows who only thought they were humanists. Nevertheless, there is much in both Dostoevsky's life and writings that either of these designations would only serve to confuse and to render inexplicable.

Like most creative artists Dostoevsky was not a consistent thinker. The rooted dualism of his creative spirit was reflected likewise in his political and religious thought. The constant warfare of conflicting forces in his soul never ceased, not even in those last years of his life when the conservatism of age and surfeit with the struggle turned his thoughts towards eternal peace.

Without attempting to formulate any consistent system of thought, we find it possible to trace the development and fluctuation of Dostoevsky's ideas. But this must be done through the medium of his creative works. The extent to which the novels reflect the whole course of his intellectual and spiritual growth has never been sufficiently insisted upon by critics. It is not simply that much biographical material is to be found in them, but his most cherished ideas and hopes, his thoughts about religion, politics, and international affairs are interwoven into the fabric of his fiction. With his letters and journalistic endeavours, such as *The Diary of a Writer,* as a constant check, one can ascertain, by a study of the short stories and novels, the true stature of the man. In the last analysis, it is Dostoevsky the artist with whom we should be concerned. As in the case of Tolstoy, his immortality rests upon his great masterpieces of fiction and not upon his philosophy. It is in his creative art, in a study of its inception and growth, that we shall find the key to the real Dostoevsky.

DOSTOEVSKY

I

Creative Beginnings

There is a continuity in an artist's total production that often evades the critic who is bent upon slicing and separating for purposes of analysis. Each work reflects the varied elements of the author's artistic consciousness much as each element of the individual's consciousness, according to Bergson, is tinged with the colouring of all the others. However, the latent danger in criticism of mistaking development for change may result in missing the continuity in artistic growth which is so important for an understanding of the author's complete creative personality. Thus critics of Dostoevsky often slight his youthful works, written before he was exiled to Siberia, in the belief that they are of little worth intrinsically, and because the supposed change he underwent in prison turned his creative efforts in a different direction. There may be an honest difference of opinion concerning the literary value of the early fiction, but it is certain that his later and more famous novels represent a consistent development of his earlier endeavours. Hence any attempt to study the creative art of Dostoevsky must concern itself, to some extent, with these early productions.

Dostoevsky was born in 1821, at a time when the poet Pushkin was just beginning to climb to fame, when Gogol had not yet been heard from, and when the mystical-minded Alexander I was still on the throne. In 1837, when the great Pushkin died, the sixteen-year-old Dostoevsky wept, for the poet was his hero at that time as he was with so many youths. Forty-three years later, when he delivered his thrilling oration at the unveiling of the Pushkin statue in Moscow, Dostoevsky had himself become the literary hero of Russia. Less than a year after this occasion he was dead.

Socially, the Dostoevsky family was perched insecurely on the lower rung of the Moscow middle-class ladder. The constant striving after respectability on the part of the father, an ex-army surgeon, betrayed his dubious position in society. The family had no pretensions to culture. In Dostoevsky's early youth, Russia was still enjoying her Golden Age of poetry, and the predominant foreign literary influence was that of romanticism. Yet none of this appears to have made any particular impression on the boy. Indeed, before he entered the engineering school, his education had been pitifully inadequate. He read Pushkin, Karamzin's *History*, and a few of the popular romantic writers, but the actual books assigned in the formal instruction which his father procured for him seem to have been mostly religious. The striking contrast between this early shoddy background and that of his later rivals, Turgenev and Tolstoy, indicates the significant social and cultural advantages which they possessed. They were noble born, and everything that was fine in Russian breeding and culture went to inform their youthful years. This disparity in social position and educational training had a decided influence on Dostoevsky's intellectual climate, and unquestionably upon his literary interests and the subjects of his novels, so utterly different from those of Turgenev and Tolstoy. Class distinctions in the Russia of those days were strongly marked and could be powerful determining factors in a novelist's career.

It would be wrong, however, to infer that Dostoevsky was an uneducated man. There is no need to labour the customary confusion between education and culture which results in the persistent fallacy that genius can dispense with formal instruction. Despite the common conviction that educational discipline is an obstacle to the free expression of a literary genius, the cases in which it can be proved to have acted as an insuperable barrier are hard to find. Once the opportunity presented itself, Dostoevsky indulged a natural fondness for books. Throughout his life he read enormously, and this broad, if undisciplined, self-education is fully substantiated by the unusual amount of knowledge he displays in his writings. It is true that he was never cultured in the sense that Russians employed the word in his own day. He did not have the fine taste and sense of artistic form which Pushkin, Turgenev, and Tolstoy possessed. These qualities, however, were almost as much a part of the accident of their birth and background as of their inherent talent. Dostoevsky had the talent, but circumstances had deprived him of the breeding.

At the age of seventeen, Dostoevsky was sent to a military engineering school at St. Petersburg. Once away from the stuffy, confining influence of his parents' home in Moscow, he began to manifest that high degree of intellectual curiosity which was a part of his intense nature. The engineering school, of course, was hardly an intellectual foster-mother for this avid nurseling. Here he received little else besides humiliating hazing, scientific studies, and endless dull drill, all of which he hated. Yet it was during this period that he plunged into a wide variety of reading and at the same

time began his life-long habit of sitting up half the
night poring over books by candlelight and taking mul-
titudinous notes.

Naturally, it was belles-lettres that he turned to at
once. Homer, Shakespeare, Corneille, Racine, and
Goethe were eagerly devoured. Gothic novels, which
he had perhaps tasted of in his childhood, now vicari-
ously satisfied his youthful delight in adventure. The
lurid fiction of Ann Radcliffe, "Monk" Lewis, Maturin,
and Hoffmann had a great vogue in Russia, and he
succumbed to the charm of their weird melodramatic
scenes. Other novelists were not neglected, such as
Scott, Balzac, George Sand, Victor Hugo, and Eugène
Sue; and the popular romantics, Rousseau, Byron,
and Schiller, were read, the latter with a youthful enthusiasm that Dostoevsky retained for years. His interest in foreign literature did not prevent him from
paying equal attention to native authors at this time.
Besides the poets Derzhavin, Zhukovsky, Pushkin,
and Lermontov, he read Russian historical and fiction
writers, such as Karamzin, Narezhny, Zagoskin, and
Gogol.

The predominance of authors of the romantic period among these early favourites is significant. Although one generally regards his novels as realistic,
the romantic elements in them are considerable and
important. There can be no question that this youthful
reading encouraged his taste for the melodramatic,
and suggested those plots of adventure and crime
which he adorned with the original element of philosophical dialogue.

The stimulation he received from this intensive
reading is fully reflected in the glowing letters he
wrote at this time to his older brother Mikhail, who
was then a student at Reval. To be sure, he mistakes
enthusiasm for serious judgments and lays about him
with a fierce critical flail, but his ecstatic schoolboy reactions are of the forgivable type. Victor Hugo as a
lyric poet he holds greater than Schiller or Shake-

speare, whose sonnets he had read in French. Only Homer is worthy of comparison with the French poet. Schiller, however, he knew by heart, and he swears that nothing more significant could have happened to him than to "learn of this great poet at such an epoch in my life." A new world was opening up before him. The career of military engineer grew more and more unattractive as the secret wish to be a writer took hold of his expanding mind. He felt that he had something to say, and he began to study how best to say it. The pleasure of contemplating the career of writing was somewhat dampened by the uncertainty of success and by the lurking fear that he was lacking in talent. But youth is ever unwise in the material concerns of life, and impracticality becomes a positive asset in the game of chance in which glory is the stake. By 1843, when he had finished his studies, every notion of becoming a military engineer had vanished. He would be a writer! His mind was full of plans for great works. He had already translated Balzac's *Eugénie Grandet*, and a story of his own was fermenting. A year after graduation he resigned from the army. Literature had his heart in tow, and, of more consequence at the moment, his purse.

In September 1844, in the course of discussing various translation schemes in a letter to Mikhail, Dostoevsky suddenly interpolates: "Here is my hope. I am finishing a novel of the size of *Eugénie Grandet*. The novel is rather original. I am already copying it . . ." [1] This is the first mention we have of *Poor Folk*, Dostoevsky's initial attempt at fiction. The succeeding references to it in his letters indicate the extensive effort he bestowed on the novel, and the excessive fear of the beginner over its chances of success. The impression exists that he was hurried in his workmanship and quite blind to the niceties of form and style. It is true that during most of his writing life he was obliged to work with haste, often under the pressure of an immediate need for funds—circumstances that frequently betrayed him into slipshod performances. On the other hand, it would be a great mistake to imagine that Dostoevsky did not possess the genuine artist's profound feeling for every detail of his work. Essentially he belongs to that group of authors who are much more interested in what they are saying than in how they say it. No doubt his novels would gain from pruning, but they might also lose some of the direct, nervous, impulsive quality which contributes so much to make them stimulating reading. However, it is of consequence to observe that at the beginning of his career he displayed the infinite capacity for taking pains with his art that is one of the hall-marks of genius.

Thus, in the next letter to his brother, he writes again about his novel: "I had just about finished it in November, but in December I took it into my head to recast the whole: I recast and recopied, but in February I began again to strip it, pick it bare, to insert, and to omit. About the middle of March I was ready and satisfied." [2] Yet his artist's conscience was not really satisfied. He still found "terrible deficiencies" in *Poor Folk*. As late as May he again writes to his brother about the novel: "I took it into my head once more to correct it and, by God, for the better . . . But now it is finished and this is the last correction." [3]

The finished manuscript did not easily find a publisher. There were delays. He could print for the glory of it, without remuneration, not an unusual condition laid down by Russian publishers in those days in the case of first productions. "But what is glory to me when I write for bread!" [4] he complained. It was a complaint that was to sound like a litany through most of his writing career. He could hire himself out to do hack work, but with the bravado of youth he scorned this form of artistic prostitution of his talents. "I wish," he proudly declared, "that every production of mine should be distinctly fine." And he fortified this stand by recalling that Pushkin and Gogol had received top prices for their works and had published only when they were ready, even though, especially in the case of Gogol, fame was achieved only after years of hunger and poverty. These pious exaggerations did not sustain him for long, and time and experience in such matters eventually softened the stern artistic code of the neophyte.

The happy accident that finally brought about the publication of *Poor Folk* is one of the best-known stories in the annals of Russian literature. Thirty-two years after the incident, Dostoevsky recalled it with extraordinary freshness in his *Diary of a Writer*. His account is worth translating with some fulness:

At the beginning of winter I suddenly began *Poor Folk*, my first tale, not having written anything up to this time. The tale being finished, I did not know what to do with it or whom to give it to. I had no literary acquaintances at all apart from perhaps D. V. Grigorovich, but he had not yet written anything, except a certain short article, 'St. Petersburg Organ-grinders,' for a miscellany. It seems he was then getting ready to go to his village for the summer, but for some time he had been living with Nekrasov.[5] While on a visit to me he said: 'Fetch your manuscript (he himself had not yet read it). Next year Nekrasov wants to publish a miscellany. I shall show it to him.' I brought it, saw Nekrasov for a minute, and we shook hands. I was abashed at the thought that I had come with my own work, and I quickly departed, hardly speaking a word to Nekrasov. I thought little about success, and I was afraid of this 'party of the *National Notes*'[6] as they then spoke about it. I had been reading Belinsky with enthusiasm for several years, but he seemed menacing and fearful to me—'and he will ridicule my *Poor Folk!*' I thought at times. Yet, I wrote it with passion, almost with tears—'is it possible that all this, all those minutes I have lived over this tale with my pen in hand—that all this is a lie, a mirage, a false feeling?' But no doubt I thought thus only for a few minutes, and my anxiety immediately revived.

On the evening of the very day I had handed over my manuscript, I went some distance away to one of my former comrades; we talked the whole night about *Dead Souls* and read it, up to what time I do not recall. There was then

a custom among youths; two or three of us would gather:
'Gentlemen, why don't we read Gogol?' And we would sit
and read, if you please, all night . . . It was four o'clock
when I returned home in the Petersburg night, as white
and bright as day. It was beautiful balmy weather, and,
entering my apartment, I did not sleep but opened the
window and sat by it. Suddenly the bell rang, surprising
me very much, and there were Grigorovich and Nekrasov
rushing to embrace me, quite in ecstasy, and both almost
in tears. They had returned home early that evening, taken
my manuscript, and begun to read it to try it out: 'In ten
pages it will be obvious.' But after ten pages they decided
to read ten more, and then, not being able to leave it, they
sat the whole night until morning, reading aloud by turns
as one got tired . . . When they finished they decided
with one voice to come to me at once. 'What if he is asleep?
We will wake him! This is superior to sleep!' . . . They
remained with me for half an hour, and for that half hour
God knows how much we discussed, understanding one
another with half-words, hurrying along with exclamations;
we talked about poetry, truth, about the 'present situation,'
no doubt about Gogol, quoting from the *Revizor* and *Dead
Souls*, but chiefly about Belinsky. 'Today I shall bring him
your tale and you will see—ah, indeed, what a man, what
a man! You will be introduced, you will see what a soul he
has!' Nekrasov rapturously said, grasping my shoulders
with both his hands. 'Well, now, go to sleep, go to sleep,
we are leaving, but tomorrow come to us!' As though I
could sleep after this! What rapture, what success, but
chiefly, the feeling that was precious I clearly remember:
'For some there is success, they praise, they meet, they
congratulate, but they had run to me with tears at four
in the morning to wake me up because this was superior
to sleep. Ach, splendid!' This is what I thought. How could
I sleep! [7]

True to his word, Nekrasov showed the manuscript
of *Poor Folk* to Belinsky, presenting it with the por-
tentous announcement: "A new Gogol has appeared!"
But the stern critic coldly countered: "With you Go-
gols spring up like mushrooms." When Nekrasov returned that evening, however, the critic, "in agitation,"
demanded that the author be brought at once. The

shy Dostoevsky appeared before the "menacing and fearful" Belinsky. His important mien and natural reserve quickly vanished as he harangued the young author: "Do you really understand what it is that you have written! You only with your immediate sense, as an artist, could have written this, but have you yourself comprehended all this terrible truth that you have shown us here? It is not possible that you, with your twenty years, can have understood this." Then in a torrent of words he extolled the infallible artistic instinct with which Dostoevsky had revealed the hidden nature of his hero, how by the most inconspicuous details he had brought out the tragedy of the wretched copying clerk. And with flashing eyes he concluded: "That is the secret of high artistic value, that is truth in art! That is the artist's service to truth! The truth has been revealed and announced to you as an artist, it has been brought as a gift; value this gift and remain faithful to it, and you will be a great writer!"

Enraptured, the young Dostoevsky departed. Over the long passage of years he recalled the sensation of his heart at that moment:

I halted at the street corner by his house, looked up at the heavens, at the bright day, at the people passing, and at everything, and felt with all my being that a solemn moment had occurred in my life, changing it forever, that I had begun something entirely new, but something that I had not surmised even in my most passionate dreams (I was then a passionate dreamer). 'Can it be possibly true that I am so great,' I shyly thought with a certain timid rapture. O do not laugh, because later I never thought that I was great; but then, was it possible to withstand it! . . . I recall that moment with complete clarity. And never could I forget it. It was the most delightful moment in my whole life. In prison, recalling it, it strengthened my spirit. Now I still recall it with rapture every time.[8]

2

Poor Folk

It has become traditional for famous authors to disparage their early artistic efforts. Not infrequently, however, an initial performance bears the impress of future greatness, as well as the youthful faults that time and fully developed talent never entirely eliminate. Dostoevsky, on the other hand, never ceased to recall with pride and pleasure the publication of his first work. Critics hailed *Poor Folk* as something new. The story was suffused with a mood that came to be regarded as characteristically Dostoevskian. The language and thought, and particularly the treatment, bore little relation to what had preceded in Russian fiction and were quite unlike Tolstoy. In his first production Dostoevsky hit upon the exceptional modernity which brought him closer to the more popular writers at the beginning of the twentieth century—Andreev, Artsybashev, and Gorky—than to the writers of the classical period in Russian literature.

The narrative of *Poor Folk* is not easy to follow. Apart from the interpolated fragmentary diary of the heroine, the story is told in an exchange of letters between Makar Alekseevich Devushkin and Varvara Alekseevna Dobroselova. The names were obviously selected with care. The Russian *devushka* means a "young girl" or a "maid," and its application in Devushkin's name suggests the virtuous and virginal aspects of his character. And the first part of Dobroselova connotes the Russian word *dobry*, which means "good," "kind," "gentle," adjectives that are precisely descriptive of the nature of the heroine.

Devushkin, a man presumably middle-aged, is a copying clerk employed in the government service. He appears to have had a smattering of education, likes to read, and is an extremely faithful civil servant. His whole life is centred in himself, in his work, and in Varvara. Although the dominant strain in his nature is obsequiousness, at times he grows querulous over his humble lot and is quite capable of resenting it.

Varvara is a girl of twenty-five, attractive but sickly. From her diary we gather a few hazy facts about her life. At the age of twelve she had moved from the country to St. Petersburg with her parents. For a time she attended a boarding school, but she had to give this up because the family fell into debt and the father died. Mother and daughter were taken in by a distant relative, Anna Fedorovna, a dominating female who treated her pensioners harshly. In the home boarded also a poor student, Pokrovsky, and his story and that of his drunken father are told in some detail. Although only a girl of fifteen at the time, Varvara developed considerable feeling for Pokrovsky which was eventually reciprocated. But the student suddenly died. Shortly after, Varvara's mother died, and the daughter continued to live on with Anna Fedorovna, who tried to interest the girl in her friend Bykov, a wealthy landowner. Bykov's proposals, however, were not honourable, and Varvara was obliged to flee the house with her old servant Fedosiya. Meanwhile, they try to make both ends meet by sewing, and all the time Varvara is persecuted by the malicious gossip of Anna Fedorovna and the dishonourable attempts of Bykov. It is at this point that the correspondence between her and Devushkin begins.

The letters give us very little insight into what is taking place in the separate lives of the hero and heroine or in their relationship to each other. We learn simply that Devushkin is desperately poor and is struggling in an impractical way against all the forces of poverty that are beating him down. His feeling for Varvara appears to be purely platonic, almost fatherly. He writes to her about the people in his rooming-house and of his miserable situation in the office, where fellow-workers heap insults upon him. Continually he complains of his degraded position, and we learn also that he has occasional lapses when he takes to drink in an effort to forget his sorry plight.

Varvara's few letters are even less revealing, and it is clear that she exists primarily to bring out the character of Devushkin. She asks his advice in everything, tells of her efforts to earn a livelihood, of her frequent illness, and of the persecution of Anna Fedorovna. Although she plies Devushkin with invitations to come and see her, for the most part he seems to prefer to write her letters.

Their curious but harmless intimacy becomes the subject of gossip among the neighbours. Varvara fears for her reputation, and Devushkin seeks the consolation of drink and sinks still deeper in poverty. When everything seems utterly hopeless, his superior calls him in for a reprimand, but, touched by his wretched situation, gives him a gift of a hundred rubles.

After this piece of good fortune, Bykov turns up again and this time offers Varvara a proposal of marriage. His change of heart is dictated by the unsavoury reason that he now desires an heir in order to frustrate the expectations of his relatives. Although she has many misgivings, Varvara consents because it is her only escape from poverty. At first Devushkin concurs, and she employs him to run errands in preparation for the marriage. After the ceremony, however, he is heartbroken and writes Varvara a farewell letter. He suddenly seems to realize that his love for her is not entirely platonic, or that his lonely life will be unbearable without her. In his final letter he frantically beseeches Varvara not to go away with her husband, not to forget him.

This brief and bald outline of *Poor Folk* does not suggest the complexity of the narrative, but it provides the necessary material for an analysis. The modern reader finds it impossible to share the extraordinary enthusiasm of Belinsky over the tale. Such a difference of opinion, however, should carry no reflection on Belinsky's powers as a critic. In most cases his judgment was uncommonly correct. Critics are inevitably circumscribed by their times, conditioned by all the temporal factors that undermine the judgments of men in matters affecting the future. In truth, there was not a little justification for Belinsky's approval, and one must admit that his prophecy of Dostoevsky's great future, amazing enough on the basis of an author's first performance, has been amply fulfilled. The justification was precisely the result of these temporal conditioning circumstances, for against the background of the development of Russian fiction up to that time, Belinsky had some cause to be enthusiastic over *Poor Folk*.

When Dostoevsky began writing, the development of Russian fiction could in no sense be compared to that in the countries of Western Europe. In the eighteenth century the magnificent flowering of the realistic novel of manners in England and to some extent in France had no counterpart in Russia. And many Western European novelists of the nineteenth century had already achieved international fame by the time *Poor Folk* appeared.

As a matter of fact, during the last half of the eighteenth and the first half of the nineteenth century, Russians had been more or less content to read the originals or translations of English, French, and German novelists. Imitations of these foreign works were written, but, with few exceptions, they never rose above the level of mediocrity.

Some twenty years before Dostoevsky's *Poor Folk*, Pushkin's *Eugene Onegin* began to appear, and it is not entirely a paradox to say that this famous narrative poem was the first Russian realistic novel. Pushkin liked to regard his poem as a novel, and it contains the first thoroughly realistic group of characters in Russian literature and the first realistic picture of Russian life. Further, in the persons of its hero and heroine, Pushkin created types that were to have a profound and lasting influence on the future course of the Russian novel. This same talent for realistic characterization and detailed descriptions of Russian life Pushkin projected into his prose stories, such as the *Tales of Belkin* and *The Captain's Daughter*. In short, in his realism, in the type of characters he created—the landowning gentry—in his best studies of the life of country estates, and in his terse, clear, unadorned prose, Pushkin may truthfully be said to have inaugurated a school—the Classical Realistic School of the Russian novel. One detects an obvious similarity in the fiction of Pushkin, Turgenev, and Tolstoy. The style and form of each seem to make a logical transition from one to the other, changing, of course, over the years, and growing in depth and impressiveness, but remaining essentially the same throughout. The directions of composition and the simplicity of the artistic development of themes are the same. And the Eugene and Tatyana of *Eugene Onegin* reappear with variations in the works of Pushkin's followers, as does also the quiet provincial life of the landed gentry to which class these characters belong.

Dostoevsky, on the other hand, does not belong to

this traditional development of the Classical Realistic
School. He had very little in common with Pushkin,
Turgenev, Tolstoy and their many minor followers. On
all his works lies the impress of a powerful individuality, opening up its own special paths. Anyone reading
his novels for the first time is struck by this special
feature of originality. You may be uncertain about
your admiration for him, but you always feel that before you is an artist whose like you have not encountered before. Between him and the novelists of the
Classical Realistic School there is an impassable gulf.
Not one general feature of Dostoevsky's novels resembles anything in the works of these other writers.

Although Dostoevsky's originality is more than suggested in *Poor Folk*, it must not be supposed that his
first production was totally uninfluenced by previous
fiction. The question of this influence throws a good
deal of light on his creative method in its initial stage
of development. Nekrasov had been quick to see in
him another Gogol, and on the strength of *Poor Folk*
Belinsky did not hesitate to include its author in the
Naturalistic School of Russian fiction (he used this
term to describe Gogol and his followers). The distinction, however, is not entirely justified, for in many respects Gogol was also a follower of Pushkin. He too
returns to the historical past or treats the provincial
land-owning gentry. However, there were certain externals in Gogol's literary method and a few important
characters and tales which patently distinguish him
from the followers of Pushkin. Now it is exactly in
these features that he chiefly resembles Dostoevsky,
and Belinsky had them in mind when he dubbed Gogol
the founder of the Naturalistic School and Dostoevsky
one of his followers.

In *Poor Folk*, the hero is concerned with the subject
of literature to a surprising degree, and the significance
of this fact has perhaps not received sufficient attention from critics. About half of Devushkin's letters contain references to his reading and his opinions on the

style and content of these works. He even dreams of a career of writing. Although Dostoevsky has been praised for his objective approach in *Poor Folk*, so unusual in the initial production of a young author, it is clear that he is projecting himself in describing Devushkin's yearning after the career of authorship and in his judgments on matters of literary taste.

Two short stories that Devushkin singles out for special comment are Pushkin's "The Station Master" (1830) and Gogol's famous "The Overcoat" (1842). The first is a distinct exception to Pushkin's usual vein, for in this tale he is concerned with the sad fate of lower-class people. It is the story of an army officer's seduction of the pretty young daughter of a humble station master whom he encounters on the post road. With deep feeling and sympathy, Pushkin describes the seducer's cruel treatment of the heart-broken father and the subsequent death of the lonely old man from drink after the loss of his daughter. The tale makes a powerful impression on Devushkin because of its simple subject and characters, and because it is all so natural and lifelike. He identifies himself with the aggrieved father and almost weeps over his unhappy fate. This is obviously Dostoevsky's own opinion, and it is just such simple, lowly people, crushed by circumstances, that he portrays in *Poor Folk*. His method, however, is entirely different.

The humble people and sympathetic treatment in "The Station Master" were exceptional for Pushkin and do not appear again in Russian literature until Gogol's "The Overcoat." With him, too, they were somewhat exceptional, but they were features of his art that most charmed Belinsky. He discovered these same features in *Poor Folk* and promptly accepted the author as a follower of Gogol and a member of the Naturalistic School.

The hero of "The Overcoat" is also a ragged copying clerk, and he has sunk still lower than Devushkin in the scale of downtrodden mortals. For him all ambition is dead. He has so completely forgotten life that he accepts his beggared condition as entirely normal, and his whole existence is devoted to his menial task, to submissive drudgery. Like Devushkin, he is the butt of the ridicule and offensive remarks of his fellow-workers. A semblance of hope enters his life over the thought of purchasing a new overcoat. With infinite sacrificing and saving, the fine fur-collared coat is eventually obtained. Almost at once the humble clerk takes on a new dignity with his new garment, and his comrades, and even his superiors, appear to treat him with a respect he had never known before. His circumscribed life now becomes wholly centred in the miracle-working overcoat. Then one cold night he is suddenly set upon by thieves as he is going home from a party, and the overcoat is stolen. With it goes all his interest in living, and the poor clerk takes to his bed and dies.

The copying clerk in Gogol's story undoubtedly influenced Dostoevsky's conception of Devushkin. But apart from a general similarity, in human tendencies, in surface features, and in a few details, the influence does not go any further. Of course, there is also the possibility that the significant part that the overcoat plays in the life of Gogol's hero suggested the psychologically similar situation that arises out of the important role that Varvara plays in Devushkin's existence. All through his life, and especially in this early period, Dostoevsky had a boundless admiration for Gogol, and his first productions unquestionably owe something to the inspiration of the older writer. Yet he was severely critical of Gogol and, perhaps because of the commonly accepted notion that he was an imitator, he takes every occasion to point out the differences between them. Certainly any detailed comparison of "The Overcoat" and *Poor Folk* at once brings out the originality of Dostoevsky's method. He puts in Devushkin's mouth a pointed criticism of Gogol's tale. He condemns the whole situation as an "insignificant example from vulgar, everyday life." And he continues, "Why, it is a book of an evil tendency, Varenka; it is untrue to life, for there cannot have been such a clerk."

It is clear that what Dostoevsky essentially objects to in "The Overcoat" is that the hero is a mere externalization, whereas all Dostoevsky's emphasis in the characterization of Devushkin is in psychological analysis. Belinsky also recognized this fact. In a letter to his brother at this time, Dostoevsky comments upon *Poor Folk:* "Some find the novel prolix, but there is not a superfluous word in it. They (Belinsky and others) find in me a new and original spirit in that I proceed by analysis and not by synthesis, i.e., I plunge into the depths, and, while analysing every atom, I search out the whole; Gogol takes a direct path and hence is not so profound as I. Read and see for yourself. Brother, I have a most brilliant future before me!" [1]

This new approach—and it was entirely new in Russian literature—was no doubt the chief reason for Belinsky's enthusiasm over the appearance of *Poor Folk*. In lavishing brilliant external effects in order to bring out the poor clerk's nature, Gogol has missed his soul. And it was the soul of Devushkin in which Dostoevsky was chiefly interested—an interest that remained uppermost in all his great characterizations. For Gogol, the individual was important only as a representative of society or of some social group; for Dostoevsky, in his artistic scheme of things, society was of consequence solely because of its influence on the personality of the individual.

This unique emphasis in *Poor Folk*, which distinguishes Dostoevsky from practically every Russian novelist who had preceded him, became a definite feature of his characteristic method. Neither the hero nor the heroine is presented to us before the real action of the tale gets under way. The action begins at once, and its exposition is not logical; it conceals rather than reveals. The focal point is not in the incidents, nor does the dramatic and tragic interest depend upon the action.

The centre of interest is placed in the characters, and more specifically in Devushkin. In the whole tale, however, we find no complete description of the two principals. Concerning the past and even the present events of their lives we have to guess much. Thus, we are told nothing about the childhood of Devushkin or how he came to meet Varvara. And we are left wondering why he persists in writing her so many letters since he appears to live almost next door. This neglect of the customary external details is intentional. The author's efforts are concentrated almost entirely upon a record and an analysis of Devushkin's feelings and emotions.

As the first of a series of characters in this vein, Devushkin is extremely interesting to the student of Dostoevsky's creative art. The author is a poet of the city, and Devushkin is analysed against the background of St. Petersburg, or, more specifically, against the background of those poverty-stricken city corners where dwell poor beggared individuals who are but one step from the bottom of society. Devushkin, it appears, has been destined to a life of poverty from birth. Although he works hard, he can make barely enough to exist, and the feeling gradually takes possession of him that he will eventually succumb to these adverse circumstances. Like Varvara, however, he fortifies himself in this struggle by the conviction that there is no crime in poverty. If he must sink to the bottom, he will accept the conditions forced upon him by a power beyond his control.

As his economic situation grows worse, what worries Devushkin most is the consequent loss of his self-esteem before society. He fears to be an object of laughter and mockery. The impression that he makes upon other people becomes a matter of major concern. When his boots wear out, he worries excessively, for he is convinced that his good name and honour will depend upon the condition of these same boots. Such concentrated introspection and self-pity drive him, at times, into a state of morbid anxiety. There are rare moments, however, when hope inflates the crushed ego of Devushkin. Then in his thoughts, at least, he rises above his depressed state. Suddenly sure of himself and convinced that he will overcome his poverty, he experiences a feeling of pride and independence. But this elation quickly gives way before the ever-present reality of his hopeless state, and he submits once more to his customary dissatisfaction with his lot and to morbid anxiety over his dwindling self-esteem.

Although not clearly presented, this dualism is the central problem of Devushkin's character. His furtive pride and self-esteem conflict with the predominant humility and submissiveness in his nature. He dreams of power and happiness and yet in real life he lacks every means of achieving them. This is the tragedy of his existence.

In Devushkin, Dostoevsky created his first "Double," a type he was to develop with infinite artistic refinement and profound psychological insight in a whole series of more famous characters that followed. Such a generalization is not the usual deplorable critical failing for reducing the complexities of the creative mind to the simple terms of fixed categories that may be easily apprehended. Many critics, notably the Russian V. F. Pereverzev,[2] have pointed out the pervasive dualism of Dostoevsky's characters. And the Double or *Doppelgänger* type, perhaps in its more pathological aspects, may be found in the works of such distinguished authors as E. T. A. Hoffmann, Poe, Jean Paul Richter, Maupassant, and Stevenson, not to mention others. Further, modern psychologists, as is well known, have indicated the prevalence of the Double in real life in their extensive investigations of the schizophrenic, or split personality. In *Poor Folk* the young Dostoevsky by no means comes to grips with the problem. Of course, there is no suggestion that he regards Devushkin as a clinical case. Modern psychology did not exist to define symptoms for him and to arm him with scientific terminology, although in his very next tale he approaches much closer the pathological manifestations of the split personality. The unhappy Devushkin interested him simply as a subject for analysis. How much of himself Dostoevsky projected into this character it is hard to say. He complained of those readers who insisted on seeing the "ugly mug of the author" in a work, and he protested that he had not shown his in Devushkin. But he protests too much. Resemblances have already been pointed out, and it is more than likely that the youthful introspective author unconsciously drew upon the struggle of contending forces in his own nature in portraying the dualism of Devushkin.

The intrinsic literary merit of *Poor Folk* may not justify the space accorded it here. The performance has obvious faults. It is prolix, despite Dostoevsky's claim to the contrary, and prolixity was a literary vice of which he never entirely cured himself. There is also an annoying sentimentality in the tale, which may derive in part from the sentimental foreign epistolary novels of the eighteenth century or their Russian imitations, which no doubt suggested also the epistolary form of *Poor Folk*. However, the historical importance of the work in the development of Dostoevsky's creative art justifies attention. Details and observations in *Poor Folk* reappear in a number of the short stories that followed and also in several of the larger works. The incident of the heroine's father is taken over in *The Insulted and Injured*, and the character of Bykov vaguely suggests Svidrigailov in *Crime and Punishment*. More important still is Dostoevsky's characteristic method of psychological analysis which appears, however imperfect, in *Poor Folk*. This concentration on the feelings and emotions, on the internal world of men and women, was the method he was to develop in all his succeeding works. Finally, in Devushkin he projected the first of his long series of Doubles. These were original departures in fiction, and it is little wonder that *Poor Folk* was hailed by the critics as the prophecy of a coming new force in Russian literature.

3

The End of
the First Literary
Period

The young Dostoevsky, his head a bit turned by the success of his first story, began to have illusions of social and literary grandeur. There were some adverse criticisms of *Poor Folk;* its originality assured that, but everybody was buying the magazine in which the tale had appeared. With laughable complacency he writes to Mikhail: "Well, brother, I think my fame will never reach such a height as now. Everywhere there is incredible esteem and a terrible curiosity on my account . . . All accept me as a miracle. I cannot even open my mouth without it being repeated in every corner that Dostoevsky said so and so, Dostoevsky wishes to do such and such." [1] He describes how the youthful Turgenev, just back from Paris, already loves him and, along with Belinsky, cautions him about the disorderly life he is leading, as though fearful of the harm he may do his precious talent. And with evident pride he records for his brother's benefit how the well-bred nobles and literary celebrities of St. Petersburg vie with one another for the favour of his presence at their *salons* and dinners. One thinks of Jonathan Swift (who did not have the excuse of youth) bumptiously writing to Stella of the manner in which the lords and lordlings of London society fawned on him and competed with one another for his attention.

Dostoevsky's illusions of social success quickly vanished. He cut a sorry figure in this polished Petersburg society. Shy and awkward in his behaviour, and an intellectual proletarian at heart, he felt ill at ease in the company of the elect. He either remained stubbornly silent at these affairs or, when stirred by some remark, he suddenly became impulsive in speech and action, betraying the bad manners of a twenty-five-year-old youth who had been leading a lonely, unsociable existence. His habitat had not been the glittering *salons* and the fine homes of the people who now pampered him, but the streets, the slums, and filthy corners of the city where he wandered on solitary walks and observed the men and women who live in his pages.

Dostoevsky quickly recognized this unexpected social success for the illusion that it was. He could forgo it without any regrets, for he was not naturally gregarious and much preferred his own company. The few young literary friends he had satisfied his limited desires for sociability. He was not disposed, however, to allow his sudden literary popularity to vanish in the same fashion. The fame might turn out to be illusory, but literature was now his only commodity, and he was everlastingly in need of funds.

Fortunately, Dostoevsky possessed an unusual creative vitality. Like Pushkin, he did not feel it necessary to search for inspiration; it sought him out. For him, inspiration was simply a disposition of the soul to a lively acceptance of impressions, and his mind was ever open to new ones. Ideas for stories came in abundance. Once he had fully thought out the idea, his powers of concentrated work were considerable. Anxious now to follow up the success of *Poor Folk*, he wrote twelve more pieces between 1846 and 1849, the year of his arrest. These are all sketches, short stories, or novelettes, with the exception of *Netochka Nezvanova*, an unfinished novel. They vary considerably in literary worth, but a few possess qualities of a high order. For during these three years, before Siberia put an end to his writing for a long time, his art matured. He improved over the methods of *Poor Folk* and enlarged the scope of his character portrayals. An explanation of the nature of this development is important for a full comprehension of his later productions.

Even before he had published *Poor Folk*, Dostoevsky had begun his second story, "The Double," which was also printed in 1846. References to the hero Golyadkin appear in letters to his brother as early as August 1845. The characterization caused him trouble at the outset, but the running comments to Mikhail indicate the author's growing artistic confidence and his mounting enthusiasm over the new production, which was rapidly taking on the proportions of a novelette. Belinsky drives him on to finishing it. And in one of his unabashed moments of youthful self-glorification he writes: "I have a thousand and one ideas: but it is impossible for me to tell anything of them, even to Turgenev, for example, for fear that the next day, in almost all the corners of Petersburg, they will know that Dostoevsky is writing this or that. Well, brother, if I should enumerate to you all my successes, I would not be able to find enough paper. I think that I shall have money. Golyadkin gets along excellently; it will be my *chef-d'oeuvre*." [2] Soon he was able to announce to Mikhail that the new work had just appeared, and he proudly declared: "Golyadkin is ten times superior to *Poor Folk*. Our crowd say that since *Dead Souls* there has never been

anything like it in Russia, that the production is one
of genius, and what do they not say! With what hopes
they all look upon me! Really Golyadkin has succeeded beyond what I thought possible." [3]

In some three months after the publication of "The
Double," the young author's inflated notions of the
work had been punctured. The great Belinsky's initial
enthusiasm waned. The public, Dostoevsky sadly admitted, found it boring and condemned its excessive
length. In a spirit of self-criticism that contrasts admirably with his youthful self-praise, he writes to his
brother: "I have a terrible vice: unlimited pride and
ambition. The idea that I deceived expectations and
spoiled a thing which could have been a great affair
has crushed me. Golyadkin has become repulsive to
me. Much of it was written in haste and when I was
weary. The first half is better than the second. Along
with brilliant pages there is nastiness, trash, and vomit-
ing, which one does not wish to read. This whole
business created a hell for me for a time and I fell ill
from anguish." [4]

Despite this frank admission of failure in the execution, Dostoevsky never wavered in his conviction
that the idea of "The Double" was a good one. More
than thirty years later, in his *Diary of a Writer*, he
reaffirmed his faith: "This story positively did not
succeed, but its idea was quite clear, and I never
projected a more serious idea in literature. But for me
the form of this tale was entirely unsuccessful." [5]

Dostoevsky was right. "The Double" is the story of
Yakov Petrovich Golyadkin, a government clerk, who
lives with his servant Petrushka. Despite Golyadkin's
timidity and submissive nature, there are moments
when he likes to think of himself as a commanding figure, endowed with all the social graces, respected by
his superiors, and held in high esteem by his fellow-
workers. As in the case of Devushkin, we are given
very little specific information concerning his past. The
story opens dramatically with the hero displaying signs

of a persecution mania that develops as the narrative unfolds. The reasons for his distraught state of mind are only mysteriously suggested. Several misfortunes, which he brings upon himself, deepen his suspicion that everyone is conspiring to blacken his reputation. It is at this point that he encounters a man who looks exactly like him and bears the same name. Golyadkin at first befriends him, and the man secures the position of clerk in Golyadkin's office. The remainder of the story relates the hero's adventures with his Double. With mounting indignation Golyadkin is obliged to follow his success at the office and to watch him gain the admiration of his fellow-workers and the praise of his superiors. To his deranged mind, the Double becomes the leader in the conspiracy against him, and he makes unsuccessful efforts to denounce the insolent fellow. After a final series of events in which he is miserably humiliated while his rival triumphs, the tale ends with the Double helping Golyadkin into a carriage on his way to the insane asylum.

Contemporary critics and Dostoevsky himself were no doubt correct in believing "The Double" to be prolix and considerably overwritten, but as a psychopathological study it is quite fascinating. The story has naturally stimulated the keen interest of modern experts, who have expended much effort in psychoanalytic investigations of Dostoevsky and his works. Although nowadays no one seriously questions the efficacy of psychoanalysis as a valuable instrument for revealing the mysteries of personalities in literature, few have gone further astray than the psychoanalytic critics of Dostoevsky. To explain away all his productions by the Oedipus complex is neither aesthetically satisfying nor scientifically sound. It is difficult, for example, to discover any sexual significance in the word "Slavophile," yet one critic reaches the startling conclusion that Dostoevsky's marked Slavophile tendencies were a result of his Oedipus complex. For his Slavophilism, explains this investigator, simply represents Dostoevsky's impassioned love for his "mother," the "mother" in this case being Mother Russia! [6]

In their studies of the psychic abnormalities in Dostoevsky's life, the psychiatrists and psychopathologists have considerably advanced our understanding of the novelist. But the attempts of the literary psychoanalysts to apply much the same methods in an effort to relate the abnormalities of Dostoevsky's imaginary characters to the psychic disturbances of their creator have not been so successful. Although he was a pioneer student of the abnormal, Dostoevsky was utterly opposed to systematic psychology. Unlike Proust, he does not give us detailed realistic descriptions of pathological conditions as such. After all, his literary psychological interest preceded the modern schools of formal psychology. His method, on the whole, is to dramatize the psychopathic experiences of his character from within, and he hardly ever indulges in extended psychological comment. The very emphasis upon the unpredictable in the abnormal impulses of his imaginery creations is entirely inimical to the mechanistic theories of volition of the modern psychologists. Rarely does he provide us with any of the necessary data of the past life of a character which are so essential to the psychoanalyst in reconstructing by analysis a consistent behaviour-pattern. Hence, any attempt to psychoanalyse his characters is sheer speculation, and the effort, often made, to read back the results of such speculation by way of explaining Dostoevsky's own habits of mind is most unscientific indeed.

The character of Golyadkin, it must be admitted, provides the richest material for the literary psychoanalysts. Once again, however, the data are incomplete. The all-essential traumatic experience of Golyadkin's past can be only suggested or invented. Nor has Dostoevsky conceived the character on the basis of positivist psychology, as Otto Rank implies. [7] That is, Golyadkin is not a deliberate study of a recognized paranoiac.

Of course, Dostoevsky was certainly acquainted with literary presentations of the *Doppelgänger* from various sources. It is a leading motif in a number of E. T. A. Hoffmann's tales, which may have had some direct bearing on the conception of "The Double." However, in deliberating on the provenience of Golyadkin, one need go back no further than the hero of Dostoevsky's first story. "The Double" differs in subject-matter from *Poor Folk,* but the psychological approach is pretty much the same, only intensified. In social position Golyadkin is simply a more successful Devushkin, and they resemble each other in their ambitions, thoughts, and feelings. Golyadkin differs mainly in the conviction that it is impossible for him to uphold his position while at the same time he struggles for a higher one. They are both Doubles, only the two personalities existing in Golyadkin are more irreconcilably opposed, and for this reason he feels his lowliness more sharply and reacts against it more forcefully. The Golyadkin with notions of grandeur mocks at the submissive Golyadkin who likes "to efface himself and slink away in the crowd." Unlike Devushkin, however, the emotional disharmony has got such a firm grip on him that he will lose his mind if he takes one more step in the wrong direction in order to resolve his ambivalence. He takes this step, and the dualism of his existence reaches the point where he has hallucinations, like Ivan Karamazov, who belongs to this same group of characters. His Double appears, and, again exactly prefiguring the unhappy situation of Ivan Karamazov, the Double carries on extensive conversations with him. The hero's sense of reality becomes utterly confused, and his persecution mania is eventually embodied in the person of his Double. Naturally, the Double achieves the very success, power, and general esteem which Golyadkin had been striving for. The outcome is assured: Golyadkin, in the hopeless position of a rival defeated by his Double, frets himself to madness.

"The Double" is a masterly literary study of the split personality, and the clearly defined intention of the characterization proves convincingly, even thus early in Dostoevsky's creative development, his preoccupation with this type. The ability with which he sustains the illusion of the Double, and the subtleness of his psychological insight into the deranged mind of Golyadkin, are impressive indications of the artistic skill of the young author. He never again pushed the pathological aspects of his Double characters quite so far, but experience increased his understanding of the more significant relations of the split personality to society at large. Abnormal psychologists could easily find independent evidence in "The Double" for their own case-studies. Except in a most general way, however, it would be highly uncritical to see in Golyadkin the abnormal aspects of Dostoevsky's own nature. To be sure, an author may put into his creations more than he knows, and Dostoevsky's literary career was in part at least an expression of his own pathological condition. But his pathological condition has never been determined with any scientific certainty, and anything more than a reflection of Dostoevsky's admitted dualism in Golyadkin would be hard to prove.

In 1846 Dostoevsky published one more story, "Mr. Prokharchin." Critics have detected the influence of Balzac's *Eugénie Grandet* and Pushkin's *The Covetous Knight* in it, but in most respects it is quite in the spirit of the first two tales. Once again we have the character of the poor clerk, but now with a difference. For Prokharchin, apparently an impoverished creature, is really a miser, and the story is essentially a psychological study of greed. He lives in a filthy corner and half starves himself in order to hoard. His fellow-roomers plague him on the score of his niggardliness, and they jokingly lead him to suspect that they are aware of his hidden treasure. Prokharchin literally goes insane at the thought of losing his money, and he dies. His hoard of some two thousand rubles is then discovered concealed in his mattress.

Dualism, of course, is implicit in the miser-type. Prokharchin remains poor, humble, and condemned by all, and yet he has in his mattress two thousand rubles. The obvious explanation is that his hoarded wealth gives him both the feeling and actuality of power. He willingly surrenders the actuality, for by exploiting it he would lose his money. Clearly one aspect of his nature concentrates solely on this feeling of power: while he possesses it he can create another world which represents an escape from the tawdry, beggared condition in which he lives. The ambivalence is neatly balanced. However, the loss of his hoard, or even the fear of losing it, deprives Prokharchin of his world of power, and without it he cannot live in his world of poverty.

In the following year (1847) Dostoevsky published two pieces. The first, "A Novel in Nine Letters," is a very brief sketch of no particular importance which he had written a couple of years earlier. The second is a rather long story, "The Landlady." A strange performance and unlike anything he had done hitherto, the weird, romantic subject-matter suggests that he wished to try his hand at something new and had gone for inspiration to the shilling-shockers of the West. There are vague echoes of Hoffmann and Balzac in "The Landlady," and the curious atmosphere of unreal realism recalls the similar effect in Gogol's famous tale, "The Nevsky Prospect." Although "The Landlady" is outside the regular tradition, the story is not devoid of certain characteristic Dostoevskian features that had already become associated with his fiction.

Thus Ordynov is one of Dostoevsky's typical heroes who lives in a dream world in order to escape from the realities of his present existence. He is a young recluse, unsociable, yet filled with a desire for love and sympathy, and convinced that a highly original

idea is dawning in his mind. Just what the idea is we
never discover. He takes lodgings with a queer old
man called Murin and a strikingly beautiful girl, Katerina. Then occurs a series of adventures which are
filled with melodrama and mystification. They defy any
logical analysis, apparently a part of Dostoevsky's design, for he deliberately keeps the whole tale shrouded
in a mist that is intended to heighten the sense of
mystery. Ordynov falls in love with Katerina and for
a time she appears to respond. But she soon displays
a well-defined streak of madness. One night she begins to tell Ordynov her history, which is all compounded of extraordinary elements—brigands, incen-
diarism, murder, elopement, and as many horrors as
Ann Radcliffe ever packed into her Gothic tales. Katerina appears to be suffering from a feeling of guilt,
presumably because she imagines herself the cause
of the death of her parents. (Dostoevsky was to make
more extensive use of the guilt-complex in later
works.) She declares that she has been corrupted by
someone and has committed an unpardonable sin, but
the exact nature of the corruption, who corrupted her,
and precisely what was her unpardonable sin are all lost
in the mist. Murin interrupts the narrative by calling
her away. It develops that this strange old man, who
reads books of a religious nature, exercises some hyp-
notic power over the ravishingly beautiful Katerina.
There is just a slight suggestion that he is the brigand
of the amazing story of her life. The climax of the
tale is reached in a burst of horrific events. Murin
fires a shot at Ordynov, who in turn threatens to knife
him. To add to the confusion, the old man has an
epileptic seizure, plunges into incantations, and then
Katerina herself falls into a fit. The upshot of all this
is that Murin orders Ordynov to leave the house. He
rationalizes the baffling situation by explaining to the
hero that Katerina is really his wife and is insane,
and that one form her madness takes is in promiscu-
ously falling in love with young men. For you see, he

declares, "her soul is simple." With this Ordynov and the reader find no difficulty in agreeing. The hero reluctantly withdraws and takes refuge once again in his dream world, only now it has lost much of its former rosy hue.

Belinsky poked all manner of fun at "The Landlady" and condemned it as something "monstrous." Probably most modern readers will concur with this opinion. Dostoevsky had a fondness for melodramatic effects, but they are acceptable only when combined with the finer stuff of his realism and psychological analysis. These qualities are all but lacking in "The Landlady," and it is easy to understand why he did not return to the tale of pure terror. The dreamy Ordynov, however, is a prototype of a later hero, and the eerie Murin contains a faint suggestion of dualism in which the criminal aspect is dominant, a feature developed in a more realistic manner in characters that are to follow.

Dostoevsky took to heart Belinsky's severe criticism of "The Landlady," and the seven sketches and short stories that he published in 1848 represent a return to the manner of *Poor Folk*. The first of these was "Polzunkov," a slight thing in which the hero is portrayed as a society buffoon. Polzunkov makes his living by playing the fool, repaying the generosity of his audiences by his ability to entertain them with anecdotes and tales. In the course of the narrative he tells his own story, which explains how he ruined himself. Despite its brevity, the tale is a fine example of Dostoevsky's analytical method by which he brings out the fact that, while making a clown of himself to amuse others, the hero is desperately trying to gain their respect.

The next production, "A Faint Heart," is important in the development of Dostoevsky's creative art, for in this short story appears a new and highly significant character-type. Unlike his first two tales, "A Faint Heart" is a simple, straightforward narrative. The hero is once more a poor copying clerk, Vasya Shumkov, who lives with his friend Arkadi. Vasya's employer honours him by giving him some extra copying for which he will receive additional remuneration, but the work must be finished at a definite date. Meanwhile, Vasya has fallen in love and wishes to be married. So preoccupied is he with the subject of his future bride that he neglects his copying. The consequence is tragic, for he becomes obsessed by a sense of ingratitude towards his employer. His mind cracks under the strain and he goes insane. Vasya's madness takes the form of a conviction that he is to be sent off to the army for failing to perform his duty. And in this belief he is led away to an insane asylum.

The friend Arkadi plays a subordinate part. Up to this point, Dostoevsky had displayed little of the care he was to lavish on his minor figures in later works. To be sure, there had been few of them, and the length of these early tales precluded any extensive treatment of secondary characters. But the few strokes he devotes to Arkadi bring him very much to life. In his impulsive, generous nature and in the vigorous manner in which he enters into Vasya's joys and sorrows, one gets more than a suggestion of a similar but infinitely greater and more complex character that Dostoevsky drew almost thirty years later, Dmitri Karamazov. The scene of the two friends pouring forth their hopes of future bliss when Vasya shall marry shows a real flash of the power of the mature Dostoevsky.

The important advance in "A Faint Heart" is the characterization of Vasya Shumkov. He resembles the hero of *Poor Folk* in most respects, but there is one significant difference: he has absolutely nothing of Devushkin's will to protest, however slight that may be. The struggle between pride and submissiveness—the dualism of Devushkin's personality—does not exist in the nature of Vasya Shumkov. He not only fails to protest against his enslaved condition, but he even regards it as entirely normal. The kicks and cuffs of misfortune he gratefully accepts. It never occurs to him to complain of the drudgery that has crippled his soul: in fact, he rather reveres his irksome copying tasks. One might suppose that the elevating experience of love would drive him to rebel against the hopelessness of an existence in which there was no place for love. On the contrary, he condemns himself as a criminal precisely because he dares to forget the task of his employer while indulging himself in dreams of love. Arkadi observes that gratitude drives Vasya insane, and this is essentially true. In the end, Vasya is destroyed without a struggle, without a murmur. He actually seeks his destruction as something he thoroughly deserves.

It is clear that in Vasya Shumkov, Dostoevsky presents the first representative of another group of his more notable characters. Critics have often designated this group in his fiction as the "Meek" type. The endless struggle of the Double is foreign to the Meek character; he is completely passive and submissive, traits that usually comprise one aspect of the split personality of the Double. In a sense, the Meek character may be considered as one solution to the ambivalence of the Double. The moral force of meekness and passive humility was to become a major factor in much of Dostoevsky's later theorizing, and its importance in his future fiction is evidenced by the series of great characters that followed Vasya Shumkov—the meek Sonya Marmeladova, Prince Myshkin, Zosima, and Alyosha Karamazov.

After two brief and humorous sketches which Dostoevsky later combined to make one tale, "The Wife of Another and the Husband Under the Bed," he published an effective short story called "The Honest Thief." Here again is an example of the Meek type, only in this case Emelyan Ilyich is even more submissive, if possible, than Vasya Shumkov. It is the story of a retired soldier, Astafy Ivanovich, who has turned tailor. He becomes acquainted with a drunken

beggar, Emelyan Ilyich, who follows him around like
a faithful hound until, out of compassion, he takes
him in. He does everything possible to reform the
drunkard, but he is finally forced to accept Emelyan's
vice as incurable. Despite the constant scolding of
the tailor, Emelyan always manages to placate him by
his utter humbleness and submissiveness. But one day
the tailor notices that a pair of riding breeches is missing and he accuses Emelyan of the theft. The drunkard
protests his innocence; but aware of the pain he has
caused his benefactor, he is overcome with remorse
and a poignant sense of ingratitude. Emelyan finally
worries himself into illness, and on his deathbed he
confesses to the theft.

In discussing "The Honest Thief," one of the psychoanalytic critics explains the theft as a transformation
of homosexuality into kleptomania! [8] Of course the
reason Emelyan steals the riding breeches is to obtain
money for drink. The resemblance of Emelyan to
Vasya Shumkov is obvious enough. Emelyan is a
special type of the Meek character, but he exemplifies
certain aspects of it admirably. Although "The Honest
Thief" is an unpretentious effort, Dostoevsky fills it
with an intense inner feeling of compassion for the
unfortunate and unhappy drunkard.

A curious and brief sketch, called "A Christmas Tree
and a Wedding," followed "The Honest Thief." The
principal guest among the older people at a children's
New Year's Eve party is a designing middle-aged man
who deliberately singles out for his attention the
eleven-year-old daughter of the wealthy host. He has
already calculated that in five years she will fetch a
dowry of five hundred thousand rubles. Sure enough,
in five years the schemer is seen at church being married to the young girl. It was "a good stroke of business," the author cynically remarks as he attentively
watches the face of the sixteen-year-old girl, whose
youth, he says, seemed "mutely begging for mercy."
Dostoevsky's latent powers as a satirist are revealed

for the first time in this narrative. And in his brief but penetrating treatment of the children at play there is more than a hint of the powerful insight into child psychology which he was to display in later works. The strange attraction of a very young girl for an older man is also noteworthy, for it is a relationship bordering on the abnormal that was to have a strong fascination for Dostoevsky.

"White Nights" is the last of this group of tales published in 1848. It is the story of a poor young clerk who lives entirely in himself and idealizes everything. His life is singularly dull, and he compensates for his lack of experience by dreaming of the striking roles he might play under different circumstances. He enjoys roaming the city streets at night, and on one of these strolls he befriends a young girl. Several meetings follow and, delighted with this unexpected listener, he pours out to her the imaginings of the dream world in which he lives. In return, she tells him of her love for a young man who had promised to marry her when he returned from a journey. However, she knows that he has been back for some time and yet she has heard nothing from him. The dreamer gallantly offers advice and aid, but his efforts are unavailing. In their mutual worry and sorrow over the situation, they both argue themselves into love for each other. To the hero it seems as though one of his cherished dreams were about to come true. As they are walking along in a blissful state, the first lover suddenly appears and she flies to embrace him. All is over for the dreamer. The next day he receives a letter from her in which she begs his forgiveness and explains that she can marry only her first lover. The dreamer bears her no grudge. After all, she has brought into his lonely existence a moment of perfect happiness, and he enthusiastically exclaims: "Is that too little for the whole of a man's life?"

"White Nights" is a whimsical tale and is well sustained throughout in this manner. The hero is a variation of the dreamer-type of Double that Dostoevsky portrayed in Ordynov in "The Landlady." He forgets the reality of his dull existence in dreams of luxurious *salons* where he plays the part of a hero of high society. There, in the flower-laden atmosphere of warm Italian nights, he loves and is loved. His humble position and poverty vanish and he feels himself a proud and powerful personality. In a sense, this ability to escape allows him to become the artist of his own life and he creates it to suit himself. But it also causes him to confuse the clear limits that separate his unreal world from the world of reality, for his dreams actually begin to seem real to him.

In the statement already quoted, in which Dostoevsky tells of the reaction of Nekrasov and Belinsky to the manuscript of *Poor Folk,* he mentions parenthetically that in his youth he too was a dreamer. No doubt, like Ordynov and the hero of "White Nights," he vividly realized in the rich fantasy of daydreams the unfulfilled ambitions and pride which, he tells us, were his failings at this time of his life. Certainly in the dreamer-type of character of these early tales there is much of the young Dostoevsky.

These short stories occupied by no means all of Dostoevsky's attention during 1848. They were written to satisfy pressing financial needs. Meanwhile, the larger design of a novel had taken form in his fertile mind. In fact, the idea of a full-length novel in four parts, *Netochka Nezvanova,* occurred to him as early as 1846, for in a letter to his brother in October of that year he remarks: "I am writing another novel and the work proceeds as it formerly did with *Poor Folk,* freshly, easily, and successfully." [9] He regarded the work with much seriousness, for it was by far his most ambitious project up to this time. The first instalment, consisting of two parts, did not appear serially until the beginning of 1849, and at the time of his arrest during the same year he was busy on the next part, which was published while he was in prison. He never returned to the theme, but he allowed the unfinished novel, with some revision, to be included in his complete works.

In intention at least, *Netochka Nezvanova* was to be as extensive as the novels of Dostoevsky's maturity. It is idle to speculate on what the finished work would have been, but on the basis of the last printed section, which represents a distinct falling off, it is perhaps just as well that he did not complete it. His failure to do so may indicate his realization of its faults.

The plot is rambling and complex. It opens with the unhappy story of the musician Yefimov, which may well have been suggested by the similar theme in Balzac's *Gambara*. Yefimov possesses great talent but lacks the ability, or rather the moral strength, to realize his ambitions. He is strikingly contrasted to his friend, a young German musician, who has little of his talent but succeeds largely by virtue of steadiness and moral courage. Yefimov marries and leads a wretched existence with his wife and her little daughter by a former husband. The child, Netochka Nezvanova, is morbidly attracted to her drunken stepfather. She believes in his genius and takes his side in the many family quarrels. In fact, she learns to hate her severe mother, who really loves her, and dreams of the time when her mother will die and she and her stepfather will go off and win fame and riches. Through drink and poverty, Yefimov sinks lower and lower, and finally dies a victim of the mania that he is a great but unappreciated violinist. Netochka is adopted into the family of an aristocratic prince. She falls passionately in love with his young daughter, whose reactions to Netochka are those of mixed love and hate. The situation grows so extreme that Netochka is removed to the home of a relation of the prince. In this final printed section of the novel, Netochka grows up to the age of seventeen. Little space, however, is devoted to the heroine. Most of the narrative is concerned with the suspected infidelity of her new benefactress, and in this situation

Netochka takes the part of the wife. By means of a mysterious letter, melodramatically introduced, the husband's suspicion is shown to be false.

In the revision of the novel for his complete works, Dostoevsky deleted a whole incident in which he provides Netochka with a male counterpart, a poor orphan whose unhappy childhood bears some striking psychological resemblances to her own. The boy labours under a guilty feeling that he has caused the death of his parents, and this feeling awakens in Netochka her dormant sense of guilt in the death of her mother.

It has been conjectured by critics that *Netochka Nezvanova* is replete with biographical details of Dostoevsky's childhood. It would be a difficult matter to substantiate on the basis of the story alone. His mixed childhood feelings for his mother and father may have been drawn upon, but at best this can only be conjecture, for we have very little positive information about this period of his life. Despite the artistic lapses in *Netochka Nezvanova,* one is impressed by Dostoevsky's already advanced technique in the complex matter of child psychology, which is everywhere apparent in the altogether excellent first and second parts of the novel. As a child, Netochka is brilliantly drawn, and the guilt feeling she is to undergo is subtly foreshadowed in her hatred for her mother which grows out of her deep devotion to her wayward stepfather. An uncanny insight into human behaviour is manifest in the love-hate relations between Netochka and the temperamental daughter of the charitable prince. In its intensity and sensual manifestations, the relationship of these two young girls amounts to a study in sexual perversion. Indeed, in the psychologically parallel series of love-hate situations in *Netochka Nezvanova* we have a real foretaste of a favourite subject of the mature Dostoevsky.

To complete this survey of the first period, a word should be said of "The Little Hero," a short story which Dostoevsky wrote while he was in prison in 1849. It is another study in child psychology, for the tale presents a profound analysis of the first love experience of an eleven-year-old boy. His childish but deep affection for a beautiful young married woman is developed with a restraint, understanding, and sympathy which never overstep the accepted limits of reality, difficult enough to ascertain in such an unusual situation. With delicate skill Dostoevsky analyses the sensitive feelings of the child and his intuitive but confused understanding of the new experience in his life. "The Little Hero" is unique in some respects among Dostoevsky's works. The background is the country estate of a wealthy land-owner. The jollity and amusements of the various visitors, and the bright out-of-doors atmosphere never again appear in his fiction. He has not been credited with any skill or fondness for nature descriptions, but the scene of the secret rendezvous at the end of the tale, with its ideal nature setting, is described with an effectiveness that rivals Turgenev, a master in this respect. These happy people and the bright gay atmosphere suggest a deliberate imaginative flight from his dreary prison cell and the hopeless future that awaited him.

For various reasons, some of which have been mentioned, it has been necessary to devote this much space to the works of Dostoevsky's first period of literary creation. These early tales are not generally known to non-Russian readers, and for this reason, as well as for purposes of analysis, the brief summaries seemed desirable. No mention has been made of his journalistic efforts, at least four articles of the feuilleton type, or of unfinished short stories that we know he worked at. But in less than six years of creative effort the young author had produced thirteen works of fiction which had earned him the reputation of one of the most promising Russian novelists of the time.

It is important to emphasize the fact that these productions indicate pretty clearly his characteristic narrative method, literary devices, and character types. Of course, he refined and developed all these features, and added much to them later, but Dostoevsky the great artist of the 1870's and 1880's exists in miniature, as it were, in these tales of the 1840's. Thus, in one of his notebooks, Dostoevsky once wrote: "They call me a psychologist: it is not true. I am merely a realist in the higher sense of the word, that is, I depict all the depths of the human soul." [10] Although this remark was written rather late in his life, its application dates from his first story, *Poor Folk*. It is this "higher realism" which is at the bottom of his surprising originality, and it differentiates him from the realists in the novel who preceded him or who were his immediate contemporaries. He had learned something from Gogol, perhaps a bit from Pushkin, in these first efforts; the English and German writers of tales of terror had influenced him; and the French realists, especially Balzac, were laid under contribution. But his realism began where theirs left off. In realism he created a fourth dimension which concerned the souls of men and women. His characters live through their feelings, in the chaos of passion.

Dostoevsky's narrative method is somewhat confusing to the reader. He invokes at the outset an atmosphere of mystery, foreboding, and expectation. We are suddenly introduced to characters whose relations are not at once clear, and to a series of events the import of which is not immediately grasped. But behind this atmosphere of mysteriousness is a world of reality which eventually emerges. The method applies to the later works as well as to these early tales. In fact, at the very beginning of "A Faint Heart" he informs us of his customary method of composition. He starts with the action *in medias res*, studiously avoiding the long, careful buildup for either characterization or events, a method quite the reverse of that employed by his great contemporaries in Russian fiction. The mysterious atmosphere is largely a result of this approach, and it is further intensified by various literary devices. Chronology and logical sequence are slighted; incidents are presented before the conditions governing them; relations between people are explained before the characters themselves are introduced; or the behaviour of a character is described before the character. As a consequence the action develops with extreme swiftness, for there is nothing to slow it up. The method is essentially dramatic; it resembles the modern detective story which starts with the murder and then works backward and forward in order to explain the motivation. One is not surprised, in fact, to find a good deal of the detective-story element in Dostoevsky's works. The immediate effect of this whole method on a reader is perhaps not unlike that which a person would experience if he should suddenly enter a room and over-hear a group of people in the middle of an exciting conversation about an extraordinary event involving those present. The uninvited guest knows none of the principals, but his curiosity carries him through the conversation while he strives to make logical connections between the events described and the people present. Finally, the people are introduced to him, and from their own explanations, which fill in the gaps, he pieces the whole story together.

Many of the characters of these early tales are simply preliminary studies of the great characters to come. They are mostly wretched clerks and poor students who live in unsavoury corners of St. Petersburg. They are dreamy, unpractical, and suffering people. From among them emerge two well-defined types—the Double and the Meek characters of *Poor Folk,* "The Double," "A Faint Heart," and "White Nights." Further, there is a vague suggestion of a third type that appears prominently in the later works—the criminal or Self-Willed character. They are not creatures born of literary influences, nor are they entirely the result of Dostoevsky's observation of the life around him. The intense inner analysis of the feelings

of these characters belies the experiences of a young
man who as yet had seen little of life. For the stuff of
these creations he plumbed the depths of his own emotional, spiritual, and psychological self. His own ago-
nies of spirit and mind were transferred into the creatures of his imagination. However, an experience was
awaiting him in far-off Siberia which would deepen
his perception of human nature and develop his genius for revealing the eternal struggle that goes on in
the souls of suffering men and women.

4

Revolution and Prison—The Spirit and Art

In the famous section "Pro and Contra" in *The Brothers Karamazov,* Ivan and Alyosha sit in a tavern. Ivan is preparing the way for his tremendous confession of religious doubt, and in one place he says to his younger brother:

Of course I am just such a little boy as you are, only not a novice. And what have Russian boys been doing up to now, that is, some of them? Here, for instance, in this stinking tavern they meet and sit in a corner. They have never known each other in their lives before, and after they leave the tavern it may be forty years before they meet again. Well, what do they talk about in that momentary halt in the tavern? Of the eternal questions, nothing else; Is there a God, is there immortality? And those who do not believe in God talk of socialism or anarchism, of the transformation of all humanity on a new pattern so that it all comes to one and the same thing; they're all the same question only with a different aim. And masses, masses of the most original

Russian boys among us do nothing but talk of eternal questions in our time.

It is not necessary to subscribe to the common generalization that the Russian is a tireless talker in order to accept the bare truth of Ivan Karamazov's observation. For Russians do not possess any greater predisposition to chattiness than the peoples of other nations. The fact is that in Dostoevsky's lifetime, and for generations before that, problems of religion, politics, and social thought were vivid realities to the majority of thinking people in Russia, for such problems had been thrust upon them by a despotic government and a reactionary Church. The hope of reform was the sustaining hope in the lives of thousands of oppressed people. Nor were they content merely to talk about their hopes, as the series of terrorist acts during this period indicates.

When he came up to St. Petersburg, the young Dostoevsky was not unlike the questioning Russian youths whom Ivan Karamazov described to his brother. The iron regime of Nicholas I provoked just such questions. The Decembrist Revolt of 1825 had ushered in the reign of Nicholas. In that terrible catastrophe the ringleaders were hanged, and scores of Russia's nobility and intelligentsia were exiled to Siberia. This first attempt at reform in an absolute despotism had received a crushing defeat and left the tsar complete master of the situation. Nicholas I improved on it, for he built up a bureaucracy that carried out his every wish. All intelligent public opinion was stifled; the regime became not merely conservative, but downright reactionary. Strict censorship laws were rigorously enforced, and through the secret police a spy system was developed which made it extremely dangerous to carry on even the most harmless kind of political activity. Every manifestation of liberal thought was suppressed and the country was plunged into semi-oriental despotism. In the Crimean War Russia reaped the whirlwind that Nicholas I had sowed, for the nation's defeat was largely a result of the grafting, obscurantism, inefficiency, and disloyalty into which his bureaucratic government had degenerated. And some sixty years later the whirlwind of revolt, like an avenging fury, destroyed the whole family of descendants of Nicholas I.

In the early 1840's the young Dostoevsky was drawn into the orbit of discontent. To be sure, the opposition at first amounted to little more than a gentle murmur. Its first mouthpiece among the intellectuals of St. Petersburg was the critic Belinsky. The liberal Westerners whom he gathered around him concealed beneath their advocacy of a Russia modelled on the more advanced civilization of Western Europe a restrained protest against the worst abuses of the autocratic rule of the tsar. The protest had to remain muffled at this time; except by way of satire and allegory, which would escape the dull-witted censors, it rarely appeared in print. Most of the protest was confined to private correspondence and to endless confidential discussions.

Dostoevsky had been attracted to Belinsky by his critical articles even before the eventful meeting with him in 1844 apropos of the manuscript of *Poor Folk*. And the formative stages of his social beliefs as well as of his artistic development were influenced by Belinsky. One reason why the critic had admired *Poor Folk* was that he believed it to contain the social content that he upheld as a touchstone of the Naturalistic School of fiction. But with the appearance of "The Double" he grew cold towards his writing, and after "The Landlady" he professed to be disillusioned with the young author. More on personal grounds than for reasons of his adverse criticism Dostoevsky also grew hostile to Belinsky. Long after the great critic's death, however, he continued to play a vital role in Dostoevsky's thought and art.

Even in the case of *Poor Folk*, Belinsky was hardly correct in attributing a social content to Dostoevsky's

fiction at this time. Neither in his early period nor
later was he concerned with the novel of social purposes as we understand this genre among the writers
of Western Europe. Some of the heroes of his early
tales are the poor, downtrodden clerks and students
of the city slums, but he is not interested in them as a
class, and certainly not as representatives of the de-
caying petty bourgeoisie, a familiar Marxian interpretation. Gogol had already popularized the poor clerk
in "The Overcoat," and Dostoevsky had accepted the
type for his own purposes. The relation of society to
his characters or the economic reasons for their poverty-stricken condition did not as yet concern him. He
was interested in the souls of his unhappy creatures.
As a novelist he had shifted the action from the external world to the mind and heart of his men and
women, an approach that left little place for social
reformation.

To convey the feelings he experienced was always
a major objective of Dostoevsky's art. Of course his
feelings, which developed from his relation to life and
from his observations of life, were not disassociated
from the reasoning process. There have been few
keener analysing minds in the history of fiction. But
what he thought about the social abuses he saw all
around him he did not allow to creep into his imaginative productions during this early period. That he reacted to these abuses is most certain, and it is highly
important to understand the nature of his reactions,
for the history of Dostoevsky the thinker over these
years of apprenticeship and up to the time he returned
to St. Petersburg from his Siberian prison marks the
first stage in the growth of those ideas that were to be
of such vital consequence in his future development.

No doubt his associations with Belinsky and his followers had infected Dostoevsky with the dangerous
virus of social reform. By 1847 he had gravitated towards the Petrashevsky Circle, a group of liberals who
met every Friday evening, like the youths in Ivan

Karamazov's description, to discuss a variety of questions—recent trends in literature, the evils of poverty, the peasant question, abuses in State and Church, and, above all, Utopian schemes for the regeneration of society. Their favourite authors were the social theorists of Western Europe, especially Proudhon and Fourier, and the disputants speculated on the possibilities of applying the ideas of these foreign thinkers to conditions that existed in Russia. The host Petrashevsky, for the better political and social education of his guests, set up in his house a lending library of banned books, most of them published abroad.

Seven frequenters of the Petrashevsky Circle, because they felt the need for more serious discussions and even for action, formed their own group which met at the house of a writer, Sergei Durov. Dostoevsky was one of the Durov Circle, and he took an active part in a plan to obtain a lithograph outfit with which they intended to produce secretly articles of political and social significance. This was a particularly dangerous project in the Russia of those days, for the government regarded illegal printing as a crime short of high treason against the State.

It has been the custom of critics to dismiss the members of these circles as fluffy idealists and their plans of reform as pure fantasies. The role Dostoevsky played among them has also been disparaged, and the importance of the whole experience in his mental and social development has been underestimated. Nearly any movement against constituted authority is usually dubbed "idealistic," and its programme of reform is always "ineffectual" unless it meets with success. The startling results of modern political movements against authority have somewhat corrected this customary attitude, but the time-lag among literary critics in matters of this sort is traditional.

In the first place, it was a hazardous business to engage in even the most pious manifestations against the autocratic regime of Nicholas I, and the enthusiastic

members of the Petrashevsky Circle were aware of
the fact. Forces in France were rapidly moving towards the Revolution of February 1848, and the secret
police of the usually well-informed Russian government were on the lookout for any repercussions at
home. Despite the apparently unpractical substance
of the talks and papers delivered amidst an infinite
amount of tobacco smoke at the Friday evenings at
Petrashevsky's, there was an undercurrent of active revolt which justified, in the government's eyes, the stern
measures it eventually took.

Recent studies in Soviet Russia have shed fresh
light on the practical purposes of these reformers and
on the real significance of the experience in Dostoevsky's life.[1] There were mere visionaries among the Pe-
trashvsky Circle, but there were some who thought
only about action, and Dostoevsky inclined to this extreme. Many years later, when he felt able to speak
more frankly about these matters, he told his wife,
who he knew would preserve his words for posterity,
that "Socialists sprang from the Petrashevskys. The
Petrashevskys sowed many seeds. Among them was
everything that existed in succeeding conspiracies . . .
a secret press and a lithography, although of course
they were not employed."[2] He added that they believed the people were with them, and that if the
circle had not been liquidated they would have gone
on to take revolutionary action.

Most members of the circle based their social views
on Fourier, but not all of these theorists—and Dostoevsky was one of them—subscribed to the Frenchman's
notion that social change could be achieved by peaceful methods. Although Fourierism accepted religion,
many of the circle actively spoke and wrote against
religion. For Petrashevsky himself, Christ was a well-
known demagogue who had ended his career somewhat unsuccessfully. That is, some of the members
who saw any hope in the practical application in Russia of the phalansteries of Fourier intended to estab-

lish them on an atheistic basis. The revolutionary nature of the Petrashevsky Circle is suggested by the fact that the tsar's Commission of Inquiry condemned the members not for advocating Fourierism, but for an intended blow at the Russian social structure.

It was probably the failure of this intention to crystallize quickly enough into a forthright programme of action that inspired the formation of the Durov Circle. Its members consisted of the hottest heads among the Friday night visitors to Petrashevsky's house. The real leader of the group was N. A. Speshnev, a wealthy landowner and by conviction an atheist and a communist. It seemed that nature had endowed him with all the qualities of leadership necessary for the dangerous task of political conspiracy. He was unusually handsome, silent, contemplative, a keen observer, and possessed of a powerful will. An air of mystery surrounded him and he appeared capable of any sacrifice to achieve his ends. Speshnev had an irresistible attraction for the young Dostoevsky, and it is possible that many years later he served as a prototype for the character of Stavrogin in *The Possessed*.

The Durov Circle was a secret society, and its avowed purpose was to promote revolutionary action in order to bring about the freeing of the serfs. There is reason to believe that all the members, including Dostoevsky, agreed on this purpose. A kind of constitution for the society was debated which included a by-law threatening death to anyone who betrayed the members. In fact, the whole project bears a curious resemblance to certain aspects of *The Catechism of a Revolutionist* which was embodied in Pyotr Verkhovensky's conspiratorial plan in *The Possessed*.

Dostoevsky apparently accepted his part in the Durov Circle with great seriousness. On one occasion he went to spend the night with his friend Apollon Maikov, the poet. His object was to invite him to join the group, and he told him that a secret printing press had already been set up. The account that Maikov has

left of this visit makes it clear that the Durov Circle
had resolutely determined upon action. He tells how
Dostoevsky sat in his nightshirt, like dying Socrates,
and held forth eloquently on the holiness of their
conspiratorial undertaking on which, he declared, the
whole fate of Russia depended.[3] Dostoevsky also promised to write an article on socialism for the secret press.
And with enthusiasm he read to the members of the
society, and later to the Petrashevsky Circle, the famous contraband letter of Belinsky. It was the critic's
indignant answer to a reactionary book of Gogol. The
letter, which circulated widely through underground
channels, contained vehement passages aimed against
the government and the reactionary Church. In the
light of the deep religious faith attributed to Dostoevsky, it is difficult to understand his willingness to read
such sentences as: "If you observe more intently, then
you will see that they [the Russians] are by nature a
profoundly atheistic people. In them is still much
superstition but there is no trace of religiosity." [4]
There is reason to believe, however, that his faith in
the Orthodox Church during this early period was not
as solid as is commonly supposed. His close association
with the avowed atheist Speshnev, under whose influence and in whose debt he was, is perhaps indicative
of the surface character of his religious convictions at
the time.

Early in the morning of 23 April 1849, Dostoevsky
was aroused from his sleep by the police and packed
off to the prison in the Peter-Paul fortress. The night
before he had been to a meeting of the Petrashevsky
Circle. The police had had the group under surveillance for some time, and that same morning many
other visitors to Petrashevsky's house were also
arrested.

The long-drawn-out investigation by the tsar's special Commission of Inquiry took place. Dostoevsky
was summoned twice to testify and he was obliged to
fill out affidavits. There has been a tendency to accept

his testimony too literally. Certainly it would be a mistake to judge his activities in this whole affair and to appraise his social thought at this time solely on the basis of the evidence he presented to the tsar's Commission.

The prisoners had little expectation that justice would be rendered; the record of Nicholas I in cases of political offenders was notoriously cruel. If the guilty conspirators had been "hopeless idealists," they might have told the whole truth. In the circumstances however, they wisely felt that the truth would not gain them any mitigation of punishment. With the exception of the strong-willed Speshnev, the testimony of the prisoners is suspiciously all of a piece—they were engaged merely in discussing an "ideal" of social reform and had no intention of trying to put it into practice.

Dostoevsky hewed to the same line. He quickly realized that the Commission had not uncovered the true facts about the Durov Circle and knew nothing of the secret press. He gave his testimony accordingly, trying to put in the best light possible the only two offences that the government was aware of—his association with the Petrashevsky group and his reading of Belinsky's contraband letter. From this point of view his testimony is an astute piece of deception. The Utopian ideals of Fourier he could honestly ridicule, which he did. And in the end he represents himself as a loyal subject of the tsar and a faithful son of the Church. Any act or word of his against either Church or State had been quite unpremeditated. Like so many people in Russia, he was desirous of certain reforms, but he was convinced that these should come about through the proper governmental channels.

His testimony and that of the others availed them little. Fifteen of the prisoners, including Dostoevsky, were condemned to be shot. The story is well known of how Nicholas I allowed all the grisly preparations for the execution to be gone through with maddening punctilio before a courier dashed up with the tsar's commutation. Dostoevsky could never forget the horrible experience he underwent that cold December morning as he stood on the platform in Semenov Square waiting to be shot, and the memory of the event haunted the pages of his later novels.

The chief point, however, in this consideration of so important an experience in Dostoevsky's life is to arrive at some understanding of his social beliefs and political philosophy at this time. The commonly accepted view that his association with the Petrashevsky and Durov groups was a flight of youthful skin-deep radicalism must be somewhat modified. Dostoevsky was engaged in a real political conspiracy, and its main endeavor was to agitate for the freeing of the serfs. If the police had not arrested the group, it is very probable that the members would have become involved in active revolutionary work. At this time in his life, the young Dostoevsky felt deeply the necessity for social change in Russia. It was not a question of his advocating the regeneration of the country through the medium of some Utopian scheme such as Fourierism. He observed real abuses and deliberately joined a secret society with the definite intention of remedying them by illegal tactics. In writing *The Possessed* in the 1870's, he drew upon these experiences of his youth for material. And in answering a criticism of the novel in *The Diary of a Writer*, he frankly admits what he failed to admit to the Commission of Inquiry: "I myself am an old Nechaev," that is, a conspirator like the real revolutionist Nechaev whose political crime of murder helped to inspire the subject of *The Possessed*. Then he goes on to ask his critic: "How do you know that the Petrashevskys could not have become Nechaevs, i.e., pursue the Nechaev road, *in case the affair had taken such a turn?*" The italics are significantly those of Dostoevsky. Finally, as though the memory of the radicalism of his youth was struggling against the reaction of age, he cautiously

concludes: "Probably I could never have become a
Nechaev, but a *follower* of Nechaev, I am not certain;
it may be I could have . . . in the days of my youth." [5]
These statements, in the light of the evidence on the
radical intentions of the Durov Circle, leave little reason to doubt the sincerity of his youthful revolutionary
convictions.

It is generally believed that Dostoevsky underwent
a significant spiritual experience during his four years
as a convict in the Siberian prison of Omsk. But the
exact nature of the experience and what effect, if any,
it had on his political and social views and on the development of his creative art is a difficult matter to
determine. In the absence of facts the temptation to
speculate is unavoidable. The facts, however, will be
our main concern.

The unexpected news of the commutation of his
sentence when he believed himself to be standing on
the brink of the grave left Dostoevsky in a kind of
stupor. Once back in his prison cell he gave vent to a
deep feeling of joy at being alive. The few letters he
was able to write to his brother Mikhail before setting out for Siberia reflect this happiness of a man
who, loving life, has been brought back from the dead.
He declares that he is not sad or depressed in spirit,
for everywhere is life, in him in his prison if not outside him. "Never has there seethed in me such an
abundant and healthy kind of spiritual life as now.
Whether it will sustain the body I do not know . . .
Now my life will change, I shall be born again in a
new form. Brother! I swear to you that I shall not lose
hope and shall keep pure my mind and heart. I shall
be born again for the best. That is all my hope, all my
comfort." [6]

Such incredible optimism in the face of blackest adversity was instinctive with Dostoevsky. Acute misfortune merely served to fill him with a boundless enthusiasm for a new life which, he was convinced,
shortly awaited him. The surprising fact is that neither

in these letters nor in his later correspondence does he even intimate that his punishment is unjustified. On the usual supposition that his offence was inconsequential, critics often explain the uncomplaining acceptance of his severe penalty as the psychological manifestation of a guilt-complex. There may be some justification for this view, but the likelihood that he had been actually involved in a potentially dangerous conspiracy makes his frank acceptance of punishment seem more rational. The characters of his novels who achieve salvation by suffering really sin, morally or criminally. Dostoevsky knew that he had sinned, and he willingly accepted his punishment as atonement for his crime and as a purification of his conscience.

Despite the tsar's "infinite mercy" in commuting the death sentence, which had been recommended by the highest tribunal, by imperial order Dostoevsky, as a nobleman, was not spared any of the rigours of prison life. He served his term like any of the common murderers and thieves among whom he lived, although presents of money and contacts with respected citizens in the town of Omsk did bring him small privileges. Filth, lice, cockroaches, stench, chains, hard labour, and the hatred of low-born fellow-convicts were his unvarying lot. The hard labour took his mind off his own complaints, often imaginary, which had been frequent in his St. Petersburg life. The rough existence greatly benefited his general health, although he dates his first epileptic seizures from this time.

A hypersensitive individual, however, Dostoevsky endured profound spiritual suffering during this ordeal. In the remarkable account of his prison life in *The House of the Dead*, one detects the undercurrent of spiritual agony that was the daily accompaniment of his existence among these ruffians. The loss of liberty was terrible enough, but his human dignity was crushed and his sensitivities constantly offended by the brutal prison discipline and the actions and insults of his fellow-convicts. Try as he might to bridge the social gap that separated him from these murderers and thieves, for them he was always the gentleman, and as such kept strictly outside the pale of their comradeship. Despite the many fine things that have been said about Dostoevsky's discovery of the Russian people in his prison, the chapter called "Grievances" in *The House of the Dead* clearly states his conviction that between the nobleman and the people there could never be any ideal kinship or complete understanding.

Although he had willingly taken up his cross, it was hard to bear in this hostile milieu. Religion was a solace and a support which he eagerly grasped. The religious training of his childhood may have been shaken by the arguments of the atheistic members of the Petrashevsky Circle, yet one of the first books he requested from his brother while still in the Peter-Paul prison was the Bible, and especially the New Testament. And the New Testament was the sole book allowed him at Omsk. He read it at every opportunity. Like Bunyan in Bedford Gaol, Dostoevsky sought and found spiritual sustenance in the words of Christ. Unlike Bunyan, however, he could not successfully struggle through despair and doubt to the distant and perfect vision of truth. All his life was to be a holy pilgrimage, an endless search for God. But for a man of his peculiar psychological ambivalence the search itself was the end, the sustaining spiritual bread of his existence and, one may add, of his artistic powers.

In prison he rediscovered Christ, and his passionate reading of the New Testament enabled him spiritually to rationalize his misfortunes. In the life and teachings of Christ he found every spiritual comfort for the persecuted and suffering. As he looked round him at these human derelicts of society, he seemed to realize that Christ was their only hope. Only He could raise up the sinner, comfort the fallen, and promise the humble of heart a new life on earth. A sinner himself, Dostoevsky yearned for this divine forgiveness that held forth the ultimate hope of salvation. In the end his firmer faith brought him a new serenity, and the bitterness of his prison existence was assuaged by this spiritual anodyne.

It must not be concluded, however, that this elevating religious experience stilled the incessant worm of doubt that gnawed at Dostoevsky's belief in God. His will to believe never ceased to be torn between the contending forces of his nature. Not long after his release from prison he writes to a woman who had befriended him during this severe period, and in one passage of the letter he records the spiritual change he experienced and the doubt it failed to destroy:

I tell you this not because you are religious but because I myself experienced and felt it keenly, that in such minutes you thirst as 'the parched grass' for faith, and you find it simply because the truth shines forth in misfortune. I tell you about myself that I am a child of the age, a child of unfaith and doubt now and (I know it) shall remain so to the grave. What terrible tortures has this thirst to believe cost me, and still costs me now, a thirst which is all the stronger in my soul the more proof I have against it. However, God sometimes sends me moments in which I am entirely serene; in these moments I love and find that I am loved by others, and in such moments I have formed in myself a credo in which everything is clear and holy for me. This credo is very simple. Here it is: to believe that there is nothing more beautiful, more profound, more sympathetic, more reasonable, more manly, and more perfect than Christ, and not only is there nothing, but, I tell myself with jealous love, there can be nothing. Besides, if anyone proved to me that Christ was outside the truth, and it *really* was so that the truth was outside Christ, then I should prefer to remain with Christ than with the truth.[7]

This is a highly important statement for any understanding of Dostoevsky's religious belief. Rarely did he reveal so frankly the struggle of belief and unbelief that went on in his soul. For unbelief is implicit in his very assertion of belief. His religious dualism would not allow him to reconcile the truth of man's suffering existence with Christ. In his great novels this struggle for faith, irrefutable faith, was profoundly reflected. More than twenty years later he resurrected the very words of this letter and placed them in the mouth of one of his characters whose soul, like his own, longed for the peace that complete faith brings to the doubt-racked mind of man.

Although the image of Christ grew brighter and His teachings helped Dostoevsky to endure, almost with the martyr's fervour, his bodily pain and mental misery, this spiritual regeneration was not the only significant development during his four years of imprisonment. The stuff of life is the bread and meat of an artist's existence, and in his communal prison he found a slice of life peopled by a level of society about which he had hitherto no intimate knowledge. The novelist in him could never lie dormant, and in prison he was never more alive to the material for art that he saw all around him.

While Dostoevsky was still in the Peter-Paul prison, with the long road to Siberia ahead of him, the hope for his future in art grew dim, and he sadly wrote to Mikhail: "That head which created, lived the higher life of art, which experienced and grew accustomed to the higher necessities of the spirit, that head has already been severed from my shoulders. The memory has remained, and the figures created and those not yet embodied by me." [8] Of course, in the prison at Omsk he was not permitted to do any writing; he was, as he remarked later, "buried alive and shut up in a grave." But over those four years his imagination was actively at work on literary schemes, plots, and characters. In the long sleepless nights, ideas flashed into his mind and rough conceptions of characters struggled for birth in his imagination. Even the spiritual transformation he had undergone was sublimated in a vision of a great future work—possibly the initial idea for his famous unwritten masterpiece, "The Life of a

Great Sinner." He tried to develop these fugitive ideas for plots and characters by sheer cerebration. His one fear was that he would forget or lose interest in this stuff of fiction before he got an opportunity to work it out in writing.

The simple natures of his fellow-convicts perplexed him. He feared these rough peasants, cutthroats, and bandits more than the complex people he had known in his sophisticated St. Petersburg circle. Although he was conscious of the wide chasm that separated him from them, he saw in them, as he said, in the chapter "Freedom" in *The House of the Dead,* "perhaps the strongest, and, in one way or another, the most gifted of our people. There was all that strength of body and of mind lost, hopelessly lost. Whose fault is that?" The answer to that question was a challenge. It stirred his literary impulse as did the stories of these convicts which he never wearied listening to. He wrote to Mikhail later: "How many native types, characters, did I take with me from prison! I got accustomed to them and therefore, it seems, I know them pretty well. How many tales of vagabonds, robbers, and, in general, of the whole gloomy, wretched existence. There is enough for entire volumes. What a wonderful people! On the whole, I did not lose my time. If not Russia, then I have come to know the Russian people well, as well as only a few know them." [9] And no one can fail to recognize the influence of this "wonderful people" of the Omsk prison on the novels written after his release.

In truth, the experiences of these four years as a convict played an important part, perhaps the most important part, in Dostoevsky's entire development. He entered the prison a young radical, and he left it with a heightened respect for the authority of the crown and for the established order of things. He entered it something of an agnostic and left prison with a firmer faith in the teachings of Christ and a stronger belief in the saving grace of the Orthodox

Church in the troubled existence of Russia. And in the growth of his creative art prison played not a negative, but a positive role. It did not change his creative process; there was no essential break with the past in this respect, as critics often maintain. Prison defined and deepened his creative process. His own experience had taught him the doctrine of salvation by suffering, and the New Testament had fortified his faith in it. His prison life provided him with rich material for further study of the suffering individuals in whom he had been interested from the beginning. In his early works he had been concerned with an analysis of the souls of the insulted and injured; in prison he succeeded in learning, feeling, and analysing the souls of the insulted and injured more profoundly than ever.

5

Uncle's Dream and *The Village of Stepanchikovo*

Nearly ten years elapsed between the time Dostoevsky entered his Siberian prison and the publication of his next literary effort. Ten non-productive years out of the best part of a novelist's life might appear to be a difficult handicap to overcome. Although the continuity of literary reputation had been sacrificed, this period, as already indicated, was by no means a barren one in his development. His spiritual horizon had been broadened and his artistic imagination enriched by memorable experiences.

Intellectually, of course, his growth ceased for the time being. The ban on all reading material, except the New Testament, in prison was one of the hardest deprivations to bear. News of the world outside rarely penetrated the walls, for newspapers and magazines were also forbidden. Once, during a siege of illness, he managed to procure in the prison hospital translations of *Pickwick Papers* and *David Copperfield*, which he read with the delight of a book-starved man. Upon his release in 1854, the first eager demand he made upon his brother Mikhail was for "books, books, and more books." The list he asked him to choose from is the curious, frightening jumble of a man who feels that his mind has stagnated, and that four empty years must be filled at a gulp: "Send me the European historians, economists, the Church Fathers, as far as possible all the ancients (Herodotus, Thucydides, Tacitus, Pliny, Flavius [i.e., Flavius Josephus], Plutarch, and Diodorus, etc. They are all translated into French). Finally, the Koran and a German lexicon." [1] He also asks for books on physics and physiology, and earlier he had demanded the philosophical works of Kant and Hegel, and contemporary magazines. Books were sent, and he eagerly set to work to remedy the gaping holes in his reading.

There were not many quiet hours for intellectual effort at his disposal. The terms of his sentence required that he serve as a private in a line regiment after his release from prison. He was ordered to the wretched little Siberian garrison town of Semipalatinsk, where he remained a common soldier until 1856. A private in the Russian army in those days led a dull, often brutal existence, not far removed from the kind of life that Dostoevsky had endured as a convict. Yet he accepted these further tribulations as part of his punishment. In keeping with the attitude of patient Christ-like suffering which he had developed in prison, he wrote to Mikhail of these new trials: "I do not complain; this is my cross and I have deserved it." [2] An acquaintance of this time remarked that he would speak of Christ with a moving rapture. He actually worked hard and faithfully as a soldier and strove to win the approbation of his superiors.

Life was boringly uneventful in Semipalatinsk. Dostoevsky read hard and began once again to get the feel of the pen. He became intimate with a young man, Baron A. E. Wrangel, who had arrived from St. Peters-

burg to take over the post of district attorney. With
him he projected translations from Hegel and a version of the *Psyche: Zur Entwicklunsgeschichte der
Seele* (1846) of the German zoologist and physician
C. G. Carus. Nothing came of the translations, but it
would be interesting to know whether Dostoevsky
read this latter work with care. Despite his reputation
for anticipating in a remarkable manner certain ideas
of modern psychologists, it has already been pointed
out that he placed little faith in positivist psychology.
However, in this pioneer work of Carus is information
that may have turned his thoughts to particular psychological manifestations that appear in the great novels. The theory of Carus that mental disease results
from maladjustment between the psyche and its environment must have attracted Dostoevsky, although
he would not have accepted it in its entirety. Then the
notion of Carus concerning the periodic throwback of
all conscious activity into the unconscious is reflected
in the actions of several of Dostoevsky's characters and
directly echoed by Prince Myshkin in *The Idiot*. Carus
also dwells upon magnetism as the intermarriage of
two nervous systems which draws people together, a
theory that may account for the special emphasis
placed upon the magnetic attraction between such
characters as Raskolnikov and Svidrigailov in *Crime
and Punishment*, Nastasya Filipovna and Rogozhin in
The Idiot, Pyotr Verkhovensky and Stavrogin in *The
Possessed*, and Ivan and Smerdyakov in *The Brothers
Karamazov*. Finally, Carus's interesting theory that abnormal states of mind may be the gateway to super-
normal experiences that are very close to divine, and
also his belief in the symbolism of dreams, may well
have influenced Dostoevsky. Indeed, it is very likely
that he profited much from the positivist psychology
in Carus's *Psyche*.[3]

Dostoevsky's reading and his efforts to pick up again
the threads of his literary life were suddenly interrupted by his first serious love affair. It ended with his

marriage in 1857 to a frail blonde widow, Marya Dmitrievna Isaeva. She was already infected with incipient tuberculosis, and she brought him the additional responsibility of her young son. Meanwhile, he had been promoted to an officer's rank as a result of the rewards dispensed by Alexander II on the occasion of his coronation in 1856, and ultimately he had restored to him his rank in the gentry.

Married life increased his ever-present financial needs. With the possibilities of borrowing finally exhausted, he had nowhere to turn but to his pen. Literature, indeed, had never been out of his mind from the moment he arrived in Semipalatinsk. The deep conviction in his own powers had been strengthened, if anything, over this period of enforced inactivity. Come what may, he was sure that his star would rise once again and with a brilliance that would outshine the uncertain brightness of his youthful productions. He had lived and suffered a whole lifetime of experiences during those four years in the Omsk prison, and he felt a powerful creative urge to embody this new material in art.

Various literary designs crowded his brain, and he built upon the ideas he had thought out in prison. His letters at this time (1854-8) are filled with demands for literary information and with criticism of works fresh from the press. It was necessary to renew his old contacts with the editors of magazines, and he liberally mentions plans for future short stories and novels. He refers to his "great final novel" which has been taking form in his mind while at Omsk, but this he must put aside. The conception of the central character, he felt, would take several years to mature in his imagination, and he feared to spoil the whole design by starting to write prematurely.

The business of getting into print once again was beset with difficulties. In the first place, as an ex-convict, he must obtain permission from the government to publish, and such permission was not easy to secure. Then he felt it incumbent upon him to make his first bid to retrieve his literary position a work of real consequence. Yet he feared the hostile attitude of the government towards anything he wrote, and this fear, coupled with the conviction that he had not thoroughly digested the material and plans he had taken with him from prison, filled him with agonizing uncertainty.

He began to suggest to his friends a "patriotic article" on politics and one on Christianity and art. Although he appears to have done some work on them, they were obvious gestures aimed at securing the coveted permission to print and were soon discarded. His heart was in fiction. Finally, in a letter to a friend in 1856, he wrote: "I have worked, but I put aside my chief production. I need more peace of mind. I jokingly began a comedy and jokingly conjured up so many comical circumstances, so many comical figures, and grew to like my hero so much that I abandoned the form of comedy, despite the fact that it succeeded, for my own proper satisfaction, in order that I might further follow the adventures of my new hero and laugh over him myself. This hero is somewhat like me. In brief, I am writing a comic novel, but up to this time I have been composing separate adventures; I have written enough now to sew it all together." [4]

This is Dostoevsky's first comment on the work with which he intended to re-establish his position in Russian literature. It is *The Village of Stepanchikovo and its Inhabitants*, better known to English readers as *The Friend of the Family*, the title given to it by Constance Garnett in her translation. The brief description of the contents indicates that he was not yet ready to trust himself to a work that would draw upon the heart-searchings and tortured spirit of his prison life. He wrote at it intermittently through the next two years, and, as so often proved to be the case with his greater productions later, this "comic novel" grew on his hands.

Its tone became more serious, its substance more complex.

But there were many interruptions. His married life in Semipalatinsk was not going too smoothly, and his need for money was often desperate. Suddenly in January 1858, he wrote to a friend that he was putting aside *The Village of Stepanchikovo* for the time being. He explains that he loves this work and expects much from it, but the very thought of finishing it in haste for money makes him ill in body and mind. Work agitates him so much that he cannot write coolly and swiftly. Accordingly, he has turned to a shorter piece which is progressing well.

His protestations were ingenuous, to say the least, for the length of *The Village of Stepanchikovo* (less than two hundred pages) and its quality hardly justify the amount of time he had already expended on it. Even the shorter piece in which he had sought relief required over another year to finish. These inexplicable delays must be attributed largely to his uncertainty concerning the kind of production with which he wished to make his second debut in literature, for some six years passed after his release from prison before he appeared in print once more.[5] Yet there is evidence to indicate that he worked on seven different projects during this period.

The short piece mentioned above, really a long short story, was the first to be finished and published. It appeared in 1859 with the title "Uncle's Dream." In the light of his vivid prison experiences and of the vague promises in his letters of mighty things to come, "Uncle's Dream" may seem quite disappointing. The critics apparently thought so and passed it over in complete silence. At any rate, it was not a very auspicious start for a man who hoped to take his place among such writers as Turgenev, Tolstoy, and Goncharov, who had already done great things. Turgenev's *Nest of Gentlefolk* had just appeared (1858), and Dostoevsky

angrily asks his brother why Turgenev should be paid
four times as much for his work than he. "I know very
well," he declares, "that I write worse than Turgenev,
but really not that much worse . . ." [6]

Despite the chilly reaction of the critics, "Uncle's
Dream" is one of the best-wrought tales Dostoevsky
ever wrote. Russian readers often select it as their
favourite among his shorter stories as distinguished
from the novels. Perhaps critics do not value it very
highly because it is out of line with his characteristic
work. Yet this tale suggests the versatility of which he
was capable, and if there is nothing in it, with one
possible exception, of the complex brooding figures of
the great novels, the master's touch is felt throughout.

"Uncle's Dream" is the story of Marya Moskaleva,
the leading lady in the society of a small provincial
town. She is excellently portrayed as sustaining her
position through her ability to be more clever, spiteful,
and designing than her rivals. The daughter Zina is a
beautiful woman of the queenly type, completely removed from the pettiness of the town, scornful of her
mother's schemes, and utterly incapable of insincerity.
In her appearance and passionate nature there is a
strong suggestion of Grushenka in *The Brothers Karamazov.*

As the story opens, a certain old Prince K is introduced. He is one of the best portrayals of Dostoevsky,
the sort of caricature that Dickens would have delighted in, and one that he may well have inspired.
Prince K lives entirely in the past, when he was a
prominent dandy. He is represented as a kind of mechanical corpse, all tricked out with false wig, beard,
moustaches, and teeth, and he goes about handsomely
bedecked, pomaded, and scented. Filled with old-
fashioned graces, he has pretty much lost his wits and
is easily led astray. Dostoevsky deliberately uses the
prince's senility and *naïveté* to expose the foibles of the
provincial social climbers.

The mother determines to marry Zina to this old

fool, not only because of his title, but in order to save her from a poor consumptive teacher whom Zina loves. The scene in which she tries to persuade her daughter of the advantages of such a match is written with much of the skill of Dostoevsky's later dialectical method. For the mother reveals her cynical, designing nature completely, yet she convinces both the reader and Zina that her motives are dictated only by her love for her daughter. Zina consents solely in order to obtain money to send her consumptive lover abroad—a suggestion of the mother. The old prince is then made thoroughly drunk and easily led to propose to Zina.

The denouement comes with suddenness, and Dostoevsky makes it a rich scene, filled with mingled comedy and pathos. A foppish suitor for Zina's hand wakes the weakminded prince from his drunken sleep and convinces him that his proposal had been merely a dream. The news of the proposal has spread through the town, and when the prince comes downstairs, Marya Moskaleva's living-room is filled with spiteful women who are determined to thwart their rival's plans. They oblige the mother to announce prematurely the engagement of her daughter. But the befuddled old prince insists that there is no engagement, that it had all been a beautiful dream. Zina, filled with scorn for the assembled people, suddenly steps forward, admits the whole plot, and contemptuously storms out of the room.

Dostoevsky unquestionably drew upon his long residence in Semipalatinsk for this excellent picture of the snivelling society of a provincial town. And no doubt his intense dislike for the place is reflected in the cutting satire on the customs, manners, and stupidity of the various character-types. In one place he remarks: "Everybody in the provinces lives as though he were under a glass bell. It is impossible for him to conceal anything whatever from his honourable fellow-citizens. They know things about him of which he himself is ignorant. The provincial, by his very nature, ought to

be a profound psychologist. That is why I am sometimes honestly amazed to meet so few psychologists
and so many imbeciles."

In the exposure of the cynical motives of these characters, one is reminded of the similar treatment of
provincial types by the famous contemporary drama-
tist Ostrovsky. Indeed, "Uncle's Dream" might easily
be cast in the form of a play in the Ostrovsky manner.
It has many sheer dramatic qualities, and several of
the scenes, especially that in which the old prince declares his proposal to have been a dream, would require little adapting for the stage.

In studying the development of Dostoevsky's creative art, one is surprised at the striking contrast between "Uncle's Dream" and everything that had been
written before. He had indicated his satiric power in
"A Christmas Tree and a Wedding." And the character of the poor consumptive teacher recalls the unhappy, poverty-stricken clerks and students of the
early tales. But apart from these two features, there
are more differences than resemblances. There is a
new sophistication in the approach and an externalization in the treatment of character that is reminiscent of
Gogol's method. Further, one is struck by Dostoevsky's
use of humour in this story. He is not a natural hu-
mourist in either character portrayal or dialogue. In
"Uncle's Dream," however, he provides a considerable
amount of amusement by creating humorous situations, although it must be admitted that the quality of
the humour is nearly always ironic. There is no feminine character in the early tales who remotely resembles Zina, unless it be the unfinished portrait of Netochka Nezvanova. Rather she looks ahead to the great
female figures of the novels, and in the brief analysis
of her nature there is a strong suggestion of the fiercely
contending forces of love and hate which struggle so
disastrously in the later heroines. In one of the last
scenes of "Uncle's Dream," where Zina steals away to
her consumptive lover to forgive him on his deathbed

for an offence he had committed, there is all the atmosphere of pity and that inner quality of throbbing feeling which we associate with similar scenes in the masterpieces.

"Uncle's Dream" served its immediate purpose: it brought Dostoevsky a quick financial return and provided a necessary respite from a larger and more exacting work. He thought highly of the performance, but he had no illusions about its literary significance. On the other hand, he did have a rather exalted notion about the worth of *The Village of Stepanchikovo*, to which he now returned with zest. He finished it shortly after "Uncle's Dream," and it was brought out in the same year (1859).

He chides Mikhail for hurrying him, and reminds his brother that Pushkin achieved his crystal clarity only by constant polishing, and that Gogol's *Dead Souls* took eight years in the writing. "They say that there was not a blot on Shakespeare's manuscripts. That is why there are so many enormities and much bad taste in him, and it would have been better if he had worked. You clearly confuse inspiration, i.e., the first, instantaneous creation of a scene or of an impulse in the mind, (which always takes place so) with work. I, for example, set down at once a scene as it has occurred to me, and I rejoice in it; but then I work over it whole months, years, and I am inspired by it *several times*, and not merely once (because I love this scene) and either lengthen or shorten it several times . . ." [7]

The work on *The Village of Stepanchikovo*, however, now went on apace, and he is soon declaring it to be "incomparably above 'Uncle's Dream.'" Finally, in May 1859, he writes enthusiastically to his brother:

Listen, Misha! this novel has the greatest insufficiencies, and the principal one, perhaps, is prolixity; but in it I am convinced, as I am of an axiom, that it has at the same time great worth, and that it is my *best production*. I wrote it over the course of two years (interrupting it in the middle with 'Uncle's Dream'). The beginning and the middle are

well-fashioned, the end was written in a hurry. But in it
I have put my heart, my flesh and blood. I do not wish to
say that I have unburdened myself in it entirely; that would
be nonsense! There will be much more yet to say. In this
novel there is little of the warm-blooded (i.e., of the passionate element, as, for example, in *The Nest of Gentlefolk*),—but in it there are two tremendously typical
characters, created and set down now for five years,
faultlessly fashioned (in my opinion),—characters entirely
Russian, and until now badly described in Russian literature. I do not know whether Katkov [editor of the *Russian
Messenger*] will appreciate it, but if the public receives my
novel coldly, then I confess I shall perhaps fall into despair.
Upon it rest all my best hopes, and chiefly the strengthen-
ing of my literary reputation.[8]

An author is rarely his own best critic. It may be
mere aesthetic snobbery or a natural desire to protect
a crippled brain child from the unfeeling scorn of the
public that prompts him to praise or condemn his work
in defiance of popular judgment. In general, Dostoevsky was an acute critic of his own productions. But
in the actual course of creation his artistic intentions so
often exceeded his accomplishments that he sometimes erred in evaluating his novels during this stage.
We have already seen an example of it in the case of
"The Double." And this appraisal of *The Village of
Stepanchikovo* appears to be another. The novel is not
"incomparably above 'Uncle's Dream'"; his expectation of popular approval was a vain one—both critics
and public ignored it; and it did nothing to strengthen
his literary reputation. However, he was quite correct
in a few of his comments—the novel is prolix; it has
great insufficiencies; and it does possess two typical
Russian characters, the like of which had not appeared
in native literature. Finally, he was quite justified in
believing that the novel has great worth and was the
best complete work he had written. Although *The
Village of Stepanchikovo* does not deserve a place beside his masterpieces, it has some importance because,
unlike the first tale he finished after his imprisonment,

it preserves a close connection with the fiction of his early period and continues this line of artistic development which was to lead to the great novels. After some ten years he picked up the thread of his youthful tales, and from this point on he never really relinquished it.

It will be recalled that Dostoevsky originally described *The Village of Stepanchikovo* as a "comic novel." The general atmosphere is genial enough, there are some amusing incidents, and the story ends happily. Whatever his initial intention may have been, the comic aspects must have been sacrificed to the more serious psychological analysis of the chief character as the work progressed. For there are frustration and suffering in this story of a man whose human dignity is outraged to the point where he makes an utter fool of himself when circumstances place him in a position of authority. Dostoevsky's besetting sin of wordiness and the admittedly weak ending are serious faults, but the work contains much more intellectual substance than its immediate predecessor, "Uncle's Dream." However, it is difficult to appreciate his statement that he had put his heart, flesh, and blood into this novel. These are weighty words in the light of the profound contents of the later works, and at best they seem inappropriate when applied to a relatively slight performance.

What Dostoevsky had in mind, no doubt, was the effort he expended on the "two tremendously typical characters." Unquestionably he means here the uncle, Colonel Egor Ilich Rostanev, and Foma Fomich Opiskin. The other figures are merely touched on; there is some depth and breadth to the mother, but nearly all the people who make up the mad household of Rostanev are like briefly described pieces of furniture intended to provide a proper setting for the extraordinary Foma Fomich. And the supposed narrator of the story, the nephew, is even more shadowy than the others.

As a Russian type, Rostanev deserves the adjective

"typical," but he is certainly not "tremendous." The description of him at the very beginning of the novel strikes a familiar note: "It is difficult to imagine a man more peaceable and in everything more ready to agree. If you should ask him jokingly to carry someone on his shoulders for two versts, he would perhaps have done so. He was so kind that at times he was positively ready to give away everything at the first request, and to share almost his last shirt with anyone desiring it." So excessively humble is Rostanev that he is ready to accept any blame even before he is accused. That there is something amiss with him he is sure, and in every adverse situation he displays all the patience of a donkey.

Clearly Rostanev resembles Vasya Shumkov in "The Faint Heart" and the poor wretch Emelyan in "The Honest Thief." In his passivity, submissiveness, and voluntary abasement he takes his place among the growing group of characters of the Meek type. His incredible gullibility and infinite forbearance, however, do not lessen our belief in his reality. Yet if one compares him with Nikolai Rostov in *War and Peace*, a character whose status in life as a nobleman and landowner is exactly the same, one immediately perceives the difference in realistic approach between Tolstoy and Dostoevsky. Tolstoy's character, in externals, actions, and thought, would at once be recognized as highly typical. Rostanev awakens our sympathy and interest through the author's concentration on the character's inner life, on the feelings and emotions of his soul. It is true that Rostanev finally does kick over the traces just long enough to throw his tormentor Foma Fomich out of the house. This unexpected act of rebellion is a flaw in Dostoevsky's psychological treatment, a flaw difficult to detect in his later representatives of the Meek type.

But it is Foma Fomich Opiskin who saves *The Village of Stepanchikovo* from being a mediocre work. In this unusual figure Dostoevsky has added another portrait to the gallery of Doubles which he began before his imprisonment. The painting of Foma, however, is more subtle, the colours are stronger, and the image altogether more lifelike than the earlier figures in this group. Foma Fomich presents the first solid evidence of the maturing artistic skill and developing psychological powers of Dostoevsky after his release from prison.

Foma Fomich had been a literary failure in his youth, and finally had sold himself as a hired companion to the decrepit General Krakhotin. The general had degraded him to the position of a family buffoon, and he daily heaped upon him every manner of human indignity. Upon the general's death Foma obtains complete control over his widow and dominates the whole household of Colonel Rostanev, a son of the widow by a former marriage. It is this phase of dualism that Dostoevsky analyses. He makes it clear that Foma, who had been oppressed and crushed all his life and had abjectly played the fool for a crust of bread, is secretly vain and a despot at heart. "A base soul escaping from oppression becomes an oppressor," Dostoevsky observes. "Foma had been oppressed, and he at once had a craving to oppress others." One would suppose that once he had established himself in the home of Rostanev, the object of everyone's admiration, the struggle between the two opposing tendencies in his nature would cease. But the struggle must go on. The more he feels himself abased, the more he desires to express his own independence. When Foma believes that people esteem him, he is happy; but then he quickly imagines that they are laughing at him and he begins to humble himself. The very struggle becomes a kind of enjoyable self-torture. And out of this contradiction of self-esteem and self-abasement in Foma, Dostoevsky formulates the psychological urge of the split personality to suffer and to make others suffer. His analytical treatment indicates an advance over the Doubles in the early tales. For now he appears to suggest that in the conflict between self-esteem and self-abasement there is a kind of reciprocity that is almost psychic; the two states of mind aid and abet each other. This dominant aspect of Foma's dualism—the desire to suffer and to make others suffer—Dostoevsky developed in a more profound manner in later characters.

It has been conjectured that Foma Fomich is a parody of Gogol, that is, of the religion-goaded Gogol of the later years when he wrote a book of moral preachments intended to reveal his message to the world. (This is the very book that Belinsky lashed so fiercely in his famous letter.) There may be some truth in this suggestion, for the naïvely pompous Gogol, spouting moral and religious platitudes which everybody ridiculed, resembles Foma Fomich in his obvious struggle of boundless self-esteem and pietistic humility. It will also be remembered that Dostoevsky, in his first description of the contents of *The Village of Stepanchikovo*, mentioned that the "hero is somewhat like me." It is difficult to know whom he had in mind at that time, for in the completed novel both Foma and Rostanev play leading roles. In reality, he probably drew upon himself for certain traits in both characters. The large-souled generosity, humbleness, and impracticality of Rostanev and the essential dualism of Foma Fomich recall similar features of Dostoevsky's own nature.

Over the years 1854 to 1859 the drift towards conformity with Church and State which Dostoevsky had manifested in prison assumed a more positive direction. Of course, all the circumstances of his life during this period forced compliance to the existing order of things. He was an ex-convict struggling for existence in a workaday world, and his marriage—not a very happy one—simply intensified the struggle. It is hardly an exaggeration to say that sheer economic necessity only served to hasten the religious and political transformation that had begun in prison. He wished to get

out of the army, to regain his social status, to obtain
permission to print, and above all to secure the right to
return to St. Petersburg, where he would have the
stimulus of his intellectual friends. These favours from
the government were not easy to obtain, and the fact
that they required some six years of persistent effort
on his part and on that of friends indicates the difficulties he laboured under.

The means he employed were deplorably abject, and
the degree to which he humbled himself is understand-
able only on the basis of his desperate situation. He
wrote patriotic poems, one celebrating the birthday of
the Dowager Empress Alexandra, another on the coronation of Alexander II, and a threnody on the death of
Nicholas I. Begging letters were addressed to people
in power and to the new tsar himself. In them he protests that he adores the young monarch whom he describes as a sun shining on the just and unjust alike,
and he declares he is ready to give up his life for him.
The crime for which he was convicted he readily confesses to, but insists that he has repented and is now
suffering for opinions that he had abandoned.

Although some of this sycophantic crawling may be
discounted in the light of the exigencies of his situation and of the peculiar conditions of autocratic Russia at that time, it is interesting to speculate on the extent to which he had actually discarded his political
beliefs of the days when he conspired against the
government. In a remarkable letter that he wrote to
Apollon Maikov in January 1856, he clearly expressed
his state of mind at this time on matters political, and
we may be fairly certain that he was sincere with this
old friend. In his St. Petersburg days he had been a
frequent visitor at the home of the Maikovs, and there
he had heard a great deal of discussion about the nationalist ideas of the Slavophiles which were then going the rounds—that Russia was utterly different from
and superior to Western Europe; that the West was
doomed because it lived by violence, whereas Russia,

with its voluntary compact between people and tsar, would develop and thrive peacefully; that the Roman Catholicism of the West was a religion of the reason and Russian Orthodoxy a religion of the true spirit of Christ. Apollon Maikov had put little faith in these Slavophile ideas at that time, and it will be recalled that Dostoevsky had trusted him enough to ask him to join the conspiratorial Durov Circle. But over the years of Dostoevsky's imprisonment Maikov had changed, and in a letter he had explained the change and enclosed some patriotic verses. A part of Dostoevsky's reply is worth translating with some fulness, for it dates the line of political thought that he had now assumed much earlier than it is commonly dated in treatments of this subject. In fact, the letter suggests a real connection between the ideas of his youth and those of his maturity.

You say [he writes] that you were thinking about me warmly, and you were saying why, why? [a reference to Dostoevsky's youthful political activities]. I myself have been remembering you warmly, and to your word: why?— I say nothing—it would be superfluous. You say that you have experienced much, have done a great deal of thinking, and have arrived at much that is new. It could not be otherwise, and I am convinced that even now, in ideas, we would come to an understanding. I have also thought and experienced, and the circumstances and influences were of such a nature that I had to live through, to think over, and to ruminate too much, more than one could stand. Knowing me very well, you will truly do me justice in that I always followed what seemed to me best and more direct, and did not act against my heart in what I gave myself to, and I gave myself eagerly. Do not think that with these words I am making any hint at the reason why I am here. I speak now about what followed it; this is not the place to speak about what happened before, and that was nothing more than an accident. Ideas change, the heart remains the same. I read your letter and did not understand the chief part. I speak about patriotism, about the Russian idea, about the feeling of duty, of national honour, about everything which you speak of with such rapture. But my friend!

Is it possible that you were otherwise at any time? I always shared precisely these same feelings and convictions. Russia, duty, honour—yes! I was always sincerely Russian— I speak to you frankly . . . I read your verses and found them excellent; I fully share with you the patriotic feeling of the *moral* freeing of the Slavs. This is the role of Russia, of noble, great Russia, of our holy mother . . . Yes! I share with you the idea that Europe and its destiny will be fulfilled by Russia. For me this has long been clear. You write that society has awakened from some apathy. But you know that in our society a general manifestation does not take place. Yet who has concluded from this fact at any time that it is without energy? Illumine well your thought and summon society and society will understand you."

In this unusual statement we have an expression of Dostoevsky's Slavophilism as early as 1856, and this was essentially the direction of his thought for the remainder of his life. His remarks make it clear, however, that it was not the narrow-minded Slavophilism of the nationalist party. What he is vaguely aiming at is a synthesis of the ideas of both Westerners and Slavophiles. When he says, "I was always sincerely Russian," he pointedly refers to his feeling in the 1840's when he was involved in a political conspiracy, as well as to his feeling after his experience in prison. This was also the feeling of such revolutionary thinkers as Herzen and Belinsky in the 1840's. It explains his opposition to the social theories of Western Europe even in his youth. And his conviction that Europe's destiny depended upon Russia was held by certain of the Westerners as well in the second half of the 1840's. The real difference between the Westerners and the Slavophiles was rooted in their different approaches to this historic mission of the Russian people. The Slavophile approach was at once religious and mystical, that of the Westerners realistic and historical. The Westerners, however, believed that the future path of Russia's historical growth would be European, whereas the Slavophiles were convinced that it would be purely Slavic. Their ultimate aim was the same, and

Dostoevsky had already begun to think along the lines of a synthesis of both ideals.

His various attempts to move the government in his favour were at last successful. He was finally permitted to resign from the army, and in July 1859 he left the hated Semipalatinsk for the city of Tver. After some months of languishing in this provincial town, his plea to the emperor that he was in urgent need of medical aid succeeded. Just ten years after he had set out for Siberia in chains he was back once again in his beloved St. Petersburg, a free man.

6

Time
and *The House*
of the Dead

Prison did not teach Dostoevsky the wisdom of silence on political and social questions. During his dark days of exile he had thought long and hard about many matters that affected the Russian people, and he now speculated on the medium best calculated to convey his ideas to the public. In fact, the notion of founding a large review had been in his mind for some time. Such a magazine would be an outlet for his own fiction, and would also enable him to express his views on national questions which were being discussed on every side. The financial returns from a successful magazine were a further incentive.

The year of Dostoevsky's return to St. Petersburg (1859) was a period of difficult readjustment for him. Not only had he developed considerably since he left the capital ten years before, but the political and social ideology of Russia had changed. The Crimean War had been fought and lost. The disastrous conflict

revealed to the world the corruption and abuses of the
bureaucracy of Nicholas I, and the national outcry for
reform was heeded by his successor, Alexander II. For
a Russian ruler, he was an extreme liberal, at least
during a part of his reign. In 1861 serfdom was abol-
ished, but the act brought little alleviation in the miserable existence of the peasants. And the emancipation was quickly followed by a whole series of judicial
reforms of consequence. Belinsky and his Westerners
of the 1840's would have felt that a tremendous step
forward had been made by these reforms of the 1860's.
Certainly Dostoevsky himself was favourably impressed.

Belinsky, however, was dead, and meanwhile the
revolutionary movement had advanced much beyond
the pious hopes of this father of the Russian intelligentsia. Augmented by many ruined landowners and
members of the lower middle class, the intelligentsia
had become political-minded. Under such leaders as
Herzen abroad and Chernyshevsky in Russia, the revolutionary movement gained hundreds of ardent
youths who were prepared to defy the government.
This rising generation was stronger and fresher and
closer to the people. It possessed an advantage over
the young radicals who had lived through the hopeless
stagnation of the 1840's, for it had the experience of
the Crimean War and the vigorous reforms that followed. And now the ideas of Karl Marx and Bakunin
were already beginning to make themselves felt in Russia. In effecting their revolutionary programme, the
new generation of radicals could be hard, cold mate-
rialists who scorned sentiment and worshipped science.
They formed secret political societies and demanded
action, and the terrorist acts that soon occurred bear
bloody testimony to this demand. Turgenev was to
call these revolutionists "nihilists," a generalization
quite inappropriate. Dostoevsky was to condemn them
vehemently.

Such was the political climate when Dostoevsky returned to St. Petersburg. He found the revolutionary element of the capital eager to glorify him as a former political prisoner. But he had no desire to accept this halo. It was not so much that he had learned the one lesson of conformity to constituted authority during the years that he had been buried in Siberia. The rebel in him was never very far beneath the surface. Nor as a member of an older generation was he jealous of the more advanced views of a younger group. His social and political opinions had not remained static in exile. He had simply grown to distrust the extremes of radicalism, and especially of a radicalism that now openly ridiculed religion. Besides, he was formulating his own panacea for the ills of Russia.

At this precise juncture, however, his thoughts were entirely occupied with the project of the magazine. There was not a little competition to be feared from well-established journals. And he encountered an additional difficulty: to an ex-convict under police surveillance the authorities would not give permission to run such a publication in his own name. (He was to remain under police surveillance until almost the end of his life!) Nothing daunted, he went busily ahead; permission was secured in Mikhail's name. With the brother as business-manager and Dostoevsky as the anonymous directing force behind the whole project the first issue of the magazine *Time* (*Vremya*) appeared in 1861. He was very fortunate to have among his faithful advisers and contributors the amiably drunken but brilliant critic Apollon Grigorev and the clever young philosopher Strakhov. *Time* quickly won popular approval, and by the second year of its existence was able to compete on equal terms with the most successful magazine in the capital. For some months Dostoevsky was in easy financial circumstances.

Much of the success of *Time* must be attributed to Dostoevsky's skilful editorial policy and to the political and social views he promulgated. For years journalism in Russia had been dominated by extreme partisanship. The rival magazines literally justified their existence by advocating one or the other side of the political and social struggle between Westerners and Slavophiles, for of course various shades of public opinion could be gathered under the banners of these two camps. It was not merely journalistic astuteness or any awareness of a popular demand for a compromise that influenced Dostoevsky in laying down a middle-of-the-road policy in *Time*. In his letter to Apollon Maikov, quoted in the preceding chapter, it was indicated that as early as 1856 he had been meditating upon the possibility of reconciling the programmes of both Westerners and Slavophiles.

The platform of *Time* rested on the assumption that the intellectuals among Westerners and Slavophiles were really working towards the same end—the ultimate salvation and glorification of Russia. One vital factor that both groups were overlooking was the vast mass of Russian people. The well-intentioned reforms of Peter the Great, Dostoevsky maintained, had split asunder the educated class and the common people. He now urged the intellectuals of both factions to join with the common people and seek in these children of the soil the true national spirit and salvation of the nation. For in the people, he felt, existed a spiritual force that would bring order out of the Russian chaos, and eventually harmonize the contradictions between Russia and the West. In the pages of *Time* he gave no indication of the *modus operandi* by which this national and international harmony was to be brought about. He was ever impatient of definitions and intellectually deficient in considering the practical aspects of his theorizing. Rather he dealt with large conceptions and eternal truths after the fashion of the philosopher or prophet, and he dramatized these political, social, and religious ideas very much as his great characters were dramatized ideas of human experience. Yet this platform of *Time* is substantially the programme he adhered to for the remainder of his life, and if we can believe the remarks in his letter to Apollon Maikov in 1856, he had dimly glimpsed these ideas even before his Siberian exile. In the succeeding years, of course, he elaborated and developed them in a more comprehensive fashion, and again and again he introduced one phase or another of this vast harmonizing scheme into his novels.

In *Time* he did not hesitate to criticize both Westerners and Slavophiles for what he considered their reactionary tendencies, and the magazine was correctly rated a liberal organ. He stood for the liberal reforms of the period, advocated the emancipation of women, and preached the spread of literacy among the peasants and schemes for their social betterment. The success of the magazine fed that desire for power which was a definite part of his dualistic nature, and he laid about him in its polemical pages with the eager and happy abandon of one whose words carried weight and authority. He had a deep interest in journalism and a high degree of talent in the practice of it, and often he transformed the material of journalism into art.

In some of the articles in *Time*, Dostoevsky utters many of his characteristic thoughts and formulates them in the very language that he used later in his novels and journalistic writings. That vehement faith in Russia and its people, and his emphasis upon their complete difference from the people of Western Europe, are reiterated again and again. Although it was axiomatic in his system of thought, this persistent notion seems to amount almost to a rooted sense of national inferiority which had been engendered by the low opinion of Russia and its people widely entertained in Western Europe. "We believe," he writes, "that the Russian nation is an unusual manifestation in history of all humanity. The character of the Russian people up to now is unlike the character of any contemporary European peoples . . . In it [the Russian character], for the most part, is a highly synthesizing capacity, a capacity of universal reconcilability, of universal humanity." [1] Even his views on art, to which he devotes much space in *Time*, he manages to express in terms of this curious chauvinism which is really not chauvinism because of its universal implications. "And do you know this," he writes, "we are convinced that in Russian society this inclination to the humanitarian, and consequently the response of its creative talents in everythng historical and common to mankind, and in general in all these varied themes, was the most normal condition of this society, at least up to now, and perhaps it will remain in it forever." [2]

The popular success of *Time* was to some extent dependent upon the purely literary works of Dostoevsky that appeared in its pages. The two most important were *The House of the Dead* and *The Insulted and Injured*. Although the instalments of the latter were actually completed first in the magazine, the literary history of *The House of the Dead* antedates it. Nearly everything that Dostoevsky wrote was first published in magazines. In Russia, as in most of Europe at this time, serial publication of fiction was much favoured by authors. It offered attractive financial returns, for an author was usually free to bring out his novel in book form after magazine publication. Serialization, however, often had a deleterious effect on the form of a novel, and this was as true in Dostoevsky's case as in the cases of certain of the English Victorian novelists. Although he usually had a fairly complete idea of the whole novel in his mind when he began to write, the plan often changed as he proceeded, with the unfortunate consequence that he could not make the necessary alterations in the earlier parts which had already appeared in print. In these circumstances, the remarkable fact is that his novels are as well formed as they are.

Dostoevsky very probably conceived the idea of *The House of the Dead* as early as 1855, even before

The Village of Stepanchikovo. It was one of the several projects he contemplated after his release from prison, and why he put it aside in favour of the other works is not precisely known. It may well have been a desire to give this performance his most careful consideration, for it is clear that he early became convinced of its striking, even sensational literary possibilities. From the critical vantage point of the present, *The House of the Dead* would have been the most effective work with which to re-introduce himself to the reading public. When he took it up again in 1859 he worked hard through the whole autumn, and finally the first chapter appeared in a weekly newspaper in September 1860. Difficulties with the censor may have interfered at this point, for the work was discontinued and began to appear again in the following year. By then his own magazine had materialized and *The House of the Dead* was issued afresh in *Time* in 1862.

Dostoevsky represents *The House of the Dead* as the memoirs of a man who had been condemned to ten years in prison for killing his wife. The book, of course, is a faithful record of his own experiences in the Siberian prison of Omsk. With deliberate intent, however, he kept the narrative quite impersonal, for he seemed to realize that it would gain in impressiveness if he avoided parading the personal element through its pages. With inconsequential exceptions, he refrained from preaching or moralizing. Nevertheless, while admiring the effectiveness of the stark realism, readers have often wondered how he could have been so impersonal about an experience that seared his soul. And in any case they did expect him to preach something of a crusade for reform in prison life. Yet there is very little suggestion for reform, and with an artist's instinct he resisted the temptation to indulge in either the usual pious admonition or the bitter invective against man's inhumanity to man which are so frequent in the prison exposé. Nor should it be forgotten that Dostoevsky accepted his imprisonment as a punishment deserved, one that had taught him the justification of salvation through suffering.

Critics very often dismiss *The House of the Dead* as a piece of superb reporting and nothing more. They praise its grim, detached realism, but they profess to see in this book nothing of Dostoevsky the artist, the creator of the great characters of the novels. It has even been suggested that Tolstoy was displaying a contempt for Dostoevsky as an imaginative writer when he placed *The House of the Dead* at the head of all his rival's works. To be sure, the book is free of certain of the characteristic aspects of Dostoevsky's fiction which Tolstoy disliked most, but his high praise was no doubt inspired by artistic qualities quite other than those of a super-reporter.

The business of selection, a most important function of the artist, is everywhere apparent in *The House of the Dead*. A reporter would not have singled out from the maze of experiences undergone in four years of prison precisely those features which provide the greatest interest for the reader. Not mere observation, but artistic re-creation accounts for such vivid scenes as the convicts in the communal bath and the highly diverting theatrical performance. And what might be considered an artistic purpose is skilfully woven into the narrative of prison life. Without obtruding the fact, Dostoevsky sustains the theme that many of these criminals possessed qualities of calm courage, real goodness, and even a certain nobility of soul which he associated with the common people. In this interaction of the artist and his material one can detect Dostoevsky's growing faith in the Russian masses.

In keeping with the criticism that *The House of the Dead* is only a piece of reporting is the usual stricture that the situations and not the characters compose the significant feature of the work. Quite the reverse seems to be true. Dostoevsky purposely describes the most striking personalities of the prison. They are not described with an obvious emphasis upon externals and the place they fill in the prison community. He imaginatively apprehends these personalities; he presents them psychologically. He peers into their souls and tries to discover what they think, why they committed crime, and how they react to their punishment. Whatever claims the originals may have had on human sympathy and interest, a few of these convicts, passed through the alembic of Dostoevsky's art, emerge as memorable characters in *The House of the Dead*.

In his early tales Dostoevsky had evinced a fugitive interest in the criminal type. The shadowy figure of Bykov in *Poor Folk* has elements of the criminal in him; and Murin, the strange old man in "The Landlady," is definitely of this stamp, although at best the characters betray a lack of knowledge of the criminal type which must have been abundantly augmented by Dostoevsky's thorough observation of his fellow-prisoners at Omsk. In at least two of the convicts in *The House of the Dead* he obviously displays a deep psychological interest.

The first of these is Orlov, who was famous among the convicts as a criminal capable of murdering old men and children in cold blood. Dostoevsky particularly emphasizes his perfect command over himself, his boundless energy and thirst for vengeance. He possesses an indomitable force of will that shirks no obstacles in the path of his desires, and an innate pride that enables him to regard with haughty disdain the weaker convicts of the prison. He is a "brilliant example of the victory of spirit over matter," declares Dostoevsky.

The other convict, Petrov, has a nature that resembles in certain respects that of Orlov. Dostoevsky describes him fully, for he had apparently been friendly with him. Petrov is the most dangerous criminal in the prison. As a common soldier, he killed his colonel for striking him on parade. The psychological picture Dostoevsky draws is of a man who is quiet, reserved, and

strangely curious. But suddenly, for some unaccountable reason—a fancied slight, a wretched object he desired—he will instantly kill a man. Reason has no
power over Petrov, for he is urged on by will. He is
born with one idea which pursues him all his life. For
twenty-five kopeks he will murder a man simply to get
a pint of vodka, yet he is also capable of disdaining
thousands of rubles.

Dostoevsky's interest in this proud indomitable criminal type that acts on impulse, by sheer will rather
than by reason, is manifested in his analysis of other
convicts in *The House of the Dead*. Even a superficial
knowledge of certain of the characters in the novels
indicates the extent to which he uses this fuller psychological understanding of the criminal type. With
convincing reasons, one Russian critic concludes that
in such figures as Orlov and Petrov, Dostoevsky found
a psychological answer to the struggle of submissiveness and pride or self-will in the dualistic natures of
the characters of his early tales.[3] If it is possible to con-
ceive of a split personality in which self-will gains complete ascendancy, then the character's nature would
resemble that of the criminals, Orlov and Petrov.
Everything would be subordinated to the fulfilment
of one's desires. The social instinct would be atrophied,
human sympathy could be completely absent, and
normal joy and suffering would therefore find no outlet
for expression. Like Orlov and Petrov, such an individual would be more like a wild animal than a human
being, for with savage energy every criminal impulse
of the will would be transformed into action.

In his future works Dostoevsky did not simplify to
this extent, unless he was treating an utterly criminal
type, such as Fedka in *The Possessed*. But his observations in prison did lead him to see a connection between criminality and the dominance of self-will in
human nature, and the fact eventually inspired him to
create a new type of character—the Self-Willed type.
Just as he perceived a generic connection between the

Meek character and the Double in whose nature submissiveness had got the upper hand, now he observed
a similar relationship between the Self-Willed type
and the Double in whom pride and self-will dominate.
In the split personality of Foma Fomich, for example,
exist cruel, antisocial, amoral elements such as we find
in Orlov and Petrov. The criminal in the soul of Foma
Fomich, however, is confused and weakened by his
timidity and submissiveness. In characters that he
created later, the desire to be evil prevails, and the
mysterious, resolute Self-Willed type appears.

In any study of Dostoevsky's creative art, one must
conclude that *The House of the Dead* is of considerable importance. In this book is the first tangible evidence of his deep interest in the criminal type. He
probed the careers of these convicts; he turned the
powerful searchlight of his psychological analysis on
the dark recesses of their crime-laden souls in an effort
to illuminate for his own uses the reasons why they
had sinned. And some of the great characters in the
novels that followed represent symbols in a world of
free men resurrected from his experiences with these
prisoners in *The House of the Dead*.

7

The Insulted and Injured

While Dostoevsky was still in Semipalatinsk, stewing in his indecisive creative ferment, he wrote to Mikhail in May 1858: "I have put aside writing a novel until my return to Russia. I did this out of necessity. The idea in it is quite happy, the character new, not having appeared any place as yet. But as this character is no doubt in great vogue in Russia in real life, especially now, judging from the movement and ideas with which all are full, then I am convinced that I shall enrich my novel with new ideas when I return to Russia." [1]

This is apparently his first mention of *The Insulted and Injured*. The new movement and ideas he felt necessary to observe in Russia proper were no doubt connected with the altruism which seized people at the end of the 1850's in anticipation of the freeing of the serfs. For in this emotional sphere is conceived the noble-minded hero of the novel and its main theme —the free love of a woman and the recognition of her right to this love. In another letter, shortly after the one just quoted, he mentions the novel as something that, "according to all indications, will be my *chef-d'oeuvre*." [2]

By October of the next year he had left Siberia for Tver, and yet the most he could report to his brother about the new work was: "I have resolved then: to begin to write a novel (a large one—this is already decided)—it will take me a year to write it. I do not desire to hasten it . . . I wish to write it freely. This is a novel with an *idea* and it will bring me into fashion. But in order to write it, I must have security." [3] And to obtain funds to guarantee the necessary leisure for the work, he proposes to issue a collected edition of his fiction. Actually *The Insulted and Injured* did not appear until 1861, when it was published serially in the pages of *Time*.

Critics have never thought highly of this novel, but in dismissing it with faint praise or no praise at all, they have perhaps accorded it less than justice. If it had not been followed by greater works, with which it must bear comparison, *The Insulted and Injured* might have won a more favourable hearing. For in many respects it was an improvement over anything he had written previously and it should be regarded as transitional between his earlier efforts and the series of masterpieces that began with *Crime and Punishment.* With a certainty that does not exist in the case of the earlier productions, one can detect in *The Insulted and Injured* something of the authentic feel and atmosphere of the great novels.

Despite its faults, *The Insulted and Injured* appears to possess most of the aspects of a novel, although nowadays one enumerates them at one's peril. It has a story plot, and characters; but it would be difficult to find those more tenuous aspects—fantasy, prophecy, pattern, and rhythm. An apologist might unearth some semblance of pattern, but rhythm in any form is undiscoverable. All the staple ingredients of a story, however, it surely has, and one is tempted to remark that it has too many of them. If the story of a novel is the "chopped-off length of the tapeworm of time," then the tapeworm of *The Insulted and Injured* was never chopped off soon enough. That is, the story is altogether too complex with relation to the thinness of the other elements.

The eternal-triangle plot would ordinarily cause no difficulty, but this familiar design in *The Insulted and Injured* seems to flatten out into a parallelogram and before the end of the novel the reader feels as though the plot is leading him in a circle, and a vicious one at that. Vanya loves Natasha, but he does everything in his power to aid her love for Alyosha; Alyosha in turn loves both Natasha and Katya, and each girl is willing to further the suit of the other. This love in triplicate, which soon shifts to a four-cornered situation, eventually becomes confusing. Further complications of the plot make for confusion worse confounded—the story of Natasha and her mother and father strangely paralleling that of Smith and his daughter; the amazing adventures of little Nellie and her dawning love for Vanya; the mysterious relations of Valkovsky to all the principals in the case; and then, the perplexing muddying of the intrigue by the shady but well-intentioned plotting of Masloboev and the mysterious letter strung about Nellie's neck. Nor does this complexity in plot-structure go down any the easier because of the thick garnishing of melodrama and its accompanying sentimentality. Dostoevsky also falls afoul of the old stumbling block of the novelist: the conclusion of his tale. For the conclusion of *The Insulted and Injured* is a lame and impotent one. He avails himself of the time-worn device of death and marriage to cut the stout knot of intrigue—marriage is at least suggested as the solution of the affair between Alyosha and Katya. The reader, however, feels that he has been left suspended in the weak evasion of the ultimate fate of Vanya and Natasha. And the fact that vice is allowed to triumph over virtue in the behaviour of the dastardly Valkovsky may puzzle the morally exacting reader, although under the circumstances it is not an artistic fault. But that Dostoevsky should have allowed this important character to drift so inconclusively from the scene at the end is a real lapse of artistic judgment.

To go beyond these strictures would amount to carrying critical depreciation too far. The surprising fact is that more characters were not slighted in such an intricate plot. On the whole, Dostoevsky threads his way through the maze of intrigue with sure craftsmanship. There is some confusion in the order, which happens rather frequently with him, largely because of his method of composition. The intricate plot, however, has one excellent justification—mystery. Mystery is a genuine, and may be a highly artistic feature of the plot of a novel. Various devices—the suspension of time-sequence, holding back important information, and reversing the order of events—are legitimately used. However one may cavil over the details, the element of mystery in *The Insulted and Injured* grips the reader's attention from the beginning to the end of the story.

Dostoevsky made it clear in the letter to his brother that the work was a novel "with an *idea*." The idea, which concerns the right of the heroine to offer her love in defiance of convention and family control to the man of her choice, is not well sustained, and like so much else in the novel, is lost in the complicated intrigue. In writing a novel about an idea, however, he had adopted a new approach. It became a favourite one in much of his future fiction in which the ideological and psychological contradictions of his great characters are embodied ideas. An explanation of the artistic development of this process may be profitably postponed until the consideration of his more famous works.

As in any novel, the real excellence of *The Insulted and Injured* must be sought for in its character portrayals. For a novel may have all the so-called aspects, but if it lacks characters who are real, living beings, it is hardly a novel. It is not enough to say that the characters, in that hackneyed phrase, "come to life." The novelist must reveal the hidden existence of his imaginary men and women, and he must convincingly show how their thought develops into action. All the characters of *The Insulted and Injured*, judged by this severe test, do not come off very well, but a few of them are portrayed with satisfactory completeness.

The hero Vanya (Ivan Petrovich) is an exasperating creation, and largely so because he belongs to that category of Meek characters. He is an author, and it is interesting to observe that Dostoevsky drew directly upon his own early career in describing that of his hero. Vanya's literary life in St. Petersburg and his sickness and poverty are faithful transcripts from Dostoevsky's initial experience in the capital. Even the nature of Vanya's first story, the circumstances of its publication, and the reaction of critics and public resemble closely the known facts concerning *Poor Folk*.

It would not be surprising if Dostoevsky, having stood as the model for Vanya to this extent, should have further drawn upon the circumstances of his own life in portraying the hero. Such appears to be the case. The curious situation in which Vanya, despite his love for Natasha, makes every effort to aid the cause of his rival, bears a close resemblance to the facts of Dostoevsky's courtship of Marya Dmitrievna Isaeva in Semipalatinsk. While passionately in love with this woman, he did not hesitate to encourage and even assist the suit of the young teacher who in the end almost married her. And the psychological basis—his complete willingness to sacrifice his happiness for her sake—is repeated in the case of Vanya. That he had his own situation in mind gains additional support from the fact that in external appearance at least Natasha is modelled directly on Marya Dmitrievna.

The love of Vanya for Natasha Ikhmeneva is a

strangely sexless one. She treats him as something less than a man, and yet she admires him for the quality of passive devotion which grows out of his endless submissiveness, the hallmark of the Meek type. Although his excessive and unrequited devotion passes all accounting, Vanya does not fail to gain the reader's interest and sympathy, for Dostoevsky fully reveals his unusual nature. It is a nature ennobled by all those rare virtues which take on saintlike proportions in the Meek figures of the more famous novels.

The paucity of female characters in the works of Dostoevsky written before his exile to Siberia, and the insufficient treatment of the few that do appear, are no doubt a reflection of his lack of interest in women during these early years. To be sure, he would write to his brother of gay parties with pretty actresses, but there is a false note in this boasting, for he appears to have led a peculiarly sexless existence up to the time of his marriage at the age of thirty-six. Varenka in *Poor Folk*, it will be remembered, exists largely to bring out the character of Devushkin, and in the short stories in general the emphasis is almost entirely upon male figures. The one considerable exception is the central character of *Netochka Nezvanova*, and it is perhaps a bit indicative that he never finished this work. After his release from prison, he clearly became more interested in women in his life at Semipalatinsk, where he experienced his first serious love. The fact that after this event women began to play an increasingly larger part in his imaginative writing argues a deeper knowledge of the sex. In "Uncle's Dream," written at this time, Marya Moskaleva and her daughter Zina give us really the first hint of the powerful insight he was later to display in female psychology. And Natasha Ikhmeneva in *The Insulted and Injured* is his first fully-drawn heroine, and she is a worthy forerunner of the great female figures of the masterpieces.

Dostoevsky's principal women characters fall into the same general types as his men, although their dis-

tinctive traits are not drawn so sharply and their
sphere of psychological variation is not so broad. For
him, women appear to be largely women in love,
and it is noticeable that in his fiction he concentrates
chiefly on this phase of their existence. Such an emphasis does not necessarily indicate an artistic short-
sightedness or limited powers of observation. He never
subscribed to the notion that a woman's life is peculiarly a life of love, although in her this experience may
be more significant, more lasting, more emotionally and
spiritually enriching or destructive. The simple fact is
that the Russian woman had not yet entered into the
world of broad social life, activities, and careers. Consequently her world of intimate relations, the inner life
of the heart, had a more profound and important significance, and hence became the centre of her psychological life.

Then the type characteristics of Dostoevsky's male
figures—their dualism, meekness, or self-will—manifest
themselves in the female characters principally in the
experience of love. The essential dualism of Natasha
Ikhmeneva is revealed through the story of her love for
Alyosha and Vanya. The female Double in love, who
wavers between cruelty and tenderness, between self-
abasement and self-love, had been vaguely suggested
in previous works—in "The Landlady," *Netochka Nezvanova*, "The Little Hero," and "Uncle's Dream." Natasha Ikhmeneva, however, is the first completely portrayed representative of this emotional dualism, and
she is also one of the most finished characterizations in
the group. With such women there can be no equality
in love, for love is either complete slavery or complete
mastery, and often the dominating emotion is maternal.
Caught between these opposing forces, she suffers and
makes her beloved suffer. After the final break with
Alyosha, Natasha sums up her feelings: "You see,
Vanya, I decided that I did not love him as an equal,
as a woman usually loves a man. I loved him as a . . .
almost as a mother." (Part IV, Chapter III) That is, her

love for Alyosha was not concerned essentially with
mutual happiness or with the growth of her own personality. In this strange love, compounded of pity, sacrifice, and suffering, are mingled the joy of dominating and the pleasure of torturing. "Natasha instinctively felt that she would be his master, his sovereign,
that he would even be her victim. She anticipated with
pleasure the happiness of loving endlessly and torturing the man she loved simply because she loved him,
and that was why perhaps she hastened to give herself
to him first as a sacrifice." (Part I, Chapter IX) This
type of the female Double in love is developed with
subtle variation and deeper psychological insight in future portrayals, such as Polina Alexandrovna in *The
Gambler*, Nastasya Filipovna in *The Idiot*, Liza in *The
Possessed*, and Grushenka, Katerina Ivanovna, and
Liza Khokhlakova in *The Brothers Karamazov*.

Despite his particular concentration upon Natasha's
emotional dualism, Dostoevsky does not neglect the
other aspects of her nature which he reveals with extraordinary thoroughness. She possesses a feminine
wisdom or intuition which enables her to perceive
clearly the whole nature of the man she loves, and to
understand perfectly her own position in relation to
Alyosha. She has known him but a short time and is
ready to desert her family for him, yet she is able to
prophesy with despairing clarity to Vanya, who deeply
loves her, all the misery of the step she is taking:

'Yes, I love him as though I were mad,' she answered,
turning pale as if in pain. 'I never loved you like that,
Vanya. I know I have gone out of my mind and do not
love as I ought to. I don't love him in the right way . . .
Listen, Vanya, I knew beforehand, and even in our hap-
piest moments I foretold that he would bring me only
misery. But what is to be done if even torture from him
is happiness to me now? Do you suppose I go to him for
happiness? Do you suppose I don't know beforehand what
to expect from him and what I shall have to bear from him?
Why, he has sworn to love me, has given me all sorts of

promises; but I don't trust one of his promises, I don't set any value on them and didn't before, although I know he didn't lie to me and can't lie. I told him myself, that I don't wish to bind him in any way. That's better with him; no one likes to be tied, I less than any. And yet I'm glad to be his slave, his willing slave; to put up with anything from him, anything, so long as he is with me, so long as I can look at him! I think he could love another if only I were there, if only I might be near . . . Isn't it abject, Vanya?" (Part I, Chapter VIII)

With all her sure understanding of her feelings and of Alyosha's, Natasha is powerless to avert the anticipated outcome of her passion. The dualism of her nature prevents her achieving happiness. She is condemned to sacrifice for her love and she fully realizes it. But she is willing to suffer, for in suffering alone does she see any hope of salvation. "We shall have to work out our future happiness somehow by suffering; pay for it somehow by fresh miseries. Everything is purified by suffering." (Part I, Chapter xv) Here, incidentally, we have the first expression of this famous doctrine in Dostoevsky's fiction. And Natasha finally makes the last and greatest sacrifice for the man she loves—she surrenders him to another woman in order to secure his happiness. One may experience a modicum of unreality in her extreme actions, however psychologically convincing is the motivation for her behavior. Yet these wide-hearted, self-sacrificing, long-suffering Russian women have a great literary tradition behind them that goes back to Tatyana in *Eugene Onegin,* and is verifiable in real life in the patient forbearance and suffering of those noble women who followed their husbands, condemned in the Decembrist Revolt, into Siberian exile.

The incredibly wise though childlike Katya is a successful rival for Alyosha's affection, but she has nothing of Natasha's deep moral feeling and emotional complexity, despite Dostoevsky's efforts to portray her as a convincing foil. Katya gives the impression of a second-

thought invention in fulfilling her function of presenting the only way out of the Natasha-Alyosha impasse.
Either he did not expend enough effort on her or else
the long build-up for the characterization leads us to
expect more from Katya than she is capable of giving
when we are finally introduced to her. Before he has
gone very far, he appears to suspect her unnaturalness,
and he offers up an observation by way of extenuation
for the unusual behaviour of this seventeen-year-old
girl: "I cannot refrain from a strange and perhaps entirely inappropriate remark. From my three hours' conversation with Katya I carried away, among other
things, a strange but profound conviction that she is
still such a child that she knows nothing at all of the intimate relations between men and women. This gave
an unusually comic flavour to some of her reflections, and in general to the serious tone with which
she talked about many important matters." (Part III,
Chapter IX) His deliberate explanation, however,
adds little to the convincingness of the characterization, for the comic flavour persists throughout Katya's
worldly conversation which finds no justification in
her extremely limited experience with life.

The reader may well react in a similar fashion to
that weird fourteen-year-old creature Nellie. But another observation, which Dostoevsky makes about
Katya, should be applied to Nellie if we are to understand her strange, unchildlike actions: "She was quite
a child, but somewhat strange, a child entirely with
convictions, with steadfast principles and a passionate,
innate love of goodness and justice. If she could really
be called a child, she belonged to that class of *thinking*
children who are fairly numerous in our Russian families. It was evident that she had already pondered
much. It would have been curious to peer into that
little pondering head and to see how quite childish
ideas and fancies were mixed with seriously surviving
impressions and observations of life." (Part III, Chapter IX) Obviously the important difference between

Nellie and Katya arises from the unusual circumstances surrounding the life of the younger girl. Dostoevsky carefully describes the mature and harsh experiences to which Nellie has been subjected and they go far towards making credible her unique behaviour.

In the early works, such as "A Christmas Tree and a Wedding," *Netochka Nezvanova*, and "The Little Hero," Dostoevsky had already evinced a special interest in the complexities of child psychology. Nellie provides further evidence of his unusual insight in this respect. And Polenka in *Crime and Punishment*, the children in *The Idiot*, the early life of the hero of *A Raw Youth*, and the well-known sections of *The Brothers Karamazov* concerning Kolya, Iliusha, and the gang of boys provide brilliant proof of Dostoevsky's acute understanding of child behaviour. Indeed, the subject might be made one for special investigation, for he obviously had definite theories on child psychology, some of which are suggested in *The Diary of a Writer*. In most of his characterizations the children may appear to be too grown-up, too mature for their age. But it is well to remember that he is nearly always portraying, as he indicates in the quotation above, "thinking children" who have been victims of the sadder and more mature experiences of life. He was convinced of the innate wisdom, the intuitive comprehension of children, and psychologically his treatment is exceptionally sound and wonderfully penetrating.

The conception of Nellie was unquestionably suggested by Dickens's Little Nell. It will be recalled that Dostoevsky had read certain of Dickens's works in the prison hospital at Omsk, and he continued to read and admire them for the remainder of his life, and in some cases was much influenced by them. There is a vast difference, however, between Dostoevsky's Nellie and her prototype in *The Old Curiosity Shop*. Like Dostoevsky, Dickens was deeply concerned in his fiction with the problems of children, but his creations can hardly be called "thinking children." He is more intent upon wringing our hearts and draining the last tear of pity for his abused minors. In the depiction of Nellie, Dostoevsky also comes very close to the border of sentimentality, and perhaps on occasions he crosses the border. Nevertheless, against an unusual background her puzzling nature and strange actions seem true to the experiences of life, and the characterization remains convincing and altogether absorbing.

Alyosha Valkovsky, the last figure in this complicated four-cornered love-duel, does not fall readily into any of the established character-types. There are traits of both the Double and the Meek types in his makeup. At that memorable meeting of Natasha and Katya, both girls discuss with utter frankness the virtues and faults of Alyosha in an amazing effort to discover who shall surrender him. They completely understand this eternal child who has no will of his own. Thoroughly attractive to women, and always with the best intentions, he seems fated to win and then to forego their love simply because he has no control over the constancy of his affections. Love is not even a matter of will with him, beyond the restraint of his reason; it amounts to an irresistible pursuit of any pretty face that makes an impression on him. Yet he brings to each occasion all the fine qualities of his nature—kindness, generosity, and a sincere willingness to sacrifice. He is selfish but only from the best motives, in his own eyes, and it is difficult for him to understand why, with his infinite capacity for affection, he cannot be in love with all women at one and the same time. If one accepts these psychological premises, the character of Alyosha is an effort of subtle delineation. He may be an impossible creature, he may entirely lose the reader's sympathy because of his quixotic actions, but he is always vital, for Dostoevsky never fails to be convincing about the reasons for his aggravating behaviour.

Alyosha's father, Prince Valkovsky, is not an artistic success. Although he plays an important role in the novel, he is a mysterious shadow who never at any point takes on the substance of reality. In Dostoevsky's literary development, however, Valkovsky is perhaps the most significant character in the novel, for he is the first sophisticated representative of the Self-Willed type which Dostoevsky had observed in his Siberian prison and portrayed in a somewhat elementary form in the persons of Orlov and Petrov in *The House of the Dead*. In Valkovsky he attempts to improve upon this criminal type by conceiving a more complex personality and subjecting it to a deeper psychological analysis.

Valkovsky at once strikes the reader as rather absurd, for he is a prince who belongs to a high, worldly society, yet he is rarely presented in situations which bring him in contact with his own social level. As a matter of fact, he seems much more at home with the lowly, poverty-stricken, underground life of the city. Nor do these humble associations appear in keeping with the fact that he is unusually clever, an astute sophist, and quite a dialectician. In his sophistry is revealed a rooted, antisocial nature, one of the essential traits of the Self-Willed type. His philosophy of life amounts to a complete negation of every social obligation and truth, and his manner of thinking entirely corresponds to his actions. Apart from himself, he loves and esteems no one and feels that all the world was created for him. He is ready to stoop to crime not merely for personal gain, but because he derives an evil satisfaction out of it. He destroys for the sake of destruction.

In his extraordinary confession to Ivan Petrovich (Part III, Chapter x), Valkovsky reveals his vile nature completely. He glories in the nastiness of his past, and with unfeigned pleasure describes his licentiousness and contempt for decency. "I have long since freed myself from all shackles, and even obligations . . . At the root of all human virtues lies the utterest egoism. And the more virtuous anything is, the more egoism there is in it. Love yourself, that's the one rule I recognize." In short, he has a positive dislike for ideals and for everything moral that society stands for. Unlike the criminals Orlov and Petrov, his enmity to society is not instinctive, but reasoned. He is convinced that all people are like him, only they refuse to be as frank about their immorality and criminal instincts.

In this further development of the Self-Willed type, the psychological ambiguity is obvious. Valkovsky possesses very much the same traits as Orlov and Petrov, but these lowly convicts wreaked their vengeance on society because society had beaten and condemned them. Their reactions were elementary and instinctive. Prince Valkovsky, a member of high society, manifests this same self-willed determination to trample on everything and commit crimes. But his hostility to society is conscious and a matter of principle. Dostoevsky suggests a reason for this unique behaviour in a man of Valkovsky's sophisticated background. He explains that the absolute power Valkovsky possessed over his serfs had developed in him a strong despotic sense which eventually degenerated into a lack of respect for all law, order, and morality. Such reasoning would seem to be exceptionable. The serf-owner was often cruel and despotic, but it would amount to a supposition contrary to fact to imagine him devoid of all sense of human decency and convinced of his moral right to commit crime. To this extent Valkovsky fails as a characterization, for it is impossible to accept the far-fetched motivation for his extreme actions. Yet Dostoevsky clearly learned much from this attempt at a sophisticated representation of the Self-Willed character, and he put his knowledge to good use in further creations of criminal types.

It is hardly necessary to consider the remaining characters in *The Insulted and Injured,* such as the Dickensian caricature Smith, the genial sleuth Masloboev, and the appealing parents of Natasha. None of these falls into the several types I have been describing and they suggest no difficulties in interpretation.

Despite its technical defects, it should now be obvious that *The Insulted and Injured* represents some advances in the delineation of character over anything Dostoevsky had written up to this point. And it is indiscreet and uncritical to overlook any work of a genius that indicates progress along the special line of his literary development. Finally, it may be noted that the publication of *The House of the Dead* and *The Insulted and Injured* in 1861-2 virtually regained for Dostoevsky the reputation he had enjoyed before his imprisonment. The critics hailed these works, and once again he was regarded by the public as one of the leading novelists.

8

Notes from the Underground

Much of consequence took place in the life of Dostoevsky between 1862 and the publication of his next important work, *Notes from the Underground*, in 1864. They were agitated and sorrowful years. The material circumstances that radically altered his daily existence contributed also to the further development of his creative art.

For a time his magazine continued to be successful, and financially his situation was better than ever before. The sale of the book rights to *The House of the Dead* for a large sum augmented his good fortune, and he seized upon the opportunity to realize a dream that had titillated his thoughts ever since his youth. Like all educated Russians who had drawn heavily upon the culture of Western Europe, he yearned to see those countries and peoples about which he had read and thought so much. The time was now ripe and at last the means were available. He left the magazine and his ailing wife in charge of Mikhail and with feverish anticipation set out for Western Europe in the summer of 1862.

The journey was a momentous one. In controversial articles in the pages of *Time,* Europe had already become a significant factor in his theorizing on the political, social, and religious problems of Russia. His attitude to the West had been antagonistic, but his knowledge of its civilization had been drawn from books and hearsay. Now he had an opportunity to observe at first-hand. Although he was never to surrender his conviction of the historical value of Western European culture in the development of Russian civilization, the unfavourable impression he experienced on this first visit tremendously influenced his whole future attitude.

There are many external and even purely whimsical factors which determine the reactions of foreigners abroad. No set of experiences is better calculated to arouse prejudices than those the traveller undergoes outside his own country. Unlike the average American innocent abroad who fails to appreciate the fact that one cannot live by bathrooms alone, Dostoevsky seemed to be vastly annoyed at the higher European standards of living because he felt that they indicated a weakening of the moral fibre. Nevertheless, there was a certain method, if not justification, in his criticism which he made amply clear in an account of the trip, "Winter Notes on Summer Impressions," published in his magazine in 1863.

This narrative is not simply a splenetic confession of intolerance, as it is so often represented. He did not come to these countries to inspect the drains and then return home to express his surprise at finding them filthy. Neither was he particularly interested in the monuments of art and architecture. He was concerned with the people and the faith they lived by, with the governments and the principles by which they ruled. His visit, of course, was impossibly brief to form any

considered opinions on these matters, but what he did
see filled him with hostility. The people of Paris he
found a money-grubbing lot of petty shopkeepers. Perhaps he still retained some of his youthful ideals
about the French Revolution and hence expected to
find liberty, equality, and fraternity written on the
brow of every Frenchman. The bourgeois aspects of
the population sickened him. "A strange creature, this
bourgeois," he wrote. "He directly anounces that
money is the highest human virtue and duty, and at
the same time likes very much to play at the highest
goodness." [1] In the French bourgeoisie he saw nothing
but servility which was accepted by them as a virtue.
His reflections on the French people in "Winter Notes
on Summer Impressions" led him to a consideration of
this country as the principal source of socialist thought
and action. He wonders why these money-loving bourgeoisie seem always frightened. Are they afraid of the
arguments of pure reason? Pure reason does not exist,
and if it did, it would prove worthless before the exigencies of reality. Are they afraid of the workers?
"However, the workers are also, in spirit, property-
owners: their whole ideal is to become property-
owners and to hoard as much as they can; such is their
nature." [2] Are they afraid of the socialists? Yes, they
scorn and yet fear them. But the socialists in the West,
Dostoevsky maintains, are no better than the bourgeoisie. For liberty there meant to do what one wished
within the limits of the law, and money alone gave
one the power to do as one wished. Equality also was
equality before the law which each Frenchman accepts as a personal offence. Finally, fraternity cannot
exist in the West, for the selfish instincts of this society
prevent the voluntary surrender of the individual for
the benefit of the community.

The trouble with socialism in the West, Dostoevsky
explains, is its attempt to legislate by reason those sac-
rifices that should come from the heart. True brotherhood demands utter selflessness, and this spirit the so-

cialist tries to inculcate by reason in a society which is accustomed to demand its rights with the sword in hand. "One must sacrifice," he writes, "to the extent of giving everything and not even wishing that anything be given in return . . . How is this to be done? It is impossible to do it, but it must be done in and for itself, it must be in one's nature, unconsciously existing in the nature of the whole tribe. In a word, there ought to be a foundation of brotherly love—there ought to be love." [3] Dostoevsky concludes that in the end the bourgeoisie will prevail.

In London also he found conditions which offended him. He was shocked by the contrast between the misery of the London slums and the hypocritical respectability of the better sections of the city. The poverty and rampant vice in the Haymarket were only emphasized in his eyes by the complacent attitude of the well-dressed gentlemen and fat, contented ministers of the Church. These impressions coloured his whole judgment of the city which not even a visit with Herzen and an excursion to the famous Crystal Palace could efface. From England he went to Switzerland, where he met his friend Strakhov, and together they travelled to Florence. Already bored with the trip, he did not bother to go on to Venice and Rome, and returned directly home.

In his radical youth Dostoevsky shared the opposition of the Petrashevsky Circle to capitalism. This first visit to Europe, in which he saw all around him the visible evidence of the abuses of capitalism, inspired a real fear in him, for Russia too was beginning to manifest signs of capitalist growth. Even the liberated peasants were falling into the evils of petty capitalism. The inevitable class struggle that would grow out of this new development represented in his eyes a terrible danger for Russia. He already saw signs of the struggle in the thriving revolutionary agitation. In the contradictions of capitalism he foretold the future destruction of Western Europe, and he already felt the necessity of pointing out that the same fate awaited his own country. The proletariat had not yet developed as a class in Russia, but in Western Europe he saw it as one of the most vicious aspects of the bourgeois organism.

Clearly this first visit abroad cannot be dismissed as just another biographical fact in Dostoevsky's life. He carried with him a more or less idealized picture of his own countrymen, and by contrast his observations in Europe seemed to strengthen his faith in the future high destiny of Russia if it could be kept free from the poison of the West. To be sure, he reasoned like a romantic. He arbitrarily opposed the historic path of Russia to the historic path of Western Europe. With the same arbitrariness he constructed a special character for the Russian people, for he was already beginning to believe that his country could remain free from the influence of the materialistic elements of Western capitalistic civilization, from the influence of the stock exchange, railroads, and factories. He had the hope, which later developed into a conviction, that Russia could escape this bloody class struggle in the West and could preserve its spiritual purity while its moral purity would enable it to select its own historic path and avoid the catastrophe of capitalism. The line of thought is only implicit in "Winter Notes on Summer Impressions," but the account frankly declares a militant opposition to Western Europe which was to play an increasingly larger part in his future theorizing. It also reflects a further drift in the direction of Slavophilism which soon became apparent in his outspoken hostility to what he considered the destructive influences of Western European thought in Russia.

Upon his return home he resumed his editing, and apart from "Winter Notes on Summer Impressions," he wrote only one other piece of consequence. This is a short story, "A Vile Tale" ("An Unpleasant Predicament" in the Garnett translation) which appeared in *Time* in 1862. Technically it is a perfect performance in this genre, and there is a timelessness about it that keeps it always fresh and interesting. In the character of the poor clerk and in his adventures the flavour of the early tales is mingled with the satiric and ironic humour of "Uncle's Dream." It is the story of a high official who fancies himself devoted to the brand of humanitarianism that was then much in vogue. On his way home from a party the tipsy official suddenly decides to attend the wedding celebration of one of his humble clerks. By favouring these wretched underlings with his company he imagines that he will be giving proof of his magnanimity and humanitarian feelings. The reaction is quite contrary to his expectations. The guests resent his butting in on their party. At the supper one of the more headstrong revellers tells off the official in no uncertain terms: "Yes, you came to show off your humanity! You have interfered with the enjoyment of everyone. You've been drinking champagne without realizing that it is too expensive for a clerk with a salary of ten rubles a month. And I suspect you are one of those high officials who are a little too fond of the young wives of their subordinates!" The climax is reached when the intruder rises at the table to reply to the charge and to plead his humanitarian motives. At this juncture, however, he is overcome with liquor. Amid the hoots and derision of all present he falls face forward into a plate of blancmange.

In an interesting passage in this amusingly satirical tale Dostoevsky observes: "It is well known that whole trains of thought sometimes pass through our brains instantaneously, like sensations, without being translated into human speech, still less into literary language." Then there follows a broken recital of the drunken official's thoughts which is clearly built up on an associative pattern. The whole passage suggests a deliberate use of the technique of the contrapuntal phase of the stream-of-consciousness.

A year after the appearance of "A Vile Tale" Dostoevsky underwent a series of misfortunes. A Polish rebellion had broken out and public feeling ran high. *Time* published an article on the question by Strakhov. The intention of the young philosopher was to take the government side, but unfortunately the article was so vaguely written that it permitted the contrary interpretation. A storm of patriotic criticism arose and the magazine was quickly suppressed by the government. It was a severe blow, for it left Dostoevsky and his brother in debt and with no immediate means of repairing their fortunes.

Strangely enough, in the midst of this trying situation, Dostoevsky suddenly decided to go abroad again. The reason he gave was to seek treatment for his epilepsy, which had been growing more severe. Although this may have been a contributory factor, the actual reason seems to have been a desire to repair his fallen fortunes at the famous gambling resorts of Western Europe. Another, and perhaps more irresistible reason, was to keep a rendezvous in Paris with a beautiful girl with whom he was in love. In August 1863 he borrowed money from the Fund for Needy Authors and went directly to the gambling tables of Wiesbaden.

On this second trip the significant experiences that eventually found their way into the creative stream of Dostoevsky's art require some explanation. For different reasons the visit was perhaps more important than the first in its influence on his fiction. The story of his unhappy passion for gambling, which he indulged to excess on this and other occasions, has been made much of by biographers. The conviction that he had devised a system to beat the game was an irrational notion which he made literary capital of. The gambling passion was no doubt compensatory, a substitute for some other strong emotional disturbance. He thoroughly understood the psychology behind his obsession and he made excellent use of his experiences in *The Gambler* and briefly in *A Raw Youth*. After a few temporary gains at Wiesbaden, he lost a good deal more than he won, and he probably would have lost all if his rendezvous in Paris had not proved the stronger of the two passions.

The girl was Polina Suslova, a handsome devotee of the new type of emancipated woman. She coquetted with the revolutionary movement and seemed to believe that flouting social conventions was the logical way for a woman to express her individuality. She bobbed her hair, wore dark glasses, and never went to church. Her offences against decency, however, have been highly coloured by biographers and critics, and the usual picture of her giving herself to one student after another in her enthusiasm for the new civilization is an unwarrantable slander. It was probably by way of getting a short story in Dostoevsky's magazine the previous year (1862) that she became acquainted with him.

Dostoevsky fell passionately in love with this girl half his age, and in the initial stage of the affair they were apparently on very intimate terms. Without any hesitation he followed her to Paris, deserting his wife, who was already far gone in consumption and with whom he scarcely seemed to be living at this time.

While waiting for him in Paris, Polina fell in love with a young Spaniard who quickly jilted her. Either as a pretext or because the new affair had genuinely affected her feelings, she used it as a reason for severing the intimate bond between her and Dostoevsky. Nevertheless, they decided to go to Rome as they had previously planned, but now as "brother and sister." It was a wretched adventure for both, and particularly for Dostoevsky, whose passion had by no means cooled. After weeks of torturing each other, they finally separated, and Dostoevsky returned to Russia. Polina had steadfastly remained a "sister," and she exploited their relationship in a literary way by basing several short stories on this unhappy journey.

The whole situation might have come out of one of his novels. Dostoevsky's strong feeling for Polina re-

mained with him for years. Yet she ultimately learned
to hate him, a hate not unmingled with vestiges of her
original love. The reasons for her strange reactions are
obscure. It is said that she blamed it all on his unwillingness to divorce his wife and marry her. Dostoevsky
suggested, and perhaps correctly, that her feeling was
the hate of a woman for a man who had first sinned
against her and whom she never entirely possesses.
Their relations, by way of correspondence at least, did
not break off after this journey to Italy. Polina eventually married and deserted the well-known critic Rozanov. And eventually she also deserted her revolutionary sympathies for the camp of the reactionaries.

This experience deeply affected Dostoevsky, both
emotionally and creatively. The dualism which was
not entirely absent in his wife's behaviour, and which
he had developed in the character of Natasha Ikhmeneva in *The Insulted and Injured*, existed in an intensified form in the unusual nature of Polina Suslova. He
had been made a victim of the love-hate emotion of a
female Double in real life, and the experience enriched his understanding of the type. The results are
immediately apparent in *The Gambler*, which is literally an imaginative rendering of much that happened on his Italian trip with Polina Suslova. This
strange woman unquestionably contributed to the portrayals of those remarkably strong-willed, fiercely hating and fiercely loving heroines—Polina Alexandrovna
in *The Gambler*, Dunya in *Crime and Punishment*,
Nastasya Filipovna in *The Idiot*, and Katerina Ivanovna in *The Brothers Karamazov*.

Dostoevsky returned home deeply agitated and far
from well. He found his wife slowly dying from consumption, and he took her to the drier climate of Moscow. Meanwhile, a stroke of luck brought a small
legacy which enabled him and Mikhail to revive the
suspended magazine, for the authorities had finally
relented. It appeared in 1864 under a new name, *The
Epoch* (*Epokha*). In this same year his wife died after

a protracted period of terrible suffering. Some four months later Mikhail, a confidant and mainstay in all his literary endeavours, also died. As a final blow he had to abandon the magazine at the turn of the next year despite heroic efforts to keep it going.

Dostoevsky had been able to do little writing during these two years of domestic and business woes. *The Epoch* got off to a bad start. While he was at the sickbed of his wife in Moscow, Mikhail had to shoulder most of the responsibility. Money was lacking and the censors wantonly mutilated contributions. The magazine won none of the initial popularity that had greeted the appearance of *Time*. Furthermore, the programme of *The Epoch* indicated a significant retreat from the liberal position of the earlier magazine, a retreat in keeping with the changed views he had announced after his first trip abroad. In its pages war was waged against the so-called nihilists, and a perceptible leaning towards some of the more reactionary ideas of the Slavophiles was noticeable.

While Dostoevsky was nursing his dying wife, subject to all manner of privation and to the torments of a sick woman out of her mind most of the time, he courageously set to work on a production which was intended for the opening issue of *The Epoch*. This work was *Notes from the Underground*, which he may well have conceived in the emotionally agitated frame of mind induced by the frustrations he endured on his "brotherly" excursion with Polina Suslova. He began it with the idea of writing a short piece, but it grew on his hands in both length and importance. In a letter to his brother in April 1864, he writes: "The story lengthens. Sometimes I dream it will be trash. However, I am writing with fervour. I do not know how it will turn out. Yet in this matter what is needed is much time." A little further he concludes rather unfeelingly: "I am afraid that the death of my wife will take place soon, and this will cause a necessary interruption in the work. If there should be no interruption, then it seems that it ought to be finished." [4] A little later he again writes to Mikhail, expressing his hopes and fears concerning *Notes from the Underground:* "What am I to do? Surely it is not possible to print it unfinished. It is impossible. It cannot be divided. However, I do not know what will become of it—perhaps it will be trash. But personally, I place strong hopes in it. It will be a powerful and frank thing; it will be truth. However bad it may be, yet it will produce a powerful effect. I know it. Perhaps it will be very fine." [5] Actually, the first part came out in the first and second numbers of *The Epoch* (January and February 1864), and the second part in the fourth number (April 1864).

Notes from the Underground is in some respects a remarkable work which reveals a concentrated power of psychological analysis unique in literature. Its relatively short length (about a hundred pages) is no indication of the real importance of this production in the creative development of Dostoevsky. Critics often divide his fiction into the works written before and after his imprisonment, and the statement is frequently made that there is little or no connection between the short stories and novels of these two periods. The unsoundness of this view has already been indicated, and it should now be apparent that up to 1864 his fiction reveals that there has been a consistent development in theme, characterization, and form. The few exceptions only serve to emphasize this general conclusion. Of course he improved tremendously, over this stretch of almost twenty years of writing, in technique, in a broader understanding of human nature, and in psychological insight. It is necessary to go even further with this generalization, for one purpose of the present study is to demonstrate the fact that Dostoevsky's fiction maintains a consistent pattern of development to the end of his creative life. From beginning to end there are certain constants in his creative art—type-characters, psychological problems, ideological themes, and an undercurrent of consistent though constantly developing philosophy.

If Dostoevsky's total production can be separated into creative periods at all, the dividing date should be 1864, when *Notes from the Underground* was published. For with this work the previous uniform pattern of his fiction changes in one important respect. The change parallels the sudden shift, at this same juncture, from the liberalism of *Time,* which he had more or less sustained from the days of his youth, to the conservatism of *The Epoch.* The fundamental reasons for the change are difficult to ascertain, but undoubtedly the events of his life from 1861 to 1863, particularly his first trip abroad, the affair with Polina Suslova, and the death of his wife and brother, were contributing factors.

One critic has pointed out[6] that if we consider the five famous novels—*Crime and Punishment, The Idiot, The Possessed, A Raw Youth,* and *The Brothers Karamazov*—as the five acts of a great classical tragedy, then *Notes from the Underground* would stand as a kind of prologue to the drama. The basic motifs of the five acts appear in this prologue, not very pointedly or in much detail, but almost as convincingly as in the great novels.

The change in the uniform pattern of Dostoevsky's creative art in *Notes from the Underground* is quite obvious. The preceding heroes of his short stories and novels are not particularly complex in either their thinking or emotional lives. With the possible exception of the unreal Valkovsky, they exist more for their feelings and instincts than for their convictions. One is always aware of the absence of any deep moral consciousness, and this fact seems to interfere with a fundamental sense of personality. Their very inability to analyse their feelings indicates a vague understanding of their own personalities. Now in this respect the hero of *Notes from the Underground* marks an abrupt change in Dostoevsky's approach to characterization. The underground man is a profound analyst of his own feelings and of those of others. He is deeply, morbidly conscious of his personality and an astute logician in explaining its complex nature. Like the heroes of the great novels, he argues endlessly as he minutely dissects his thoughts, emotions, and actions. This underground man is Dostoevsky, the engineer of human souls. In short, *Notes from the Underground* fully reveals what had only been suggested in earlier works— Dostoevsky's searching dialectic, his unique ability to dramatize the conflicts of human minds. This dialectic is not so much the power of discursive thought; it is a kind of omniscient consciousness expressed in compelling language.

Although Dostoevsky called *Notes from the Underground* a novel, this description finds little support in either the form or content. It is cast in his favourite form of a confession, or better still, a diary, a deliberate narrative device which enables him to maintain suspense and create mystery by the simple trick of having the events appear as mysterious to the imaginary writer of the diary. In a footnote at the beginning he announces that his purpose is "to expose to the view of the public, more clearly than is usually done, one of the characters of the recent past. He is one of the representatives of a generation still living." The first part, entitled "The Underground," presents a microscopic self-analysis of the underground man, an unhappy individual of about forty who has been in the government service. The second part relates a few striking experiences in the life of this character, and they become doubly significant against the background of the thorough self-analysis of the opening section.

It is immediately evident that the underground man is a Double, and the ambivalence of his nature is not far removed from the intense pathological aspects of Golyadkin's dualism in "The Double." All the conflicting forces in the split personalities of the early heroes

exist in the underground man—he thirsts for power
and is powerless, he desires to torture and to be tortured, to debase himself and to debase others, to be
proud and to humble himself. Every positive human
attribute seems to inspire its negative quality in him.
Like several of the early Doubles, he is an inveterate
dreamer, and in his dreams he achieves all those ambitions of power, pride, and self-esteem which he is
incapable of realizing in actual life. The one important
difference between the early Doubles and the underground man is that he is fully aware of his dualism. In
truth, a morbid consciousness of all the contradictions
in his distorted personality appears to be the whole
story of the underground man, the entire substance of
his searching analysis.

From the underground man's own account we gather
a few facts about his early life which illuminate the
problems of his unintegrated personality. An orphan
and a dependent of unsympathetic relatives, he had
led a miserable, lonely existence at school. His comrades snub and mistreat him, and he tries to show his
independence, and at the same time gain their praise,
by leading the class in studies. He treats the one friend
he makes at school with all the cruelty and spitefulness
which are his own lot. Forced in upon himself, he becomes a dreamer and imagines himself in a position of
grandeur while he eats out his heart in abject misery
over the failure of others to appreciate his cleverness
and refined feelings. This whole experience recalls
Dostoevsky's schooldays, and it was repeated in fiction in the case of the hero of *A Raw Youth*.

After he leaves school the underground man enters government service. During this period he seeks
relief from his poisoned existence in furtive debauchery. When he realizes that such an escape cannot satisfy the rational man, he takes for his ideal the man of
action. He begins to wonder whether the rational man
can ever respect himself, and he ends by ridiculing
modern thinkers who propound theories designed to

set people on the path of normal interests. Does not man prefer to act as he chooses and not as reason dictates? And he concludes that man wants independent choice; he will choose pleasure even though reason oppose the choice. The only gain of civilization for mankind, the underground man decides, is a greater capacity for variety of sensation.

As time goes on the conflicting forces of his nature crystallize. "I felt that in me raged opposing elements." His recognition of this fact and all its implications takes a clearer form in his mind as he analyses his reactions. He knows that he is cowardly and obtains an intense enjoyment from his own degradation, yet he also realizes that he is impossibly vain. More than anything else he wants power and respect, for he is convinced that he is more clever and intelligent than the people around him. His analysis leads him to the conclusion that the conflict in his personality is based on one fundamental opposition—an opposition between will and reason. Will negates reason and in its turn is negated by reason. Reason tells him that he is an insect, a mouse, and that it is no one's fault that he is these things. His abasement does not depend upon himself or his surroundings, but upon certain elementary forces over which he has no control. However, his will does not reconcile itself with such a conclusion, and therefore he feels that he must get rid of his reason, since reason paralyses his activity. But he cannot get rid of his reason.

Thus the underground man continues through life, wallowing in the hopeless contradictions of his personality, aware of his worth, yet incapable of making it effective or of impressing it upon others. In his heart he yearns for the approval of people whom he secretly scorns. While dreading humiliation, he goes all out of his way to seek it. In this confusion of cross-purposes he retreats into himself and stores up venom and spite for all and sundry.

In the second part the underground man relates cer-

tain experiences which serve as vivid illustrations of
the actual workings of his dualistic nature. He thrusts
himself into a convivial party of former schoolmates.
They do not desire his company and he despises them,
but he desperately wants them to like him. After undergoing terrible humiliation from his companions, he
follows the party to a brothel with the intention of
slapping the face of the ringleader in order to prove his
own pride and worth. He fails to find them there and
consoles himself with one of the entertainers of the
house. When he wakes up in the early morning, he lec-
tures his pretty bedfellow on the evils of her calling.
His macabre picture of the terrible fate that awaits her
reduces the girl to tears and penitence. For a moment
he is carried away by his own eloquence and the apparent sincerity of his desire to reform the prostitute.
Then he quickly realizes that he does this for the sense
of power it gives him, and that he is actually trying to
compensate himself for the humiliation he had suffered
at the hands of his schoolfellows by humiliating this
unfortunate girl. In his momentary elation he invites
her to his lodgings and leaves the brothel well pleased
with himself.

For days he indulges his inflated ego over his success and even imagines that he might marry the girl.
This notion alternates with the fear of what might
happen if she should really visit him and see his
wretched quarters and learn of his pitiful existence.
When she does unexpectedly come, she surprises him
in a degrading scene with his own servant. Suddenly
convinced that he has lost his lofty position in her eyes,
he furiously blurts out that his eloquent sermon of
that night had been false, and that he had merely been
making fun of her, for now he longs to make her suffer
again in order to reassert his former feeling of superi-
ority. With swift feminine intuition, however, she perceives his true wretchedness and suffering and pities
him in an embrace of real love. After responding, his
hypersensitive, self-torturing nature tells him that she,

in her sincere love for him, has envinced the very nobility of soul which he is incapable of. With black envy in his heart he deliberately offers her money as though he has understood her pure affection to be the common solicitation of a prostitute. Still she conquers in the end, for she rejects his money and runs out, leaving him a prey to the baseness of his soul in an experience which had touched his finest instincts.

The inner struggle of Dostoevsky's own nature, intensified and deepened by his experiences abroad and with Polina Suslova, are clearly reflected in this extraordinary characterization of the underground man. More than this, it is very likely that the work is a deliberate and cruel parody on the social and political ideas Dostoevsky had held previous to the change which becomes noticeable after his first trip abroad. In 1865, the year after the appearance of *Notes from the Underground*, he published in his magazine an amusing skit, "Crocodile." Although he vehemently denied it later, the charge has often been made, and with much justification, that this short piece is a satirical allegory on Chernyshevsky's arrest in which the radicals and their ideas are ridiculed. In a similar fashion the underground man pours forth his accumulated bile on the radical followers of Chernyshevsky. The line of reasoning is very similar to that expressed by Dostoevsky in his attack on the socialists in "Winter Notes on Summer Impressions." With transparent satire, the underground man inveighs against the egoism of socialists who believe that human beings can be governed by rational self-interest. Human nature is not so simple, he argues, and anyway man is essentially irrational. The futile struggle between his own will and reason proves this. Reason no more determines the path of a man's life than the path of history. If society could be established on a perfectly rational basis, he declares, and man had to live by it, then man would rebel. The implication is obvious. The socialists are wrong in their reasoned Utopias. Man must have

something else to fall back on. This had already become Dostoevsky's own position.

The substitute for reason is not mentioned in *Notes
from the Underground,* although there is evidence to
indicate that it had been included but was deleted by
the censor. The answer, however, had been emphatically stated in "Winter Notes on Summer Impressions."
Man must have religion, faith, and Christ to fall back
on. To carry the thinking of the underground man to
its logical conclusion, he would have to surrender his
reason to a love of Christ if he is to achieve peace of
mind and ultimate salvation. The contrast between the
underground man and the prostitute turns on the fact
that she possesses pity and love and hence can be
saved; he has only reason to fall back upon, and from
reason spring his own everlasting contradictions. He is
cut off from life and is damned.

Like all the Doubles, then, the tragedy of the underground man is that he wishes to be something that he
is unable to be. And he cannot find a way out of his
dilemma because he has no faith. The disharmony between will and reason remains with him to the end,
and from thinking too much on it, he believes the same
disharmony to exist in all men.

Up to this point in the development of Dostoevsky's
creative art, the underground man is the most finished
picture of the Double. Unlike all his predecessors,
however, he is a thinking, a highly intellectual Double.
As a piece of self-revelation the work is one of the most
powerful in literature, and it is a long step to certain of
the great characters in the novels that followed. Hitherto Dostoevsky had never dissected a human soul so
completely and so convincingly.

9

In the Author's Laboratory

Dostoevsky's misfortunes did not cease after the deaths of his wife and favourite brother and the failure of his magazine. The years from 1864 to 1866 were among the most wretched in an existence that had been solaced by few of the amenities of life. He was overwhelmed by debts and the many demands made upon him. Not only was he held responsible for the large sums owed to the creditors of the bankrupt magazine, but he had dutifully taken upon himself the support of his brother's widow and her numerous brood as well as of Mikhail's mistress and her child. Added to this burden was the maintenance of his stepson and pressing requests for aid from his younger brother Kolya. Dostoevsky regarded such obligations as sacred and he did his best to fulfil them. In darkest adversity he had a wonderful power of looking forward to a time that would be bright, and these periods of incurable optimism were sustaining factors in his life. As during those black moments in the Peter-Paul prison, when hard labour in Siberia awaited him, he now called up hidden reserves of vitality, and despite the lack of any palpable resources, actually felt that he was about to begin a new and happier existence.

Throughout the whole of 1865 creditors dunned him, and at one point he narrowly escaped being thrown into a debtor's prison. Once again he borrowed from the Fund for Needy Authors; and for an advance on a projected novel, he signed an incredible contract with an unscrupulous publisher. Failure to deliver the promised manuscript on time gave the publisher the privilege of printing everything Dostoevsky might write for the next nine years without payment to the author.

Much of the money went to clear up debts and to help his dead brother's family. With the remainder he set off in August for Germany. Despite his dislike for Western Europe, he believed that his health improved abroad and that he worked better. As on his last trip, however, what probably lured him from Russia was a desire to try his luck at the gaming tables and, once again, the possibility of meeting Polina Suslova. Since his wife's death he had been dwelling upon the idea of marriage, and he had already had several unsuccessful love-affairs in St. Petersburg.

At Wiesbaden he found Polina and the gaming tables, and with both his luck was execrable. At the end of five days he had lost everything and was reduced to pawning his watch and to sitting as quietly as possible in his room in order not to work up an appetite which he did not have the means to satisfy. To make matters worse, Polina deserted him for Paris, after treating him in her usual tactics of leading him on and then coldly denying him. Although he was now ready with an offer of marriage, the hatred in this strange woman had gained an ascendancy over her love, and she seemed to have no desire other than to make him suffer. In desperation over his financial plight, he sent appeals for funds in all directions. Finally, he obtained a loan from Turgenev, one that he was always to regret, and he received money from his old friend Baron Wrangel also. With this assistance he returned to St. Petersburg in October.

As early as June 1865, Dostoevsky had written to a friend that he had begun a new story. "It is necessary for me to finish this work as quickly as possible in order to get money to pay off my debts." [1] Two days later he wrote to A. A. Kraevsky, editor of *National Notes*, asking for an advance of three thousand rubles on this work, a short novel, which he promised to deliver by October 1865. "My novel is called *The Drunkards*, and it will be concerned with the present question of drunkenness. It concerns not only this question, but will present all its ramifications, especially the picture of a family and the bringing up of children in these circumstances, etc., etc." [2]

Kraevsky did not express any interest in *The Drunkards*, which was Dostoevsky's original version of the novel that eventually became *Crime and Punishment*. At this stage he obviously intended it to be the story of the drunkard Marmeladov and his family. It has already been observed that this was not an unusual procedure; in the course of composition his novels often changed, and in some cases so radically that the finished product bore little relation to the original design.

About three months later, while he was in Wiesbaden frantically trying to raise money, he wrote to Katkov, the editor of the *Russian Messenger*, to plead for an advance on the same work he had unsuccessfully offered to Kraevsky. He now describes it as a performance of about a hundred pages and is certain that it will be finished within a month. In an effort to convince Katkov, he outlines the plot with some fullness:

It is a psychological account of a certain crime [he writes]. The action is contemporary, in the present year. A young man, expelled from the university, bourgeois in

origin, and living in extreme poverty, because of his gid-
diness and instability of thought, having submitted to
certain strange 'incomplete' ideas which float on the wind,
has resolved at one stroke to get out of his vile situation.
He resolved to murder an old woman, the window of a
titular counsellor, who lends money at a percentage. The
old woman is stupid, deaf, ill, greedy, charges exorbitant
rates, is evil, and wrecks the life of her younger sister while
tormenting her as her workwoman. 'She is worthless.' 'What
does she live for?' 'Is she of use to anyone?' etc. These
questions perplex the young man. He decides to murder
her, rob her, and with the plunder make happy his mother,
who is living in the provinces, and deliver his sister, a companion in a landowner's family, from the lascivious attentions of the head of this family, attentions threatening her
ruin. Then he will complete his studies, go abroad, and for
the rest of his life be honest, firm, and steadfast in fulfilling
his 'humane debt to society,' by which of course he will 'expiate his crime,' if only this deed against the deaf, stupid,
evil, sick old woman can be called a crime, when she herself does not know what she lives for in this world, and
who perhaps may die a natural death in a month.

Dostoevsky has almost comically stressed the "ripe-
ness" of the old pawnbroker for murder. He may well
have been unconsciously suggesting his own sympathy
for the crime, or he may have had a justifiable fear that
the normal scruples of Katkov would revolt against an
"unreasonable" killing. In an effort to satisfy the editor
on this score, possibly, he adds a paragraph to the
letter in which he mentions the psychological problem
of the murderer; how he is obliged to denounce himself and accept his punishment as the only possible
expiation for his crime. Then he concludes his outline
as follows: "In my novel, besides this, there is a hint at
the thought that the legal punishment inflicted for a
crime intimidates a criminal infinitely less than law-
makers think, partly because *he himself morally demands it.* I have even observed this in most undevel-
oped people on the most accidental occasions. I should
like to show it particularly in the case of a well-devel-

oped person of the new generation in order that the idea may be seen more clearly and tangibly." [3] To prove that the "subject is not eccentric," he cites several recent attempts and actual murders of this sort that have appeared in the newspapers.

From this outline it is clear that Dostoevsky had dropped his original idea of *The Drunkards*. Marmeladov and his family are skilfully worked into the main theme which is now that of Raskolnikov and his crime. In the short scope of a letter, the outline is pretty inclusive, but it hardly suggests the extraordinary superstructure that he raised on the bare foundations of Raskolnikov and the murder.

Dostoevsky wrote to Katkov under the impression that the novel was to be a relatively short one, and he also indicated that the work was well under way. In reality he had little of it finished, and the manuscript eventually grew into a long novel. Katkov agreed to publish it. The first part appeared in the January 1866 issue of the *Russian Messenger*. Dostoevsky had to race against time for a whole year with the successive instalments. Fortunately, the magazine itself rarely came out on time, and the last section of *Crime and Punishment* was published in December 1866. The public rewarded his efforts, for the novel enjoyed an enormous success and created a powerful impression. In all seriousness, one contemporary commentator tells how people with strong nerves become almost ill over the novel, and people with weak nerves were obliged to cease reading it.

In his letter to Katkov, Dostoevsky remarked that he was writing the novel with zeal. As it developed in length and complexity, he realized that he was engaged in a major effort. During that whole year he literally ate and slept with the work on his mind. There is a fairly authentic story that a servant who was detailed to remain with him at night in the event of an epileptic seizure finally refused to do so any longer on the ground that the master had murder on his mind and walked the floor all night, talking to himself about it.

As the first of his famous masterpieces, the composition of *Crime and Punishment* has a special interest for the student of Dostoevsky's creative art. The conception and his original outline have already been mentioned, but the care that he expended on the planning and writing of the novel is an effective answer to those critics who consider him a slipshod author, with little regard for the severe discipline demanded by great art. Happily, Dostoevsky left behind him a series of notebooks which contain a large amount of material that has important bearing on the composition of his principal novels. During the last few years these notebooks have been published. Nothing could give one a deeper insight into the creative process of a literary genius than a comparative study of these rough drafts, preliminary sketches of characters and scenes, and above all his corrections and observations, extending to the minutest details, of the material he designed to go into a novel. We are taken into Dostoevsky's laboratory, as it were, and allowed to see the creative mind in operation. The notebooks are proof positive of the infinite pains he took with everything that made for artistic perfection.

The three notebooks containing material on *Crime and Punishment* print up to over two hundred pages.[4] Here, among addresses, irrelevant notes of things that he wanted to remember, and drawings of men's heads and fragments of Gothic buildings, are scattered plans, drafts of chapters, outlines of characters, notes on the plot, and a variety of other material concerning *Crime and Punishment*.

Dostoevsky rarely lost sight of the entertainment value of his fiction, and this element plays an important part in his creative process. In the letter to Katkov he had said of the theme of the projected novel: "I vouch for its interest. Of the artistic fulfilment of it I do not take upon myself to judge." [5] The efforts he made to sustain the interest of the story are obvious from particular changes and corrections in the variants in the notebooks. But this preoccupation by no means excluded an even greater emphasis upon the purely artistic, and what might be called the ideological, aspects of the work. In the same letter he remarked: "Too often it has happened to me to write very, very bad things while hurrying to meet a time-limit. However, I've written this piece slowly and with ardour. I shall try, although it may be *only for myself,* to end it as well as possible." [6] Indeed, so arduously did he slave for perfection in all the artistic details of *Crime and Punishment* that he strictly warned Katkov, in a later letter: "I beg the editor of the *Russian Messenger* not to make *any* corrections in it [the manuscript]. *In no case* can I agree to this." [7] The evidence of the notebooks testifies to the manner in which he meditated over every word.

The mass of corrections and annotations of the margins and between the lines often concern simple facts or single words—changing the age of a character, the amount of a sum of money, substituting a proper name for an indefinite pronoun, or a more precise adjective for one with vague connotations. Sometimes the word-order of a sentence is transformed for purposes of greater emphasis or the whole sentence is reworked.

The notebooks indicate that he experienced much difficulty in deciding upon questions of form and narrative technique. He fluctuated among no less than three methods—narration by the omniscient author, by the hero in the form of a diary, and by the hero in the form of reminiscences. Arguments for the preference of one form over the other are set down, and in the case of two forms several trial flights are attempted, as though he wished to test their comparative effectiveness. There is even evidence that he considered in addition two other methods of narration, partly combinations of the first three—the murder told in the form of a confession by Raskolnikov, and the remainder of the story by the omniscient author; and finally a reversal of this process. In the end, of course, he selected the method of the omniscient author.

One interesting device of composition is the manner in which he drafts an outline of a sequential series of events covering several chapters. With the intention at first of writing the novel in the form of a diary, he sketches the following outline:

N.B. A hole under the window-sill.
1. Went to pawn watch and *to inspect*. Reasoning.
   N.B. (that the reader should be informed he did not go to pawn it, and that there is something behind this.)
2. Meets Marmeladov in the tavern.
3. Home. Relations with the *landlady*. Letter from mother about the bridegroom. No, they must not suffer. Consideration sceptical. Lizaveta at the Haymarket.
4. Before the preparation [reminiscences] reasoning. Murder.
5. In the police station. Under the stone. On the boulevard. 20 kopeks. Translations returned.
6. Illness. Letter from mother. Money.
7. Escaped. The tavern. Terrible arrogance. Dispute with workers. Death of Marmeladov.[8]

Apart from a few explanatory words and phrases in the margin on certain items, this is the complete outline for practically the whole of the first three parts of the novel. Of course, such reminders as "No, they must not suffer" will invoke long passages of careful reasoning in the finished performance. And he is rarely content with the first presentation of such outlines. They are often repeated and the situations elaborated and varied as he searches for the most successful skeleton, which he later arrays with the solid flesh of the complete narrative.

One fact that is clearly brought out by the mass of material in these notebooks is the importance to Dostoevsky of having a complete plan of the novel in mind before he could write with any ease. Once he had grasped the plan in its entirety, the writing flowed smoothly and swiftly. The false starts and frequent experiments in compositional features in the notes on *Crime and Punishment* suggest his inability to see the novel as a whole. This difficulty appears to be connected with a certain vagueness in the conception of the hero. He once wrote to Apollon Maikov: ". . . many conceptions of artistic thoughts keep flashing through and making themselves felt in my mind and soul. But these are only flashes; what is necessary is a complete fulfilment, which always takes place unexpectedly and suddenly, but it is impossible to estimate when, precisely, it will take place; for only after having conceived a complete character in one's heart, may one proceed to artistic fulfilment." [9] The evasiveness of the total personality of Raskolnikov prevented Dostoevsky from quickly integrating the various strands of the novel.

In the consideration of *The Insulted and Injured* it was pointed out that the "idea" of the novel became an increasingly important factor in Dostoevsky's later fiction, for his chief figures are often embodied ideas. This is true in the case of *Crime and Punishment*, and his confusion about the character of Raskolnikov may be traceable to a confusion about the idea he represents. For the struggle of his intellectual heroes for a faith, for a way out of the dilemma of life, usually takes the form of an idea which represents a solution of the character's spiritual existence. He is concerned with this living idea in both the individual and the social consciousness, for in each case he believes it to be a definite factor in intelligent society. It must not be supposed, however, that he wrote what are commonly referred to as "novels of ideas," or even tendentious or philosophical novels. Rather he wrote novels about ideas. Of course, an idea as a dominating factor in the creation of a hero leads to the disintegration of the customary world of the novel, and in its place we have a world of men and women organized according to the ideas which possess them. The aim of the novelist is to orient the hero to his surroundings which in turn reveal the form of his ideological relations to society. It is a noteworthy feature of Dostoevsky's great novels that the world of the hero appears to have a special aspect which corresponds to the way he himself is formulated. There is little objective description of the external world as we know it. Thus the world of *Crime and Punishment* strikes us as almost bizarre. The material of which it is composed is original and its hero, the would-be superman Raskolnikov, is an idea.

In the plan which Dostoevsky outlines in the letter to Katkov he evinces some uncertainty about the idea of the novel. It is to be a psychological story of a certain crime, and he goes on to add that the criminal willingly accepts his punishment partly because he himself morally demands it. Dostoevsky's experiences in his Siberian prison had awakened in him a profound interest in crime and criminals which had already been reflected in *The House of the Dead* and in the character of Valkovsky in *The Insulted and Injured*. Towards the end of his life, in answering a critic who had censured this morbid interest, he defends himself on humanitarian grounds, and no doubt with Raskolnikov in mind: "I say that I have actually succeeded in my novels and tales in *unmasking* some people, who reckon themselves in health, by proving that they are ill. Do you know that many people are ill precisely because of their own health, i.e. because of an excessive conviction of their own normality, and thus are infected by a most fearful self-opinion, by a shameful self-admiration, amounting almost to a belief in their own infallibility? Well, it has sometimes happened to me to point out to my readers, and even perhaps to demonstrate, that these healthy people are far from being as healthy as they think, but on the contrary are very ill and that they ought to go and be cured." [10] The murderer in *Crime and Punishment* is also ill in this sense and convinced of his own infallibility. A member of the new generation, he has been afflicted with "certain strange 'incomplete' ideas" which lead him to believe that he can justifiably commit a crime on a purely rational basis. In the end he becomes convinced of the falseness of his reasoning and morally seeks punishment for his crime. Apparently this was the initial idea of the novel.

Even in the letter to Katkov, however, Dostoevsky develops an idea tangential to the one mentioned above. It concerns the moral reasons why a criminal such as Raskolnikov confesses his crime and accepts punishment. At this point the letter is highly important, for these reasons are made use of in the final version of the novel. Dostoevsky writes of his hero:

He passes a month after this [the murder] to the final catastrophe. There can be no suspicions of any sort connected with him. Then the whole psychological process of crime unfolds itself. Unsolvable questions arise in the murderer's mind. Unsuspected and unexpected feelings torture his heart. The truth of God and earthly law take their toll of him, and he ends by feeling *obliged* to denounce himself. He feels obliged, for although he perish in prison, he will once again be with people; the feeling of being roped off and separated from humanity, which he had experienced immediately after committing the crime, had tormented him. The laws of truth and human nature have affected his convictions. The criminal resolves to accept his punishment in order to expiate his deed.[11]

These reasons explaining why Raskolnikov morally welcomes his punishment suggest traits of his nature which are at variance with the outline of the character in the earlier part of the letter to Katkov. Obviously the image of Raskolnikov was not yet fully developed in Dostoevsky's mind, and hence the idea he represents of the criminal who achieves salvation through moral enlightenment is also confused. It is perhaps important to point out that, among other things, Dostoevsky mentions the "truth of God" as one of the factors that helped the murderer to see the light. Here he was touching on a favourite theme.

It may be urged that at this early stage Dostoevsky

could hardly be expected to have the hero and the idea of the novel fully in mind. As he progressed on the work, however, the uncertainty actually grew. In one place in the notebook, under the heading: "Chief Idea of the Novel," he writes: "All the time in conversations with her [Sonya] he always insists that he can atone, that perhaps he is good and that this is mathematics." [12] This idea is in line with that in the letter to Katkov. But further on in the notes, and again under the caption: "Idea of the Novel," he suggests a new and interesting approach: "The Orthodox meaning is in what is Orthodoxy." Then he develops this thought: "There is no happiness in comfort; happiness is brought by suffering. Man is not born for happiness. Man earns his happiness and always by suffering. Here there is no injustice, for life's calling and consciousness (i.e. the immediately-felt in body and spirit, i.e. in the whole vital process) is acquired by experience *pro* and *contra* which must be felt in the process of living." And an annotation follows: "By suffering, such is the law of our planet. But this immediate consciousness, felt in the process of living, is such a great joy, for which one may pay by years of suffering." [13]

The development of the notion—earning one's happiness by suffering—as the chief idea of the novel suggests the growing importance of this doctrine in Dostoevsky's mind. One is immediately tempted to draw the parallel between his willing acceptance of suffering in the Omsk prison as an atonement for his crime and as the only way to happiness and ultimate salvation with the roughly similar situation of Raskolnikov at the end of the novel. For Dostoevsky wrestles mightily with this doctrine in *Crime and Punishment*, and in the end the police inspector in the novel preaches it to Raskolnikov: "I am convinced that you will decide to 'take your suffering' . . . For suffering, Rodion Romanovich, is a great thing . . . Don't laugh at it, there's an idea in suffering." (Part VI, Chapter II)

As a human embodiment of the idea of salvation

through suffering, however, Raskolnikov leaves much to be desired. In the letter to Katkov, in the notebooks, and in the final version of the novel, Dostoevsky attributes qualities to his hero which are inimical to the successful artistic fulfilment of this idea. The humility of Christ, which he inevitably connected with the doctrine, was difficult to integrate psychologically with the proud, satanic character of Raskolnikov. Throughout the whole course of composition, and in the printed novel itself, there is an obvious dichotomy in both the character of the hero and in the idea he represents. There were deep-seated reasons for this artistic dilemma. It must not be imagined that Dostoevsky simply conceived an idea which he embodied in the person of his hero, and then, standing outside it, spun out a narrative about this idea with the notion that he was writing a novel. His great works, it is true, are conceived in the spirit of religious and philosophical thought. His thought, however, was rarely attracted to proving a thesis in his novels. He does not try to prove ideas by religious or philosophical argument; in the majority of cases he is concerned largely with indicating and demonstrating all their consequences. In this respect, his masterpieces irresistibly reach out to the chief question with which he consciously or unconsciously tortured himself all his life—the existence of God. But a theological attempt to prove the existence of God in the novels did not concern him. What vitally concerned him was the relation of this question to the human consciousness of his characters and how it revealed and conditioned their destinies. He rarely allowed religious and philosophical problems or the polemics they often inspired in his fiction to interfere with his inherent objectivity as a literary artist. Dostoevsky always remained the artist, and in his imaginative creations he was primarily concerned with artistic problems. In the notebooks he recognizes as an artistic problem his inability to formulate clearly the character of the hero and the idea of *Crime and*

Punishment. As he analyses the idea in terms of the hero, he appears to come to the conclusion that the ambiguity results from the inevitable dualism in Raskolnikov's own nature.

10

Raskolnikov

Critics neatly label Raskolnikov and safely deposit him among the "distorted personalities" of fiction. Such simple generalizing is more than an admission of defeat; it indicates an unawareness of the essential complexity of the character and of the manner in which the creative process sustained the complexity without sacrificing truthfulness to the experience of life. To Dostoevsky Raskolnikov was a tremendously difficult problem —as he is to all thoughtful readers and critics—and the way in which he coped with that problem contributes largely to the fascination of the character and to the intense interest of the novel.

Categories are helpful in criticism when they do not misrepresent the parts that go to make up the whole. It is not particularly clarifying to call Raskolnikov, in the fashion of the psychologists, a "*demi-fou*" or a "cyclothymic type" or a victim of "lucid-madness" unless these labels find positive justification in the total

personality as Dostoevsky understood it. Raskolnikov
may act irrationally at times, but he is not mad nor
even half-mad, and his creator never intended him to
be mad. Western European literary critics often label
the defining essence of Dostoevsky's more complex
characters as their "spirituality." Curiously enough,
they find it in such figures as Raskolnikov and Ivan
Karamazov, whose chief fault in Dostoevsky's eyes is
their lack of spirituality, which he attributes to their
submission to the unholy intellectualism of the West.

In generalizing about the great characters, one cannot afford to lose sight of the substance of reality out
of which Dostoevsky created them. It has already been
indicated that he had his own notion of realism. Although he persistently emphasizes the fact that his
characters are not mere poetic phantoms, it is often
difficult to accept them in terms of modern realism. In
commenting on the subject of realism, he once wrote:
"I have an understanding of reality and realism entirely different from that of our realists and critics. My
idealism is more real than theirs. Lord! To relate
sensibly all that we Russians have experienced in our
last ten years of spiritual growth—indeed, do not our
realists cry out that this is fantasy! Nevertheless, this
is primordial, real realism!" [1] And in a letter to his
philosopher-friend Strakhov he sheds some light on
this rather cryptic statement: "I have my own special
view on reality in art; what the majority call almost
fantastic and exceptional sometimes signifies for me
the very essence of reality. In my opinion the com-
monness of the manifestations and the public view of
them are not at all realism, but quite the contrary.
In every issue of a newspaper you meet accounts
of the most real facts and amazing happenings. For
our writers they are fantastic; they are not concerned
with them; nevertheless, they are reality because they
are *facts*." [2]

These statements—and he never tired of reiterating
the point—indicate clearly what he considered to be

realistic material in the domain of life and art. In his fiction he depicts not fantastic inventions, but actual happenings—however fantastic they may seem—which have a place in the life of society. In a well-known passage in *The Diary of a Writer*[3] he gives an example of how he and Tolstoy would differ on this question of realism. He refers to an incident in Tolstoy's *Childhood and Youth* in which an offended child dreams of killing himself and imagines what a furor such an act would create among his family and playmates. Of course the child does not commit suicide. Then Dostoevsky retells a recent newspaper account of a twelve-year-old boy who actually does kill himself because he had been punished for doing poorly at school. For Dostoevsky the latter is the more real action, and he is vitally interested in the spiritual and psychological factors that could compel one child to take the extreme way out, whereas the child in Tolstoy's book eventually submits to the traditions and breeding of his class. Although the crime of Raskolnikov may seem unreal, shortly after the appearance of the first part of the novel Dostoevsky was able to point out to unbelieving friends, and with not a little artistic satisfaction, a newspaper account of the murder of a pawnbroker by a Moscow student under circumstances uncannily similar to those in *Crime and Punishment*.

Within this sphere of reality he creates characters, psychological types, that embody in their actions these real facts of life and at the same time reflect the constant peculiarities of a common spiritual habit of mind of the Russian people or of separate social groups of them as they exist at a definite historical moment of social development. In his great novels he is usually concerned with characters who belong to the intelligentsia, and he depicts their spiritual life at a time when they are tearing themselves away from the people. This fact is of peculiar significance, for it goes far towards explaining both the intense spiritual and intellectual conflicts of his heroes and their unusual actions.

Dostoevsky was fully aware of this special concentration in his art. He apprehends his characters at the moment when they rebel against all that life has meant for them. They may be exceptional, but the fact of rebellion is real, and hence they often do exceptional things. These intellectuals become introspective and take refuge in their thoughts and dreams. They wish to think their own ideas because they experience an urge for something new, for a way out. In such creations Dostoevsky remained one of the greatest single influences on many of the Russian writers who succeeded him. Now Raskolnikov is imaginatively apprehended as one of these intellectuals, and Dostoevsky portrays him at the moment of the birth of a terribly destructive idea which is the fruit of his rebellion against life and society.

In the letter to Katkov in which he outlines the plot, Dostoevsky is quite definite about the reasons why Raskolnikov commits the murder. The original motive might almost be described as altruistic: with the plunder he wishes to remove himself and his family from a burdensome situation, and he will then atone for his sin by leading an honourable life and fulfilling his "humane duty to mankind." Consistent with these intentions, Dostoevsky deliberately instils admirable qualities in the nature of his hero. The crime, projected with a worthy purpose, presupposes a love for the weak and oppressed and a hatred for the powerful and for oppression. At times Raskolnikov is represented as a man of noble impulses, ready to sacrifice his last penny to aid a distressed person, and he does precisely this in the case of the Marmeladov family. The expression of love for him by Polenka, Sonya's little sister, awakens all his fine qualities and fills him with a momentary desire to go on living in the hope that he may be useful.

Dostoevsky had not gone very far with the characterization before he departed from his outline to Katkov and introduced a different set of reasons for the crime which in turn necessitated a strikingly new development in the nature of Raskolnikov. The unusual article which the hero writes contains a new motive for his murder of the old pawnbroker. Raskolnikov explains that mankind in general may be divided into two categories. The first is composed of ordinary people who serve only to reproduce their kind. They are conservative and desire to be controlled. The second category consists of extraordinary people, Napoleons, who transgress the law and seek the destruction of the present for the sake of something better. Without remorse or pangs of conscience they will wade through blood if necessary to achieve their ends. Raskolnikov commits the murder to convince himself that he is one of these extraordinary people.

To support this new motive, Dostoevsky feels it necessary to portray one side of Raskolnikov's nature as dominated by satanic pride. This feature emerges more clearly in the notebooks than in the finished novel. Thus, in one place in the notes he writes of the hero: "In his person will be expressed in the novel the idea of immeasurable pride, arrogance, and scorn towards society. His idea: to get power over this society. Despotism is his trait."[4] Dostoevsky emphasizes this trait again and again in the notebooks. Raskolnikov is described as not simply scorning people, but hating them.

It is obvious from the notes, however, that both motives for the crime and both sets of traits in the character of Raskolnikov fused in Dostoevsky's mind. He vainly struggled for a way out of this artistic impasse as though convinced that it would make for confusion with his readers. In the notes he jots down a reminder: "To dig out all the questions in this novel."[5] Then, believing that the principal difficulty is the ambiguity in the motivation for the crime, he writes under the heading, "Chief Anatomy of the Novel": "After the illness, etc. Must establish the course of action on a real point and eliminate the uncertainty, i.e. to explain *one way or the other* the whole murder and set up its nature and relations clearly. Then begin the second part of the novel. The collision with reality and the logical outlet to the law of nature and duty." [6]

But Dostoevsky never did eliminate the uncertainty. Neither Raskolnikov nor the reader of the novel ever knows precisely why the crime is committed. After the murder the hero feverishly racks his brain for some justifiable motivation. His bold theory of ordinary and extraordinary people disintegrates under his own searching analysis; or at least he had placed himself in the wrong category. He is not a Napoleon but an aesthetic louse, he tells himself. A Napoleon does not split open the skull of a loathsome pawnbroker and crawl under her bed for a few rubles. In killing her he killed his principle. Then he says that he murdered simply because he wished to convince himself that he had the power of will, the daring to kill. But he sees that the very fact that he had to test himself proved that he was not made of heroic stuff. Finally, in utter confusion, he confesses to Sonya that he did not commit the crime to help his mother, to gain wealth and power and become a benefactor to mankind; he did it because he wished to prove that he had the right to kill. When she doubts this right, he concludes that in murdering the old woman he murdered himself. Starting from what he thought was a direct and singleminded motive for a crime, Dostoevsky has allowed his character to lose himself in the cross-purposes of a nature perplexed in the extreme.

Now it is evident that this conflict in the character of Raskolnikov was enforced by that compelling necessity in Dostoevsky's creative process which literally obliged him to portray the split personality. And it is against the background of the previous Doubles that Raskolnikov's puzzling nature becomes entirely explicable. Fortunately, in this case, we have the additional and significant evidence of the notebooks to support the point. His various drafts, observations, and arguments in these notes testify to the fact, suggested in the treatment of the earlier Doubles, that the dualism of his own nature fed the creative stream out of which came such characters as Raskolnikov. In one fragment of dialogue in the notes Raskolnikov argues a specific motivation for the murder: "There is one law—a moral law. Agreed, agreed! Well, sir, and this law? Why, if conscience does not accuse me [continues Raskolnikov], I seize authority, I acquire power—whether money or might, and not for evil. I bring happiness. Well then, because of a paltry screen, to stand and to look over to that side of the screen, to envy and hate and to stand still. That is ignoble!" [7] Under no circumstances could one expect Dostoevsky to agree with this reasoning. But the other side of his nature, the side that secretly sympathized with Raskolnikov's design for power, asserted itself, for in the margin opposite this dialogue he wrote: "Devil take it! This is partly right."

Raskolnikov, then, is a typical Double. Dostoevsky makes this perfectly clear in Razumikhin's description of his friend in the novel. "He is morose, gloomy, proud, and haughty; of late (and perhaps for a long time before), he has been mistrustful and depressed. He has a noble nature and a kind heart. He does not like to show his feelings, and would rather do a cruel thing than open his heart freely. Sometimes, however, he is not at all depressed, but simply cold and inhumanly callous; in truth, it is exactly as though *he were alternating between two opposing characters.*" (Italics mine; Part III, Chapter II)

This "alternating between two opposing characters" is the most sustained feature of Raskolnikov's nature. His feelings, philosophy, cares, and agitation identify him with the group of Doubles to which Devushkin, Golyadkin, and other characters belong. Like the underground man, however, he differs from them by virtue of his intellect. Raskolnikov is a thinking, analysing Double. Although no one in the university loves him, all respect him—an advantage which none of the previous Doubles enjoyed.

Against the background of the poverty-stricken city slums, Raskolnikov's nature develops the inner contradiction of self-will and submissiveness. Although the underground man loses himself in an endless analysis of his mental and spiritual dualism, Raskolnikov decides to act. He projects his dualism into society in general, which is a natural psychological manifestation of the split personality. All society he divides into the ordinary and the extraordinary people. The first category is entirely submissive, devoid of any will of its own; the extraordinary category contains self-willed people to whom all is permitted. Here we have the same struggle in society that the underground man discovered in individual personalities. On one side is unlimited self-abasement, on the other unlimited power. Raskolnikov sees no possibility of harmonizing this fundamental opposition. Accordingly, he takes his place among the strong self-willed members of society, and to prove his title to it he murders the old pawnbroker. The act, no doubt, was a conscious fulfilment of an unconscious desire to resolve his ambivalence.

The crime, of course, solves nothing, unless it be to convince Raskolnikov that he was never intended to be a superman. The struggle must go on; his dualism, as in the case of all the Doubles, admits of no solution. In fact, after the murder he begins to believe that his proper place is with the submissive people. He wonders whether it is possible that he has made the mistake of those "ordinary people" who, in his own words, "In spite of their predisposition to obedience . . . through a playfulness of nature sometimes vouchsafed even to the cow, like to imagine themselves advanced people, 'destroyers,' and to push themselves into the 'new movement,' and this quite sincerely." (Part III, Chapter v) He even recalls that the deed was done accidentally, almost involuntarily, and not with the firm decision of a man who belonged to the "extraordinary people" of his category. Dostoevsky is insistent upon this point in the notes. He repeats it several times and it adds to the complexity of the characterization. In one of these notes he writes: "Admits and realizes that the whole business [the crime] was done almost accidentally (to be persistently attracted, to be drawn), that now perhaps he would not risk it again if it were still not finished, not even for any guarantee." [8] The utter uncertainty concerning his motivation for the crime also serves as an indication that he could not resolve the contradictory forces of his nature that pulled him now to unlimited power, now to unlimited submissiveness. It remains to point out that this same ambivalence was even operative in his struggle to convince himself that he must expiate his sin.

In the letter to Katkov, Dostoevsky reviews the general reasons for his hero's desire to atone. Raskolnikov experiences a moral demand to suffer for his crime. He cannot bear the feeling that he is an outcast from society, a man regarded with horror by every living thing. There is a hint in the outline that the truth of God enters his heart and illuminates for him the purification to be obtained through suffering.

Sonya is the effective agent in this apparent reformation, and it is to her alone that he first admits the murder. She tells him that he must expiate his sin. For a moment his faith in the idea of obtaining unlimited power deserts him, and he entertains the notion that Sonya's path of submission is the only way out. The momentary feeling suffuses him with a kind of ecstatic tenderness for her and her lot of suffering. The famous scene in which he bows down and kisses her foot symbolizes his acceptance of the saving grace of salvation by suffering. "I did not bow down to you," he declares to Sonya, "I bowed down to all the suffering of humanity." (Part IV, Chapter IV) He asks her to read to him the passage in the Gospels, concerning the raising of Lazarus from the dead. Like the Jews, he, too, had refused to believe. He had murdered his soul, and its resurrection would come only through faith in Christ. He would earn his future happiness like Sonya, who embodies Christian love, by suffering. Raskolnikov follows her advice: he confesses his crime, bows down and kisses the earth to symbolize his newly found humility, and finally accepts his punishment in Siberia. This is Sonya's path of submission, a path that one aspect of his nature had prepared him to follow.

It must not be supposed that Raskolnikov willingly or completely surrenders to his decision. The incessant dualism of his egotistic personality quickly reasserts itself and he is once again caught between contending forces. His towering pride wars against his desire to repent. To the very end he cannot get himself to admit that he was wrong in killing the old woman. In fact, in the notes Dostoevsky actually has him contemplating a new crime! [9] A moment after he has kissed the feet of Sonya, he fiercely turns and accuses her of destroying herself for nothing. Her prostitution helps no one, he savagely declares, and he wonders how shame and degradation can exist side by side with the holy feeling in her. He concludes that it would be a thousand times better and wiser if she were to jump into the water and end it all. How could he earn salvation through suffering when, as Svidrigailov cynically explains to Raskolnikov's sister after the murder, "He is still suffering from the idea that he could make a theory, but was incapable of boldly overstepping the law, and so is not a man of genius. And that's humiliating for a young man of any pride . . ." (Part VI, Chapter V) In the last chapter but one in *Crime and Punishment,* just before he sets out for Siberia, Raskolnikov gives the lie to his submission. As his sister praises his determination to expiate his crime, he suddenly exclaims in fury: "Crime? What crime? That I killed a vile noxious insect, an old pawnbroker woman, of use to no one!" Then he reverts to his theory of "extraordinary people." He had shed blood, but benefactors of mankind had shed blood in streams. And if he had succeeded, he too would have benefited mankind. If he had succeeded, he would have been crowned with glory; because he failed, everybody calls his crime stupid. But everything seems stupid when it fails. "I've never, never recognized this more clearly than now, and I am further than ever from seeing that what I did was a crime. I've never, never been stronger and more convinced than now." He concludes by a repudiation of the faith that Sonya had helped to teach him: "They say it is necessary for me to suffer! What's the object of these senseless sufferings? Shall I know any better what they are for, when I am crushed by hardships and idiocy, and weak as an old man after twenty years' penal servitude?"

To the very end of the novel, and even in prison, the dualism of Raskolnikov pursues its relentless course. It is impossible for him to accept either path as a solution: the path of blood and crime to power or the path of submission and suffering to a Christ-like salvation. He loves and hates both, the meekness and submission of Sonya and the self-will and desire for power of a Svidrigailov. Indeed, both these characters represent the extreme poles of his dualism, and it is psychologically inevitable that he should be drawn to each of them. Dostoevsky himself recognized this very fact, for there is a brief observation in one of the notebooks which clearly suggests the whole pattern of dualism in the characterization of Raskolnikov that has been argued here. He writes: "Svidrigailov is desperation, the most cynical. Sonya is hope, the most unrealizable. (These must be expressed by Raskolnikov himself.) He is passionately attached to them both." [10]

If one may judge from the remarks and the revealing "thinking out loud" which he scribbled in the notebooks, Dostoevsky felt much perturbation of spirit over Raskolnikov's ultimate fate. The artistic and psychological problems connected with the final resolution were not easy to solve in the face of the involved dualism of the character. Had he allowed the self-willed aspects of Raskolnikov's nature to predominate —and the notes suggest that he considered this possibility—then there was only one psychological solution. Like that truly self-willed character Svidrigailov, Raskolnikov should have killed himself. The complete frustration of his pride and the humiliating failure of his theory on achieving power make this outlet a logical one. Even as an artistic solution, suicide would be aesthetically more satisfying than the fate Raskolnikov meets in the printed novel. As his own name intentionally indicates (from the Russian *raskolnik*, meaning "dissenter"), he is one of those characters who does not become reconciled to life and never adjusts himself to it. And Dostoevsky actually considered suicide as the natural way out for his hero. Under the heading, "Conclusion of the Novel," he writes in one of the notebooks: "Raskolnikov goes to shoot himself." [11]

As is well known, the conclusion of *Crime and Punishment* is managed quite differently. Raskolnikov goes to prison, and there by patience and suffering he eventually loses his pride. His soul is prepared for the resurrection of faith and love which Sonya symbolically foretells in her reading of the story of the raising of Lazarus from the dead. Through the ministrations and unselfish example of Sonya, he also experiences this love. Dostoevsky writes of the revelation at the end of the Epilogue: "They wanted to speak but could not. Tears stood in their eyes. They were both pale and thin; but in those sick, pale faces already shone the dawn of a new future, of a full resurrection into a new life. Love renewed them; the heart of one held infinite sources of life for the heart of the other." That night the New Testament lay under the pillow of Raskolnikov. In his infinite love he had learned selflessness. The implication is that the meekness and submissiveness of his dualistic nature triumphed in the end, and that a new and happy life of pious humility awaited him in which he would make his peace with his fellowmen.

The Epilogue is manifestly the weakest section of the novel, and the regeneration of Raskolnikov under the influence of the Christian humility and love of Sonya is neither artistically palatable nor psychologically sound. It would be interesting to know why Dostoevsky set aside the logic of events in rejecting the ending of suicide for his hero. Raskolnikov is the first of the Doubles to resolve the ambivalence of his nature and achieve the unified purpose that will bring peace to his tortured spirit. An obvious reason, of course, was the desire to satisfy the public preference for a happy ending. Although this may have been a factor, it would hardly have weighed heavily with Dostoevsky. Unfortunately, there is not much in the notebooks to indicate why he decided on the actual ending of the novel. The notation on earning one's happiness by suffering has already been pointed out, and in one place there is a relevant note applying to the hero: "Finally he makes his peace with all. A vision of Christ. He asks forgiveness from the people. Pride. It goes. Sonya and love destroy [it]. Can it be that such a person would be unhappy? Indeed, is this justice?" [12] In the novel itself there is considerable preparation for the preferred denouement, although the fluctuations of Raskolnikov's thought leave us uncertain until the very end.

The final accounting of the hero, however, was plainly suggested by Dostoevsky in his letter to Katkov. At that time, when the novel was still in the process of gestation, he did not grasp all the complications of the character which eventually led him to consider an act of suicide as the logical outcome of Raskolnikov's deed. In returning to his original design at the end, he was very likely influenced by strong subjective rather than artistic reasons. It has been shown that the central idea of the novel became confused in his mind as the character of Raskolnikov developed in the course of composition. In the letter to Katkov he describes Raskolnikov as "having submitted to certain strange 'incomplete' ideas which float on the wind." His obvious intention was to represent his hero as one of the younger generation who subscribed to the nihilist ideas which Dostoevsky was coming to abominate. Raskolnikov's theory of ordinary and extraordinary people and the crime that resulted from it were products of what Dostoevsky considered to be the extreme and distorted thinking of the young revolutionary-minded generation. The notion is not well sustained in the novel, but there is enough scornful and ridiculing reference to socialists and socialism to show that his original intention was not abandoned. Nor is there much in the notebook material of *Crime and Punishment* on the subject. A few observations, however, suggest that the theme was on his mind, and their pointed nature indicates their application to the ideas that drove Raskolnikov to commit murder. In one place in the notes, for example, he drafts a conversation between Svidrigailov and apparently Raskolnikov which is entirely omitted in the novel. Svidrigailov says of the socialist: "For him conviction is the principal thing. But what is conviction? The chief idea of socialism—this is a *mechanism.* Here man turns himself into a mechanical man. There are rules in everything. Man himself does not exist. The living soul is taken away." [13] Raskolnikov also lived by convictions. He tried to arrange his life by a theory born of the intellect, as though man's existence could be predetermined like that of a machine. Elsewhere, in one of the notebooks, Dostoevsky set down the following observation, no doubt as a reminder of a line of thought he wished to develop in the novel: "Nihilism—this is servility of thought. A nihilist is a lackey of thought." [14]

It was Dostoevsky's growing belief that the fundamental error of socialism was its conviction that it could organize a social system on a rational plan, that reason could take the place of human nature, of the living process of life. Life will not submit to mechanical rules, he felt, or the living soul to logic. He had already advanced this opinion in "Winter Notes on Summer Impressions," in articles in *The Epoch*, and he had more than hinted at it in *Notes from the Underground*. This belief, adapted to suit the circumstances of the plot, was pretty certainly the central idea of *Crime and Punishment* in his original conception of the novel. Raskolnikov's crime is a crime of the intellect. He is a child of nihilism who tries to order his life on a self-willed plan of reason. Although the central idea became confused in the developing conflict of Raskolnikov's nature and because of Dostoevsky's own sympathy for the very reasoning behind the crime, he returns to it with conviction at the end of the novel. In the Epilogue, Raskolnikov has a strange dream on the eve of his conversion. A fearful plague spreads over the earth, caused by microbes endowed with intelligence and will. The infected people consider themselves ever so intelligent, and each believes that he alone possesses truth. Chaos reigns when these sick intellectuals try to thrust their infallible plans for new social organizations on the community, and only a few uncontaminated souls are destined to survive and found a new race.

The symbolic intent of the dream is obvious. Dostoevsky is ridiculing the socialists and nihilists (he confused the two) for believing that by reason alone they can secure the salvation of the world. Raskolnikov likewise had been infected by this same intellectual virus. For him dialectics had taken the place of life. Instead of living life, he had substituted reason for life. In prison he will realize that happiness cannot be achieved by a reasoned plan of existence but must be earned through suffering. Dostoevsky rounds out the central idea of the novel by offering his own personal antidote to medicine the disastrous intellection of Raskolnikov, a possibility which no doubt prompted his return to the idea in the end. Both the idea and the antidote were to play their part in future novels.

The object of this analysis is not to explain the powerful human appeal that Raskolnikov has for the average reader. That is another story. The purpose is simply to show Dostoevsky's creative process at work on the material out of which a Raskolnikov was fashioned. Such an analysis provides additional proof of the existence of certain constant factors in his creative art, for the close relation of Raskolnikov to the Double type seems clear, as well as the extent to which he reflects Dostoevsky's own subjective thinking. Finally, the analysis brings out the interesting fact that some of the difficulties which readers experience in understanding the character were also experienced by Dostoevsky in creating him. The reasons why he failed to overcome the principal difficulty—the indefiniteness in the motivation for the crime—have been suggested. It is surprising that this failure does not essentially detract from the tremendous vitality of the characterization. Dostoevsky, like Coleridge, seldom felt without thinking or thought without feeling, and he applied the activities of both mind and heart to this creation to an exceptional degree. The mixed motives in his own mind, caused by the developing dualism of the character, make for psychological credibility when conveyed to the mind of Raskolnikov. The tortured perplexity of the hero inspires the very sympathy in the reader which Dostoevsky felt for him. With artistic design he places Raskolnikov in an adverse social position and endows him with such qualities of mind and heart that the horror of his crime is softened in our eyes. So convincing is the reasoning behind the mixed motivation that the reader, like Dostoevsky, finds himself at times believing that the murder was justifiable. Without being in any sense a self-portrait, Raskolnikov has much of Dostoevsky in him, and especially that boldness and originality of thought, that desire to plunge beyond the accepted limits of human knowledge. This searching intellection, which the other side of Dostoevsky's dualistic nature so fiercely condemned, is personified by Raskolnikov. In this respect the character prophesies a still greater intellectual hero—Ivan Karamazov.

I I

The Art of
Crime and Punishment

In Dostoevsky's fiction previous to *Crime and Punishment* the unified contemplative experience of his art had been expressed largely through the medium of the central figure of the story. His treatment was restrictive and intensive rather than expansive. He was never to have the large epic sweep of a Tolstoy, nor did he even pretend to the limited but inclusive "slice of life" that Turgenev portrayed. With *Crime and Punishment,* however, one detects a broadening of the base of experience that he desired to reflect in fiction. The accumulated happenings of the last twenty years of his life seemed suddenly to have thrust upon him the central problem of human thought—the relation of man to the world. Henceforth in his imaginative writings, as well as in his journalistic articles, he wrestles with various phases of the problem. In *Crime and Punishment* the hero of course holds the centre of the stage in most of this ethical and moral speculation. In this respect, however, Dostoevsky by no means neglects the secondary characters, one or two of which actually challenge comparison in artistic finish and interest with Raskolnikov himself.

Perhaps the most striking and memorable is Sonya Marmeladova. She is first mentioned in the novel by her father in his remarkable confession to Raskolnikov in the tavern. This favourite indirect method of introducing a character is employed most effectively here. The father's description of how his daughter was forced to become a prostitute makes an immediate impression which creates eager suspense until the actual appearance of Sonya on the scene. The horror of her position is only intensified by its profoundly despairing effect on her human derelict of a father. In his description of this tragic incident in Sonya's life there is an unusually clear anticipation of her whole nature. She is an outstanding representative of Dostoevsky's Meek characters and one of the most noteworthy of all his female creations.

In one of the notebooks, Dostoevsky jotted down a few brief characterizing phrases which are elaborated in the complete portrait of the novel: "Sonya is always meek and has no humour at all; she is always grave and quiet." [1] The father describes her as "a gentle creature with a soft little voice, fair hair and such a pale, thin little face." (Part I, Chapter II) She is utterly unequal to the struggle with life. It terrifies her. To all the miseries of poverty and squalor are added continual family quarrels and the extra insults reserved for a step-daughter. Yet in this Marmeladov household of drunkenness, starvation, beatings, wailing children, and screaming scenes Sonya moves like a furtive, unbidden shadow. All her actions, her very voice, suggest meekness and submissiveness. Even on those extremely rare occasions when she becomes agitated or angry—as much as she can be angry—Dostoevsky is careful to describe the emotion as indicative of the softness and humbleness characteristic of her nature:

"Sonya was agitated again and even angry, as though a canary or some other little bird were to be angry." (Part IV, Chapter IV) Joined to her fear of life is a conviction that she is a burden to everyone and ought to be helping her poverty-stricken family. Attempts at honest labour fail. Then, in a moment of despair, circumstances literally oblige her to take the other way out. The necessity to live by charity can never degrade a woman as prostitution does, and for a woman of Sonya's meek and devout nature it is the lowest form of existence.

Dostoevsky's feminine characters of the Meek type are all of lowly origin, as though he were convinced that their special attributes would seem natural and plausible only among women close to the soil or crushed by poverty. Complete passivity exists in them to an equal degree, and they accept humbly and un-complainingly everything that fate sends their way. The humility and submissiveness of Sonya, however, contain a more poignant and extreme quality because of her dishonourable calling, for she is the only prostitute among the Meek characters. This is why she experiences such horror when Raskolnikov declares that she is as honourable as his mother and sister.

There is an interesting bit of dialogue in the notes between Sonya and Raskolnikov which is only partially reflected in the novel. Sonya says to him: "In comfort and wealth you would not be able to see anything of the distress of people. God sends much unhappiness to him whom He loves very much and in whom He has much hope, so that he may learn and see more for himself, because the misery of people is more ob-vious in their unhappiness than in their happiness. Perhaps there is no God, he says to her. She wanted to reply, but suddenly she burst into tears. Why, what should I be without God?" [2]

Here Dostoevsky places in Sonya's mouth his own doctrine of earning one's happiness by suffering, the lesson that Raskolnikov is forced to learn at the end of the novel. At first the hero calls her a "religious maniac." In truth, a large element of mysticism, subtly attuned to her meekness, is deeply rooted in her fatalistic nature. Later characters in this group reflect it to an even greater degree. Sonya is convinced that the acts of her life depend upon some mysterious, all-powerful force, and in this dependence is expressed her complete incapacity. This supernatural power, of course, is God. When Raskolnikov asks her what God does for her, she whispers, "He does everything." (Part IV, Chapter IV) She unquestioningly accepts everything He sends, whether it be good or bad. If, in His infinite wisdom, He visits her with suffering, she willingly submits for she cannot pretend to judge the ways of God. This deep faith is Sonya's only hope in life, for it always enables her to entertain the expectation of something better. As Raskolnikov divines, she believes not only in God, but in all His miracles.

The relationship between Sonya and Raskolnikov is of the utmost importance, for upon it turns the ultimate fate of both. His intellectual pride forces him to hate everything she represents. In his amazing categories of humanity, Sonya would occupy the lowest place among those despised "ordinary people" who are born to be submissive. On the other hand, Sonya also appeals to all the finer instincts of his nature. The submissive aspects of his own dual personality lead him to see in this prostitute an embodiment of Christian love and the very image of chastity.

Their love for each other, however, is strangely evasive in all its external manifestations, but it is quite representative of similar relations between such characters in later novels. In his art Dostoevsky, like Tolstoy, realized that love is expansive only in hidden ways, and that its loftiest expression should be treated as a secret thing. The undercurrent of passion may run high in the lives of his characters, but the verbal expression of it is carefully subdued in his pages. Ordinarily, the experience of love for Dostoevsky's Doubles is a torturing, hopeless struggle between pride and submissiveness, which expresses itself through the conflicting emotions of love and hate. This was made clear in the discussion of Natasha Ikhmeneva in *The Insulted and Injured*. There is a suggestion of this contradiction in Raskolnikov, but his destiny is worked out on a much broader psychological basis. For artistic reasons Dostoevsky deliberately mutes every outward show of love between Sonya and Raskolnikov. In the hero's case a confession of love would have amounted to an act of submission foreign to the dominant pride of his nature. His authoritarian theory of greatness has no place for love; he can neither give nor receive it. In the notes Dostoevsky reminds himself of this characteristic for future development in the very first meeting of Sonya and Raskolnikov: "He descends with her at the Marmeladovs; behaves rudely so as not to give her an excuse to fall in love with him." [3] He is soon in love with Sonya himself, but it is an affection that never shows itself by any outward demonstration; it develops imperceptibly, like a thing of the spirit, and manifests itself only in the irresistible affinity between these strange, shy beings. Throughout the notes Dostoevsky continually warns himself not to allow any expression of love on their part, which he obviously considered to be an artistic and psychological fault in this particular situation. A note such as the following is repeated in various forms: "N.B. There is not a word of love between them. This is a *sine qua non*." [4]

With Sonya, certainly, any active expression of love would have been contrary to the characteristic emotional features of her type. All the passive and submissive traits of the Meek characters are most clearly evinced in their relations with the opposite sex. One hesitates to call this relationship love, since the sex element is virtually negligible. The Meek woman in love is utterly devoid of passion. In love, as in nearly everything else, she is destined to play the role of the sufferer. She considers herself infinitely below the person loved, and if there is any response to her affection, her happiness is not that of satisfied desire but of gratitude. Curiously enough, if her love is not returned, it appears to make no palpable difference in her life.

As a prostitute, however, Sonya's selflessness in love surpasses that of the other Meek characters, such as Darya Shatova in *The Possessed* and Sofiya Andreevna in *A Raw Youth*. Despite Raskolnikov's crime, she feels herself immeasurably beneath him in every respect, and her love is one of utter self-abnegation. She is willing to give all and she demands absolutely nothing in return. Even in that last scene in Siberia, when their intimate future together is symbolized by Raskolnikov's acceptance of their mutual lot of salvation by suffering, Sonya's role is still that of passive submission.

From the point of view of the novelist's art, the material for the characterization of Sonya would seem to have nothing more viable in it than the stuff of a picture of "still life." It is a tribute to Dostoevsky's genius that he was able to breathe the breath of real life into this exceptional figure. If she reminds one at times of an allegorical personification of some abstract virtue in a medieval morality play, she transcends her allegorical significance by the sheer force of the novelist's art. Perhaps it would be better to say that Sonya is a kind of living universal symbol of crushed and suffering humanity that bears within itself the undying seed of joyous resurrection.

The other members of the family have nothing in common with Sonya, emotionally or spiritually, unless it be her father. Marmeladov has something of Sonya's deep religious feeling, of her conviction that God will receive the lowliest sinner if only he be contrite and humble of heart. Marmeladov is a unique creation. He takes his place, although a lesser one, among that memorable company of exaggerated, off-centre heroes of world literature to which belong Don Quixote, Parson Adams, Uncle Toby, and Micawber. This may appear to be an ill-assorted group, but like all these fa-

mous figures, Marmeladov strikes us as comical, even
ridiculous, and at the same time the ridiculous in him
is never far removed from an abiding pathos that makes
us pity while we smile. It is very likely that Micawber
and his long-suffering brood were in Dostoevsky's mind
when he conceived Marmeladov and his family. The
seriousness and psychological depth in the portrayal
of this chronic drunkard, however, make him much
less a caricature than Dickens's amiable creation. The
abundant detail with which Marmeladov and his family are drawn may be accounted for by the fact that
Dostoevsky had originally intended to write a full-
length story about them.

Nothing could be more effective as a piece of characterization than Marmeladov's own revelation of his
nature to Raskolnikov in the tavern. Beneath the ver-
biage, pomposity, and unintentional humour of this
inimitable confession is revealed the soul of a man
who has experienced every feeling of degradation in
an unequal, hopeless struggle to preserve his human
dignity. Nowhere else in his fiction is Dostoevsky's intense sympathy for the poor and downtrodden more
feelingly expressed than in his treatment of Marmeladov and his family. The frequent quarrels, the dying
of Marmeladov, and the funeral feast provide an un-
exampled picture of human misery. And the last chapter of Part III, in which the deranged mother takes
her children out on the streets to beg, is almost too
excruciating in its realistic details. One experiences the
sensation of being shut up in a madhouse; the scene
is the stuff of nightmares.

The mysterious Svidrigailov, no less than Valkovsky
in *The Insulted and Injured*, gives one the eerie feeling of coming to grips with a human phantom. The
identification suggests itself naturally enough, for
Svidrigailov belongs to the same type of Self-Willed
characters. So obvious is their similarity that it scarcely
requires any pointing out. The shamelessly frank confession of Svidrigailov to Raskolnikov in the tavern is

almost an exact duplication of Valkovsky's confession to Ivan Petrovich in the tavern. The setting, thoughts, criminal adventures, frank admission of immorality, and even some of the turns of expression are repeated in the scene in *Crime and Punishment*. Svidrigailov is especially addicted to Valkovsky's dominating passion —women. Debauching young girls, which runs so strangely through Dostoevsky's fiction, is a particular feature of Svidrigailov's immoral nature.

It is clear from Dostoevsky's notes on this characterization that he kept constantly in mind the criminal type of Orlov and Petrov, which he had described in *The House of the Dead*. The notes continually emphasize the fierce, unreasoning, peculiarly instinctive criminal nature that lies behind the cynical and, at times, genial exterior of Svidrigailov. To take only one example: under the heading "N.B. Primary Point," he writes: "Svidrigailov is conscious of mysterious horrors within himself which he will tell no one but lets slip out as facts. He has convulsive, animal-like urges to rend and to kill; coldly passionate. A wild beast. A tiger." [5]

Despite their close resemblance, there is one important difference between Valkovsky and Svidrigailov. Although Valkovsky is a land-owning noble, Dostoevsky never explains how he manages to retain his high social status while he appears to spend most of his time with the riffraff of the city. This difficulty is avoided in the case of Svidrigailov. He is a noble, but a bankrupt one who has already breathed prison air. After each adventure he falls lower and lower in the social scale, and in the end he is quite alienated from his class. The descent is a logical one, and his criminal actions psychologically correspond with the loss of his original social status. This is not true of Valkovsky, whose inconclusive actions at the end of *The Insulted and Injured* seem to reflect an uncertainty in Dostoevsky's own mind concerning the psychological development of the character. There is no uncertainty about the ultimate fate of Svidrigailov. For the entirely Self-Willed type, whose rational or instinctive actions represent a criminal force directed against society, there can be only one solution—death. Svidrigailov fulfils his development by committing suicide.

If Dostoevsky has scorn for any of the characters in the novel, it is for Luzhin, the would-be suitor of Raskolnikov's sister. One gathers from the notes that Dostoevsky originally intended Luzhin to be more complex and his actions more extensive than they actually are in the novel. The notes suggest that he becomes involved in a series of intrigues which would have contributed greatly towards his fuller development along typical Dostoevskian lines. At first Dostoevsky has him "falling terribly in love with Sonya." [6] He pursues her without success and then makes indecent proposals. Her flat rejection provokes his violent antipathy. It is difficult to understand why Dostoevsky dropped this whole intrigue in the finished novel. Its inclusion would have made more plausible Luzhin's vile attempt to prove Sonya a thief, and, besides, the excluded action is all of a piece with his disgusting personality.

On the whole, the pettiness, nastiness, and money-grubbing aspects of Luzhin are strikingly portrayed. Razumikhin sees through his hypocritical humanitarianism, and his own self-communings reveal the baseness of his "noble" love for Raskolnikov's sister. In voluptuous dreams he had already possessed Dunya. She was young, pretty, of good birth and education. But she was very poor and would humble herself, worship him as her saviour. He was convinced that he would have boundless power over her and that she would be slavishly grateful to him all her life for his heroic condescension in marrying her. Besides, he would make use of her in his climb to greater business success.

The traits of Luzhin's nature were precisely those

which Dostoevsky despised in real life—the cautious, reasoned, calculating, middle-of-the-road bourgeois attitude, bourgeois hypocritical respectability, and a petty sense of self-importance. Luzhin has nothing of the largeness, generosity, intense passion, or impulsiveness which Dostoevsky admired in real men and women as well as in his imaginary creations.

These admirable qualities that Luzhin lacked are to be found in the genial Razumikhin. Once again Dostoevsky's notes indicate aspects of Razumikhin's character, and to a lesser degree of Dunya's, which do not appear in the novel itself. For in the notes Dostoevsky describes him as a "very powerful nature," [7] and he drafts a series of incidents which bring out this characteristic. The incidents have to do with the relations between Razumikhin and Sonya. At first Razumikhin becomes her protector, but apparently Dunya resents these attentions and through her instigation he insults Sonya. No reason is given for Dunya's enmity, unless it be the implied one of jealousy. Eventually the generous soul of Razumikhin is again won over by Sonya, and he has a terrible scene with Dunya on this score. These incidents in the notes do not appear in the finished novel, and Razumikhin's relations to Sonya are only briefly referred to. Clearly this dramatic opposition would have brought out the fine, generous nature of Razumikhin and would have clarified his rather vague relations to Dunya. The notes indicate that Dostoevsky had intended to throw in relief pointed contradictions in Dunya's nature which his heroines often possess. Her affection for Razumikhin, it appears, was to assume the more decided emotional expression of the split personality in love, and largely through the agency of Sonya. Although the final version of her character is not entirely clear, she emerges as a lovable, wise, but strong-willed woman. One can only guess why Dostoevsky omitted these significant incidents and additional points of character development. Either the novel had already grown too long and he could not fit in these further details, or else he felt that these incidents, involving Dunya and Razumikhin, were essentially episodic and that the architectonic features of the work demanded that he centre his attention on the main figure of Raskolnikov.

The remaining minor characters of *Crime and Punishment* do not require any special attention here. However small their roles may be, it is surprising how well Dostoevsky individualizes them with a few strokes. Raskolnikov's mother is ineffably human. Her cares, joys, and sorrows over her erring son, whose strange behaviour she cannot possibly understand, reflect a natural maternal exaggeration. The long letter she writes to Raskolnikov to tell of the proposed marriage of Dunya shows all the love and self-sacrifice for a son and daughter who have left her far behind in everything but affection.

The police inspector, Porfiri, is endowed with Dostoevsky's own powerful dialectical method. He bears little resemblance to the scientific sleuth of the modern detective story, but he is no less real for that. What he may lack in scientific technique he compensates by possessing a deep sense of human values which is never devoid of a sympathetic understanding of his victim. Not only was Dostoevsky intensely interested in criminal psychology, but he sought special knowledge in crime detection and legal procedure. This expert information is revealed in the police inspector's handling of Raskolnikov's case. Evidence of Dostoevsky's careful checking of details is to be found in the notebooks. For example, against the direction: "They place him [Raskolnikov] under surveillance," he reminds himself that the legality of this action must be checked by the note: "Is it possible to do this?" [8] In Profiri's subtle psychologizing one perceives Dostoevsky's mind at work. In fact, through the police inspector he seems to be projecting his own opinions on Raskolnikov's crime and his moral need for punishment.

On the whole, the faults of *Crime and Punishment* as a work of art are not very serious. Critics have censured the melodramatic element, but the unusual fact, in this novel of crime, is that the melodrama is rarely overdone. The murder of the old pawnbroker and Lizaveta is one of the best pieces of expository narrative in literature. This scene cannot be called melodrama. It is so intensely imagined that the author appears to be describing a vividly realized experience of his own. The cold logic of events is never sacrificed to extra-melodramatic effects. If anything, Dostoevsky consistently underwrites this unforgettable account of crime. He is not always so successful in other scenes, however, where the action crackles with horrific effects. For example, there is more melodramatic exaggeration than artistic measure in the scene in the locked room where Dunya shoots from close range at the imperturbable Svidrigailov and manages to miss him.

Coincidence is an ever-present trap for weary novelists, and in this respect Dostoevsky nodded rather frequently in *Crime and Punishment*. It is perhaps the principal artistic blemish in the work. Coincidence, of course, may be justifiable in a novel, for it is a legitimate part of the pattern of reality. In real life, however, coincidental happenings do not violate the laws of probability, and in fiction our credibility is forfeited if coincidence is overworked. Dostoevsky certainly carries the matter too far in *Crime and Punishment*. Svidrigailov is allowed to pass Sonya precisely at the moment when she asks Raskolnikov an important question. Svidrigailov overhears the reply which significantly affects the action. Lebezyatnikov bumps into Raskolnikov on the crowded city streets just when he is looking for him. Indeed, such opportune meetings in the busy city occur frequently and create the impression that Dostoevsky took the easiest way out when it was necessary to get his characters together. Following this line of least resistance, he often ignored the time-sequence. In one of the notebooks he boldly declares: "What is time? Time does not exist; time is a cipher; time is the relation of being to unbeing." [9] On occasions the action is so telescoped that time indeed does not seem to exist. And this compressed action and time-sequence literally force him to group his characters in a most improbable manner: Luzhin lives in the same house as the Marmeladovs, and Svidrigailov hires quarters in Sonya's house. The restricted stage, which recalls the misdirected application of the unities in some bad imitations of classical drama, results in forced situations and unbelievable coincidences.

Apart from these faults, however, there is little else to quarrel with in *Crime and Punishment* as a work of art. Dostoevsky's powerful dialectic admirably satisfies the realistic demands of the reader, for the author rarely fails to present, with equal persuasiveness, both sides of the intellectual, moral, and spiritual contradictions which evolve out of his hero. Although Dostoevsky may seem at times to sympathize with Raskolnikov's unique theory of murder, this fact does not interfere with his convincing presentation of the negative side. In the struggle between good and evil that goes on in the mind of Raskolnikov, Dostoevsky does not hesitate in the end to take a positive stand on the side of the good. This does not mean that he projected, in a didactic manner, his personal moral or ethical discrimination into a work of art. He clearly recognizes that the moral and artistic spheres are quite distinct from each other, for he never confuses his own morality, which is primarily concerned with the way men behave in the real world, with the morality of art which is not, or should not be, conditioned by the personal factors of ordinary life.

As a story, however, the common interest of *Crime and Punishment* does not rest in any dialectics, morality, or in the author's central idea, although these features definitely contribute to make the novel what it is. As Dostoevsky himself described it, the novel is the "psychological account of a certain crime," and it is the compelling, high seriousness of this drama of crime as it is cast against a throbbing background of real life that attracts the average reader. The intensity of the step-by-step revelation of Raskolnikov's plan, the thrilling description of the murder, and then the equally intense psychological analysis of the disintegration of all the rational forces that had driven him on to kill—this is the essential and vital story that never loses its grip on the reader's imagination and emotions. Over all radiates a spiritual glow, so characteristic of Dostoevsky's great novels, that illumines at once the darkest recesses of the minds of the proud and humble, of the criminal and morally debased and inspires them to seek a deeper meaning in life through suffering to ultimate salvation.

12

The Gambler

The actual writing of *Crime and Punishment* was an exhausting experience for Dostoevsky. To the nervous strain of composition was added worry over ill-health and lack of money. Then suddenly he awoke to the realization that on 1 November 1896—now only about three months away—he had contracted to deliver the manuscript of a novel to the unscrupulous publisher with whom he had made an arrangement the previous year. Failure to fulfil the agreement, it will be recalled, meant that the publisher had the right to print everything Dostoevsky might produce during the next nine years without paying him a kopek. Here was a serious predicament, and meanwhile he was still engaged in writing the last part of *Crime and Punishment*.

With his usual fortitude Dostoevsky struggled manfully to meet the new danger to his career. At first, he thought of attempting the difficult feat of writing two novels at the same time, working on one in the morning and on the other in the evening. When this scheme proved to be impractical, a few of his literary friends conceived the idea of a co-operative effort, each undertaking to write a section of the work. While these plans were being talked over, however, nothing was accomplished and precious time was rapidly slipping away. With scarcely a month left in which to deliver the manuscript, not a word had been committed to paper in final form, and all Dostoevsky's pleas to the Shylock of a publisher would not prevail upon him to alter one jot or tittle of the contract.

In a fever of anxiety Dostoevsky accepted the suggestion to hire a stenographer and dictate the novel. Accordingly, on the evening of 4 October he began the dictation of *The Gambler* to a plain-appearing, half-frightened girl of twenty. Her name was Anna Grigorevna Snitkina. It was her first job, and she stood much in awe of the famous author whose shabby quarters and strange, irritable behaviour did not in the least accord with her notions of great writers. In the course of twenty-six days the novel was finished—an incredible feat. Dostoevsky delivered the manuscript on time and saved himself from a dangerous situation that had threatened his sole source of income for nine years.

It was almost inevitable that *The Gambler*, composed under such trying circumstances, should contain many deficiencies as a work of art. There is much about the performance, however, which indicates that if it had been written under more favourable conditions, it might well have developed into something more extensive and profound than the present hurried long short story. Even in its present form the work is highly instructive in any study of the development of Dostoevsky's art.

The Gambler was not a sudden, heaven-sent inspiration that came in the midst of frantic efforts to find a way out of the contract with the grasping publisher. The theme of the story had occurred to Dostoevsky some three years before, while he was enduring his Odyssey of unconsummated passion with Polina Suslova, and the experiences of this adventure contributed greatly to the material of the novel. In a letter to Strakhov from Rome in September 1863, he mentioned that he had the plan of a new work in mind. He wrote in part:

The subject of the story follows: a particular type of Russian abroad. Note: there was a great question this summer in the magazines about Russians abroad. All this is reflected in my tale. And in general the contemporary moment of our inner life is reflected (as far as this is possible of course). I take a spontaneous nature, a man of varied development, but in everything incomplete, one having lost his faith and *not daring to believe*, rebelling against the authorities and yet fearing them. He comforts himself with the idea that there is *nothing for him to do* in Russia . . . He is a living figure—(entirely just as if he stood before me)—and you must read about him when he is written up. But the chief fact is this, that all his vital forces, strength, rage, and arrogance are expended on *roulette*. He is a gambler, and not a simple gambler, just as the miserly knight of Pushkin[1] is not a mere miser. (And I am not comparing myself to Pushkin. I speak solely for the sake of clarity.) He is a poet in his own way, but the fact is that he is ashamed of this poetry, for he profoundly feels its baseness, although the necessity of *risk* ennobles him in his own eyes. The whole story is the story of how he gambles for three years at roulette in the gambling houses. If *The House of the Dead* won for itself the attention of the public as a depiction of criminals whom no one had depicted graphically before *The House of the Dead*, then this story will unfailingly win attention for itself as a *graphic* and most detailed depiction of roulette gambling.[2]

Then he concludes, quite characteristically, that it will be a very short work, and that it will soon be finished.

It was probably at this time that Dostoevsky also conceived *Notes from the Underground*, but both works, born in a state of intense emotional excitement, were put aside until he had achieved some peace of mind. It is known, however, that he prepared pretty full notes for *The Gambler*, and these were put to good use three years later when he once again took up the theme. Although *The Gambler* is not a long story, in the original design it was intended to be very much shorter.

The outline in the letters to Strakhov recalls the well-known letter to Katkov on *Crime and Punishment*. There is one noticeable difference: the subject-matter of *The Gambler* is not described with as much detail or clarity. References to the hero, however, indicate that Dostoevsky had already grasped the full image of the protagonist, a stage so necessary in his creative process before he could begin actual composition. The idea of the novel is only vaguely suggested—the spiritual emptiness of a social rebel who has failed in Russia because of a lack of faith in himself and seeks an escape in a life of gambling abroad.

When he took up the tale three years later, he kept close to the outline in the letter to Strakhov. There is one important addition—the love element—which pretty certainly was in his mind in the original conception of *The Gambler*. Very likely he failed to mention it in the outline because he did not wish to betray to his friend the personal relations that inspired this vital phase of the story. Polina Alexandrovna of *The Gambler* is directly modelled upon Polina Suslova, and the hero, Alexei Ivanovich, is an exaggerated portrayal of certain aspects of Dostoevsky. Further, the relations of hero and heroine are an intensified version of the relations between Dostoevsky and Polina Suslova on their unhappy "brother-and-sister" excursion. From Polina Suslova's diary and Dostoevsky's letters one may obtain considerable information of the manner in which the stuff of real life is projected into fiction.

If Polina Suslova had never existed, Dostoevsky might well have created her in a novel. Before he ever knew her, his artistic gravitation towards this feminine type had evinced itself in Zina Moskaleva of "Uncle's Dream" and Natasha Ikhmeneva of *The*

Insulted and Injured. These are not ordinary women, but Dostoevsky never hesitated to avail himself of the licence of artistic exaggeration, although he was reasonably careful not to offend the credulity of his readers. Dostoevsky had definite ideas about the relative importance of commonplace and unusual characters in fiction. In a passage in *The Idiot* that appears to have escaped the critics he touches upon the ideas in a manner that throws some light upon his own artistic practices. He writes:

There are people about whom it would be difficult to say anything that would describe them at once and completely, in their most typical and characteristic aspects; there are people who are usually called 'ordinary' people, 'the majority,' and who do actually make up the vast majority of society. For the most part, writers attempt, in their tales and novels, to select types of society and to represent them vividly and artistically,—types very rarely met with in actual life but who are nevertheless almost more real than reality itself . . . thus, without entering into more serious explanations, we will say merely that in actual life the typical figure is apt to be watered down . . . Yet the question remains: What is the novelist to do with ordinary people, entirely 'ordinary,' and how is he to present them to his readers in order to make them at all interesting? It is quite impossible to ignore them in a tale, because ordinary people are at every moment the chief and essential links in the chain of human affairs; if we pass them over, we must break with verisimilitude. To fill a novel with certain types, or to fill it with strange and unbelievable people, even merely for interest, would be to make it unreal and even uninteresting. In our opinion a writer ought to try to search out interesting and instructive features even among ordinary people. (Part IV, Chapter I)

In general, Dostoevsky selected types that are rarely, if ever, met with in actual life, but for him they were "more real than reality itself." He was also capable of making the ordinary interesting by emphasizing particular characteristics. From all accounts, it is unlikely that Polina Suslova was a commonplace person; but as Polina Alexandrovna in *The Gambler* she becomes an extraordinary person, endowed with a magnified measure of her model's love-hate ambivalence. Like Natasha Ikhmeneva, she is a female Double in love. The total effect of the characterization is not as artistically satisfying as that of Natasha, but the dualism of love and hate in her nature is more intensely realized.

Polina Alexandrovna is the cast-off mistress of a French adventurer to whom she is obligated to the extent of fifty thousand francs. The situation at once recalls the treatment accorded Polina Suslova by her fickle Spanish medical student. Dostoevsky emphasizes in her unhappy position the heroine's imperious pride, a trait that Suslova possessed to a marked degree. On one occasion he wrote about Suslova to her sister: "Apollonariya is a great egoist. Egoism and self-love in her are colossal." [3] This description precisely fits the heroine of *The Gambler*.

The dualistic counterpart of pride is humiliation. After the Frenchman has jilted her, Polina Alexandrovna abjectly offers herself to the gambler, Alexei Ivanovich, whom she both loves and despises. The act appears to indicate a mixed desire to humble her pride and to reassert it by convincing herself that she is not to be bought by fifty thousand francs. In his ecstasy, the hero goes to the gaming tables and wins this sum in order that his beloved may throw it in the face of the Frenchman. He returns with the money, and they spend the night together. In the morning, however, Polina Alexandrovna, with a sudden revulsion of feeling, throws the money in the face of the hero and leaves him forever. Here again, the psychological motivation is mixed, reflecting the dual nature of the heroine. It will be recalled that Polina Suslova had written in her diary Dostoevsky's explanation of her hate for him, which he had attributed to the fact that she could not forgive him because she had once given herself to him. Such may have been the reason for Polina Alexandrovna's swift reversal of feeling. From her subsequent actions, however, it appears that this reason may have been connected with the desire to reassert her pride and her power over the gambler. That is, she insults and rejects her despised lover because she realizes that he has suddenly assumed her position of the magnanimous giver, just as the underground man turns on the poor prostitute who has offered him her sincere love, because he feels that she has usurped his proud dominance.

From the outline to Strakhov, one gathers that Dostoevsky originally intended the hero to hold the centre of the stage in *The Gambler*. He succeeds in this to some extent, although Alexei Ivanovich only vaguely suggests the power and depth of the leading figures of the famous novels. The autobiographical features in the characterization are obvious. He possesses Dostoevsky's passion for gambling and even his irrational notions of a system for winning. His dislike of expatriated Russians and his positive contempt for polished Frenchmen and boring Germans reflect Dostoevsky's known opinions. Nor is it unlikely that the hero's particular bitterness for the French adventurer was inspired by Dostoevsky's active hate for the Spaniard who jilted Polina Suslova. The significant biographical similarity, however, consists of his frustrated passion for Polina Suslova and the frustrated passion of the hero for Polina Alexandrovna. In fact, the intimate scenes of dialogue recorded in Suslova's diary might almost have provided the rough material for many passages in *The Gambler*.

For artistic reasons Dostoevsky had avoided any outward manifestation of the experience of love in developing the character of Raskolnikov. Alexei Ivanovich is a Double whose essential ambivalence is expressed almost entirely in the experience of love. For the Double, love stands in contradiction to itself; it can never be a source of permanent happiness while the conflicting forces of his nature war with one another.

Love is born of hate and engenders hate. In order to be successful in love, he must deny his own personality and become an abject slave to the woman he adores. He cannot do this consistently, however, for his pride and desire for domination prevent him. The more he loves a woman the more fiercely he hates her. Thus the Double in love remains balanced between slavery and despotism, between periods of humiliating submission and extravagant scorn for the object of his affections.

Alexei Ivanovich undergoes such an emotional experience. He analyses his mixed feeling for Polina Alexandrovna as follows:

And once again I asked myself the question: Do I love her? And again I did not dare answer it, or it would be better to say for the hundredth time I answered that I hate her. Yes, I hated her. There were moments (more especially at the end of our conversation) when I would have given half my life to strangle her. I swear that if there had been a sharp knife available at such moments, I would have seized the knife with pleasure and plunged it into her breast. Nevertheless, I also swear by all that is holy that if she had really said to me on the Schlangenberg: 'Leap into that abyss,' I should have leaped into it, and with equal pleasure. . . . Yes, Polina must have often taken me for something less than a man. (Chapter 1)

Such feelings are an intensified and exaggerated reflection of those that Dostoevsky experienced in his curiously frustrated relations with Polina Suslova.

The desire to suffer pain and to inflict it on others is a phase of ambivalence which Dostoevsky had described in previous Doubles, such as Foma Fomich Opiskin and the underground man. Alexei Ivanovich willingly submits to mental and physical suffering from the woman he loves. In turn, he demands that Polina Alexandrovna grovel before him and suffer under the lash of his pride. This love-duel, at once sadistic and masochistic, dominates the whole relationship between hero and heroine. He bows to her slightest caprice and would even commit murder at her bidding. When she cruelly dares him to insult the German baron, at great risk to himself, he promptly carries out her request. On the other hand, Alexei Ivanovich feels it his privilege to subject her to his will, to insult her, and at one point he contemplates murdering her. The outcome of such a twisted love is either crime or destruction for one or both of the principals. Although Dostoevsky does not actually complete the history of his hero, the fact that he is a doomed man is clearly suggested at the end.

The Gambler has some claim to distinction by virtue of this treatment of a special phase of ambivalent love, a psychological problem in human relations that concerned Dostoevsky in a more profound way in later works. Apart from this interesting concentration, however, there is not much else of distinction in *The Gambler*. The plot is unnecessarily involved for the length of the story, and there is much about it that betrays the haste in which it was written. Of all the other characters, only that of the fantastic old grandmother deserves high praise. It is very likely that the mad old gambling lady of Pushkin's *Queen of Spades* provided inspiration for the fascinating figure of the grandmother who storms belatedly into the story and scatters all about her like ninepins. Such a creation, and the power of certain scenes, leave one with the conviction that with more time Dostoevsky might have made a really significant work of *The Gambler*.

The Gambler appeared in 1866 and it was almost three years before Dostoevsky completed another novel. During this period many things happened which crowded out the possibility of writing, although the desire in him was stronger than ever and the necessity great, for he was desperately in need of funds. At this time the principal event in his life was his second marriage (February 1867). The diligent stenographer quickly proved herself indispensable to Dostoevsky—a familiar enough situation among secre-

taries and their lonely unmarried employers. To be
sure, he was twenty-five years older and had little to
give in marriage, but then he had nothing to lose and
perhaps much to gain. Anna Grigorevna Snitkina was
not pretty, but she was ever so efficient, practical, and
patient, and she had a capacity for devotion that
passes all accounting. She fully realized that she would
have a sick, nervous, impractical, irritable man on her
hands for the rest of her life. Her strong maternal
instinct, however, was equal to these difficulties, and
in her eyes, at least, Dostoevsky had the compensa-
tion of genius to offer. She could appreciate his life
and works without criticizing them—a dubious though
often desirable virtue in the wives of literary men.
Dostoevsky's second marriage was perhaps the most
fortunate event in his life.

Their married life began auspiciously enough. After
The Gambler had been finished, Anna had copied the
last instalment of *Crime and Punishment*. Along with
the enthusiastic public reception of the novel, Dostoevsky had the pleasure of hearing the critics praise it
more highly than Turgenev's *Fathers and Sons* and
Tolstoy's *War and Peace*, the latter of which was just
appearing.

Amid this success, Anna proved her devotion under
the first horrifying experience of seeing her husband
in an epileptic fit. Her patience and care were endless.
Only one difficulty arose to disturb this happiness. His
dependents—his stepson and the wife and family of
his dead brother—resented this second marriage, particularly because they feared it would diminish the
financial aid he gave them. He did not neglect them,
however, and Anna acquiesced to sharing their slen-
der earnings. When they began to treat her with cruel
disrespect as an interloper in the family, even her long-
suffering patience crumbled. She felt that the whole
future of their married life depended upon getting
away from these ungrateful people. It did not take
much persuading, for once again he was deep in debt

and feared prosecution if he remained in Russia. Further, he still entertained the secret hope that he could remedy his position by gambling, and he was convinced that his epilepsy would improve abroad and that he could work there more satisfactorily. After extending themselves to the limit to obtain the necessary funds, they set out for Germany in April 1867. If Anna had known then what was facing her, perhaps she would have preferred to fight it out at home with the resentful stepson and widowed sister-in-law. In the end, however, she never regretted this step.

This time Dostoevsky remained abroad more than four years. Their first weeks in Germany were filled with petty quarrelling. His irritability, exhibitionism, and thoughtlessness taxed Anna's patience, and for a short time his renewed correspondence with Polina Suslova aroused jealous pangs; but her deep love eventually overcame all these vexations. She thoroughly understood her husband's nature, if not his novels. He quickly became completely dependent upon her, and she seemed instinctively to realize that she would never lose his affection. If anything, their love was strengthened by his weaknesses.

They travelled from Berlin to Dresden and then to Baden-Baden. Here Dostoevsky's gambling mania took possession of him. It was a new and perhaps greater trial for his young and inexperienced wife. Anna very wisely did not try to reform him; she sensed the fact that this obsession must run its course. Even her pregnancy and his delight in the anticipation of his first-born could not divert his mind from the roulette wheel. Time and again he visited the neighbouring gambling resorts and always he lost. He cursed himself and implored Anna's forgiveness. Letters were sent in all directions begging for money; everything that could be pawned was pawned; and again and again they were reduced to the direst poverty. Still money would no sooner arrive than he would slink off, under one pretext or another, and gamble it away. Anna bore all this heroically.

It was on one of these occasions, when he had lost his last penny, that he saw Turgenev at Wiesbaden. Although he still owed him a sum of money which he had no means of paying, he felt it necessary to call on his rival for propriety's sake. The visit resulted in the famous quarrel between the two novelists. Exactly what happened is not clearly known, for both told different stories. Dostoevsky was in a bad humour. Turgenev now stood for everything he disliked in the expatriated Russian who had cut himself loose from the holy soil of Mother Russia, regarded his countrymen as barbarians, and felt that the salvation of Russia depended upon its going to school to the polished civilization of the West. According to Dostoevsky, he taxed Turgenev with the atheistic, anti-Russian, Western ideas reflected in his latest work, *Smoke*. He now saw in Turgenev a radical, one of the brood of Belinsky and Chernyshevsky, who criticized everything good and original in Russia under the guise of a condescending love for the country. Dostoevsky's account of this memorable conversation inadvertently got into print. Turgenev hastened to reply. Among other remarks he mentioned that he had regarded Dostoevsky as a sick man and one not entirely in possession of his mental faculties. On the whole, the controversy did credit to neither writer, but it was to have its repercussions in Dostoevsky's fiction.

The couple went on to Geneva, where Dostoevsky attended a meeting of the International League for Peace and Freedom. The "peace" and "freedom" advocated in the speeches of such apostles of universal destruction as Bakunin sickened him. These fiery orators, proposing Utopian schemes for the regeneration of society and the salvation of the oppressed workers of the world, recalled the pale ghost of radicalism of his youth. Their clarion calls to bloody revolution and their vehement diatribes against Christianity horrified him. This was a flaming whirlpool of destruction compared to the tepid movement of the 1840's. To achieve the brotherhood of man by decree and to legislate universal equality now seemed to him a monstrous fallacy. He realized more than ever that his path and the path of the new radicals would never meet. In their sole dependence upon reason as the panacea for all the ills of mankind, they were neglecting faith—but faith in what he was as yet quite unable to say. This meeting at Geneva, however, made a tremendous impression on him. It seemed somehow or other to be related to an idea that was struggling for birth in his brain, an idea of faith. Dostoevsky was already beginning to think about his next novel—*The Idiot.*

13

A Positively Good Man

Dostoevsky's fourth visit abroad was graced with few of the amenities ordinarily associated with a honeymoon trip, but creatively it was a period of intense literary activity. In the autumn of 1867 he began *The Idiot*, which was not finished until January 1869. Artistic uncertainties in the planning and a string of domestic misfortunes and attacks of illness delayed the work.

During the process of composition, circumstances obliged the couple to move from city to city—from Berlin to Dresden, to Baden-Baden, to Geneva, then to Vevey and Milan, and finally to Florence, where he finished the novel. While he was recovering from an unusually severe epileptic fit in Geneva, his first child was born in March 1868. Rapture over the infant, however, did not prevent him from stealing off to the gambling resorts to lose his last penny. After each catastrophe he would return to beg forgiveness for depriving his wife and child of the necessities which they so sorely needed. Barely three months after the birth of little Sonya, the baby died. Of all the many sorrows of his life, this was the hardest for him to bear. It was weeks before he could regain a semblance of calm. The knowledge that his wife was once again pregnant failed to still his grief, for he felt that he could never have enough love left in his heart for another child.

Over this troubled period in which he laboured on the novel he was also harassed by the most straitened financial difficulties. If it had not been for the patience and kindness of his publisher Katkov, it is hard to imagine how he could have survived. Katkov was giving him a monthly allowance of a hundred rubles against the promise of the novel. As frequent emergencies arose, however, Dostoevsky begged additional sums, and long before *The Idiot* was finished, he was considerably in Katkov's debt for still another work. Grimly he compared himself, as a proletarian among writers, to his well-to-do rivals Turgenev, Goncharov, and Tolstoy. In a moment of despair over his poverty, he bitterly complained: "They demand from me artistic finish, the purity of poetry, without strain, without waste, and they point to Turgenev and Goncharov. Let them take a look at the conditions under which I work!" [1] Despite all his miseries and distractions, he kept on writing. It would almost appear that his work on *The Idiot* was the only sustaining hope of these dark days.

Dostoevsky was also undergoing a period of spiritual suffering and growth during the long months of work and worry. His many letters from abroad contain frequent mention of the moral, political, and religious ideas that were troubling his mind. About a year before he left Russia, the attempt on the life of the tsar by a young revolutionist had filled him with horror. This young Russian generation that had drunk in the radical poison of the West seemed bent on the destruction of everything he held dear. At this time he wrote what was apparently a bitter critical article on Belinsky, the radical hero of his youth, which was never published and has since disappeared. His prolonged residence abroad began to crystallize his opinions concerning the religious and political opposition between Europe and Russia. Not only did Western civilization seem hopelessly bourgeois and decadent, but he believed that he could detect emphatic signs of its approaching disintegration. Although his antagonism was no doubt aggravated by acute homesickness, his critical senses seemed preternaturally sharpened by the internal corruption that he saw in the whole body politic of the West. The orthodox religion and morality of Russia appealed to him as the only answer to the cataclysmic fate that awaited the nations of Europe. It has not been generally recognized by critics, but these considerations were never out of his thoughts while he was working on *The Idiot*. A colossal plan for the artistic treatment of the ultimate salvation of a civilization at war with itself was beginning to dawn in his mind, and now he lived and created under the vast shadow of this cosmic idea. He was never to write the great work that would embody his sweeping design, but he did create several novels in which he depicted the tragedy and pain which his country was destined to suffer before it could achieve world leadership and the salvation of Europe. It is in *The Possessed* and *The Brothers Karamazov* that the facets of the huge design shine most brightly. But *The Idiot* is one of the initial links in the chain of this artistic synthesis of universal salvation.

Like *Crime and Punishment*, *The Idiot* cost Dostoevsky infinite labour. Throughout the critical period of planning, the fictive aspects were continually obstructed by a spiritual anguish out of which the main theme developed. An expansive imagination and a rich power of invention could not be entirely controlled by the discipline of the central idea which in turn evaded precise formulation for some time because of Dostoevsky's inability to grasp the complete image of his hero. The many manuscript notes and drafts of *The Idiot*, which have been published,[2] reveal strikingly the intricate pattern of his artistic efforts and illustrate once again the curious relation of his dualism to the creative process.

As early as August 1867, Dostoevsky wrote to Maikov from Geneva that he had begun work on a new story: "There is to be a novel, and if God helps, it will turn out to be a large affair and, perhaps, not bad. I love it terribly and will write it with joy and anxiety."[3] The initial inspiration for the novel appears to be connected with a celebrated court trial that had been written up at length in the newspapers. The importance of such material in his fiction has already been mentioned. While abroad, he read every Russian newspaper he could get his hands on, for he felt it vitally important to keep in touch with affairs at home. He particularly devoured the domestic tragedies, police records, and criminal processes which seemed to him more real than the common-place happenings of everyday life. These newspaper accounts were often accessories to the actions, settings, and characters of his novels. In *The Idiot* alone several well-known murder cases were drawn upon for certain scenes and they provided some hints for characterizations.[4]

The comparatively new institution of trial by jury was arousing much interest in Russia, and even provincial cases, which were often handled by famous lawyers, were widely featured in the metropolitan newspapers. An account of just such a sensational trial in the province of Tula was eagerly read by Dostoevsky as he was struggling with the conception of *The Idiot*. The case concerned a land-owning family by the name of Umetsky. Their fifteen-year-old daughter, Olga, had been accused of trying to burn down the family house on several occasions. Testimony revealed that the parents had for years subjected her to the most appalling cruelties. It developed, however, that the motives behind the crime of young Olga Umetskaya were strangely mixed, for the harsh treatment she had received had quite warped her mind. The newspaper accounts brought out fully the characters of the several principals, and the lawyers made much of the popular question of parental control in this "family drama."

Dostoevsky wrote to Maikov about the trial, and his wife subsequently indicated that "He interested himself to the extent that he had the intention of making the heroine of the trial, Olga Umetskaya (in the original plan) the heroine of his new novel." [5] That is, the original conception of *The Idiot* involved a family drama, and Dostoevsky tried to adapt several principals of the trial to the initial design of the novel. In his first sketch one of the feminine characters is called Mignon, and a few pages further in the notes he writes: "The story of Mignon is entirely the same as the story of Olga Umetskaya." [6] More and more material from the proceedings of the Umetsky trial is drawn into the orbit of the novel as the plan developed.

The draft of the first plan in the notebooks is very far removed from the scheme of things in the printed novel. The drama of a typical St. Petersburg bourgeois family is obviously intended. Lines of action are indicated and a confusing number of characters and their relations are sketched. The family is poor but has social pretensions. After a trip abroad to better his position, the father returns and commits a theft. The elder of two sons in the family is handsome, writes poetry, and is worshipped by his mother. The younger, designated solely as the "Idiot," is unloved, detested by his mother, and subject to epilepsy and nervous disorders. A practical-minded daughter, Masha, marries, and her husband's first cousin, a beautiful creature who is called the "Heroine," plays a considerable part in the action. Then there is the adopted child, Mignon, and an "Uncle," the father's brother. He is an odd person, a kind of Dickensian caricature who is given to humanitarian deeds, and it is clear that he is designed for a leading role. Several secondary characters are introduced also.

It is difficult to make out the projected course of action from Dostoevsky's compressed notes of this first plan. One fact stands out plainly: the drama of the story was to centre in the relations of the Idiot to Mignon and the Heroine. The Idiot is called such more because of his strange nature than for any positive manifestations of idiocy. In fact, he is described as a powerful, proud, and passionate individual. There is something Byronic about him, and he resembles those criminal, self-willed creations Valkovsky and Svidrigailov. He is sensual, performs extravagant actions, and perhaps his most marked trait is egotism. Although he is secretly in love with the Heroine, who is described as a proud, lofty woman, she scorns him and is really in love with his handsome brother.

The "wrathful Mignon," as Dostoevsky calls her in the notes, is a mysterious being. Her position in the household is worse than that of a servant, and he early attributes to her the characteristics of Olga Umetskaya as they had been brought out at the trial. Beaten and pushed about, she becomes deeply introspective and contemplates suicide. Although she is very shy, she is also capable of moments of terrible anger, when she vents her hatred for the family and her desire to avenge herself. Like the Heroine, Mignon loves the handsome brother, but she is strangely attracted to the Idiot. When he is falsely accused of the theft that his father had committed and is driven from the house, Mignon sympathetically follows him and shares his misery. They seem to understand each other and she tells him all her naïve dreams. His extreme actions she readily passes over, and even when he violates her in a moment of passion, she willingly forgives him.

Within this general framework, Dostoevsky, striving to hit upon a satisfactory plot, projects at least four separate intrigues in the first plan, each involving a different combination of characters. In one of these intrigues he introduces a new character, a "Son" of the Uncle, who is described as a high-minded individual with softened and benevolent traits that at once differentiate him from the Idiot, whose opposite he is obviously intended to be.

Though the sketch of this first plan is a far cry from the outline of the finished novel, it is possible to perceive certain lines of resemblance. The family recalls that of General Ivolgin, and in a number of details the father is clearly the prototype of the drunken, bankrupt general. The handsome son is the future Ganya, his sister the future Varya, and her husband has much in common with Varya's husband Ptitsyn. Although in the first plan there is no group that would correspond to the Epanchin family, in some respects the position of the Uncle suggests that of General Epanchin, and the Heroine, although she has a few of the traits of Nastasya Filipovna, is closer to the character of Aglaya. It is in the "wrathful Mignon" that one discerns something of the history, lineaments, and baffling behaviour of the remarkable Nastasya Filipovna. One striking fact that emerges from this first plan is the complete contrast between the Idiot and Prince Myshkin. Both characters have "idiocy," nervous ailments, and epilepsy in common, but the resemblances cease here. The full image and unique nature of the dominating hero of the finished novel had yet to be born in Dostoevsky's creative imagination.

For the next two months Dostoevsky struggled in feverish haste with the design and characters of the projected novel, because the first instalment was due in January. A maze of drafts of plots, character-sketches, and abundant details in the notebooks testify eloquently to the tremendous effort to discover the precise combination of cause and effect in human relationships that would satisfy his artistic conscience. Situations involving murder, suicide, rape, incest, and diabolical hatred give a vivid impression of the confused drama of violent passions that agitated his brain as he sought for the artistic constants that would bring order into the chaos that he had created.

With some difficulty it is possible to thread one's way through this labyrinth of material. In the early stage Dostoevsky formulated eight successive plans for the novel, each of which is a variation of the first plan that has already been described. In design, characters, and incidents nearly every plan marks a perceptible advance in the direction of the printed work. Although new characters are introduced, it is intensely interesting to observe how many of these are often further developments of earlier figures and take on more and more the traits of their future representatives in the finished novel. It is as though he were feeling his way towards distant images that he had not thoroughly comprehended. Thus, in these eight plans, five feminine characters are portrayed, each an extension of the other and contributing some specific feature to the complete characterization of Nastasya Filipovna, whom they all foreshadow.

It is not until the third, which Dostoevsky hopefully labels: "New and last plan," that he conceives the essential situation of the two families in the novel. The bourgeois family of the Umetsky's now has for its head a retired general who is still a closer approximation to General Ivolgin. He groups a second family around a father who is also a general, vaguely resembling General Epanchin. On the whole, as plan follows plan, Dostoevsky reveals a positive tendency to exalt the rank and social conditions of his leading characters, a marked contrast to his concentration on the lowly and oppressed figures in his fiction up to this point.

The many changes in plans, false starts, and obvious confusion in the creation of characters indicate that he was beset by an artistic difficulty not unlike that which interfered with the smooth drafting of *Crime and Punishment*. A careful study of the material in the notebooks reveals that in the early stages the "idea" of the novel evaded him and also the chief figure who would embody it. In several places in the notes, he jots down statements which are attempts to generalize on the purpose or main intention of the novel, as though this would help him to pull into focus his divergent designs. In one place he writes: "The whole novel: a struggle of love with hate"; then he changes this somewhat: "Endless pride and endless hate." Further on he introduces a new thought: "The chief idea of the novel: so much power, so much passion in the present generation and yet they do not believe in anything. Endless idealism with endless sensualism." [7]

Such ideas are plainly involved in the early drafts and are reflected in the first sketches of the character of the Idiot; but none of them plays any principal part in the printed novel. The spectre of the modern radical generation and its lack of faith troubles him at this point in the composition of *The Idiot* as it did in the case of *Crime and Punishment*. His preoccupation with this theme finds considerable expression in the finished novel, although it by no means pervades it. The solution of the main problem, as it is worked out through the various plans, affords a convincing illustration of the operation of Dostoevsky's creative process.

In the first plan it is not even certain that the Idiot was intended to be the hero of the novel, and this uncertainty continues for some time. The initial conception of the proud, passionate, vengeful man has absolutely nothing in common with Prince Myshkin. As a matter of fact, his traits and behaviour bear a close resemblance to those of Rogozhin in the printed novel, and it is more than likely that some such characterization was in Dostoevsky's mind in his original notion of the Idiot. The first suggestive variation in this egotistic, evil-working, self-willed portrait does not occur until the third plan, where he sets down a fleeting and unsupported observation on the characterization of the Idiot: "He ends with a heavenly deed." [8]

In the fourth plan Dostoevsky's growing uncertainty about the characterization takes a curious form. From the deep well of his creative mind a new figure was struggling to the surface. At first, the identification with the Idiot does not occur to him, and his obvious dissatisfaction obliges him to project certain of the dominant traits of the new figure in his mind into another character that had already appeared in the drafts. Now the Son of the Uncle is described as a meek individual, charming in his simplicity, and generous and noble in all his actions. His traits patently resemble Prince Myshkin's and are directly opposed to those of the Idiot in this plan. Although the Son is the chief figure in the fourth plan, he does not appear in the novel, having been absorbed, apparently, by the final conception of Myshkin.

The fifth plan brings no solution to the problem of the Idiot's characterization. He is still a Rogozhin-like figure who seeks his own enjoyment, hates all around him, and insists on dominating everybody. The notes only serve to indicate Dostoevsky's seemingly unconscious tendency to break down the original conception. For the first time he brings in the motive of Christianity in connection with the Idiot in a long conversation between him and the Uncle about Christ. Then suddenly he interpolates an observation: "From childhood there should be more beauty, more fine feelings, more love of one's surroundings, more breeding." [9] These are sentiments which Myshkin himself might have pronounced. And they find an outlet in Dostoevsky's persistent search for an opposite to the Idiot. Again this results in a concentration on the Son of the Uncle, who in this plan approaches still closer to the image of Prince Myshkin. The description of the Son is revealing: "Pure, beautiful, worthy, stern, very nervous, deeply Christian, and compassionately loving . . . There is no profundity or arrogance in ideas, although he is wise, educated, and a thinker. But *feeling* predominates in his nature. He lives for feeling. He lives powerfully and passionately. In one word, his nature is Christian." [10] This description recalls at once the essential features of Myshkin's nature. Yet Dostoevsky now names the Son "Ganya," who in this portrayal has nothing in common with the Ganya of the novel. As though he had discovered the real emphasis he is seeking, however, he remarks: "Ganechka must also be the most appealing, most meek, and most powerful figure in the whole novel." [11] Here Dostoevsky is very close to the idea he is seeking to formulate, but he is trying to embody in it the character of Ganya. By the time he has finished drafting the fifth plan, he appears to realize that Ganya cannot possibly carry the idea of the novel, and he laconically observes at the end of the sketch: "No good." Again his thoughts return to the Idiot, for he follows up this sharp observation with the remark: "The principal idea about the Idiot does not emerge." [12] The search for the pure image of Myshkin continues.

With new determination to plumb the depths of the character, Dostoevsky centres most of his attention on the Idiot in the sixth plan. The effort results in confusing complications but at the same time brings about a surprising development in the character. He now represents the Idiot as the Son of the Uncle. Here we see at once the anticipated identification of the Uncle's Son of the preceding plan with the Idiot! Separated from his parents, he spends his youth with the Umetsky's, marries one of them, and is sent to Switzerland. Upon his return he meets his own brother on the train and goes to the general's family. The relation of these incidents to the finished novel is plain, but the remaining notes indicate that the Idiot, as in the earlier characterizations, leads a life of passionate adventure in which he seduces Olga Umetskaya and falls in love with the Heroine.

Although the proud, vengeful aspects predominate, the self-willed nature of the Idiot now succumbs to Dostoevsky's fondness for the Double type. In fact, he describes him in this plan as: *"The dualism of a profound nature."* [13] The chief and basic idea of the whole

novel, Dostoevsky now declares, is the morbid pride of
the Idiot, who believes himself almost a god and yet
does not really esteem himself and cannot be convinced of his right or his capacity to do wrong. Despite
the titan features of his nature, he captivates all with
his childish *naïveté*, as Myshkin; he is generous and
has a real thirst for truth; finally, he believes himself to
be a Christian, but at the same time he lacks faith.
With this dualism we are on familiar ground, but it is
the change in the characterization which is of prime
significance. Dostoevsky has finally broken down his
original conception of the Idiot as a proud, Self-Willed
type by conceiving him as a Double. He has merely to
push the development one step further to arrive at the
image of Myshkin—the Meek opposite of the Self-
Willed type.

In the action of the seventh plan, there is little development over what has gone before. The problem is
still concerned with the character of the Idiot. After
involving him in a writhing knot of passions in the
notes, Dostoevsky gives vent to the baffling uncertainty in his mind by scribbling: "Puzzles, and who
is he? A fearful scoundrel or a mysterious ideal?" [14]
But towards the end of the draft a sudden inspiration
flashes through Dostoevsky's brain. It is as though all
his rebel thoughts and imaginings that had vainly
beaten against the hard and fixed form of the original conception of the Idiot now crystallize in an image
of pure light. For he jots down a cryptic note, pregnant
with meaning in relation to the finished character in
the novel: "He is a Prince. An Idiot Prince (he is with
the children)?!" [15]

The quickened tempo of composition, induced by
this resolution of the character of the Idiot, is everywhere apparent in the notes of the eighth plan. All the
characters, scenes, ideas, and action of the preceding
drafts are dynamically drawn to the new figure of the
Idiot. He now completely dominates the plot, and his
traits are essentially those of Prince Myshkin. Dostoev-

sky plunges into the details of the new conception of his hero, a simple-minded Christian, as though he were feeling the greatest satisfaction in ridding his imagination of the former proud, vengeful, and passionate Idiot. He is now ready to begin writing the actual novel. At the end of a few weeks of composition, however, he "threw all to the devil," as he wrote to Maikov,[16] and started out anew. What he had drafted up to this point would not satisfactorily adjust itself to his new conception of the Idiot. Once he had the image of the hero in mind, however, composition came easily. The first part of the novel appeared in January 1868. Many interruptions occurred, and it was not until February 1869 that Katkov published the last instalment.

In no work of Dostoevsky does the image of the hero so entirely embody the idea of the novel as in *The Idiot*. In fact, Prince Myshkin and the idea he represents are completely identified, one with the other. In a letter written to his niece, Sofiya Ivanova, after the first part of the novel was finished, he describes the idea that guided his efforts:

The idea of the novel is my old favourite idea, but so difficult that for a long time I did not dare to cope with it, and if I have attempted it now, it was certainly because I was in an almost desperate situation. The chief idea of the novel is to portray the positively good man. There is nothing in the world more difficult to do, and especially now. All writers, and not only ours, but even all Europeans, who have tried to portray the *positively* good man have always failed. Because this is an enormous problem. The good is an ideal, but this ideal, both ours and that of civilized Europe, is still far from having been worked out. There is only one positively good man in the world—Christ . . . I recall that of the good figures in Christian literature, the most perfect is Don Quixote. But he is good only because at the same time he is ridiculous. Dickens's Pickwick (an infinitely weaker conception than Don Quixote, but nevertheless immense) is also ridiculous and succeeds by virtue of this fact. One feels compassion for the ridiculous man who does not know his own worth as a good man, and consequently sympathy is invoked in the reader. This awakening of compassion is the secret of humour. Jean Valjean is also a powerful attempt, but he arouses sympathy by his horrible misfortune and society's injustice to him. In my novel there is nothing of this sort, positively nothing, and hence I am terribly afraid that I shall be entirely unsuccessful.[17]

The idea of writing a novel about an entirely good man had apparently been in Dostoevsky's mind for some time. A week before the letter to his niece, he had written to Maikov to say that he had long been tormented by this idea. Although the first part of the novel is already finished, the character, he complains, is not yet entirely imagined. "Only my desperate situation forced me to seize upon this premature idea. I risked it as at roulette: 'perhaps it will develop under the pen!' This is unforgivable." [18]

Both the image of Myshkin and the idea he embodied did develop under Dostoevsky's pen. The idea is essentially concerned with the larger problem of the ethical and moral good of the Russian nature, a problem that had deeply interested him since his conception of Raskolnikov, if not before. Later in life he contemplated writing a novel about a Russian Candide. The famous Dr. Pangloss in Voltaire's *Candide* encounters every conceivable misfortune with the conviction that all is for the best in this best of possible worlds. A Russian Candide, one may be sure, would conform to Dostoevsky's Meek type, a character whose basic features are humility and a willingness to suffer, even to justify suffering. Such an outlook on life is based on eternal optimism. The optimism of Dr. Pangloss is rational, whereas with the Russian Candide it would be instinctive. This instinct is deeply ingrained in the nature of Prince Myshkin, who seeks a rational justification for his optimism. Yet there is even a more important difference between the approach of Voltaire and Dostoevsky to the problem of the entirely good man. In his misfortunes Dr. Pangloss is rendered ridiculous; the meek Prince Myshkin is sad and tragic. Voltaire laughs over Dr. Pangloss. Dostoevsky profoundly sympathizes with the humiliated Idiot.

Perhaps more so than Dr. Pangloss, closer parallels to the entirely good man in world literature would be Parson Adams in Fielding's *Joseph Andrews* or the Vicar in Goldsmith's *Vicar of Wakefield*. In the letter to his niece Dostoevsky mentions Pickwick. But Pickwick, in essence, is a figure of fun whose sole resemblance to Myshkin is as an ideal of reality. Don Quixote is also mentioned in the letter, and he is perhaps a closer approximation to the figure Dostoevsky had in mind when he created the hero of *The Idiot*. The Knight of the Sorrowful Countenance had long held a secure place in the hearts of Russian readers, and for Dostoevsky, as well as for Turgenev and Tolstoy, the masterpiece of Cervantes was a supremely great book. In *The Diary of a Writer* he notes: "In all the world there is nothing more profound and more powerful than *Don Quixote*. Further than this, it is the last and greatest word of human thought, the most bitter irony that man can express." [19]

The influence of Don Quixote on the conception of Myshkin is palpable enough. That Cervantes's famous character was in Dostoevsky's mind is clear from the evidence in the letter to his niece and from the printed use made of *The Poor Knight*, Pushkin's poem about Don Quixote, which Aglaya Epanchina reads to Myshkin. Still, there is little similarity beyond the fact that both characters represent attempts to portray the completely good or perfect man. The differences are more striking than the resemblances. Cervantes intended the good Don to express the tragedy of his life through laughter and hence conceived him as the personification of reason and moral sense while at the same time being devoid of judgment and understanding. As in the characterization of Dr. Pangloss, Dostoevsky preferred to see in Don Quixote not the ridiculous, but the infinite sadness of life. His conception of the completely good man left no room for laughter. There is nothing comical about Myshkin.

Another and more important influence than Don Quixote is apparent in the conception of Myshkin, and one expressly indicated in the letter to Dostoevsky's niece. The image of an entirely good or perfect man at once suggests the image of Christ. In the light of the enormous part played by Christ in the moral and ethical thinking of Dostoevsky, it was almost inevitable that he should turn to Him for inspiration in this instance. The parallelism between Myshkin and Christ is everywhere apparent in the novel. The description of Myshkin on the opening page recalls the familiar features of Christ as they are ordinarily portrayed in the art of the Eastern Church: ". . . above the average in height, with very fair thick hair, with sunken cheeks and a thin, pointed, almost white beard. His eyes were large, blue and dreamy; there was something gentle, though heavy-looking in their expression." Myshkin's love of children and his implicit faith in them, his behaviour towards the Swiss Mary taken in sin, and many other surface features and symbolic actions point to the Christ-like nature of Dostoevsky's conception. In the manuscript notes his name is frequently coupled with that of Christ, and in one place he is called "Prince Christ."

To portray a character endowed with the perfect moral beauty of Christ is a hazardous task for any author and one that would seem to be doomed to failure from the outset. It is too much to expect that a character, even though only an imitation of nature, can be drawn through the wringer of life and emerge perfect. It is a curious fact of literary history that Samuel Richardson, in his prolix and stilted way, attempted to create a perfect male in the hero of *Sir Charles Grandison*. Sir Charles is adorned with every human perfection and possesses what Richardson thought was moral beauty. But a greater bore and moral prig, a more flat, two-dimensional character than Sir Charles Grandison has perhaps never been imagined in a novel that has any real pretensions to genius. He is so perfect and hence so unreal that Richardson succeeded in making a kind of museum piece of Sir Charles Grandison, a character, remarked Taine, that deserved to be canonized and stuffed.

Dostoevsky was thoroughly aware of the anomaly involved in the creation of an entirely good man. He realized that perfection in any form did not exist in real life, and hence his artistic sense led him to introduce the cracks in the otherwise perfect white marble surface of Myshkin's moral beauty. Although he eschewed the laughter and ridicule with which Cervantes justified the characterization of Don Quixote, he supported the reality of Myshkin's nature with more serious and human defects. Even the very centre of Myshkin's nature—his moral beauty—is not without its flaws. For he admits to a species of double thoughts in which low motives mingle in his mind with lofty ones, although he never really acts upon a base motive. More important, the Christ-like image of Myshkin is marred by the afflictions of idiocy and epilepsy. Although possessing the highest spirituality and the moral beauty of the Saviour, Myshkin after all is simply one of God's imperfect children, an erring son of man in his mental faculties. What he loses in divine stature by these defects he gains in human verisimilitude.

Still, Dostoevsky squarely faced the problem that Myshkin, compared to the other positively good characters of literature, might sacrifice much in appeal because of his Christ-like qualities, however marred by human frailties. In the notes he frankly asked himself the question: "How to make the figure of the hero appealing to the reader?" His answer is emphatic and interesting: "If Don Quixote and Pickwick, as virtuous figures, succeeded in gaining the sympathy of the reader because they are laughable, the hero of the novel, the Prince, if he is not laughable, then he has another appealing feature—innocence!" [20]

Apart from the figure of Christ, the conception of Myshkin was no doubt closely joined with the reality of an ancient Russian tradition. The inspired idiot, the afflicted messenger of God, was a kind of folklore type long accepted in Russian life and literature, and in the lore of other peoples. Not only the common people, but even the nobility, associated a deep spiritual nature with idiocy. It was believed that God compensated the idiot with special spiritual powers, a notion that became connected with Myshkin in the early stages of his development as the Idiot in the notebooks.

The idea of a novel, it has already been pointed out, was always apprehended by Dostoevsky in connection with the larger problem of the relation of man to the world in which he lives. In *The Idiot* the idea of the entirely good man is worked out by bringing the Christ-like character of Myshkin into contact with a world of greedy, sensual, sinning people. This problem is complicated by the fact that Myshkin, like all the Meek characters, is passive, whereas the society in which he lives is intensely active. Of course it would be easier to understand the nature of a supremely good man if he performed actual good deeds, like an American philanthropist who endows colleges, engages in slum clearance, and directly aids the poor and unfortunate of his community. Although Myshkin undoubtedly possesses a certain potentiality for accomplishing active good deeds, he does not do them. Nor is he represented as a morally perfect male Pippa who passes through the world, unconsciously transforming evil into good. In general, the spiritual passivity of Myshkin that changes the lives of people is difficult to accept, for it is so foreign to our conception of affecting the lives of others by real active deeds. Yet this passive dominance, which amounts to a spiritual control over reality, is a persistent trait in several of Dostoevsky's great characters. It is the power of spirit over matter that has its inception in primitive Christianity, or even in Russian Orthodox Christianity as opposed to Western or Catholic Christianity, which translates its influence into active good deeds. Myshkin's extraordinary influence is exercised through the spiritual perfection of his own life and the force of his radiant personality. Sinning men and women are drawn to him and transformed by the Christian beauty of his nature. They are deeply affected by a humility and patient submission to suffering that invokes the image of Christ who passively, not actively, submitted to suffering at the command of God in order to achieve the salvation of man. To appraise correctly the character of Myshkin, who lives in a world where the repentant sinner is closer to God than the ninety-nine respectable citizens who have not sinned, it is essential to understand the ethical principles behind this pervasive influence of a personal but passive morality.

14

An
Unattainable
Ideal

The Idiot is a baffling book, a composite of truly great art and of much that falls below the level of even good craftsmanship. It is also baffling because one can never be certain that the ethical and moral problems which run through it are solved or whether they admit of any solution. Dostoevsky may be correct in maintaining that his idealism is more real than the realism of his literary rivals, but the idealism in *The Idiot* is better described by Tolstoy's definition that an ideal is an ideal simply because it is unattainable in real life. Certainly the idealism of *The Idiot*, real enough in Myshkin's strange world of spiritual values, is an unattainable ideal in the world of living men.

That the heroes and heroines of Dostoevsky tend to fall into three well-defined groups which in turn are closely related psychologically, seems to gain support with every successive analysis. The additional fact emerges that each hero appears to supplement and clarify the preceding characters in the same group. It is almost an antecedent probability that the traits of the meek Vasya Shumkov, Rostanev, and Sonya Marmeladova will turn up, in one form or another, in Myshkin. And this is actually the case. He is entirely passive, willingly accepts suffering, is easily put upon, answers offences by begging forgiveness, and exaggerates the good in others while continually overlooking or rationalizing evil. In the notes Dostoevsky lists as the "Chief features in the prince's character: cowed; fearfulness; humbleness; submissiveness; complete conviction about himself that he is an idiot." [1] He particularly stresses "submissiveness," which elsewhere in the notes he describes as "the most fearful force that can exist in the world." [2] Myshkin believes himself to be "more humble and worse than all." Although he is a prince, like most of Dostoevsky's high-born figures, he seems to preserve none of the traditions of his class. In the company of his peers he acts like an outsider, and at times he behaves as though he were ashamed of the rank he bears.

For the first time a Meek character becomes the hero of a novel. In several important respects, however, Myshkin goes beyond the previous Meek figures and carries the development of the type to a point of greater psychological complexity. One trait that sets him apart is the quality of his mind. Though he has had little education, he is a thinking person, and his rational processes are supplemented by a kind of sixth sense which, as Dostoevsky indicates in the notes, enables Myshkin to see through the thoughts of everyone around him. When his heart and conscience speak to him, he is willing to follow a course of action in the face of every opposition.

Myshkin has definite opinions on a variety of subjects, and under certain unusual circumstances he displays a keenness in expressing them. Of course, he has little of the analytical powers of the intellectual Doubles, such as Raskolnikov and Ivan Karamazov. This ability is never possessed by the Meek characters and is compensated by their moral intuition and spiritual insight. But Myshkin's ideas, although lacking in logical consistency and orderly presentation, provide a pattern of thought which is quite significant, for it amounts to the Meek character's philosophy of life. Further, his theories on social, political, and religious matters, directly reflect those of Dostoevsky while he was writing *The Idiot* abroad.

In truth, *The Idiot* is the first of Dostoevsky's artistic works into which he injects a deliberate didactic purpose. In previous fiction he had rarely indulged in special pleading and it never obtruded on the unity of the total performance. His sojourn in Europe, however, was clarifying and intensifying his reactions to various problems in Russia, and *The Idiot* was conceived in an atmosphere of revolt against the liberal and nihilist forces which he felt were undermining the country. On various occasions Myshkin becomes the mouthpiece of his creator while in the process of formulating his own philosophy. Many of the ideas he expresses turn up in Dostoevsky's letters at this time, and later in his journalistic articles.

Upon Myshkin's return from his visit to Moscow he is full of something new, something confused in his mind but clearly inspired by a different understanding which he has attained of Russia and its people. He begins to love the Russian masses and vaguely recognizes as their enemies the self-willed, insolent, godless, nihilist younger generation for which nothing is sacred. The causes of this fatal division in Holy Russia take form in his mind and resolve themselves into the series of contending forces which had developed out of Dostoevsky's own incessant dualism. Suggestive comments in the notes, which serve as reminders for Myshkin's arguments, might almost stand as the titles for journalistic articles of Dostoevsky. In one place he jots down: "Speech of the prince to Aglaya at the country house: Comparison of the West with the East." [3]

In another place it is indicated that Myshkin is to speak "About foreign and Russian people, etc." [4]

These and other themes are developed most fully by Myshkin in his impassioned outbursts at that unfortunate party at the Epanchins'. He declares that there are two ways to unite society into an harmonious whole—the way of oppression through authority, which amounts to establishing equality by force, and the way of service, which achieves harmony through mutual submission of one to another. Then he elaborates this point by a thesis that was becoming a kind of credo in Dostoevsky's thinking. Roman Catholicism, Myshkin insists, has accepted the path of authority which inevitably leads to socialism—the aim of both Roman Catholicism and socialism being to subject all to their authority, and in return for this submission to promise equality. The second path is that of the Russian Orthodox faith, the aim of which is to bring about universal harmony by preaching submission and service to one another. The latter, of course, is the path that Myshkin follows.

Convinced of this pervasive contradiction, Myshkin, like Dostoevsky, seems to see all humanity dividing itself into the meek and good of heart on one side and the self-willed and offending people on the other. With the first he identifies Russia and the Russian Christ, with the self-willed and offending people the nations of Western Europe along with their Roman Catholicism and socialism. He declares to his astonished listeners at the Epanchins':

Why, socialism is a product of Catholicism and the Catholic essence. Like its brother atheism, it comes from despair, in opposition to Catholicism in the moral sense, in order to substitute itself for the lost power of religion, to quench the spiritual thirst of parched humanity, and to save it, not by Christ, but by violence. This, then, is freedom by violence; it is union through the sword and blood! 'Do not dare to have a God, do not dare to have property, do not dare to have individuality, *fraternité ou la mort,*

two millions of heads!' And do you imagine that all this is
so harmless and without danger for us. O, we need to have
resistance at once, at once! Our Christ whom we have
kept and they have never known must shine forth and
vanquish the West. (Part IV, Chapter VII)

Of course, this is Dostoevsky speaking out at the top
of his voice, and in accents that anticipate the social
and religious propaganda of *The Possessed* and of the
later journalism. In the mouth of the meek, submissive
Myshkin these militant ideas, however much they
may complement the ideological framework of his
philosophy, sound harsh and discordant. Dostoevsky's
attempt to justify this extraordinary outburst by connecting it with the nervous excitement that customarily
precedes an epileptic seizure does not wholly succeed. And he returns to the charge later in the novel
in a scene which does less injustice to the character of
Myshkin but is even more didactic in intention.

The satiric references to nihilism and its adherents
throughout the book culminate in that noisy scene
where Terentev, Lebedev's son, Keller, and others
gather on the porch to plead the cause of the young
man who claimed to be the illegitimate son of Myshkin's benefactor. (Part II, Chapters VIII-IX.) Here Dostoevsky pays his respects to the extremists and even
to the liberals of his day, men with whom Myshkin
has nothing in common. The lofty, radical ideas of
these young blackmailers are in sharp contrast to their
shabby, dirty appearance, and to their arrogant, dishonourable, petty natures. Compared to the pure-
minded hero they cut sorry figures, and their behaviour reveals their self-seeking designs. Like some prince
out of a fairy tale, Myshkin waves his spiritual wand,
and these youthful devils of revolutionary destruction
are transformed into docile creatures, confounded by
his moral perfection. Dostoevsky's triumph is a cheap
one. He allows Myshkin, like a troubadour of reactionary optimism, to dissipate the social pessimism of a
group unworthy to cope with even his weak and dis-

orderly intellect. These loud-mouthed youths by no means represent the typical radicals of the 1860's. It was a mistake that he was to make again, and on a larger scale, when he attempted to portray the revolutionists that he now regarded almost as personal enemies.

The social and religious theories that Myshkin enunciates at the Epanchins' reflect very clearly the curious dual approach that Dostoevsky propounds in much of his future fiction and journalism. The path of authority aims to destroy society and to construct it anew in order to obtain equality through despotism. Myshkin's path leads to the individual's suppressing himself, and through service and compassion establishing a rule of equality and brotherly love. This universal dualism involves Dostoevsky's supplementary contradictions between Russia and Western Europe, between the Roman Catholic Church and Russian Orthodoxy, and between faith in Christ and a belief in socialism. In a general way these contending forces suggest the opposing traits of the Meek and Self-Willed characters, and their existence in a single individual, the Double type.

Myshkin's awareness of the social and moral evils of society, however, is not attended by any active programme of reform, for he is passive by nature. Like the meek Sonya Marmeladova, who would have thoroughly understood him, he is of a mystical turn and deeply religious, and his own spiritual life must stand as the answer to the ills of society. Yet his religious faith calls for an enraptured unification with the highest synthesis of life. He appears to achieve this unification in moments of greatest weakness, usually when he has completely suppressed his own personality or, strangely enough, during that fleeting ecstatic moment before an epileptic fit, when time seems to stand still and his soul is flooded with an extraordinary light that reveals at once all that is serene and harmonious in the existence of man.

In Myshkin's ideal of society, insult and suffering will vanish from the earth, and goodness of heart will reign. With all his spirituality he strives towards this end. Despite his great faith, however, he fails. Nearly everyone looks down upon him; and his experiences are symbolic of Christ's among the Pharisees and those of little faith. The sinning people he comes in contact with or influences are almost, without exception, rendered unhappy—one is murdered. At the conclusion of the novel, he himself lapses into idiocy. Perhaps the parallel of Christ's failure upon earth and the hope of salvation by suffering and faith which He left behind were in Dostoevsky's thoughts. There is also the other possibility that he may have accepted the inevitable fact of Myshkin's failure in an unbelieving world. On the other hand, the obvious uncertainty at the end of the novel, apparent also in the notes, may well have reflected a profound doubt in Dostoevsky's own mind as to the efficacy of Myshkin's way of life as an answer to the ills of mankind. This problem of the Meek character who opposes his submissive nature, intuitive goodness of heart, and boundless faith in the common people and in the Christ of the Orthodox Church to the Self-Willed man dominated by reason, socialism, and the intellectual poison of the West, was a problem that Dostoevsky felt impelled to struggle with in future works. In truth, he never seemed to have found the answer, perhaps for the simple reason that there is none.

Dostoevsky's deep concern with the characterization of Nastasya is apparent in the manuscript notebooks where an unusually large amount of material is devoted to her. Something has already been said about the tortuous course of her development throughout the various drafts. He experienced considerable difficulty in forming Nastasya and in working out her exact relations to Myshkin. The real figure of Olga Umetskaya, as described in the newspaper accounts of her trial, contributes something, and finally the succession of wrath-

ful, passionate, and vengeful women in the early outlines of the novel are condensed into an image of
startling brilliance. With calculated artistry he excites
curiosity and anticipation about her by his favourite
device of an elaborate build-up. The use of her portrait
in this connection and Myshkin's prophetic comments
on it are extremely effective.

Nastasya's intense emotionalism and strange behaviour are somewhat justified by the unhappy experiences of her youth and by the frank admission that she
is an exceptional woman. Perhaps Dostoevsky was influenced by his own affair with Polina Suslova in describing Nastasya as unable to forgive Totsky because
he seduced her. The offence blights her life, for upon
her is thrust the social degradation of a fallen woman
while her whole spiritual and moral existence is dominated by an ideal of chastity.

In her relations with Rogozhin and Myshkin, this
strange woman alternates between love and hate, reflecting the conflicting forces of her nature. She both
tortures and allows herself to be tortured. Nastasya
falls in love with Myshkin because she recognizes the
selflessness of his morally perfect nature, and because
she knows that he is the only one to perceive her own
nobility of soul. For her Rogozhin is merely a lover,
Myshkin a human being, and her struggle to choose
between them becomes the tragedy of her life. Unlike other men, Myshkin talks to her about serious subjects—life, Russia, and religion—but never about love,
which fact satisfies a furtive but real yearning she has
for things of the mind. Yet in the end she drives him
away, motivated by a dual feeling of envy for his
moral perfection which she longs to possess, and by
the desire to save him, for she instinctively feels that
union with her would be his ruin. Their whole relationship seems to symbolize that of Christ and the
harlot.

Her rival, Aglaya, is not in any sense a foil; their
natures and even their actions, in a limited sense, are

strikingly similar. What differentiates them is largely
the matter of background and social circumstances.
One can almost imagine Nastasya acting as Aglaya if
they could have exchanged social positions. Like Nastasya, Aglaya is a passionate and proud woman. She
loves Myshkin and is jealous of Nastasya, and at the
same time she capriciously plays off her other ad-
mirers one against the other. The love of these two
women for the same man and their psychological reactions resemble the situation of Grushenka and Katerina
Ivanovna in their love for Dmitri in *The Brothers Karamazov*.

Myshkin, however, has nothing of the sensual and
passionate nature of Dmitri Karamazov, yet he is the
object of the love of two women whose affections are
scarcely less insistent and demanding than those of
Grushenka and Katerina Ivanovna. The situation created a psychological problem which Dostoevsky regarded as of first importance in the characterization
of his hero. The variant solutions in the notes indicate
the difficulty he experienced in deciding upon the
final outcome of the problem, which is further complicated by the love of Rogozhin for Nastasya. In one
place he has Nastasya marrying Myshkin; in another
she runs away on the eve of the marriage and goes
to a brothel, where she dies; in a third, she deserts him
for Rogozhin, who marries and finally kills her; in a
final variant, before she is murdered, she makes a
friend of Aglaya, whom Myshkin eventually marries.
The tremendous scene of the meeting of the rivals,
to which Dostoevsky attached much significance, also
caused him a good deal of hesitation before he settled
upon the outcome of this fateful clash of passions.
The proud and virtuous Aglaya is humbled by her
scorned and fallen rival.

The problem, obviously, was how to release Myshkin from an intricate situation which involved the psychological consistency of his nature. His pure, Christ-
like character was incompatible with marriage, and

Dostoevsky wisely abandoned this solution for the highly artistic frustration which resolves the whole complex situation of the love-duel. This way out, be it noted, is entirely in keeping with the unusual nature of Myshkin. He marries neither woman, for, like all the Meek characters, he is sexless. At the outset of the story he declares to Rogozhin that he has no knowledge of women, a fact which he attributes to his illness. Myshkin, in truth, finds it difficult to comprehend the kind of love Nastasya and Aglaya offer him. The basic elements of his nature—Christian humility, meekness, and readiness for self-renunciation and self-sacrifice—determine his behaviour in love as in everything else. The charms of Aglaya and the irresistible beauty of Nastasya he ignores, and he prefers to regard himself as their "brother." The absence of normal sexual instincts does not lead him to imagine that he might possibly offend a woman who loved him by denying himself to her. He is quite ready to marry either of them and is unable to understand why he cannot be in love with both at the same time. Nor do his feelings in the matter prevent him from lending every aid to his rivals in love. It is an infinite compassion for the unhappy and suffering Nastasya and a kind of humanitarian compliance with the designs of Aglaya that guide his relations with both women. Meanwhile, both mistake his efforts as an expression of normal desires. What his morally perfect nature seeks is a spiritual, not an earthly, union of man and woman.

The relatively few comments on the character of Rogozhin in the notebooks would indicate that he presented no special problem. All the volcanic passions and primitive psychology with which the initial figure of the Idiot and his successors had been endowed in the early drafts are now concentrated in Rogozhin. Dostoevsky obviously invented him as an opposite to Myshkin, who has a kind of magnetic attraction for him. The vagueness and horrific traits recall the mysterious Murin in the early story, "The Landlady"; and the psychological aspects of his love for Nastasya resemble the dual feelings of the hero of *The Gambler*. It has been conjectured, and with considerable likelihood, that the characterization and actions of Rogozhin were influenced by a murderer, Mazurin, an account of whose crime Dostoevsky had read in the newspapers in March 1867.[5] Although there is not much resemblance in the two figures, certain details of the crime described in the newspapers turn up in the account of the murder of Nastasya—the piece of American leather with which Rogozhin covered the body and the jars of disinfectant he placed near by. The fact is interesting, since some critics have discovered a profound mystical significance in these same curious details. On the whole, Rogozhin strikes one as a literary device, necessary to sustain the action of the plot. Certainly his mysterious comings and goings and his strange and often unexplained behaviour, though calculated no doubt to make the flesh creep, rarely rise above the level of sheer melodrama.

Young Terentev had not figured in the early drafts of the novel. He is introduced in a later sketch as one of a group of "children," including Kolya Ivolgin. The notes indicate that Myshkin's relations with this group were to occupy an important place in the action. The intention was to throw further light on the character of the hero, for Myshkin is more at home with youngsters than with grown-ups. They love and trust him, and in turn he influences them. Many projects are suggested in the notes, such as the publishing of a magazine by the young people and the formation of a club in which Myshkin takes a leading part. Most of these suggestions are not worked out in *The Idiot;* the project of a children's club, interestingly enough, appears in *The Brothers Karamazov,* where Alyosha—who resembles Myshkin in so many traits— is involved. The plans in the notes, however, are reflected in the novel in Myshkin's activities with the children in Switzerland and in his relations with Kolya Ivolgin and Terentev.

"The vanity of a weak character" [6] is the description of Terentev in the notes. But there are also reminders that he is "the principal axis of the entire novel," [7] and that it is necessary "to centre the whole intrigue in him." [8] These prescriptions are largely fulfilled in *The Idiot*. It was Dostoevsky's intention, in making Terentev so significant a factor in the main action of the novel, to justify this by attributing to him a curious dominance over several important characters. Terentev actually wields an influence over Rogozhin, Aglaya, Nastasya, and to some extent over Myshkin, although in this case the prince finally conquers him by his spirituality and trustfulness. At one point in the notes, Dostoevsky even considered the possibility of Terentev's murdering Nastasya as a solution of the impasse at the end of the novel.

The obvious psychological problem in the characterization of Terentev is to account for this unusual influence of an essentially weak nature over stronger individuals who actually look down upon him. His strength lies in his positive philosophizing, which at the same time reveals his weakness since he fails to accept entirely his own theorizing or to act upon it successfully. Although he is a thinking Double, like the underground man and Raskolnikov, neither of these predecessors had connected his dualism with the broader problem of the relation of man to the world. Terentev translates his ambivalence of pride and submissiveness into terms of a struggle between God and the world of men. To accept God, he believes, one must be submissive, and therefore he rebels against Him. He has been beaten by life and is dying of consumption, yet he defies the God who has ordained his defeat. His rebellion takes a unique form. Although he had no control over his birth, he has over his death. By committing suicide he feels that he will frustrate

God's last vestige of power over him and thus elevate himself to the position of a "man-god." His attempt to kill himself fails, but his struggle goes on until disease ends his days like those of any other mortal. An interesting aspect of the philosophizing of this minor Double about the man-god is that it appears again, in somewhat altered form, in connection with Kirilov in *The Possessed* and Ivan Karamazov.

The figure of Ganya Ivolgin presents a complex development throughout nearly all the early drafts. The notes reveal many permutations, from a character that possesses some of the violent traits of the early Idiot—in one variant Ganya shoots himself at the end —to the merely "clever" commonplace figure of the novel. He turns out to be an unoriginal young man, constantly scheming to amass a fortune and embittered by his failure with Aglaya and his inability to achieve distinction, which he knows in his heart he does not deserve. On the whole, he is a pale creation.

The other secondary figures in the rich gallery vary between brilliant character-sketches and the undistinguished human furnishings of any packed drama of literature. Among the most successful are the mother of Aglaya, General Ivolgin, and Lebedev. Madame Epanchina is expertly drawn. It is interesting to observe that Dostoevsky deliberately attributes a family resemblance, in traits as well as appearance, between her and Aglaya. They both possess a forthright scorn for any middle-of-the-road policy, and they both go all out of their way to disguise their most generous impulses. The relationship recalls that between Natasha Ikhmeneva and her father in *The Insulted and Injured*. General Ivolgin, a kind of Marmeladov in both his actions and his weakness for strong liquor, is a "poet of lying." Even on his deathbed he cannot tell the truth. His friend Lebedev, who is almost his equal in the matter of colossal fibbing, recognizes his human qualities and weeps at his death. To be sure, tears come easily to this bottle-companion of the general.

Lebedev is an amateur philosopher who thoroughly understands Myshkin and is an important participant in the action of the novel. In the notes Dostoevsky calls him a "talented man," and certainly some kind of talent is evident in his extraordinary interpretations of the apocalypse and in the bafflingly mixed motives that dictate his unique actions.

The conclusion of *The Idiot* leaves one with a painful sense of frustration. A powerful spiritual idea, magnificently developed throughout the novel, is refuted in the end by the evil forces of sinning men and women. The beautiful Nastasya is murdered, the impulsive Aglaya marries a Pole and becomes converted to Roman Catholicism, Rogozhin goes mad, and Myshkin turns into a hopeless idiot. The futility of the spirit in its struggle against the sins of humanity seems poignantly symbolized in the sharp contrast between the eager, stainless Myshkin, arriving in St. Petersburg from his quiet isolation abroad at the beginning of the novel, and the final picture of him a year later, jabbering incoherently to the mad murderer Rogozhin as they sit beside the slain Nastasya, whom he had hoped to save and restore to moral health. Dostoevsky also experienced a sense of failure. After he had finished the work he wrote to his niece: "I am not satisfied with the novel; it has not expressed a tenth part of what I wished to express; nevertheless I shall not renounce it, and I love my idea, even though up to now it has been unsuccessful." [9]

Dostoevsky was always ready to admit the insufficiencies of *The Idiot*. After the first part, which is superbly executed, the plot grows progressively complicated, sometimes to the point of confusion. Despite the many early drafts, it appears that he did not actually begin the final version with a complete outline of the action as it now exists. This fact, coupled with the pressure under which he wrote and the usual difficulties of serial composition accounts for a number of the technical drawbacks. Essentially the work becomes a collection of brilliant and powerful dramatic scenes which are loosely connected and in a few instances vaguely motivated.

With all its faults, however, Dostoevsky never failed to admit to a partiality for *The Idiot* among his works, and those who shared his view, he felt, displayed a habit of mind similar to his own. The artistic flaws he freely admitted, but the sustaining power of the novel, he was convinced, consisted of something that far transcended its technical weaknesses. In a letter to Strakhov he wrote: "In the novel much was composed in haste, much is prolix and has not succeeded, but something has succeeded. I do not stand behind the novel. I stand behind my idea." [10] Here he is on solid ground. The enduring quality of *The Idiot* rests squarely upon the treatment of its idea and the great character that embodies it. For over all the many figures and the variegated dramatic action hovers the unforgettable personality of Myshkin. His failure in an intensely pragmatic world, where things of the spirit are consumed in the flame of reality, does not lessen the appeal of his Christlike nature or the rightness of his moral principles. Myshkin is one of the supremely great "good" characters in fiction, and in many respects he is absolutely unique.

15

The Eternal Husband

The completion of *The Idiot* brought no relief to the desperate financial plight of Dostoevsky. Long before he sent off the last instalment he had used up all the profits from the novel. More discouraging, perhaps, was the reaction of the public and critics to *The Idiot*. Important magazines gave it little or no space, and comment was far from enthusiastic; the reading public was puzzled but not entirely unappreciative, if the accounts written to Dostoevsky reflect the average reaction. No doubt the tremendously successful *Crime and Punishment* had whetted the appetites of his readers for a kind of detective-story element and for swift, closely knit, and compelling narrative. In the earlier novel Dostoevsky had been more successful in reconciling the fantastic with the prosaic aspects of reality. Of course there is melodrama and excitement in *The Idiot;* but the terrific intensity of separate scenes is neutralized by the looseness of structure and general prolixity of the novel. The realism is essentially subjective. In order to transform his idea of the positively good man into a realistic creation, he had to resort to strained artistic methods of combining the real and the fantastic. His morally perfect hero is often involved in complex and improbable adventures. Nevertheless, while standing on the periphery of irrationality and often under bizarre circumstances, the characters speak their ideas and theories convincingly. But neither public nor critics seemed to appreciate the realistic features of these characters or the logic of their ideas. Myshkin did not recommend himself to the average reader of that time any more than he does today. In attempting in all seriousness to create a morally perfect hero, Dostoevsky had definitely gambled with popular interest. People in general do not take kindly to moral perfection, in or outside of fiction. Had he been willing to make Myshkin amusing, as Cervantes did Don Quixote, the public and critics might have accepted him with better grace. Nor was the quality of "innocence," which Dostoevsky had counted upon to win sympathy for his hero, wisely calculated to arouse interest in a character that otherwise had no sins, venial or unpardonable. On the whole, readers were baffled by *The Idiot* and critics were inclined to consider it a distinct falling off. What was more immediately important for Dostoevsky: this comparative lack of interest was reflected in the fact that there was no eager demand on the part of publishers to buy up the book rights of the serial, as had been the case with *Crime and Punishment*. He was keenly disappointed and began to imagine that his artistic powers were failing.

In the summer of 1869, Dostoevsky left Florence, where he had finished *The Idiot,* and took up residence in Dresden. He had wheedled an advance against another novel from the patient Katkov, and he eventually obtained a small sum for a short story for Strakhov's new periodical *Dawn* (*Zarya*). But it was difficult for him to work. His self-imposed exile was becoming unbearable; he yearned for Russia and would almost have preferred the risk of prosecution for his debts than to remain abroad any longer. Soon the expenses attendant upon the birth of his second child in September took every available penny and reduced the family again to abject poverty. Under these conditions he could make no progress on the projected novel, but he doggedly stuck to the short story for Strakhov, which, as usual, grew longer and longer. By the beginning of winter it was finished, and he had to plead for a pittance from Maikov in order to send the manuscript to the publisher, since he did not have even enough money for postage.

This short story, *The Eternal Husband,* had actually turned into a short novel by a process now quite familiar. In its comparative lightness of tone it represents a retreat from the serious work of *The Idiot,* and he regarded it as something of a relaxation before he returned to the more formidable project of his next novel. The unusually well-constructed plot and smooth narrative style of *The Eternal Husband* no doubt owe something to the fact that he had ample time to revise while waiting for the postage money. The plot concerns Velchaninov, a rather tired devotee of the science of the tender passions, who feels himself growing old although he has not yet reached forty. Unpleasant memories of his escapades have begun to vex him and induce an imaginary nervous disorder and spiritual depression. He loses his old gaiety and irresponsible habits and allows himself to become absorbed in all the trifling details of his daily existence. At this point a certain provincial official, Pavel Pavlovich, appears in the city. He is the "eternal husband," the type of spouse born to be cuckolded. Several years before, Velchaninov had been the lover of the wife and had left the provincial town unaware of the fact that he was the father of her child. The docile Pavel Pavlovich was equally in the dark and tenderly brought up the little girl as his own. After his wife's death, however, he discovers her unfaithfulness. A fierce desire for vengeance suddenly takes possession of this mild and long-suffering husband, and he goes to the city with the little girl to hunt down his betrayer. The remainder of the story relates the unusual psychological struggle that takes place between Velchaninov and Pavel Pavlovich, in which the little girl, Liza, plays an important part.

With such a situation in hand it is not difficult to understand why Dostoevsky was tempted to go far beyond the limits of the short story he had originally planned. The situation seems especially designed for the application of his characteristic psychological method, and in *The Eternal Husband*, one must admit, he presents a most convincing application of it. Critics have suggested that the theme of the betrayed husband in this story is a fictional treatment of the alleged infidelity of Dostoevsky's first wife. At best this must remain a mere conjecture, since we know next to nothing about the supposed unfaithfulness of his first wife, and in the story there is no tangible contributory evidence to the effect that he is being autobiographical. Certainly the theme of the betrayed husband is common enough in literature. Dostoevsky's treatment of it, however, is unusual.

The story is neatly balanced psychologically. So regular are the parallel sets of situations which compel the curious transverse reactions in the behaviour duel of Pavel Pavlovich and Velchaninov that one is tempted to regard the tale as a deliberate exercise piece in the finished psychological technique of Dostoevsky. For the concentration is largely on analysis, whereas scenes and characters, in a rather unoriginal fashion, echo those in previous works. Pavel Pavlovich dogging Velchaninov on the streets of St. Petersburg recalls the experience of Golyadkin being trailed by his ⸺ in "The Double"; his stealthy peering up at

Velchaninov's window goes back to the similar situation in *The Idiot* where Myshkin peers up at Rogozhin's window; the attempted murder of Velchaninov by Pavel Pavlovich reminds one of Rogozhin's attempt on Myshkin's life; little Liza is simply an attenuated version of little Nellie in *The Insulted and Injured;* and Pavel Pavlovich reflects the traits and actions of the early Doubles, particularly Golyadkin.

The husband is a Double whose ambivalence is motivated by the discovery that he is a cuckold. His desire for revenge is prompted by a longing to assert his power and throw off his habitual submissiveness which had made his married life a shameful farce of wifely dominance and betrayal. Yet Pavel Pavlovich alternates for some time between his former humble friendship for Velchaninov and his new desire for revenge. This friendship is not unmixed with a secret admiration for his betrayer, since he represents everything that Pavel Pavlovich would like to be in his relations with women—the strong, gay, confident, and successful Don Juan. In this connection one remembers Golyadkin's yearning to possess the superior abilities of his Double.

Pavel Pavlovich decides to marry again, and his desire to assert his power, mingled with the strange impulse of the injured man to finger his wound, impels him to take Velchaninov on a visit to his intended bride. It is a desperate effort to prove to himself and to Velchaninov that he can be a successful lover and no longer fear the man who had displaced him in the affections of his former wife. Yet he is also thoroughly aware of the risk he is taking. Once again he is humiliated, for the young lady heartlessly treats him like a superannuated government clerk as she succumbs to the superior charms of Velchaninov. The pitiful termination of this design revives his longing for revenge, and he attempts to murder Velchaninov in the hope of regaining his self-respect. The failure of this last anguished effort leaves him in the customary un-resolved quandary of the Double—in this instance, the eternal husband, born to be cuckolded, while at the same time trying vainly to assert his pride and power. In fact, the ending of the story, in which Velch-aninov meets Pavel Pavlovich on the train with the wife whom he finally married, suggests that he will suffer again the ignominious betrayal that had been his lot in his first marriage.

The analysis of Pavel Pavlovich's actions in the last chapter shows how carefully Dostoevsky had thought out the subtle psychological motivation of the story. In every respect *The Eternal Husband* is a keen inter-pretation of the complex impulses behind the facts of human behaviour. Despite the light tone, particularly at the conclusion, the strong suggestion of tragedy is rarely absent. The whole incident of little Liza is in the deeper, more sombre manner of Dostoevsky, and Pavel Pavlovich's mixed feelings of love and hate for this child, who is a constant reminder of his humiliat-ing betrayal, are the stuff of tragedy.

One scene in *The Eternal Husband* requires a final word. The house of Pavel Pavlovich's bride-to-be, to which he takes Velchaninov, is filled with young peo-ple. Two of these are particularly noticeable—the rude youth with the blue glasses, and his puffed-up, obnoxious friend Sashenka, who has destined Pavel Pavlovich's intended bride for himself. In these char-acters Dostoevsky once more goes out of his way to drag into a story extremists and radicals. They are al-most extraneous to the action, and in the few brief lines he devotes to them they appear thoroughly ridic-ulous and even reprehensible. The persistence of his unsympathetic attitude towards the "new generation" in his last three novels, and the obvious bias mani-fested in these characterizations of radicals are pointed indications of his mounting concern with the whole question of the revolutionary movement in Rus-sia. Almost inadvertently he was developing a state of mind and conscience which, as always with Dostoevsky, must eventually find expression through the medium of his art. *The Possessed,* his next novel, was to serve as the vehicle for this accumulating bile.

16

Conflicting
Designs

Dostoevsky's creative process worked like some powerful centripetal force. Related subjects, situations, and new characters were often irresistibly drawn to the central theme of a novel as his vigorous imagination played over an expanding field of action. One of his most difficult problems in this later period was to prevent his central theme from disintegrating into subjects for several novels. In this respect the inception and development of *The Possessed* (more correctly translated *The Devils*) cost him more effort than any of his works of fiction.

The ultimate salvation of a warring civilization had suggested itself to Dostoevsky as a possible theme for artistic treatment at about the time he had begun to think of the design of *The Idiot* (1867). This nebulous and cosmic idea may well have contained the germ of the projected plan of his next novel. On the other hand, the idea may have occurred to him as early as his prison days in Siberia, for during the years that he lived among those human derelicts in the House of the Dead, the theme of salvation, on a more personal level, agitated his mind. In fact, the sinner who finds his way back to God was a cherished conception which he could never successfully embody in artistic form.

Before he actually finished *The Idiot*, however, a plan for a new novel had occurred to him. Even a plan would help to salve his conscience at this time because of the money he was taking from Katkov for another work. He had been obliged, however, to put aside the projected novel for the comparative relaxation of *The Eternal Husband*. In the meantime (December 1868), he wrote to Maikov that he was contemplating

A huge novel, to be called *Atheism* (for God's sake between ourselves), but before undertaking it I must read a whole library of atheists, catholics, and orthodox believers. It will materialize, even with complete security for work, in no less than two years. The chief figure is a Russian, of our own social standing, mature, not very well educated, but not uneducated, and not without rank— *suddenly*, in his maturity, he loses his faith in God. All his life he had been occupied only with his job, had never altered his routine, and up to his 45th year had done nothing extraordinary. (The psychological solution: a profound feeling, a man and a Russian.) His loss of faith in God acts upon him in a colossal way. (The action itself in the novel and the environment are very extensive.) He pokes about among the new generation, among atheists, Slavs, and Europeans, among Russian fanatics, hermits, and priests. Among other things, he is thoroughly caught on the hook of a Jesuit, a propagandist, and a Pole; from this he falls to the very depths of self-abasement, and in the end he returns to find both Christ and the Russian soil, the Russian Christ and the Russian God. (For God's sake do not tell anyone); but my hope is to write this last novel, and then I can die—I shall have said all.[1]

A few weeks later, he mentions the same theme in a letter to his niece. Several of the characters have already taken shape in his mind, one of them, a Catholic priest, modelled somewhat on St. Francis Xavier. Enthusiastic comment on the project continues in subsequent correspondence, but he admits to an unwillingness to undertake the writing since he feels himself unprepared for the task. The idea, he declares, is the most precious thing in the world for him, and his chief fear is that he will botch it.

A whole year passed while Dostoevsky was finishing *The Idiot* and writing *The Eternal Husband*. Over this entire period, however, fugitive schemes for the great novel haunted his thoughts. His references to it were those of an artist intoxicated with an idea which he envisions as the culmination of his creative life. But the plan, like some huge magnet, was attracting related subjects, and by December 1869 he had shifted his ground from the theme of atheism to a more generalized aspect of the subject to which he gave the title of "The Life of a Great Sinner." The idea was still that of salvation, but the image of the hero had changed, and the field of action extended. He now envisaged the work as falling into three separate novels with a connecting theme—later he entertained the notion of breaking it up into five novels. He believed that it would take five years to write, and he felt that he must return to Russia to obtain material for monastery scenes and possibly visit Jerusalem for similar purposes. In a mood of sacred devotion to the project, he wrote to his niece: "This novel is my entire hope and the whole expectation of my life . . ." [2]

From the comments in several letters and from sketches in the notebooks, extending from December 1869 to May 1870,[3] one can obtain some conception of the projected novel, "The Life of a Great Sinner." The mature and pious hero whom Dostoevsky outlined in the letter to Maikov has given way to a proud sensitive child, an illegitimate son, who is brought up among strangers. The first novel is to begin with a description of his life at boarding-school. Here he is beaten and humiliated, yet he feels himself destined for great things. He has a crippled girl for a companion and he compensates his own injured feelings by tormenting her. His misfortunes and proud isolation contribute to a natural introspection, and he indulges in daydreams in which he imagines himself infinitely powerful. He schemes to achieve power by acquiring great wealth, but he is uncertain whether he will use his riches to satisfy his desires or, with a grand gesture, dispense with them as an assertion of his will. Eventually he runs away from school, falls into crime, and even becomes involved in a murder. At last he goes into the country to live with his stepmother and father. There he is a witness to her adultery and he sees his father killed by his own serfs. Finally the hero returns to Moscow only to plunge once again into all manner of debauchery, aided along the primrose path by a vicious old school friend. He even commits the fearful sacrilege of stealing the jewels out of an ikon. In the end, however, this young atheist confesses all and is sent to a monastery for reformation.

In the second novel Dostoevsky intended to give a detailed picture of the great sinner's life in the monastery. He planned to introduce a number of interesting people, similar to the contrasting figures he described in his sketch of "Atheism," the original design of "The Life of a Great Sinner." The centre of the stage in this volume is to be occupied by a saintly old monk. His influence on the hero is considerable. He preaches the necessity of living in the world and of removing temptation, as it were, by submitting to it. Through suffering and repentance one will finally turn to good deeds and learn the ways of God. The hero's spirit is chastened but is by no means reformed by the moral wisdom of the holy man. He is still heir to the sins of the flesh, desires unlimited power, and is guilty of pride of intellect. In the third volume Dostoevsky apparently intended that his hero should once again go out into the world and come in contact with the vast panorama of Russian life. The remainder of the design is unclear and barely suggested in the notes. One may be fairly certain, however, that the hero would travel once more the dark and narrow vale of sin before he reaches the end of his spiritual pilgrimage and achieves salvation through suffering and saintly deeds.

"The Life of a Great Sinner" was destined to remain one of the famous unwritten novels of world literature. From what we know of Dostoevsky's artistic limitations, it is doubtful whether he could have successfully realized this vast design under any circumstances. He planned to write it in the simple style and with the measured epic sweep of a *War and Peace,* a manner entirely foreign to his swift dramatic method of narration. Further, he obviously hoped to express in this huge work the full measure of his search for God. It would involve the whole canvas of Russian life. On it he would bring together the significant figures of a past epoch of vigorous orthodoxy and well-known representatives of the hostile schools of Slavophilism and Westernism. Christ and anti-Christ, Russia and Europe would wage their struggle, and the battlefield of this endless dualism would be the hearts of his men and women. It is difficult to imagine, however, how he would have treated the regeneration of his great sinner. The notes are significantly silent on this score; nearly all the extant material concerns the hero's career of sin. He would undoubtedly fall into the category of the Doubles, and this type, with Dostoevsky, never achieves salvation in a manner satisfactory to reality or to art, as the fate of Raskolnikov convincingly illustrates. Even the meek Myshkin, endowed with moral perfection and spiritual unity, fails in the end. And it is safe to assume that Dostoevsky would have failed of his ultimate purpose in "The Life of a Great Sinner." The fact that he never attempted to carry out this plan is in itself indicative. To portray the spiritual pilgrimage of a great sinner through an evil world of little faith to the distant goal of salvation, which he gains through suffering and glorifies by saintliness, stood at the end of Dostoevsky's whole creative scheme of things. The end either eluded his imaginative grasp or was inconsistent with his psychological dualism. The souls of the damned, of proud sinners, or of the insulted and injured were his province, not the souls of saints incorruptible.

Although Dostoevsky never wrote his spiritual epic, the design of "The Life of a Great Sinner" cast its shadow over everything else he did write, like some vast monolith in the background of his creative experience. The design is literally the starting point for any study of the genesis of each of the three succeeding novels. The interrelation of this plan with biographical facts and with the material in the last three novels is extremely illuminating. The life of the young sinner at boarding-school recalls that of the hero in *Notes from the Underground*. And his experiences, considerably elaborated, provide the basis for the whole first part of a later novel, *A Raw Youth*. That is, the hero of this work, Arkadi, is directly developed from the notes on the early youth of the hero of "The Life of a Great Sinner." A careful check of certain of the proper names mentioned in the notes shows that Dostoevsky drew upon his own childhood experiences in a Moscow boarding-school for various situations and for a few of the characters in this material. One is also struck by the facts that the murder of the hero's father by his serfs in the plan is similar to the murder of Dostoevsky's own father. The notes on the monastery scene for the projected second volume were used for the picture of monastic life in *The Brothers Karamazov;* and the saintly old man of God in this section undoubtedly influenced the characterization of Zosima in the last novel. Finally, certain phases of the youth of the great sinner and his vaguely suggested career after he leaves the monastery were to have a direct bearing on the conception of Stavrogin, the hero of *The Possessed*. Even the character of the crippled girl and a few of the details mentioned in the notes, such as the theft of the jewels from an ikon, turn up in this novel. Thus the plan of "The Life of a Great Sinner," by a seemingly unconscious operation of Dostoevsky's creative process, actually did grow into three novels, and its hero furnished forth suggestions for three of the main characters in these separate works. This curious pilfering from his vast design in order to piece out the imperfections of what he thought were lesser efforts may seem like an artistic tragedy, for by the time his next three novels were written there was little left of the plan of "The Life of a Great Sinner." Too, the sum-total of these works does not achieve his original objective—to portray the redemption and salvation of a great sinner in his spiritual pilgrimage through the world. It is instructive, however, to observe how this extensive plan was drawn into the scheme of his next novel, *The Possessed*.

Although Dostoevsky was still filled with enthusiasm over the initial conception of "The Life of a Great Sinner," the necessity of fulfilling his promise of another novel for Katkov was preying on his mind. He soon abandoned the idea of immediately attempting to write the projected *magnum opus*, and he cast about for a subject that he could dash off in a hurry while his thoughts dwelt fondly on the larger work. Apparently he met with quick success, for in September 1869 he announced in a letter to Maikov: "I am working energetically. I have planned a thing for the *Russian Messenger* which agitates me very much, but I fear this furious working." [4] No further information is volunteered at this juncture, but it is pretty certain that we have here the first reference to *The Possessed*.

Whatever may have been the initial theme of the novel, it assumed a definite direction under the influence of a startling event that took place in Russia a little more than a month after Dostoevsky had informed Maikov that he was beginning a new work. On 21 November I. I. Ivanov, a student in the Petrovsky Agricultural Academy in Moscow, was murdered. A few days later his body was found in a pond in the school park. An investigation revealed that he had been slain by a group of radical comrades under the leadership of S. G. Nechaev. This young revolutionist had served his apprenticeship abroad under the tutelage of that apostle of destruction, Bakunin. He had eagerly absorbed the peasant anarchism of the master and accepted with utter literalness the terrifying precepts of Bakunin's *Catechism of a Revolutionist*. As a student in Moscow, he formed a secret political society called the People's Avenger. Nechaev represented himself as a member of some mysterious Central Committee—a pure fiction—and set out to organize his followers into groups of five. With incredible energy and a passionate devotion to the cause, he preached the doctrine of Bakunin and carried it to its logical conclusions, which meant a complete willingness to use any means, however criminal or immoral, to gain his revolutionary ends. He was able to convince his fellow-conspirators that a revolt was to materialize all over Russia through the efforts of many similar though entirely imaginary groups. In his own group he enforced rigorous discipline and demanded implicit obedience. Because he falsely suspected Ivanov, who belonged to his group, of possible treachery, he had him murdered by the other members. When the facts became known, hundreds of arrests followed throughout the country.

The whole affair electrified Dostoevsky when he read about it in the newspapers abroad. He learned many intimate details of this student revolutionary movement, of the scene of the murder, and of some of the participants from his young brother-in-law, also a student in the Petrovsky Agricultural Academy, who was visiting him at that time. In his letters and fiction over the last few years he had been bitterly criticizing the young radical generation. They were the spawn of the Westerners of the 1840's, and in his mind now these contemporary nihilists and their predecessors were at one in their anti-nationalism and in their devotion to the revolutionary intellectualism of the West. In the Nechaev affair he saw material for the novel that Katkov was demanding and also an opportunity to speak out more directly and forcefully against the radical tendencies that were undermining Russia.

The main idea of *The Possessed* and the general outline of the story as it now exists did not occur to Dostoevsky directly after he heard of the Nechaev affair. At this early stage he experienced all the uncertainties in characterization and all the fluctuations in design which were so evident when he began to draft *The Idiot*. The process was further complicated by the fact that he had apparently started to plan a novel before he knew anything of Nechaev; and then characters and details of "The Life of a Great Sinner," which was ever in his mind at this time, continually obtruded upon his thoughts. The first draft of *The Possessed*, as it appears in the notebooks, bears the original title "Jealousy." The translation of a section of this first outline will serve to indicate, in the light of the finished novel, the kind of initial narrative pattern on which Dostoevsky's creative process worked.

NB. *The whole affair is in the characters.*

The story follows:

K. A. B.,[5] his mother, a lady of consequence, and a sister, (they have returned from abroad). *A foster daughter.* A little brother and a little sister.

Large landowners. V. in the manner of V. (NB. Desire to enter into the role of large landowners)—there is money. They are not in need.

Neighbours have also returned from abroad. The daughter a beauty and a wealthy heiress. Mother of A. B. (a despot, she submits to her despot of a son) hankers after a beautiful girl for her A. B.

The foster daughter is an orphan girl, poor, with very evil aunts and an uncle (mauvais genre).

A. B. started a liaison, foolishly, by an accident, a passionate, proud and inconsistent man.

The character of the foster daughter—a child, but lively,

mocking, truthful, with a big heart, and (strangely)—a timid child.

Belly. A lady of consequence in dismay. To conceal from the sisters. The girl gave herself without any resistance and coquetry,—strange how she submitted. A. B. says that he is sorry for it. But of course marriage is not a way out. Naturally, there cannot even be a question of marriage. And *she* herself does not even think about marriage and does not count on the possibility.

Our nobleman is a lackey.

Meanwhile a numerous society gathered in the country. One neighbour, a general, with whom they have a law-suit and reconciliation. A beautiful neighbour, and insignificant neighbours.

A teacher is recommended. A humble and timid character. Terribly absent-minded and strange. Partly a nihilist, does not believe. A citizen. Rapid-firing guns. He tried to serve. A fool.

NB. Another neighbour is a nihilist, very influential with students. The teacher observes that all nihilists love terribly to profit. [The Proclamation. Nechaev appears for a moment, to kill the teacher (?).]

NB. [Teach.]—A. B. prepares to play a role.

At first there are sneers for the teacher. (How he behaves with the children. A water-carrier, etc.)[6] The teacher laughs at himself, but A. B. is finally struck by the fact that he conducts himself nobly. 2000 lost.

The foster daughter is the teacher's *first* ridiculer.

She does not worry about the liaison, but suddenly her belly.

The general, having lost his wife, proposes to the foster daughter. She refused (but suddenly pregnancy). The mother scolds her: why did she refuse, still not knowing that she has been intimate with the son.

NB. The teacher meanwhile typically takes it upon himself, to compose all this and to think it out.

There is a scandal. Scenes between the mother and A. B. Meanwhile there can be no reason for the scenes: A. B. says to her: What are your fits for? Indeed you do not find fault in the morality of the act, and there is no talk of marriage.

NB. A. B. esteems the teacher, but in his own way. To

remove her of course, as if to a sick aunt. All this struck *her*, as if she were surprised, and at the same time the situation has changed from a magnificent to a disgusting one—she is sad, and for the first time there is a feeling of humiliation, yet she still has no pretensions to marriage.

An idea to offer to the teacher. They propose (for saving the belly and in good time) 15,000. He blushes, but at first says nothing about the 15,000. *She* accepts him laughingly.

The teacher visits her, friendship, he follows her. *She* even begins to open up before him, about Christ, God, and about sciences. She listens. You are a fine man. But suddenly she begins to weep. He timidly proposes an idea: if it should be without the 15,000—Why did you not speak up before?—I love you. (Humility, etc.).

Finally it happens that she says: and I love you. But he sees that this is not so.[7]

There are several more pages of notes in this first outline. They contain mostly variants of the sketch just quoted with additional situations and characters. The teacher offends Prince A. B., who strikes him in the face, a blow that is received in silence. A duel follows in which the teacher refuses to take his shot. The conduct impresses the beautiful neighbour, with whom Prince A. B. is in love, and he grows madly jealous and beats the teacher. One of the notes suggests that the prince first met the teacher abroad. The governor of the province is introduced and a certain clownish person, Kartuzov, who makes verses and sets himself up as the protector of the honour of the beautiful neighbour. The teacher also becomes involved with a group of nihilists, and again it is suggested that he be murdered. Dostoevsky indicates that the two chief figures are the prince and the teacher, and he supplies a number of characterizing features. The prince has a singular nature, is excessively proud, and has no control over himself. The teacher is humble, but he has greatness of soul, and is capable of the most noble and unselfish actions. Most of the variants elaborate the growing envy and hatred of the prince for the teacher, and at this point it is clear that Dostoevsky intended the psychological conflict of these two characters to be the central problem of the novel. His uncertainty, however, is everywhere apparent in this first outline as he casts and recasts the same situations. In fact he began to doubt the feasibility of the whole project, for in one place in this rough sketch he asks himself the question: "Is it necessary to write this novel?" [8]

The first outline has little relation to *The Possessed*, but it represents a stage in Dostoevsky's creative process when, out of the plethora of subjects contending in his mind, one begins to dominate and another to subordinate itself. The outline is essentially concerned with the romantic aspect of the future novel. In Prince A. B. one may discern a few of the traits of Stavrogin, which in turn have been carried over from the hero of the plan of "The Life of a Great Sinner." The resemblance at this stage is superficial; it consists largely of the prince's amoral nature, his inclination to evil, and his overweening pride. The "lady of consequence" is clearly the prototype of Stavrogin's mother, Varvara Petrovna. The beautiful neighbour and heiress, with whom Prince A. B. is in love, is obviously the future Liza, and the submissive foster daughter is the first version of Darya Shatova of the novel. Curiously enough, the figure of Kartuzov introduced into this outline is the hero of a story, "The Tale of an Awkward Man," which Dostoevsky had projected more than a year before, a draft of which may be found in his notebooks. Here Kartuzov serves as the starting-point of the remarkable Captain Lebyadkin, the would-be poet and self-appointed protector of Liza.

It is interesting to observe that the teacher is really the hero of the first outline of *The Possessed*, and in this figure we no doubt have the earliest form of Shatov. The second phase of the novel, the revolutionary conspiracy, is fleetingly suggested in the brief note connecting the teacher with Nechaev and the nihilists. In the conjectured murder of the teacher, Dostoevsky

pretty certainly has in mind the actual murder of
Ivanov by the conspirators which inspired the murder
of Shatov in the novel. Other episodes in the outline,
such as the slap in the face, the duel, and the meeting
of the nihilists, turn up in *The Possessed*.

In the course of the next few months, Dostoevsky
continued to hesitate between the growing importance in his mind of the Nechaev theme and the romantic aspects of "The Life of a Great Sinner." His letters reflect the fluctuation in emphasis. In February
1870 he wrote to Maikov: "I have set down to a rich
idea; I speak not about its fulfilment but about the
idea. It is one of those ideas that has an undoubted
effect upon the public. It is in the nature of *Crime and
Punishment*, but it is still closer to and more rooted in
reality and directly touches on the most important of
contemporary questions . . . Never have I worked
with such enjoyment and such facility.' [9] The idea that
concerned "the most important of contemporary questions" refers to the Nechaev affair. This assumption is
supported by a request to Strakhov, a few weeks later,
for a book on T. N. Granovsky, a well-known professor
of history and a pious liberal of the 1840's. Dostoevsky
indicated that this book was absolutely essential for
the work he was immediately engaged upon. Shortly
before he received the book he had already outlined
the character of "T. N. Granovsky" in the notes, the
first draft of Stepan Trofimovich Verkhovensky in *The
Possessed*. One may suppose that by this time (February 1870) the theme of revolutionary conspiracy had
gained the ascendancy in his design.

The hold that the Nechaev affair now took upon his
imagination is abundantly evident in the notebook material of *The Possessed*. The extent of his dependence
upon the characters and details of the real conspiracy,
about which he learned a great deal from the newspaper accounts, is fully revealed in the notes. Not only
the organization of the revolutionary group of five, its

meetings, doctrines, and the murder of Ivanov are duplicated, but the very participants in the Nechaev affair serve as prototypes for the characters in the novel. In the notes Dostoevsky employs the real names of the conspirators for his characters, thus indicating their derivation. Nechaev himself, of course, provides the model for Pyotr Verkhovensky. P. G. Uspensky, the chief assistant of Nechaev, was heavily drawn upon for the characterizations of both Liputin and Virginsky. The notes also indicate that for many other characters—Stephan Trofimovich, Shatov, Lyamshin, Karmazinov, Shigalov, and Tolkachenko—Dostoevsky had real people more or less in mind. With the exception of Karmazinov, however, who is a satirical portrait of Turgenev, none of these characters is entirely dependent upon any definite person. This was not Dostoevsky's method. Not one but often several real figures are drawn upon for specific features in a single characterization. The chief model for Stepan Trofimovich, for example, is the historian Granovsky, but in the characterization may be discerned traits borrowed from as many as four other figures, among them Belinsky and Herzen. That is, he is not presenting caricature portraits of historical figures but composite pictures, fused by his imagination and essentially his own creations.

Once Dostoevsky had seized upon the theme of revolutionary conspiracy, he seems to have altered the whole direction of the promised novel for Katkov. An instalment was almost due and he had nothing on paper except rough plans. Apparently the idea occurred to him that he could dash off a slight thing, a kind of fictionized version of the Nechaev affair. It would give him the opportunity he had been unconsciously seeking to pour out his wrath against these youthful nihilists. Meanwhile he would devote his more serious thoughts to the plan of "The Life of a Great Sinner." In fact, few of the letters at this precise time, in which he mentions his plans for *The Possessed,* fail to contain some passing reference, often couched in reverential terms, to his vaster design.

As we have observed, however, Dostoevsky's creative process did not operate in this fashion. The more he worked on the new novel the deeper he became involved. What seemed to be taking place in his mind, if we may judge from the early notes, was that the plans for both "The Life of a Great Sinner" and *The Possessed* were running a parallel course. This did not continue long, for they merged and grew into one, the themes, characters, and some of the details becoming inextricably entangled. Gone was the "facility" with which he had been able to handle the original straightforward plan. Now he was beset with perplexities that grew out of all manner of refractory material. One hero became confused with the other, and he experienced the greatest difficulty in deciding upon the opposing attractions of both subjects. In one of the early drafts in the notes he sets down the cryptic phrase: "NB. In doubt about Nechaev?" [10] which seems to indicate that he still could not decide on combining the subjects of two novels about different heroes—Stavrogin and Verkhovensky. The notes bear frequent testimony to the creative ferment that he underwent. Nearly all the characters, their relations, and separate situations are sketched again and again with numerous changes. Often he connects situations with entirely different characters, and disjointed parts of the narrative appear in the notes far out of their ultimate sequence. Then, after working for months and piling up a large amount of manuscript, he suddenly announced to his niece, in August 1870, that he had hit upon a new plan. "It was necessary to change everything radically; with not a little thought I drew a line through everything that had been written (up to 300 pages, speaking generally), and started out again with the first page. All the work of a whole year was destroyed." [11]

Dostoevsky took this heroic decision no doubt because the original slight work he had intended had assumed a new and deeper significance for him. Facts of living reality and real figures were at most only the springboard for his imagination. Upon the Nechaev affair he would build a huge superstructure, for he now hit upon a scheme which would allow him to connect Stavrogin, a character clearly suggested by the unnamed hero of the plan of "The Life of a Great Sinner" and slightly adumbrated in Prince A. B. in the first outline of *The Possessed,* with the revolutionary conspiracy. Although Stavrogin was to remain for Dostoevsky the real hero of the novel, he is now removed to the background, and the centre of the stage is held by the "devils," the nihilists. The field of action, however, is to be extended so that, besides political conspiracy it will involve some of those profound questions of religion and morality which are implicit in the plan of "The Life of a Great Sinner." The fusing process was clearer in his mind and he went to work with fresh vigour.

The short piece that he had contemplated for Katkov had now taken on the proportions of a huge novel, and still his difficulties were by no means over. The broader canvas and more complicated plot required many changes in the plan. "In a word, never has anything cost me so much effort," [12] he complained to Strakhov. For the time being all thoughts of "The Life of a Great Sinner" vanished from his mind as he became progressively absorbed in this new design of *The Possessed.* He fought for time, deceiving his anxious editor as to the amount of manuscript he had written, for his greatest fear was that he would spoil the total effect by too much haste. In a letter to his niece, already mentioned, he expressed with deep feeling the anguish he felt at this time:

O Sonechka! If you only knew how difficult it is to be a writer, that is, to suffer this fate. Believe me, I absolutely know that if I had two or three years entirely for this novel, like Turgenev, Goncharov, or Tolstoy, I could write a thing which would be talked about for a hundred years after! I do not boast; ask your conscience and your recollections of me whether I am given to boasting? The idea is so splendid, so significant that I do reverence before it. But what will come out of it? I know beforehand; I will write a novel in eight or nine months, I will make a hash of it, will spoil it. It is impossible to write such a thing unless you have two or three years . . . The details, perhaps, will not turn out badly, the characters will be sketched, but only sketched. There will be many inconsistencies and prolix passages. The utter beauty (I speak literally) will not emerge, for, in much, inspiration depends upon time. Well, nevertheless, I shall sit down to write! Indeed, is it not a torment consciously to raise one's hand against oneself?

It was not until January 1871 that the first two chapters of *The Possessed* were published. He despaired, however, of ever finishing the novel. Sickness and poverty were sapping his energies. Europe was becoming absolutely hateful to him. He yearned for Russia and was convinced that he would never be able to complete the novel successfully while he remained abroad. But he had nowhere to turn for money for the trip except to Katkov, who at last heeded his pleas. Perhaps this wise publisher finally came to believe the constant asseverations of his erratic author that the novel, several chapters of which had already appeared in his magazine, would never actually be finished unless the writer could work among more congenial surroundings in his beloved country. The return fare was a good gamble on Katkov's part. Dostoevsky, with gladness in his heart, returned to St. Petersburg in July 1871, more than four years after he had left it. The last part of *The Possessed* was finished in the autumn of 1872 and was published in the *Russian Messenger* in December, just two years after the novel first began to appear.

17

The "Devils" and
Their Disciples

The plot of *The Possessed* contains two main themes. The first concerns the romantic element built around Stavrogin and suggested in part by the plan of "The Life of a Great Sinner"; the second theme is the revolutionary conspiracy, inspired by the Nechaev affair and dominated by Pyotr Verkhovensky. Both strata are fairly well integrated, for nearly all the characters, by one means or another, are drawn into the web of the conspiracy. There are faults in the sequence and some confusion in details, which may have resulted from the usual difficulties of serial composition as well as from the combination of two distinct themes. In one conversation, Stavrogin is called "prince," a title much used in the notes but appearing nowhere else in the novel; Captain Lebyadkin is suddenly presented in the middle of the book as though nothing had been said about him earlier; and the manner of the narrative changes several times without any apparent reason. The middle and last sections were written while Dostoevsky was in Russia and had fuller access to newspaper accounts and gossip about the criminal investigations of the Nechaev conspiracy. A consequence is the overweighting of these sections with details and a deliberate elaboration of the didactic aspects. Concern for such matters may have been part of his reason for rewriting the final third of the novel.

The character with which the book begins, Stepan Trofimovich Verkhovensky, is brilliantly depicted. As already indicated, the initial inspiration for the portrayal was T. N. Granovsky, professor of history in the University of Moscow in the 1840's, a Westerner, and a friend of Belinsky and Herzen. The sentimentality, endless purposelessness, impracticality, and love for Spanish history attributed to Granovsky reappear in Stepan Trofimovich in an exaggerated degree. Traits of other well-known Westerners were also laid under contribution. The ideological significance of the character was to indicate that the nihilists of the 1870's were the political heirs of the liberals of the 1840's. The old liberal Stepan Trofimovich is the father of that bloodthirsty young revolutionist Pyotr Verkhovensky as Granovsky is the political father of Nechaev. Like a reformed radical, Dostoevsky pokes fun at the political and social sympathies of his own youth in Stepan Trofimovich, and at the same time he points the dark moral of this unbroken heresy in his son.

The large amount of material on Stepan Trofimovich in the notebooks attests to Dostoevsky's deep interest in the character. Throughout these preliminary sketches the development tends consistently to minimize the serious didactic aspects and expand the purely human and comic traits. The latter qualities are those most emphasized in the novel, and the finished portrait represents a pure and idealized old Westerner. At first he wishes to come to an agreement, in theory, with the new ideas, but he does not understand nihilism and in the end rejects it with indignation. Yet he cannot return to an active belief in the ideas of his youth, in the teaching of Belinsky. He remains a Europeanized Russian who is blind to everything real in Russian life. If Dostoevsky had regarded him as a representative liberal, he would have heaped scorn on him as he did on Karmazinov. "For our liberal," he observes parenthetically in the notes, "is first of all a lackey and is merely on the watch to clean someone's boots." [1] Stepan Trofimovich, on the contrary, is an honourable man. He imagines himself endowed with profound wisdom, and his love for champagne is rivalled only by his passion for writing lachrymose letters. He lives in an ideal world in which beauty is more important than bread, and where existence without Shakespeare would be insupportable. When this quixotic and lovable old man is off the stage, interest in the narrative noticeably wanes. At the end of the novel even the last vestige of his ancient liberalism vanishes before his new faith in the religion of the people which he had formerly scorned.

Stavrogin is the dominating figure in the romantic part of the plot, but he is not effectively integrated with both strata of *The Possessed*, a deficiency that must be attributed largely to the fact that he was never originally conceived within the sphere of the novel's polemical purpose. The basic image of Stavrogin first arose in Dostoevsky's imagination as the hero of "The Life of a Great Sinner." Although Stavrogin loses many of the identifiable features outlined in the brief sketch of the earlier plan, something of his initial significance is carried over into *The Possessed*. It is not Stepan Trofimovich or that chief "devil," his son, who agitated Dostoevsky; the character most precious to him in the novel is Stavrogin. When he sent the first few chapters to Katkov, he accompanied them with a letter in which he explains the importance of the Nechaev affair in his work, but he insists that it is not merely copied or handled in an unoriginal manner. Then he continues:

Therefore, despite the fact that this whole incident occupies a prominent place in the novel, it is nevertheless only an accessory and background for the action of another figure who can really be called the main character of the novel. This other figure (Nikolai Stavrogin) is also a gloomy individual, also a villain. But it seems to me that this figure is tragic, although many will no doubt say, after a reading: 'What is this?' I sat down to a poem about this character because I had long ago wished to portray him. In my opinion he is a Russian and a typical figure. I shall be very sad if I do not succeed in it. I shall be still sadder if I hear the judgment that the character is stilted. I took him out of my heart.[2]

In the notes this attitude is supported by frequent references to Stavrogin as the real hero of the novel, and in one place Dostoevsky sets down the following observation for his own guidance: "*And so the whole pathos of the novel is in the prince* [Stavrogin]; *he is the hero.* Everything else moves about him like a kaleidoscope." [3]

Whatever may have been Dostoevsky's original conception of the importance of Stavrogin, the real meaning of his role is less clear than that of any other character in the novel. The vagueness unquestionably arose from the fact that Stavrogin was a borrowed character. The unusual hold that the hero of the plan of "The Life of a Great Sinner" had over Dostoevsky's imagination in the initial conception of Stavrogin is clearly indicated in an early note in which he writes: "The chief idea (that is, the pathos of the novel) is that the prince and the foster daughter [Darya] are *new people,* who had undergone temptation and are resolved to begin a *new* restored life." [4] Only a faint echo of this purpose, so closely joined with the fate of the hero of his unwritten masterpiece, is reflected in Stavrogin's development in *The Possessed.* The extremely interesting fact is the manner in which Dostoevsky made an artistic virtue of this initial ambiguity. The evasiveness of the characterization has often convinced critics that Dostoevsky wished to convey some profound symbolic truth in Stavrogin. The notes, however, reveal that he deliberately made him mysterious. In the end, he never actually intended Stavrogin to become a clear image, embodying some well-defined ethical or moral idea. This may be a tacit admission of artistic defeat in a character that originally had so much potential significance for him, but the function Stavrogin ultimately fulfils is skilfully sustained and highly effective.

It has been argued that Dostoevsky modelled Stavrogin on a definite person, such as his youthful friend of the Petrashevsky days, Speshnev, or the anarchist Bakunin. One could just as convincingly maintain that he was inspired by heroes, like the Corsair or the Giaour, in Byron's verse tales. There may even be a touch of Milton's Lucifer in Stavrogin, for he is a fallen angel, or at least an angel with his wings clipped. In certain respects there is even a close resemblance to Pushkin's Eugene Onegin and Lermontov's Pechorin, for like them he is bored with life; all human endeavour seems futile. To settle on any definite prototype would be hazardous. All one can say with assurance is that Stavrogin is cast in the image of a "Byronic" hero, a descriptive epithet which Dostoevsky actually employs in describing him.

The notes are extremely rich in material on Stavrogin, and the treatment of him is in decided contrast to that in the novel. The nature of the difference reveals Dostoevsky's intention of enveloping him in a cloak of mystery. In the notes the thoughts, conversation, and actions of Stavrogin are directly described and in some detail; in the novel the method is reversed —his dominating personality is revealed indirectly by the effect he has on other people, and his ideas by sayings attributed to him. His first appearance in the novel is delayed for almost two hundred pages while our curiosity about him is excited by numerous dark hints and by reports of his acts and sayings. This indirect method was used in the case of Valkovsky, Svidrigailov, and Nastasya Filipovna, and in each instance it is employed on characters who have an element of the melodramatic in them.

Stavrogin's external appearance and surface traits in the notes are closely followed in the novel. He has beauty, charm, elegance, manly prowess, and extraordinary courage; he is aloof, inordinately proud, gloomy, passionate, demonic, and in every way an isolated individual. In his relation to other people, however, and in his attitude towards religion, politics, and social ideas the notes are extremely contradictory, reflecting Dostoevsky's initial difficulty in imaginatively apprehending the character. To a considerable degree these contradictions reappear in the novel, but there the effort is consciously directed towards sustaining the mystification which Dostoevsky finally came to accept as an artistic approach essential to the conduct of his plot. In the notes, for example, he is represented both as a believer in God and an atheist; he is an active enemy of the peasants and yet wishes to abandon all and seek solace in poverty; he turns to wanton pleasures but also finds comfort in work; he is hostile to nihilism in one note and allies himself with the nihilists in another; he is both a powerful thinker and man of ideas and then devoid of ideas, incapable of understanding common political controversies, and even so uneducated that he cannot write correctly; he is a Russian—as Dostoevsky also described him in his letter to Katkov—yet "he has mind enough to know that he in fact is not a Russian" and *"finds no necessity to be a Russian";* "since he is outside all parties, then he may dispassionately look on all and hear all, but he remains aloof." [5] These real fluctuations in the notes are, for the most part, only suggested in the novel, and the final impression which Dostoevsky creates is that Stavrogin is outside all parties but irresistibly charming to the adherents of each.

Of course, it is not possible to reconstruct with scientific accuracy the precise operations of Dostoevsky's creative process in the imaginative development of Stavrogin from the first vague conception to the final image in the completed novel. The wealth of material in this case, however, does permit the formulation of an imaginative pattern which must resemble pretty closely Dostoevsky's actual creative experience. Starting with a fugitive conception of the evil hero in the plan of "The Life of a Great Sinner," he tried to adapt the character to a different plot. The effort resulted in a period of intense uncertainty, principally concerning the spiritual, moral, and social ideology of Stavrogin. In the end he deliberately settled upon an enigmatic conception which seemed to him to serve the exigencies of the plot of *The Possessed.* The notes eventually reveal this intention. The artist cannot afford to mystify himself, but the clarifying details about Stavrogin, which he sets down in the notes for his own purposes, are studiously excluded from the novel, and on several occasions he reminds himself "not to explain the prince" and "to keep the reader in a quandary." In another place he observes, under the caption "Very important: The prince reveals himself to no one and is everywhere mysterious." [6] On the whole, he made of Stavrogin what might be called a "literary character" rather than a bearer of ideas in the fashion of the typical Dostoevskian hero.

The nature of the characterization, however, made it almost inevitable that some vestiges of the spiritual and moral struggle involved in the original conception should still cling to the final portrayal. This fact is much in evidence in the notes, but such a struggle is also reflected in the novel, and its very inconclusiveness contributes to the enigmatic nature of Stavrogin. A dualism, implicit in the rough sketch of the hero of "The Life of a Great Sinner," appears in Stavrogin in the form of a fierce opposition between good and evil. His personal magnetism draws all to him, and he exerts a tremendous influence over such individuals as Pyotr

Verkhovensky, Shatov, and Kirilov. The first two literally worship him, regard him as a born leader, and in a large measure they owe their revolutionary idealism to him. Yet Stavrogin is capable of the vilest crimes and worst debauchery. Although a noble, like Valkovsky and Svidrigailov he associates with the lowest riffraff, and he is capable of such pathological offences as biting the ear of the governor.

Even those whom he has most offended, however, find it difficult to turn against Stavrogin, although they see clearly the utter viciousness of his nature. Shatov, whose wife he has debauched, is bitter when he learns that his idol has feet of clay. "You are an atheist," Shatov shouts at him, "because you are a snob, a snob of the snobs. You have lost the distinction between good and evil because you have ceased to know your own people." (*The Possessed*, Part II, Chapter II, vii) Shatov is right. In this struggle between good and evil Stavrogin finally reaches a stage of psychological amoralism in which he fails to distinguish between them. Dostoevsky, like Shatov, would attribute the trait to Stavrogin's severance from the soil, to his isolation from the Russian masses. But it is important, in order to sustain the mysterious aspect of the character, that there should be no rationale in his position; he appears neither to understand his actions nor to offer any reasons for them. In a rather revelatory passage in the notes, Dostoevsky writes of him: "The Prince does not have any special ideas. He has only an aversion to his contemporaries, with whom he has resolved to break . . . But there are no ideas." [7] Even the crippled idiot whom he marries in a moment of moral sensuality, dominated by a mixed desire to make a martyr of himself and to outrage people's feelings, finally sees in her former hero an "owl" and a "shopman." Pyotr Verkhovensky perceives that the man he wishes to make the leader of his revolt is merely a terrible aristocrat who has turned democratic, and he further damns him as unworthy of Liza who has given herself to him.

Nevertheless, none of these characters can escape his influence or cease to worship him. After Shatov's fierce excoriation, a few sentences of which were quoted above, he bids his hero farewell with the words: "Shall I not kiss your footprints when you are gone? I cannot tear you out of my heart, Nikolai Stavrogin."

It is now a well-known fact that Katkov refused to publish a chapter of *The Possessed* because he considered it offensive to public taste. The chapter, "At Tikhon's," was probably intended to follow Chapter viii of Part ii in the novel, and it contains the "Confession of Stavrogin" which relates the story of his violation of a little girl.[8] The sequence of the chapter is plainly indicated in the meeting with Shatov, who throws in Stavrogin's face the rumour that he has decoyed and corrupted children, and he advises him to go to see Tikhon, the venerable holy man, a figure borrowed from the plan of "The Life of a Great Sinner."

This chapter is of primary importance for an understanding of the character of Stavrogin, and its omission has contributed to the unfinished and mysterious nature of the hero. Dostoevsky's failure to publish it in the later separate edition of the novel lends support to the belief that he preferred the unexplained, enigmatic quality of Stavrogin as more suitable to his artistic purpose. Stavrogin goes to Tikhon and lets him read his confession which he threatens to publish. Of late he has been having hallucinations in which he sees a devil or his Double, like Golyadkin and later Ivan Karamazov. The devil confronts him with all his ugliness and sin. In the confession, Stavrogin relates his debauched St. Petersburg life, his violation of the little girl, and a completely unmotivated theft. Then he tells of his travels abroad where he continues to indulge in loose living. In an hotel room in a little German town he has a dream of a Golden Age in which all mankind lives in the islands of the blest in a state of perfect happiness and contentment. By a trick of asso-

ciation the dream is suddenly disturbed by the appearance of the image of the little girl whom he has violated. She gazes at him silently and shakes her tiny fist
in a threatening gesture. From this point on, the image
of the child constantly recurs to Stavrogin. He feels
that he can will it out of his life, but for some reason
he does not wish to.

The facts in the omitted chapter concerning Stavrogin's past life and the emphasis upon the crime
against the little girl, which constantly tortures his conscience, contributed a great deal towards explaining
his unaccountable behaviour in the novel. There are
few references to the crime in the notes and none of
them supports the implications which psychologists
have read into this act in relation to Dostoevsky's own
life. In order to provide psychological credibility to
the extraordinary characterization, Dostoevsky apparently felt it necessary to make him guilty of what
Tikhon describes as the greatest and most fearful sin.
Stavrogin wishes to publish his confession because he
experiences the terrible need of punishment, of public
chastisement. Yet it is difficult for a man to take up his
cross when he does not believe in the cross of Christ.
Here Stavrogin is the atheist, the hero of the plan of
"The Life of a Great Sinner." He does not wish to
disclaim responsibility for his acts, but he frankly
admits that he has lost all sense of good and evil.
Tikhon disabuses him about his real reasons for desiring to print his confession. He is possessed by a desire
for martyrdom and self-sacrifice while at the same time
he is entirely devoid of sincerity and genuine humility,
for he despises his judges and does not believe in God.
Publishing the confession will only gain him ridicule,
which is the one thing Stavrogin's proud nature cannot
tolerate. Tikhon's final advice is that he forsake the
world for a time, live at the monastery as a novice,
and by sincere humility and suffering earn the right to
forgive himself. Stavrogin's refusal serves to convince
Tikhon that his purpose in coming to him is insincere

and that he is already contemplating another crime! Stavrogin does not publish his confession, a failure which is symbolic of his ultimate spiritual bankruptcy.

The deleted chapter was obviously intended to mark the turning point in Stavrogin's career. The struggle between good and evil has ceased; the forces of evil have now taken full possession of his soul. He cannot confess to the world, for this would argue a loss of pride. For a fleeting moment he dreams of finding peace by marrying Liza; but he cannot love her or anyone else. At first he rejects suicide as a way out, for to kill himself would indicate a despair which his pride cannot accept, and it would also imply a greatness of soul which his reason tells him is a sham. In that final letter to Darya, he gives a rather faithful picture of his complete spiritual frustration. He has torn himself away from the Russian masses and lost his faith in God; as a consequence, the innate goodness of his nature has utterly atrophied. Like Svidrigailov, he has arrived at the ultimate impasse of the Self-Willed man, and the solution of his enigmatic personality is inevitably the same. Despite his prejudices against the act, Stavrogin commits suicide.

In the romantic division of the novel, the feminine characters play an important part, but, with two exceptions, they have little in them of those obsessive passions which elevate Dostoevsky's heroines above the common mould. Stavrogin's mother, Varvara Petrovna, is one of those strong-minded, direct women, like Mme. Epanchina in *The Idiot,* whom she resembles to a considerable extent. She is irascible, temperamental, domineering, and a manager of things. Like Mme. Epanchina, she is generous to a fault and goes out of her way to conceal her generosity. The tragicomic friendship between her and Stepan Trofimovich, always hovering on the periphery of deeper emotions, does not prevent them from being severe critics of each other's faults. From a hint in the notes it seems very possible that Dostoevsky has a real person in mind in this characterization—A. O. Smirnova-Rosset (1810-82), the wife of a St. Petersburg governor and in her youth a friend of both Pushkin and Gogol. It is more certain, however, that A. O. Smirnova-Rosset provided the inspiration for Iuliya Mikhailovna, the governor's wife, who resembles Varvara Petrovna in many respects. She represents the humanitarian female busybody on the edge of the radical movement, a type that Dostoevsky must have been familiar with in real life.

The two exceptional female characters are Lizaveta Nikolaevna and Darya (Dasha) Shatova, both in love with Stavrogin and both familiar types in Dostoevsky's gallery. He has a variety of descriptive nicknames for Liza in the notes, such as the Beauty, Amazon, and Nihilist. She seems to have been drawn into the orbit of the novel from the plan of the same short story that contributed Kartuzov as the model for Lebyadkin. For in the plan of "The Tale of an Awkward Man," mentioned in the previous chapter, is the sketch of a heroine which is closely followed in the portrayal of Liza, and the curious relations between her and Lebyadkin parallel the relations of Kartuzov and the heroine of this projected tale. In *The Possessed*, however, she conforms entirely to the Double type, a worthy successor to Natasha Ikhmeneva, Polina Alexandrovna, and Nastasya Filipovna, and not unlike that real Double, Polina Suslova, who, if we may judge from the notes, was very much in Dostoevsky's mind as he developed the character of Liza. For long, Dostoevsky was uncertain about the nature of Stavrogin's relation with her. In several places in the notes it is mentioned that she is violated by this Don Juan, and she is also described as being in love with both Pyotr Verhovensky and Shatov. None of these suggestions is followed up in the novel in any concrete form. Her disastrous destiny in love, however, seems almost assured by the fatal ambivalence of her emotional nature. Liza is torn between extremes of tenderness and cruelty, between utter self-abnegation and a violent sense of possession.

That faithful soul, Mavriki Nikolaevich, who loves her sincerely, correctly diagnoses her divided soul for Stavrogin's benefit: "Under her persistent hatred for you, sincere and complete, love flashes at every moment—and madness! On the other hand, behind the love she feels for me, which is also sincere, every moment hate flashes forth—the greatest hatred!" (Part II, Chapter VI, vii)

In this racked existence of love and hate, Liza tortures and seeks to be tortured. At the same time she hesitates at no sacrifice for the man she loves. Haunted by the feeling that her love will save Stavrogin, she finally submits to him. He accepts her sacrifice in the hope that he will find release in her love, but this altruistic notion does not even survive their night together. In the end she becomes conscience-stricken at the thought that Stavrogin has allowed his crippled wife to be killed because of her. She runs away to ascertain the truth and in turn is killed by the angry mob. Dostoevsky makes it clear, however, that after their night together Liza realizes that Stavrogin is a lost soul who can never love.

As the "foster daughter" Darya is sketched in the very first plan of the novel, and she appears in every succeeding variant, but her position in them fluctuates considerably. She is the mistress and then the wife of Shatov; the mistress and the wife of Stavrogin, and the betrothed of Stepan Trofimovich. In the novel she is finally represented as the sister of Shatov and the lover of Stavrogin. One feature that remains constant in all these variants is the nature of her devotion to Stavrogin. An observation in the notes reveals succinctly the real touchstone of her character: "*She lost the possibility of judging him. His acts do not frighten her. Whatever he may do, she knows that she will follow him.*" [9] In short, Darya is unmistakably a sister in meekness of Sonya Marmeladova. Nothing could stand in greater contrast than her love for Stavrogin and that of Liza. Her nature is compounded of submissiveness, passivity, and a willingness to sacrifice. Although she worships Stavrogin, she does not struggle, like Liza, to win his active love in return. On the contrary, she gratefully accepts any show of attention he condescends to give her. Quite characteristic of the Meek figures in love—like Myshkin, for example—she does not resist union with another. Darya is willing to be married to old Stepan Trofimovich because, as she says, "It is all the same" to her. The contrast between the proud female Double and the Meek character in love is nowhere brought out more pointedly than in the contemptuous words of the imperious Liza to Stavrogin, after she has submitted to him and is ready to leave him forever: "Appeal to Dashenka; she will go with you wherever you wish . . . Poor little dog! Give her my greetings. Does she know that even in Switzerland you have settled upon her for your old age?" (Part III, Chapter III, i) In Stavrogin's last letter to Darya, her position of absolute subserviency and the sheer selflessness of her devotion are clearly defined. He has nothing to offer her in his contemplated retreat abroad except the position of "nurse" to him. Without a moment's hesitation she agrees to go. Her self-abnegation is comparable to Sonya's willingness to follow Raskolnikov to Siberia.

The world of revolutionary conspiracy, however, almost entirely absorbs the romantic aspects of the novel. The kind of fictionized pamphlet that Dostoevsky had originally planned slowly developed into an extended diatribe against the radical movement, which he used as a medium for expressing his own views on the present state of Russia and on its ultimate destiny. Pyotr Verkhovensky is the centre of the conspiracy, the dominating figure in this whole section of the novel. From the purely artistic point of view he must be considered something of a failure, largely because he is a symbol rather than a human being. Previous novels have demonstrated that Dostoevsky can create characters who are embodied ideas and still make them essentially real. In Verkhovensky he has embodied an idea, but he preaches it in a didactic manner. His powerful dialectical method has been sacrified to an ulterior polemical purpose. The more he strives to make Verkhovensky the symbol of a hated doctrine, the more the character divests itself of the stuff of reality. He excites our interest in Verkhovesnky by virtue of the almost superhuman vitality which he imparts to the characterization.

Under the initial inspiration of Nechaev, Dostoevsky apparently grasped at once the complete image of Verkhovensky the nihilist, but it must not be thought that he merely transferred to fiction the image of a person in real life. Apart from the original suggestion and a few of the revolutionary acts attributed to Nechaev, there is little about the final portrait of Verkhovensky that closely resembles his model. In fact, Dostoevsky deliberately avoided a slavish imitation. In the letter to Katkov, already quoted, he writes:

Except from the newspapers, I did not know at all and do not now know either Nechaev or Ivanov or the circumstances of this murder. And if I did know, then I would not copy. I only take the accomplished fact.[10] My fantasy may differ in the highest degree from the former reality, and my Pyotr Verkhovensky may not in the least resemble Nechaev; but it seems to me that in my astonished mind there has been created by my imagination a figure, a type that fits this crime. No doubt it is not unprofitable to present such a man; but he alone would not have tempted me. In my opinion these sorry deformities are not worth literature. To my own surprise this figure appears to me half comically.[11]

Historians have never suggested that there was anything comic about Nechaev, and at best Verkhovensky is a mere caricature of him. In the notes, interestingly enough, the resemblance is closer and the character less ludicrous. There Verkhovensky is pretty much represented as a sincere exponent of Bakunin's *Catechism of a Revolutionist,* and he acts on its principles.

In the novel he is stripped bare of these principles, and they in turn are foisted upon Shigalov, who burlesques them.

In reality Verkhovensky is no special exception to the creative patterns that have become obvious in Dostoevsky's fiction, and if he is examined in this light he appears to resemble certain previous characters of an established type more closely than he does Nechaev. Like the criminals Orlov and Petrov in *The House of the Dead,* Valkovsky in *The Insulted and Injured,* and Svidrigailov in *Crime and Punishment,* Verkhovensky is a Self-Willed man. Some of the same descriptive adjectives are applied to him. Like the criminal Petrov, he is utterly conscienceless, a man who directs all his powers towards accomplishing one idea. His cold, deliberate cruelty springs from his immoralism and from a complete atrophy of his social responsibilities. His part in the slaying of Shatov and his cyncial expectation of Kirilov's suicide place him in the same category as Fedka, another example of the Self-Willed type in *The Possessed,* who is willing to murder for a few kopeks. These low criminals, however, override moral obstacles and kill by instinct. Verkhovensky, like Valkovsky, is a rational enemy of society; consciously formulated principles of behaviour determine his criminal actions.

One very interesting feature differentiated Verkhovensky from the previous Self-Willed characters. He has designed a forthright solution to the social problem and he dares to act upon it. An exposition of this solution must be postponed until the next chapter, when the politics of *The Possessed* will be considered in some detail. However, it is curious that Dostoevsky did not seem to realize that he weakened his condemnation of the radicals by creating as the mouthpiece of what he thought were their views a character whose nature was no less criminal than that of Petrov or Svidrigailov, a man who was merely a caricature of a revolutionist. With the exception of Shatov and Kirilov, he presents the rest of the characters closely connected with the conspiracy in the same unsympathetic light. The extraordinary meeting of the conspirators in Chapter VII of Part II is a powerful but unjust travesty of his conception of a nihilist gathering. These followers of Verkhovensky—Virginsky, Liputin, Shigalov, and the rest—are described as fools, dolts, eccentrics, and rascals who lack the absolute conviction and criminal courage of their master. It is perhaps a reflection on Dostoevsky's own sincerity or on his understanding of the radicals when he even allows that moral bankrupt, Stavrogin, to declare in the notes: "I knew these fools (the followers of Nechaev) and was with them, but I always believed that they were fools." [12]

Shatov, the reformed radical, is the principal bearer of ideas in the novel and Dostoevsky's ideological answer to the would-be revolutionists. Not only is he one of the central figures in the novel, but in a few of the variant sketches he is clearly regarded as the hero. The large amount of preliminary material on Shatov in the notebooks reveals that Dostoevsky wavered for a long time before he settled upon the final form of this character. A variety of factors contributed to the conception which in the early stages pursued a course of dual development. Under the suggestive title in the notes: "The History of a Certain Proletarian," [13] Dostoevsky first sketched the image of Shatov as a young worker. Variants of this character were the teacher in the first plan of *The Possessed* and a poet-worker briefly outlined in the notes.

The other line of development, and the one that Dostoevsky retained, drew its inspiration from the murdered student Ivanov. Shatov becomes the counterbalance to the group of nihilists, although a few of the traits of the proletarian and of the teacher still cling to him. Ivanov, like Nechaev in the case of Verkhovensky, contributes no more than the initial suggestion in the characterization. The highly important ideological side of Shatov was much influenced by K. E. Golubov, an Old Believer and contemporary writer on religious, social, and political questions, who eventually returned to the official church. Dostoevsky had come in contact with his writings in 1868 and recognized in his ideas a surprising similarity to his own. He mentions him enthusiastically in a letter as a type of the "future Russian people." During the early planning of the novel, he introduces Golubov as a character of the first importance, and there are a number of references to him in the notes. His intention, apparently, was to represent Golubov as a formidable opponent of the nihilists. In these sketches, Shatov is described as a mere pupil of Golubov, who also powerfully influences Stavrogin and even shakes the convictions of Verkhovensky. After much effort in this direction, Dostoevsky suddenly decided to drop the character entirely. He seemed to sense that Golubov was overshadowing Stavrogin, the real hero of the novel. In abandoning the character, he transferred his role of influence to Stavrogin, and to Shatov the part of ideological opponent of the nihilists. That is, Shatov now becomes the representative of the "new Russian" and the mouthpiece of Dostoevsky.

Not only does Shatov present Dostoevsky's ideas, but in other respects he resembles his creator. Certain external features and an irritable and often gloomy disposition recall Dostoevsky, as do also Shatov's uncommunicative manner and his habit of bursting into unrestrained speech when he is aroused. Even the whole course of Shatov's political and religious development has much in common with that of Dostoevsky. He is a peasant, the only one of all the conspirators who belongs to this class. Under Stavrogin's mysterious influence, he had entered the revolutionary movement as Dostoevsky had in his youth, and like him, he has charge of the secret printing press of the conspirators. In the end this peasant, ideologically as it were, reverts to type, as though Dostoevsky meant to suggest

in this act his own conviction—a turning to the masses
—as the only path to salvation.

Shatov's faith in the radical movement had been a
passionate one, and in the novel he is presented in the
soul-torturing process of tearing himself away from his
former convictions. While abroad he had married a
governess. They had separated and Stavrogin had become intimate with her. Then Shatov and Kirilov had
gone to America for a reason that is interesting, coming from Dostoevsky: "to test the life of the American
workman on ourselves, and thus to verify by *personal*
experiment the state of man in the hardest social conditions." (Part I, Chapter IV, iv) Apparently their experience in America made them feel that the labourer
in Russia lived in a kind of paradise, and it affected
Shatov very much as Dostoevsky's prison experience
reacted on him. Shatov's thoughts turn to a different
solution of Russia's social ills. Stavrogin had sent him
the necessary funds to enable him to return to Russia.
Meanwhile he has become so involved in Verkhovensky's conspiracy that the members plot his death for
fear that he may expose them. It is really at this point
that he begins to play the role of the unfortunate
Ivanov in the Nechaev affair.

Stavrogin also is an important factor in Shatov's
break with his radical convictions. When Shatov strikes
him fiercely in the face, he secretly hopes that his
idol will make the most of this act and reassert his
immense power over him. Stavrogin, however, receives
the blow in silence, and the disillusioned Shatov understands that his former teacher and all his revolutionary
doctrines are a living lie. Stavrogin had formerly
taught him to believe in the destiny of Russia and of
its people, and that only through revolution could this
lofty mission be realized. At the bottom of Stavrogin's
theories had been his assumed faith in the Russian
Christ, and all his pupil's activities were predicated
on this same faith. For Shatov, belief in the Russian

people is absolutely inseparable from belief in Russian Orthodoxy. He recapitulates these convictions to Stavrogin. They might have been lifted directly from Dostoevsky's letters of this time, and later they appear in nearly the same form in a number of articles in *The Diary of a Writer*. More startling is Shatov's repeating Stavrogin's statement: "But did you not tell me that if it were mathematically proved to you that the truth is outside Christ you would prefer to remain with Christ than with the truth?" (Part II, Chapter I, vii) This is remembered almost word for word from the letter that Dostoevsky wrote to the wife of the Decembrist, who had aided him on his way to prison, almost twenty years previously.[14] Stavrogin does not deny that he said this. Yet now Shatov discovers that his idol is an atheist and has been inculcating Kirilov with atheism, and it is on this rock that his faith in Stavrogin splits.

Although Stavrogin insists that he had not been lying when formerly he had won Shatov over to his beliefs, he now has no reason to offer for discarding them. This instability is in keeping with his mysterious nature. His convictions, apparently, had been artificial, and he had assumed them simply because they suited the expediency of the moment. For Shatov, however, faith in the world destiny of Russia and its people has meaning only as a part of his faith in the Russian Orthodox God. Stavrogin's former revolutionary idealism has become godless and Shatov now rejects them both. A man cannot be a Russian and an atheist at the same time. Shatov's repudiation in the first chapter of Part II is a remarkable statement, unfortunately too long to quote. Like Myshkin in *The Idiot*, he expounds here Dostoevsky's own religious and political beliefs. Science and reason, he declares, recalling Stavrogin's words, have never played more than a subordinate part in the life of nations, yet socialism, an atheistic organization, establishes itself exclusively on the elements of science and reason. Nations, however, really survive by virtue of another force, unknown and inexplicable, which Shatov describes as "the seeking of God." God is the synthetic personality of a whole people, and when nations share their faith in the same God it is a sign of growing weakness, for the stronger a people the more individual is its God. And every nation has a religion, that is, a conception of good and evil, and again when nations share this conception it is a sign of decay; they begin to lose the distinction between good and evil. Nor can reason or science distinguish between good and evil. In fact, they confuse good and evil in a hopeless manner.

The artist in Doestoevsky, even where his own convictions are concerned, will not permit Shatov to have it all his own way. His searching dialectic asserts itself, and, one is inclined to think, his lurking religious doubts, which he concealed in his polemical writings, are forced from him by the demands of art. Stavrogin refuses to accept entirely Shatov's version of his former teaching, and he accuses him of reducing God to a simple attribute of nationality. Shatov replies that, far from reducing God to an attribute of nationality, he would raise the people to God. On his own premise, however, this could be achieved only by a universal negation of reason. And Shatov is a reasoning creature whose faith, as Stavrogin perceives, is no better than the half-truths of science which his former pupil so bitterly condemns. With diabolical persistency he puts to Shatov the terrible question: " 'Do you believe in God, yourself?' and the frantic Shatov is forced to reply: 'I believe in Russia . . . I believe in her Orthodoxy . . . I believe in the body of Christ . . . I believe that the new advent will take place in Russia . . . I believe . . .' 'And in God? In God?' Stavrogin demands. 'I . . . I will believe in God.' " (Part II, Chapter I, vii)

Dostoevsky was also a reasoning being, and like Shatov, who so much resembles him, he never seemed to transcend the *desire* to believe in God. Although he searched for God all his life, reason and faith never ceased their struggle in his mind. He never attained to the infinite faith that passes all understanding, that absolute faith which negates evil in the world or accepts it as the work of the devil, or as the result of man's will as expressed in sinning, or as the suffering of man divinely ordained as a means of eternal salvation. Later he was to argue these questions through the brilliant mind of Ivan Karamazov, and again the answers brought him no solace. Whatever may have been the anguish of Dostoevsky's search, the gnawing doubt it affirmed was a state of mind in which his genius seemed to thrive best.

Shatov renounces Stavrogin and his radical teaching, but he admits that he is condemned to believe in him through all eternity. Like Stavrogin, however, he is also a doomed man. The scene that presages his fate, that in which his wife gives birth to her baby, is one of the finest in the novel. It is as though Dostoevsky, with extraordinary artistic prescience, contrived to make all the previous actions of Shatov contribute to the success of this scene. For the first time this irritable, uncommunicative, and disillusioned peasant's son is transformed from a bloodless image of didactic dissidence into a living man with natural feelings and homely cares. His whole nature flowers under the emotion of an intensely realized but common experience. Stavrogin is the father of the child, but the mystery of life, of seeing a new spirit finished and complete come into the world, opens up the well-springs of love in Shatov's obdurate heart—love for both the newcomer and his estranged wife. Perhaps Dostoevsky may have remembered his own feelings upon the birth of his first child. What immeasurably intensifies the effect of this chapter, however, is our knowledge of the impending fate of Shatov. The ecstasy of this tortured soul over the arrival of the babe and over the new life of peace and love which he anticipates with the wife whom he believed irretrievably lost is heightened by the terrible human irony of the death which we know shortly awaits him. It is altogether a compelling and ominously beautiful scene.

The engineer Kirilov, another pupil of Stavrogin, has learned from his teacher a God-defying thesis that turns him into an ideological foil, a kind of religiophilosophical antithesis to Shatov. The genesis of this character is difficult to trace. He is introduced relatively late in the notes, and it is evident that he did not figure in the earlier plans of the novel. The first mention of him in the notes, some ten months after the draft of the first plan of *The Possessed,* runs: "An engineer smuggled in proclamations, disseminated [them] in the South in a factory with Fedka and others. An *agent* of Nechaev [Verkhovensky], reasoning thus: If they learn, then they will seize me alone. I will testify in writing and will shoot myself, for it is all the same to me." [15] The lack of characterizing remarks in the notes supports the theory that Kirilov was originally introduced for a purely functional purpose in the plot—to use his suicide to cover up the murderers of Shatov.

Suicide, however, was a subject that much interested Dostoevsky. Given the act, it was almost inevitable that he should speculate on the motivation behind it. Out of such speculation, the "idea" of Kirilov develops, for it is apparent that there is little more to the characterization than the embodiment of an idea. The idea itself Dostoevsky has been concerned with earlier. Terentev, the consumptive youth in *The Idiot,* had thought to defy God's power by taking his own life, and he had felt that this act of final revolt would elevate him to the status of a man-god. In the notes on the plan of "The Life of a Great Sinner," a statement is made of the hero which reverts to this idea of Terentev: "In the diversions of his fantasy are infinite dreams pertaining to the overthrow of God and the putting of himself in His place." [16] This statement describes the essential position of Kirilov, but Dostoevsky now works out his idea of the man-god in a manner that is both metaphysical and mystical at once.

Kirilov carries out the relation of the individual, as a cosmic entity, to the world in a fashion that represents the fullest development of the Self-Willed character. For Kirilov, the world is a cipher, and the elimination of it in the name of the individual is an inevitable and logical corollary to his ultimate fate. He is convinced that man is unhappy because he believes in the existence outside himself of a world the laws of which he must obey. Hence, he insists, it is man who has created the world and God and they exist only to the extent that the individual wills them to exist. If the individual wishes, he can make the world and God vanish or become something other. If man only understood this fact, declares Kirilov, he could abolish the world and obtain his complete freedom. In short, he could become a man-god. To achieve this beatific state, all that man has to do is to conquer the fear of death which everlastingly condemns him to submit to the world-god. In Kirilov's mind, God is identified with the fear of death, and his aim is to eliminate this fear and thus take the place of God. There is no world, then, no God, nothing except the individual, unlimited if only he will assert his self-will. Kirilov envisions the salvation of all humanity in the realization of his idea, for, he asks, how can man suffer when he knows that there is no death and that he is entirely free?

Kirilov pushes his idea to its logical conclusion with the terrifying persistency of a madman. The end for the completely Self-Willed man is suicide, for if he does not act upon this conclusion he suffers from a fear of death. When everyone learns that there is no death, universal suicide will destroy the world, and the rule of the absolutely free human personality, of the man-god, will begin. Someone must initiate this process, however, and Kirilov feels himself elected. By showing his contempt for death, he will become a man-god and thus set an example for the rest of mankind. Accordingly, he decides to kill himself.

The similarity of Kirilov's idea to that of Terentev is patent, and Ivan Karamazov was to develop its various phases much more subtly. But Terentev fails miserably in his attempt to become a man-god, and Ivan never gets beyond the philosophical implication of his idea. Kirilov, however, kills himself with discouraging punctuality and dispatch. He is a rebel against God, but the religious instinct in him is powerful though perverted. He denies God for the sake of man and almost in a Christ-like sense he offers himself as a sacrifice for the greater glory of man. In order to save man, however, he must be a superman. Dostoevsky's profound concern with religious thought in *The Possessed* clearly indicates its growing significance in his mind. In *The Brothers Karamazov* the whole subject of religion was to find even fuller expression.

Dostoevsky's gift for caustic satire, very little in evidence in his previous fiction, is fully revealed in *The Possessed*. The real figures in Russian life who contribute to the characterizations of certain of the conspirators are ridiculed in both their actions and radical ideas. The brunt of the satire, however, is borne by Turgenev in the person of Karmazinov, the fashionable novelist who comes to the provincial town where the action of the story takes place. This characterization is often described as a spiteful and vicious calumniation of Turgenev, provoked solely by his unfortunate quarrel with Dostoevsky abroad. No doubt the quarrel had much to do with whetting Dostoevsky's appetite for the kill. However, there is more to the point of the satire than personal spleen. By the time he had begun to write *The Possessed*, he had reached the stage of identifying with what Turgenev stood for nearly everything he considered inimical to the religious, political, and social welfare of Russia. In his eyes, Turgenev had become one of those renegades, more European than

Russian, who were doing the greatest disservice to their native land by preaching the need of westernizing Russia. That Turgenev's latest works powerfully reflected this attitude simply made him all the more dangerous. Dostoevsky is in deadly earnest in the matter, and the satire clearly transcends the level of mere personal enmity. In a novel the aim of which was largely to oppose those convictions which he firmly believed Turgenev championed, it was most natural that he should harshly satirize and expose his popular rival.

The real element of unfairness in the satire is that Dostoevsky mistakenly or wilfully confuses Turgenev's position with that of the caricatured nihilists of the novel. He virtually represents the vicious young radical Verkhovensky as the spiritual son, not of that old-fashioned liberal, his father, but of Karmazinov. Turgenev, of course, would have had no more sympathy with Verkhovensky's murderous extremes than Dostoevsky. In fact, Turgenev stood closer, ideologically, to Stepan Trofimovich than to his radical son. The only mitigating factor is that Karmazinov's enthusiasm for the cause of the young nihilists is described as emanating from his vanity rather than from honest conviction.

Apart from the serious concern with Turgenev's political and social ideas, his personal foibles and literary mannerisms are fair bait for the satirist. If Dostoevsky is malicious in this respect, it can be said in his defence only that most personal satire is malicious from one point of view or another. The introduction of Karmazinov is somewhat crude, but as Dostoevsky warms up to the subject he makes his satire of the great novelist's appearance, voice, and habits both effective and amusing. Gradually the intensity of the attack increases. Karmazinov tells young Verkhovensky that he has lost faith in the Russian God, who is scarcely to be relied upon since the emancipation of the serfs. And in his description of Russia as a sinking ship which all the rats are deserting, he unwittingly takes his place among the fleeing rodents. Russia has no future, he declares, and therefore he has become a German and is proud of it. One has merely to read Turgenev's *Smoke* to appreciate the full intention behind this hit. Dostoevsky carries his satire too far, however, when he has Karmazinov say, "The whole essence of the Russian revolutionary idea lies in the negation of honour . . . For a Russian honour is only a superfluous burden. And it always has been a burden throughout his whole history. The open "right to dishonour" will attract him more quickly than anything else." (Part II, Chapter VI, v) Young Verkhovensky seizes upon this as a delightful morsel to repeat to Stavrogin, for he feels that it aptly sums up the attitude of his conspirators. Dostoevsky is on fairer ground in his description of Karmazinov's swansong *Merci*, which he reads to that impossibly mad gathering engineered by the governor's mad wife. This is a satire of Turgenev's piece *Enough*, and with unerring perception Dostoevsky selects those wishy-washy features of his writing which most lend themselves to ridicule.

The Possessed is richer in characters that powerfully reflect the positive or negative aspects of Dostoevsky's own views on Russia than any previous novel. Stavrogin, Stepan Trofimovich, Pyotr Verkhovensky, Shatov, Kirilov, and Karmazinov, to mention only the most notable, express a great deal of his accumulated thinking on the social, political, and religious questions which were close to his heart. The pattern of this thought is extremely varied, but out of it emerges one unassailable fact—his profound concern for the future of Russia. While engaged in writing the novel abroad, he had observed some of the effects of the Franco-Prussian War. Although he was no pacifist, this struggle and everything connected with it served merely to increase his contempt for both the French and the Germans, whose corrupt civilizations alone, he felt, led them to these extremes of destruction. When the Paris Commune ended in bloodshed and defeat, he

saw in it a symbolical object lesson for those Russian
Westerners who preached this kind of violence in their
efforts to achieve socialism. All these people, he was
convinced, had turned away from God and put their
faith in force and reason. Catastrophe for Russia would
be the result if they continued. This concern, suddenly
intensified by the Nechaev affair, prompted him to
spew forth all his fiery convictions against the radicals
of his novel. If he had clung to his original purpose,
however, *The Possessed* would have turned out to be
an extensive satirical pamphlet on the Russian revolutionary movement. By an artistic miracle the work was
saved from this fate, for the compelling force of his art
made of *The Possessed* a great novel in spite of its
didacticism. A throbbing vital intelligence informs the
thrilling action and elevates it infinitely above the
average level of the purpose-novel.

18

The Politics of
The Possessed

When Dostoevsky began *The Possessed* he had written his niece that he could make of it a book that would be talked of a hundred years hence if only he had the time and means at the disposal of his great rivals in fiction. The artistic imperfections which he worried about have never seriously endangered the immortality of the work, but he could not anticipate then the world events which have made *The Possessed* perhaps his most discussed novel today. The socialist revolution in Russia has directed the attention of modern critics to the novel, and they have found it a remarkable prophecy of many recent happenings in that country. Literary critics, journalists, and students of political science have frequently cited it, largely by way of supporting their condemnation of events in Soviet Russia. Often such criticisms reveal a misunderstanding of both Dostoevsky's political thinking and its relation to the social history of his age.

History is no doubt an unfailing and obligatory condition of sociological analysis, but it is not easy to interpret Dostoevsky's political beliefs in terms of the class struggle and its national surroundings in Russia between 1840 and 1880. Soviet critics have contributed a number of studies of Dostoevsky from the Marxian point of view and the results are peculiarly contradictory. Some concepts in his political thinking seemed to have been arrived at by a process of divination, and the panaceas which he offers for Russia's social ills resemble incantations rather than rational cures. Further, the functional role of his creative process is so often a matter of feeling rather than reason that it is difficult to relate it to the practical problems of his times.

It is uncritical to dismiss Dostoevsky as a confirmed reactionary, as is so often done, for the temperament of the conservative was essentially foreign to his nature. The dualism reflected in so many of his great characters was simply a projection of the constant struggle that went on in his own mind. In this endless warfare of reason and feeling, the quality of his thought remained dynamic. These characteristics conditioned his political thinking. I have said elsewhere that the rebel in him was always just beneath the surface. It could erupt in moments of extreme conservatism. No man suffered more inwardly because of his convictions, for he was constantly undergoing the painful process of changing them. In 1876, at a time when he was supposed to be engrossed with reactionary friends and ideas, he wrote in the foreword to the first part of *The Diary of a Writer*: "I reckon myself more liberal than all, although it may be only in this one thing that I do not wish to be lulled." [1] These facts must be kept in mind in considering his political beliefs as they are reflected in *The Possessed*.

The outlines of Dostoevsky's previous political development have already been sketched. The liberal activities and ideas of his youth, influenced by Belinsky and by his association with the Petrashevsky and

Durov groups, were not simply sloughed off in prison. In fact, the Utopian idealism which he imbibed in those days, a kind of idealism which Marx and Lenin valued in the history of the revolutionary struggle, never entirely deserted him. It was directed into different channels, inspiring his later dreams of world harmony.

After Dostoevsky's release from prison and his return to St. Petersburg, he evinced his liberalism in many ways. The emancipation of the serfs he welcomed, and the whole direction of his first magazine was a liberal one. His initial trip abroad in 1862 seems to date the beginning of a momentous change in his political views. In his youth, influenced by the theories of Fourier and Saint-Simon, he had no doubt been unsympathetic to the capitalism of the West. The hypocritical bourgeois morality, political corruption, and the suffering of oppressed people that he observed on this first trip abroad turned him into an open and bitter critic of European capitalism. All the forces which he believed had contributed to these conditions in Western Europe—Roman Catholicism, imperialism, and materialism—also came under his lash. More important, however, was his identification of the European radical movement, designed to cure these ills, with the ills themselves. The revolutionary movement of the proletariat he regarded as a moral sickness which presaged the last convulsion of the bourgeois world.

To turn with his fears to the situation in Russia was a natural transition. He observed that the freeing of the serfs was quickly followed by manifestations of the hated capitalism of the West, which seemed to render worse the conditions of both peasants and landowners. And the growing Russian revolutionary agitation of the 1860's, which he did not clearly understand, now appeared to him, like capitalism, to be entirely an importation from the West. At this point, he looked back on Belinsky and the early Westerners as the original purveyors of dangerous European ideas. Their successors, such as Chernyshevsky, were their intellectual sons, advocating the same materialism and socialistic changes, but in a more intensive and more practical manner. With horror he viewed the growing violence, the first attempt on the life of Alexander II, and the strange fires in St. Petersburg in 1862, which he attributed to the young revolutionists. He was convinced that Russia was in grave and immediate danger from the radical movement, and his successive trips abroad in the 1860's served only to increase his alarm over this Western influence and his hostility to those Russian intellectuals who submitted to it. This was Dostoevsky's political position when the Nechaev affair took place, and he decided to deal the radicals a blow by writing *The Possessed*, a frankly tendentious novel.

Dostoevsky's understanding of the theoretical background of the Russian revolutionary movement of his day was most imperfect, and his knowledge of its practical operations extremely limited. This fact, almost as much as his uncompromising hostility, accounts for the mistakes and patent exaggerations of the doctrines and actions of the conspirators in the novel. He admitted that he knew very little about Nechaev, and his information of the actions and personalities of the other conspirators was drawn largely from newspaper reports which, in the circumstances at this time in Russia, were much compressed and by no means unprejudiced. Yet Nechaev inspired the image of Verkhovensky, who represented Dostoevsky's idea of the young radical of the age. In his mouth is placed a political programme which Dostoevsky apparently believed to be typical of the revolutionists. It will be instructive to examine this programme.

Shigalov is the theoretician of the conspirators in *The Possessed*. From the notes to the novel, it appears that his system was suggested by Bakunin's *Catechism of a Revolutionist* which had been introduced into

Russia by Nechaev. Any contemporary student of the radical movement knew that there was a world of difference between the popular evolutionary socialism of Herzen and his followers and the destructive peasant anarchism of Bakunin. Whatever may have been the similarity in ends, Bakunin's anarchistic means and totalitarian concepts found little favour among the socialists of this period.

Shigalov declares: "I am perplexed by my own data: my conclusion is a direct contradiction of the original idea with which I start. Starting from unlimited freedom, I end with unlimited despotism." His solution of the social question is to divide mankind into two unequal parts. "One-tenth receives freedom of individuality and unlimited power over the remaining nine-tenths. These must surrender all individuality and become, so to speak, a herd, and, through boundless submission and by a series of regenerations, they will attain a primitive innocence, something like a primeval paradise, although they will have to work." (Part II, Chapter VII, ii)

Shigalov is prevented from developing his bizarre notions by the many interruptions at the nihilist gathering. He has given a cue to Verkhovensky, however, who also claims to know the full text of Shigalov's system. What he advocates is not Shigalovism or any socialist theory, but the revolutionary tactics of Nechaev, wildly exaggerated in all their reprehensible features. He takes for his slogan freedom, equality, and socialism. For him, these words have special meanings which are not the commonly accepted ones, either as abstract definitions or as descriptions of these terms as they were used in Russian revolutionary theorizing. He explains his meaning to Stavrogin: "Everyone belongs to all and all to everyone. All are slaves and equal in their slavery. In extreme cases there are slander and murder, but the chief thing is equality. To begin with, the level of education, science, and talents is lowered. A high level of science and talents is suitable only for great intellects, and great intellects are not wanted . . . Slaves are bound to be equal. Without despotism there has never been freedom or equality, but in the herd there is bound to be equality, and that's Shigalovism!" (Part II, Chapter VIII)

Verkhovensky's conception of socialism is all of a piece with his notions of freedom and equality. He pictures the millennium for Stavrogin: "Culture is unnecessary; we've had enough of science! Without science we have material enough for a thousand years, but one must maintain discipline. The only thing that is lacking in the world is discipline. The thirst for culture is an aristocratic search. The moment you have a family or love you get the desire for property. We will destroy that desire: we will make use of drunkenness, slander, spying; we'll make use of incredible corruption; we'll stifle every genius in its infancy. Everything to one common denominator, complete equality." Then in his effort to induce Stavrogin to be the leader of the projected revolt, Verkhovensky's imagination soars and his language becomes violent. He acts like a man drunk with a sense of power, and one for whom intrigue is an end in itself. In his new State, he tells Stavrogin, a Cicero would have his tongue cut out, a Copernicus would be blinded, and a Shakespeare stoned. Even the Pope will come to terms and help lead the rabble on to victory. Every element of crime and vice will be put to the service of the cause. "One or two generations of debauchery are essential now," he continues, "unparalleled, vulgar debauchery, when man turns into a filthy, cowardly, cruel, selfish reptile. That's what we need! And what's more, a little 'fresh blood' that we may get accustomed to it . . . We will proclaim destruction . . . Why, why has this idea such a fascination? But we must have a little excuse; we must. We'll set fires . . . we'll set legends going . . . Every mangy 'group' will be of use. From these groups I'll search out for you such fellows who will not shrink from shooting, and will remain grateful for the honour. Well, the upheaval will begin! There's going to be such an overthrow as the world has never seen before . . . Russia will be plunged into darkness. The earth will weep for its old gods." (Part II, Chapter VIII)

Now, it was pointed out in the preceding chapter that Verkhovensky definitely falls into the Self-Willed group of characters, and it is highly significant that Dostoevsky should have made such a type the leader and mouthpiece of the radicals. Obviously, Verkhovensky's solution of social problems is bound to be an antisocial solution, for his social feelings are dead, as are those of the other criminal Self-Willed characters, such as Orlov, Petrov, Valkovsky, and Svidrigailov. For Verkhovensky, freedom and equality without despotism are unthinkable; they are simply the theoretic expressions of self-will and immoralism. He even admits to Stavrogin that he is not a socialist and that he is a scoundrel. If those prize criminals in *The House of the Dead*, Orlov and Petrov, had been able to express their relations to society and their notions of freedom, equality, and socialism, their formulation would have been quite similar to that of Verkhovensky. His ideas on freedom and equality amount to the destruction of society in the name of his own personality. Society becomes an absolute zero in his scheme of things. Verkhovensky, then, is a monster and not a radical, and his social ideology is the criminal creed of the absolutely self-willed man. Dostoevsky went completely out of his way to present him in the most unfavourable light possible. His vain, deceitful nature has scarcely a single redeeming feature, and he even stoops to the base treachery of the *agent provocateur,* for it is hinted at the end that he betrays his own followers to the government.

The social ideology of Verkhovensky is no doubt consistent with this Self-Willed type, but in allowing it to typify the general aims of the Russian revolutionary movement in the 1860's Dostoevsky committed a serious error and one that the radicals of the time were quick to condemn. That he was serious in his intention is indicated by a letter to the future Alexander III; in it he says that the novel virtually represents a historical study in which he tries to show that the radical movement resulted largely from the fact that Russian intellectuals were out of touch with the masses and unsympathetic to them.

Dostoevsky's error is rooted in the general confusion in his mind concerning the aims of the radical movement and in his indiscriminate mixing of nihilists and revolutionary terrorists. Much of his point of view in understanding the 1860's was hopelessly distorted by the radical experiences of his own youth. He seemed to regard Nechaev as the final violent manifestation of the revolutionary movement that began in the 1840's. In the notes, he calls him the last Russian conspirator, when in reality he was one of the first of the revolutionary-democratic workers in the cause, and one whose extreme tactics were repudiated by his successors. Even Bakunin rejected the tactics of his pupil and eventually broke with him. Yet Nechaev and his followers are often construed in terms of the members of the Petrashevsky group, for Dostoevsky seemed to think it important to prove that the radical youths of the 1860's had nothing more to offer than the impractical programme of the old liberals of the 1840's. This intention is plainly manifested in the notes where he reminds himself by the observations: "Nechaev partly Petrashevsky" and "To keep closer to the type of Petrashevsky." [2] Such an approach was probably dictated by his passionate desire to deny any progress in the bourgeois-democratic revolution, which he had come to fear and hate. Nihilism, which had taken on the proportions of a fad in his day, he excoriated in the burlesqued meeting of the conspirators in the novels. Yet he did not understand that nihilism was the result of the despair of all productive action felt by thwarted subjects who possessed absolutely no rights in a state governed by police. The nihilists, however, were crass egoists and had no constructive programme, and there was some justice in Dostoevsky's condemnation of them. It was vicious misrepresentation, however, to confuse them with the revolutionary terrorists whose acts had aroused his ire. These radicals were often men of lofty ideals, and their definite programme was not designed to create a social system that reduced men to the equality of slaves. Their deeds, however futile, compose one of the greatest stories of selfless, sacrificing activity in the whole history of the Russian revolutionary movement.

Dostoevsky either did not know or wilfully maligned the real Russian revolutionists of his time. The underground type of revolutionist who put his faith in the proletariat and ultimately brought about the Revolution of 1917 did not exist in Dostoevsky's day. As yet there was no class-conscious proletariat. In actuality the radical movement was made up largely of followers of Herzen whose programme had developed into the widespread Populism of the period. In a sense this amounted to a synthesis of the position of the two old rival camps of Westerners and Slavophiles. The revolutionary theories of the West, when applied to peculiarly Russian peasant conditions, would bring about a social revolution through gradual and non-violent means until finally the communized peasantry would fulfil its universal subversive mission in Europe.

Dostoevsky's positive programme, his answer to the social anarchy of the conspirators in *The Possessed*, is placed mostly in the mouth of Shatov. The argument was not unfamiliar to his readers. It is simply an elaboration of the statement of Myshkin in *The Idiot*, and it derives partly from the Slavophile doctrine. Shatov himself is represented as a Slavophile. The answer has Dostoevsky's own peculiar idealistic colouring. Prophecy takes the place of logic, spiritual postulates are substituted for historical analysis. By forsaking Christ,

Roman Catholicism has ruined the whole Western world. Out of it has grown socialism, which is predicated on atheism, materialism, and reason. Like the Catholic Church, it strives to achieve equality by despotism. It is only Russian intellectuals, the liberals and radicals, who have been infected by this noxious virus of the West. They must return to the soil, to the masses and to the Russian Christ. Shatov, a peasant by birth, symbolizes the "new people" who will not only save Russia, but the world. In the notes there is a bit of dialogue between him and Stavrogin that does not appear in the novel. Yet it pointedly states Dostoevsky's formula of salvation for all Russians afflicted by the disease of Western intellectualism, and prophesies the world-mission of the Russian people. Shatov declares to Stavrogin:

'To be with the soil, to be with your own people, signifies to believe that precisely through this people all humanity will be saved, and finally the idea will be born into the world and a heavenly kingdom in it.'

'I cannot force myself to believe.'

'It is clear,' says Sh[atov], 'if you were really a Russian, then you would believe without noticing it, you would simply accept, even without reasoning that it could not be otherwise—without arrogance and with humility, as any Russian would.'

'Indeed, does every Russian believe this?'

'Without fail.'

'But in your opinion only peasants are Russians. Is it possible that a peasant even believes that all humanity will be saved through him?'

'Without fail. Is it possible that you have not noticed this? Of course he does not think about it, and such a question cannot enter his head, but if this question could suddenly enter his head, whatever form it might be in, then he could not think about it in any other fashion. Man for him is a Russian only, God for him is only the Russian God, custom only Russian custom.' [3]

This is too much, even for Stavrogin, and he dismisses it all as "fanaticism." The word is not inappropriate. Dostoevsky's picture of revolution in *The Possessed* has been commended as a startling prophecy of what has happened in Soviet Russia. Parallels have been drawn between Pyotr Verkhovensky's Shigalovism—its freedom and equality through despotism, its atheism, its sacrifice of the dignity of the individual, and its complete justification of any means to achieve the end of purely imaginary socialism—and conditions of life in socialist Russia today. On the other hand, certain elements of Dostoevsky's own programme suggest a parallel with the doctrine of Nazism. While Shatov tries desperately to find some spark of the former faith in Stavrogin, he says to him, among other things: "If a great people does not believe that the truth is to be found in it alone (in itself alone and exclusively in itself), if it does not believe that it alone is fit and destined to raise up and save all by its truth, it at once ceases to be a great nation, and at once turns into ethnographical material and not into a great people. A truly great people can never reconcile itself with a secondary role in humanity or even with the first, but without fail must exclusively play the first role. A nation which loses this belief ceases to be a nation." (Part II, Chapter I, vii)

It is only fair to say, however, that Shatov's extreme nationalism, which was Dostoevsky's profound conviction, was intimately connected with religious beliefs that verged on mysticism. The truth is God, and Russia is the only "God-bearing" nation, destined to save the whole world through this symbol of faith. He also associates this truth, by way of refuting the rational truth of socialism as the salvation of nations, with the "seeking for God," and the "spirit of life." This is the truth that dawns upon Stepan Trofimovich at the end and points the moral of the novel. Just before his death, the evangelical Bible-seller reads him the passage from Luke on the devils that enter into the Gadarene swine—a passage that stands as the epigraph to *The Possessed*. He imagines the devils as all the sores, impurities, and foul contagion that will leave the sick body of Russia and enter the swine—the nihilists— and be drowned in the sea. Holy Mother Russia will be healed, and all will "sit at the feet of Jesus." Stepan Trofimovich dies, happy in the thought that he has discovered something infinitely great before which he can bow down.

Neither the extremes of Dostoevsky's reactionary convictions nor his own brand of socialism—for he had one—are fully revealed in *The Possessed*. The novel gives the impression of having been written in anger over a stupid crime that symbolized for him the vicious excesses of the young radical generation. Yet he did not know and hence failed to understand the radical youths of the 1860's who sacrificed all for a futile cause. Like Turgenev, he was incapable of creating a positive revolutionary hero. Nor does the novel reveal any of his profound sympathy for the down-trodden and oppressed of Russia whose bitter lot these same radicals strove to alleviate. His answer was to idealize their suffering and make out of it a way of life. Instead of practical reforms, he offered them religious and mystical consolation. Yet the ultimate of his solution was the brotherly love and universal happiness of primitive communism, and, like the more enlightened socialists of his own day, he placed his hope for the salvation of Russia in the masses. He would achieve this end, however, by faith in God and in the innate goodness of man, not in revolution and in a planned society. Perhaps more clearly than anything else, the novel reflects the internal contradiction and fear among the mass of bourgeoisie of the time before the spectre of revolt and radical change.

In the first part of this chapter, however, the danger of tagging Dostoevsky with any unqualified political beliefs was pointed out. His position in *The Possessed* is no exception to this rule. Before long, one can detect a definite drift away from this stand. Even before the novel was finished—he worked on it for over three years—there was a shift in his point of view towards the hero and the pupose of the work. At the end of this period, he criticized the novelist Leskov for his unfair treatment of the nihilists in a recently published work. Only a few years later, he took to task a critic who dismissed Nechaev as an idiotic fanatic, supporting his point by mentioning that he himself, in the Petrashevsky days of his youth, had been a kind of Nechaev. And in the notes to the last part of *The Possessed*, there is a brief draft of a foreword which he never used. He wrote: "In Kirilov is a national idea— to sacrifice oneself immediately for truth . . . To sacrifice oneself and everything for truth—that is a national feature of the generation. May God bless it and bring to it an understanding of the truth. For the whole question consists in what to regard as truth. For this reason the novel was written." [4] This statement indicates a considerable retreat from the intransigeant attitude in which he began the novel. Before he had reached the end, the whole problem had been swept back into the cauldron of his mind—was God the truth, to be achieved by faith, or was truth at the end of man's rational quest?

19

A Raw Youth

Debts and domestic difficulties were Dostoevsky's immediate worries when he returned to St. Petersburg in 1871 from his long sojourn abroad. For the moment such cares seemed trifling in the excitement and pleasure of being once again among familiar scenes and old friends. It took him almost a whole year after his return to finish *The Possessed*. As the chapters appeared in the *Russian Messenger*, they were eagerly read and much talked about. He made the most of his renewed popularity by going out into society rather frequently. It is noticeable that he now favoured conservative circles in which he was beginning to be regarded as a formidable literary support to a reactionary government. He regularly attended the Wednesday gatherings at Prince V. P. Meshchersky's. There he met the eminent Senator K. P. Pobedonostsev, one of the most powerful and sinister influences on the internal policies of Russia during the reign of Alexander

III and part of the reign of Nicholas II. He remained friendly with Dostoevsky until the death of the author in 1881. A writer on jurisprudence and translator of *The Imitation of Christ*, Pobedonostsev detected much in Dostoevsky's religious and political convictions that was similar to his own and hence of value to the aims of the government. In *The Diary of a Writer* and in the whole ideological conception of *The Brothers Karamazov*, one can find traces of Pobedonostsev's religious and nationalist ideas, although their inception is apparent in Dostoevsky's works earlier. Indeed, it is difficult to say which man influenced the other in this strange and unequal friendship.

With *The Possessed* finished in the autumn of 1872, Dostoevsky's new conservative friends soon made use of him. He could be helpful in the government's struggle against the revolutionary-democratic movement, commonly called "nihilism." Prince Meshchersky needed an editor for his paper *The Citizen* (*Grazhdanin*). The salary was attractive and Dostoevsky accepted. Meshchersky was a writer of small ability and a faithful partisan of the conservative cause. His connections in government circles were very influential, and his unpopular paper enjoyed official protection.

Dostoevsky slaved at this task for about a year. It gave him an opportunity, in a weekly piece he contributed under the title of *The Diary of a Writer*, to develop many of the ideas on religion, politics, and social questions which had been occupying a prominent place in his letters and fiction over these last few years. He varied this procedure by occasional sketches, sometimes amounting to short stories, which lend a literary significance to *The Citizen*. These special weekly contributions he was later to continue as a separate publication. He quickly realized, however, that he had undertaken a thoroughly distasteful task in editing *The Citizen*. His employer, who had lofty notions about his own literary and journalistic ability, was a continual source of annoyance. Despite the reactionary policy of the paper, Dostoevsky tried at times to steer a course between the conservative and progressive camps. The break came when Meshchersky sent in an article which recommended that the government provide dormitories for university students. The real purpose behind this suggestion was the opportunity it would give the government of keeping the students under surveillance and thus prevent the spread of radical propaganda. The prince did not hesitate to state as much. Dostoevsky deleted the passage on surveillance, protesting that he had a reputation to maintain and also children of his own, and he added that such a practice was entirely contrary to his own convictions. The upshot of this difference of opinion was his resignation. He was heartily glad to be released, for apart from the uncongenial nature of the position, he was eager to get to work on another novel.

Financially, his situation was a bit brighter, for Dostoevsky's wife had set up a publishing business, issuing separate editions of his novels and making a substantial profit on them. He settled down to a quiet life with his growing family. During the summer months he was now able to hire a country house at Staraya Russa, some distance from the capital. Although he had passed his fiftieth year, he eagerly looked forward to much creative effort before he died. The uncertain life of the previous years was to return no more.

Even before he concluded his editorial work on *The Citizen* (April 1874), his thoughts had begun to dwell upon another novel. At this precise time he was favoured by a visit from Nekrasov, the distinguished editor of *National Notes*, one of the best periodicals of the day. This friend of his youth, whose enthusiastic encouragement some thirty years before had helped to launch *Poor Folk*, had long since parted company with him by becoming a leader in radical literary circles. He had now come to offer Dostoevsky a handsome rate for his next work. The meeting seemed to portend another shift in Dostoevsky's political sympathies, for *National Notes* was the principal progressive review. With his strong sense of moral obligation, Dostoevsky first insisted on offering the projected work to Katkov. This faithful publisher had just bought up *Anna Karenina* and hence did not feel able to commit herself to another advance. With some reluctance, Dostoevsky accepted Nekrasov's tempting offer. The work on this next novel, *A Raw Youth,* went along speedily. The first instalment appeared in the January number of *National Notes* in 1875, and the final part in December of the same year.

By general consent *A Raw Youth* is usually ranked beneath the four famous novels, a position all the more surprising since it was written almost at the height of Dostoevsky's greatest creative period. Turgenev, whose reactions may have been somewhat biased by the treatment accorded him in *The Possessed,* utterly damned the work as psychological excavation and sour stuff. Contemporary criticism was by no means so harsh—the reception of *A Raw Youth* was not unfavourable. Yet the fact remains that it is the least read of all his full-length novels. Only in recent times, in Soviet Russia, has an interest in it been revived, and largely for reasons not connected with its indubitable, although unsustained, literary merits.

What makes the novel particularly interesting for students of Dostoevsky's creative process is a special treatment of the ambivalence that had dominated so many of his characters up to this point. In several passages he theorizes on emotional dualism and presents such pointed examples of its manifestations that there can no longer be any doubt concerning this pervasive psychological influence in the whole course of his creative efforts.

The Dostoevskian quality of inwardness, however, is noticeably lacking in the novel. The customary concern of his characters with profound social, religious, and political problems, while occasionally evident on the surface, never penetrates to the core of their relations to life. Action does not develop into thought but often becomes an end in itself. This failure, no doubt, arises from the absence of an "idea" which in the masterpieces provides the dynamics of thought and contributes so much to the artistic integration of the total production.

The genesis of *A Raw Youth* throws some light upon its complex structure. In *The Diary of a Writer* for January 1876, Dostoevsky tells us something about the origin of the story:

> When Nikolai Alekseevich Nekrasov invited me to write a novel for *National Notes* a year and a half ago, I was just about to begin my 'Fathers and Children,' but I called a halt, and thank God for it: I was not ready. Meanwhile, I wrote *A Raw Youth*,—this first trial-flight of my thoughts. But there the child had already emerged from childhood, and appeared simply as an unfledged youth, timidly and then boldly desirous of quickly taking his first step in life. I took an innocent soul, yet one already touched with the terrible possibility of corruption, with an early hatred for his insignificance and 'accidentalness,' and with that wideness with which a soul still pure consciously entertains vice in his thoughts, nourishes it in his heart, and is caressed by it in his furtive yet audacious and wild dreams—all this naturally connected with his strength, his reason, and even more truthfully, with God. These are all the abortions of society, the 'uprooted' members of 'uprooted' families.[1]

The "Fathers and Children," which he put aside for *A Raw Youth,* may possibly refer to an early design of *The Brothers Karamazov.* For the general theme of the new novel, however, and for the conception of the hero, Dostoevsky once again dips into the plan of "The Life of a Great Sinner." In fact, the sketch of this plan in the notebooks was no doubt directly drawn upon, including even minor details, for the first part of *A Raw Youth.* The novel is cast in the form of the memoirs of the hero, Arkadi Dolgoruki, and the extensive action covers about a year in the precisely planned time-sequence. Dolgoruki is the illegitimate son of Versilov by one of his house serfs. Up to the age of twenty-one, when the story opens, he has scarcely seen his parents. His lonely school days at Moscow, inspired by Dostoevsky's own childhood experiences, had been a brutal existence. The stigma of his birth and his hypersensitive nature bring down on him the taunts and cruelty of both teachers and students. An only solace is his "idea." He has a scheme to become fabulously wealthy simply by practising the self-denial of a miser; he even makes several tests of his ability to go hungry and is convinced that he has the strength of will to achieve his objective. At the conclusion of his schooling, a summons to St. Petersburg from his father fits in with his plans. In the capital he finds Versilov and his mother and sister living in a poverty-stricken condition. He has an intense desire to ferret out everything about his mysterious father. Both a yearning for the parental affection so long denied him and a feeling of hate for a father who has cruelly neglected him possess the son.

The general theme mentioned in the quotation above is abandoned at this point. In the remainder of the novel, the emergence of the Raw Youth into society and his struggle between the forces of good and evil receive only an adventitious development. What there is of the characterization of Dolgoruki, however, is presented with an extraordinary awareness of the thoughts, confusion, bravado, sensitiveness, and idealism of the boy and adolescent. There is an appealing freshness about the picture which Dostoevsky always seemed capable of invoking in his treatment of childhood and youth. Towards the end of the first part, the tendency to overload his productions begins to manifest itself, and soon he almost strangles the plot in the excessive motivation forced upon him by the profusion of new characters. Only in one other novel has he so many characters and yet so few that leave a lasting impression on the mind of the reader.

In a letter to his wife he remarked despairingly that there were four novels in *A Raw Youth*, and this is virtually true. Besides the theme already mentioned, at least three more well-defined ones are introduced, and a fifth is adumbrated. The part of Versilov, who is a widower, is narrated at some length. He had taken the hero's mother, Sofiya Andreevna, abroad on his restless wanderings. There he had vainly fallen in love with a beautiful married woman, Katerina Akhmakova. Back in St. Petersburg, in a ruined condition, he appears to have forgotten this affair until Dolgoruki develops a passion for the same Katerina Akhmakova. This fact awakens Versilov's former feeling for her, and a love-duel takes place between father and son. It ends only when Dolgoruki falls desperately ill and Versilov wounds himself in an attempted suicide.

The third theme involves old Prince Sokolsky, the doddering father of Katerina. The legitimate daughter of Versilov, Anna Andreevna, schemes to marry the old man for his money, but she is opposed by Katerina, who is entirely dependent upon her father. The fourth theme concerns an affair between Dolgoruki's own sister, Liza, and Sergei, the son of the old prince. Dolgoruki becomes friendly with Sergei and takes money from him at first, unaware of the fact that he has seduced his sister. Sergei eventually falls into the hands of sharpers and ends in prison.

The device that Dostoevsky employs to connect these separate subjects is the ancient one of the mysterious letter. In this respect he may well have been influenced by the similar device in Lesage's *Gil Blas*, a work very much on his mind, if we may judge from remarks in his notebooks during the time he was writing *A Raw Youth*. Dolgoruki has a letter sewed in his clothes which has come into his possession by chance. It had been sent by Katerina Akhmakova to her lawyer some time before, and in it she requests legal advice as to whether her queer father may not be put away in an insane asylum. All the chief characters scheme to obtain the letter—Katerina, because if it falls into the hands of her father she fears he will cut her off without a kopek; Anna Andreevna, because it will enable her to end the daughter's control over her father and remove this obstacle to her marriage with him; and Versilov, since possession of it may force Katerina to submit to him. Finally, Dolgoruki prizes the document because it places the beautiful Katerina in his power.

About this letter Dostoevsky spins a bewildering web of intrigue. Once in St. Petersburg, Dolgoruki soon forgets his plan to obtain great wealth, succumbs to the temptations of the city, and turns into a veritable dandy. An old school friend takes him to a meeting at the house of Dergachov, where he meets Kraft and Vasin, who are very tenuously connected with the plot of the novel. In this incident Dostoevsky once again comes to grips with the radical movement. The meeting is made up of revolutionary conspirators, and the Raw Youth listens to their arguments and attempts to confute their views.

The whole incident is based upon an actual case, the Dolgushin trial, which took place in July 1874. It is known that Dostoevsky assiduously followed the newspaper accounts of this group of radicals, who were charged with the dissemination of proclamations designed to provoke rebellion. The parallel with the Nechaev affair is striking, and some of the convicted men had actually been involved in the earlier conspiracy. Dolgushin is the model for Dergachov, and several other principals and certain of the details in the newspaper reports were made use of in the characters and situations in the novel.

In the original plan of *A Raw Youth*, it is very likely that the Dolgushin affair was intended to play as large a part as the Nechaev conspiracy in *The Possessed*. It has been conjectured that the chief psychological aspect of Dolgoruki, emphasized in the first part of the novel—his desire to obtain great wealth in order to avenge himself on society—corresponds exactly to the feature that Dostoevsky later attributed to Nekrasov, the radical editor of *National Notes*.[2] That is, Dolgoruki, cast in the image of Nekrasov, was to become a member of the Dolgushin group of conspirators. The reason why this scheme was abandoned and the whole incident cut down to a minor, almost digressive, chapter of the novel is not difficult to ascertain. From his letters, it is clear that Dostoevsky worried excessively over the possibiltiy of Nekrasov's objecting to the unsympathetic treatment of progressive themes in *A Raw Youth*. If he had handled the Dolgushin affair in as extensive and hostile a manner as the Nechaev conspiracy, Nekrasov would most certainly have been obliged to reject the novel for *National Notes*, a leading radical organ.

The surprising fact is that Dostoevsky portrays these radicals almost as heroes, at least compared with those "devils" he had depicted in *The Possessed*. Unlike the mad gathering of nihilists in the previous novel, the meeting at Dergachov's house seems to exude that Christian Utopianism and humanitarian ideology of Dostoevsky's youth. The leaders of these radicals are described as selfless, serious, intellectual reformers who willingly suffer for the cause of humanity. In his attempt to refute their arguments, Dolgoruki is clearly worsted. Although Dostoevsky may have toned down this section because he feared Nekrasov would edit it, it is more likely that his treatment of it indicates a change in his views from the reactionary stand in *The Possessed*. Subsequent facts seem to bear this out. At all events, he could not expect the approval of his conservative friends, such as Pobedonostsev and Meshchersky, for this aspect of the novel.

The mysterious letter leads Dolgoruki into a variety of adventures. He secretly enjoys the power over Katerina which the letter gives him. She treats him disdainfully at first, but when she suspects that he has the letter, she encourages his youthful ardour. His feeling for this beautiful woman is a mixed one: he idolizes her on the one hand and imagines the noble gesture he will make by voluntarily turning over the document and relieving her anxiety; then her haughty nature provokes his hatred and he longs to humble her. There is a dualism in him which is not fully brought out, for after the early part of the novel, he ceases to be the central figure. In an unusual dream his dual thoughts are strongly suggested. In much of his fiction Dostoevsky employs the dream with artistic effectiveness and with almost a scientific understanding of its psychological implications. Dolgoruki has fallen into the power of Lambert, an old school friend in league with blackmailers who finally steal the letter. In his dreams Lambert appears and Dolgoruki perceives that he intends to blackmail Katerina. She, too, appears, but completely transformed; she makes shameless advances to him which he reciprocates with an agonizing thrill, continually urged on by Lambert. When he awakes, he realizes that he has been secretly imagining the idealized Katerina as a wanton creature, and that all this time he has been subconsciously desiring her willing submission. His relations with Versilov are determined by this dualism to an even greater extent. While manifesting hatred for his father, he protects his honour and strives to create in his own mind an image which will magnify the virtues of the man whose affections he desires.

Very early in the novel, however, the interest shifts from the Raw Youth to the strange character of Versilov and to his stranger love for Katerina. Versilov is a composite figure in whom may be found traits of various characters in the other novels. In the main, his mysterious personality recalls the enigmatic Stavrogin, and he is developed in very much the same indirect manner—by flashbacks, second-hand accounts, and by the effect he has on other people. Like Stavrogin again, the final portrait leaves an incomplete but vaguely powerful impression.

Versilov is a Russian nobleman. As in the case of
Stavrogin, unmentionable acts are connected with his
name, but they seem to be largely the products of
rumour. After a crowded youth of adventure, he suddenly abandons Russia for Europe, because he is a victim, so he says, of the melancholy of the upper class.
Dolgoruki jumps to the conclusion that he does this
in order to take part in revolutionary propaganda
abroad. Versilov, however, seems incapable of anything deeper than a light cynicism in matters political.
He believes that no class is so fond of idleness as the
toiling masses, and that the delights of labour have
been invented by the idle from virtuous motives. At
all events, he intends to stick to the ideals of his class.

In the course of his wanderings through Europe,
Versilov appears to have lived through a period of
religious asceticism, but the nature of his faith is
clouded with almost as much uncertainty as his political convictions. Vasin's explanation of the report that
Versilov had once turned to God is singularly perti-
nent. He is a very proud individual, says Vasin, and
proud people "turn to God to avoid doing homage to
men . . . to bow before God is not so humiliating.
From them come the most fervent of believers—or to
speak more accurately—the most fervently desirous
of believing; but they take this desire for belief itself."
(*A Raw Youth*, Part I, Chapter III, v) This acute observation might well be accepted as an unconscious
revelation of Dostoevsky's own relation to religion. It
certainly is the author speaking when he has Versilov
declare to his son that the idea of virtue without Christ
is the idea of all modern civilization.

More specifically, Versilov admits that he is a philosophic deist who has a kind of sentimental attachment
for God, as though he felt it necessary to be a Christian
in order to appreciate the beauty and significance of
life. He cannot understand how man can live without
God, but one gathers the impression that he falls back
upon Him as upon an ancient tradition, because he

fears the brutality that change inevitably brings. Dostoevsky, too, feared the bloodletting in revolution, although he would be willing to admit that change involved the unmistakable striving towards ideals which were compatible with his own. Christ in his eyes was a reformer and a radical, but he effected change through meekness, love, and faith, not by violence.

In his opinions concerning the relation of Russia to Europe, Versilov also projects one of Dostoevsky's favourite ideas. The Russian is unique, says Versilov, in that he is a perfect cosmopolitan. Europe stands on the brink of destruction because of her revolutionary materialism and denial of Christ. For the Russian, however, Europe is a second fatherland, and he loves its treasures of art, its ancient relics, and its whole history. Europe itself has turned its back on all these things and is doomed, but Russia, which lives not for itself but for the whole world, will in the end lead Europe to the kingdom of God and to salvation.

Some conception of this future world harmony is reflected in a remarkable dream of Versilov which is inspired by Claude Lorrain's picture "Acis and Galatea." He dreams of a corner of the Grecian Archipelago. It appears to him as the cradle of Europe, the "Golden Age," set back some thousands of years. This earthly paradise, fixed in the smiling blue waves and ringed by a flowery shore, fills his soul with delight. The gods come down to live with this splendid race of men who spend their days in simple-hearted joy and love. Happiness and innocence reign, and when Versilov wakes his eyes are wet with tears, and he is filled with a love of humanity that he had never experienced before. This vision of the "Golden Age" is lifted almost word for word from the unpublished "Confession of Stavrogin" in *The Possessed*. The vision haunted Dostoevsky, and in one form or another it appears in nearly all his works in the last period of his creative life. Even in the days of his youth, he had seized upon the idea, no doubt influenced by the philosophy

of history of Belinsky and Herzen and by the Hegelian
synthesis of the two opposing cultures of the ancient
and Christian worlds. His ideal paradise is inhabited
by people whose source of love and happiness is the
"living life," a favourite formula, and the "idea-
feeling" which stood at the end of all his visions of
earthly bliss. The "living life" is the opposite of the
rational life and amounts to a universal wholeness
through feeling, through experiencing in a purely
sensory way the joy and goodness and spirituality of
existence. He never attempts to define this term with
any exactness, but it is clear that the conception is
similar to Rousseau's *exister, pour nous c'est sentir.*
Although Rousseau is rarely mentioned by Dostoevsky, he unquestionably had a profound influence on
his thought. Rousseau's emphasis upon the innate
goodness of man's natural feelings as opposed to the
destructive powers of reason became a central point in
Dostoevsky's theorizing. To be sure, he adapted the
idea to the problems of his own age, which he believed
to be victimized by a rationalistic or materialistic posi-
tivism. The goal of society, he felt, was incompatible
with enlightenment and the development of the mind.
The basic principle of life and human history he found
in suffering and compassion, which are the source of
all noble impulses and social virtues. Like Rousseau,
he identifies the rule of reason with the perversions of
modern civilization. His "Golden Age" is pushed back
to the dawn of mankind, when all men are happy because they are equal. The "living life" is the rule of
their existence; they care nothing for possessions, and
love for each other dwells in their hearts. Again like
Rousseau, he carried this conception into his ideas
about Christianity which both writers understood
to be founded on love and veneration before the personality of Christ. Out of this same opposition to rationalism came the conviction of both that the highest
virtues exist among simple people. One could describe
the living experiences of nearly all of Dostoevsky's

great characters as dominated by either reason or feeling, or by both in the dualistic natures of his Doubles.

For Versilov, the "living life" is an ideal which has evaded him, but he believes that it is embodied in the woman he madly loves, Katerina Akhmakova. If the novel could be said to have any central theme, it is this strange affair between Versilov and Katerina. She is even more enigmatic than he, and in the whole course of the novel she is never fully described nor does she appear above a half-dozen times. It is possible that Dostoevsky intended her to represent the ideal woman, but her vague personality contains little that is ideal and less of the "living life" that Versilov imagines to be the principal factor of her existence. Indeed, her actions seem to be dictated by rather sordid motives which are in no way mitigated by the mysterious effect which her supposed perfection appears to exercise on everyone.

Versilov had met Katerina abroad under peculiar circumstances. She was not yet a widow, and out of his deep love for her he had taken the blame for an unsavoury act connected with a member of her family. We are not told much of his love, except that it was manifested in strange ways and eventually ran its course. Only when his son expresses a boyish devotion to this imperious beauty, shortly after the novel opens, does Versilov's old love flare up, and then we are left in no doubt as to its nature. It is a fierce passion compounded of love and hate, for he is a Double, and the whole course of his baffling behaviour is explicable only in terms of a deeply rooted dualism.

In connection with the characterization of Versilov, Dostoevsky makes very clear for the first time the underlying principles that have governed his long preoccupation with split personality in his fiction. He leads up to his explanation of dualism by a statement that has been much quoted. After his revealing dream, Dolgoruki says: "It has always been a mystery, and I have marvelled a thousand times at that faculty of man (and for the most part, it seems, of the Russian) of cherishing in his soul his loftiest ideal side by side with the greatest baseness, and all quite sincerely." (Part III, Chapter III) Although hostile critics have sometimes accepted this remark as an apt characterization of the Russian, it is a generalization that will hold true for all men and was no doubt prompted by Dostoevsky's clear understanding of his own nature.

In previous Doubles the human impulses that impelled to dual actions have unconsciously manifested themselves or have been only vaguely understood. Versilov plainly recognizes these impulses. He says in one place: "Yes, I am split in two mentally and I am terribly afraid of this. It is just as though your double were standing beside you; you yourself are sensible and rational, but this other person beside you wishes without fail to do something senseless and occasionally something funny; and suddenly you notice that you wish to do this funny thing, and God knows why; that is, you want to against your will, as it were; although you fight against it with all your might, you want to do it." (Part III, Chapter X, ii) At this very moment Versilov's second self is prompting him to do an evil action which he cannot resist. He has just entered the house, full of joy, and presents a nosegay to the faithful woman who has lived with him and whose husband has just died. He picks up the ikon of this man and admits that he has a longing to break it. Suddenly he smashes it to bits, a fearful sacrilegious act that symbolizes for him a complete severance with his past life with this woman.

Dolgoruki, in turn, analyses his father's dualism: "But the 'Double' I do accept unquestionably. What exactly is a Double? The Double, at least according to a medical book of a certain expert, which I purposely read afterwards, is nothing other than the first stage of a serious mental derangement, which may lead to something very bad. And in that scene at my mother's, Versilov himself had explained to us the 'duality' of his will and feelings with strange frankness." (Part III, Chapter XIII)

It is only this dualism that makes plausible Versilov's curiously mixed feelings for his son and his love-hate relations with Katerina which conclude with his mad attempt to murder her. It explains his love for Sofiya Andreevna, the mother of the Raw Youth, who is a perfect foil for Katerina. Sofiya is the typical Meek character, and through her suffering and spirituality she appeals to those very qualities in Versilov's nature which are negated by his passion for Katerina. His divided soul is further emphasized by the studied contrast between him and Makar Ivanovich, the thoroughly integrated and deeply religious husband of Sofiya. A former house serf of Versilov, he had humbly acquiesced to the master's making a mistress of his wife. After years of wandering as a holy pilgrim, he returns to the home of Versilov and Sofiya to die. He is a kind of peasant prototype of that aristocratic symbol of moral perfectibility and goodness—Prince Myshkin, and it is very likely that the image was suggested by the hero of Nekrasov's famous poem *Vlas*. More than any of the characters in the novel, he is a representative of the "living life" which Versilov vainly longs for. Dolgoruki admires in him a "seemliness" that amounts to a dignified pattern of life based on the Christ-like virtues of humility, selflessness, and saintly deeds. It is interesting that the simple philosophy he preaches is instantly recognized by Dolgoruki as a kind of primitive communism which, as mentioned elsewhere in this study, seems to have been Dostoevsky's ideal, the "Golden Age" of a distraught civilization. Unlike Myshkin, however, the meek and pious Makar Ivanovich has achieved his blissful serenity by completely removing himself from the world of suffering men. Free from the conflicting passions of Versilov, he performs the function of a mere symbol of a radiant way of life.

From literary examples and semiscientific studies,

Dostoevsky no doubt picked up considerable information on the subject of dualism, but modern psychological investigations of emotional ambivalence, however, had not yet been published. On the other hand, his intense interest in the theme must have grown out of a realization of the dualism in his own nature, and the large part it plays in his creative process was perhaps both a conscious and subconscious reflection of this fact. His awareness of conflicting forces in his life is explicitly stated in a letter to a female correspondent in 1880. She had written to ask his advice about the dual impulses she experienced, for she feared that they continually led her to commit reprehensible acts. He replied in part:

But now to what you *have* told me of your inward duality. That trait is indeed common to all . . . that is, all who are not wholly commonplace. Nay, it is common to human nature, though it does not evince itself so strongly in all as it does in you. It is precisely on this ground that I cannot but regard you as a twin soul, for your inward duality corresponds most exactly to my own. It causes at once great torment and great delight. Such duality simply means that you have a strong sense of yourself, much aptness for self-criticism, and an innate feeling for your moral duty to yourself. If your intelligence were less developed, if you were more limited, you would be less sensitive, and would not possess that duality. Rather the reverse: in its stead would have appeared great arrogance. Yet such duality is a great torment . . . Do you believe in Christ and in his Commandments? If you believe in Him (or at least have a strong desire to do so), then give yourself wholly up to Him; the pain of your duality will be thereby alleviated, and you will find the true way out—but belief is first of all in importance.[3]

If Dostoevsky had mentioned "great meekness," as well as "great arrogance," as an alternative state of being in the absence of dualism, he would have suggested both facets of the Double which, when taken separately, seem to dominate the other two types in his creative range—the Self-Will and the Meek characters. Belief in Christ he regarded as the ultimate solvent of the conflicting forces in the Double, or even a "strong desire" to believe, a qualification that is eloquently indicative of his own position. Such a solution was unconvincingly indicated in the case of Raskolnikov; it was to be the saving grace in the struggle between good and evil in the nameless hero of the plan of "The Life of a Great Sinner."

As Versilov recovers from the wound which he has inflicted upon himself, the lower, evil side of his dualism miraculously vanishes. Dostoevsky seems intent upon a happy ending. Something of the gentle nature and religious fervour of the old pilgrim, Makar Ivanovich, has entered Versilov's soul. He is only "one half of the former Versilov," remarks Dostoevsky by way of suggesting that the struggle is over, the impulse to evil dead. This sudden shift from the conflict of the Double to the quiescence and submissiveness of the Meek character is no more convincing than the transformation of Raskolnikov at the end of *Crime and Punishment*. Religion was not the answer to the problem of the Double. Reformation of human nature in art or in reality is rarely satisfactory. Dostoevsky's solution was a wishful one, and he seemed pointedly to recognize the fact in his great Double—Ivan Karamazov.

20

The Diary of a Writer

Dostoevsky was rarely satisfied with his writing. The high hopes that sustained his creative spirit throughout the period of composition had nearly always vanished by the time the last word was set down. For him, art was a medium for conveying the wisdom of life, the emotions of the soul, and in this respect he invariably felt that he had failed to express everything that was in his mind and imagination. *A Raw Youth* was no exception. The finished work seemed like the cold ashes of all that had burned within him when he set out to write.

For several years after the appearance of *A Raw Youth*, Dostoevsky did not undertake another novel. They were quiet years, alternating between the pleasures of a happy family life and occasional and regretted trips to Ems to take the cure. He was now very much of a celebrity and often invited to literary soirées and to the homes of aristocratic families. During this period he revived his old column in *The Citizen* as a separate publication. It began to appear as a monthly in January 1876, and it ran until 1877, when he dropped it in order to start work on *The Brothers Karamazov*. A few more numbers appeared in 1880 and 1881. He had several aims in this unusual venture, of which the financial was not the least important. The publication was extremely successful, and at its height it had some six thousand subscribers, a convincing testimony of Dostoevsky's popularity. He had always felt the necessity of keeping in touch with contemporary events in order to store his mind with the material for imaginative writing. *The Diary* obliged him to inform himself on current events and national questions. Finally, he desired an outlet for his own thoughts on significant problems of the day, for he had begun to feel his importance in the Russian world and sought a following for his ideas.

After it had run for about a year, he wrote: "The chief purpose of *The Diary* has been to explain, as far as possible, the idea of our national spiritual independence, and to point it out, as far as possible, in the current facts as they present themselves." [1] This statement, however, is a poor description of the varied contents. His original intention, apparently, had been to write up impressions of contemporary happenings which seemed important to an observant diarist. To a considerable extent, the publication fulfils this function with its accounts of court trials, suicides, spiritualism, and conditions of factory children. *The Diary* was also a medium for expressing his own ideas on the broad social, political, and religious questions which meant so much to him, and among such articles he abundantly interspersed literary reminiscences, autobiographical material, and short stories.

There is a tendency to regard *The Diary* as mere journalism and even bad journalism. To be sure, there is a good deal of slipshod writing and loose thinking,

but it is well to remember that journalism and art
were closely allied in his mind. For him *The Diary* was
a means of preparing for his next novel, and as source-
material for *The Brothers Karamazov* it is of the first
importance. It is a curious anomaly that he is often
praised as a powerful thinker in the novels and condemned as a muddle-headed prophet in his journalism, although he is often dealing with the same ideas
in both. The psychological truth which we admire so
much in the mouths of his imaginary characters fails
to impress us as logical truth when he expresses it in
his publicist writings. The difficulty arises from the
fact that he remains the artist in his journalism in
which he brings to the development of controversial
ideas the attitude of the omniscient author. In dealing
with history, he ignores the facts or substitutes for
them those half-truths which Shatov had bitterly de-
nounced in *The Possessed* as despots before whom all
do homage with love and superstition. He offers up
sweeping generalizations on political and social questions with practically no concern for the economic factors that condition them. In his vehement comparisons
between Russia and the nations of Western Europe,
these countries take on almost a mythical existence,
the result of poetic rhapsodizing rather than rational
comprehension. Like the characters in his novels, he
endows these nations with personalities and subjects
them to a kind of psychological analysis. Often he
deals in paradoxes, and consistency in point of view is
unhesitatingly sacrificed for moral principles.

From many articles in *The Diary* it is clear that the
reforming zeal which had inspired the radical activities of Dostoevsky's youth never deserted him; it was
directed into different channels, but it lived on, sustained by lofty moral feelings. His prison experiences
had led him to discover the Russian masses and their
belief in Russian Orthodoxy. However imperfectly
he may have understood the social and economic
needs of the people and the abuses of the Church, his

faith in the saving power of both became the motivating factor behind all his later theorizing. In a sense, the emancipation of the serfs helped to crystallize this faith and led him to oppose the Russian world to the Western world.

The significant points in Dostoevsky's attitude towards the major powers of Western Europe had already been expressed by such characters as Myshkin, Shatov, and Versilov. In *The Diary* he further defines this attitude, embroiders it with the half-truths of history, and casts it in the form almost of a manifesto. Roman Catholicism, he declares, perverted the Christian idea at the very outset by adopting the principle of force of the ancient Roman Empire. Instead of spiritual unity on a moral basis, Catholicism attempts to achieve unity by force. For universal service the Catholic Church has substituted universal subjugation. France, he feels, is the incarnation of this idea, and although German Lutheranism effectively protested against Roman Catholicism, its protest has remained essentially negative, for it has no profound spiritual values to offer for the faith it has displaced.

In the long course of history, however, movements have arisen in Western Europe directed against the attempt of Catholicism to bring about universal subjugation. The bourgeoisie raised the banner of "liberty or death." After they had won a victory over Catholicism, the bourgeoisie in turn appropriated the same principles of rule—conquest and force. In modern times this situation resulted in the rise of the socialists against the bourgeoisie. Political socialism, Dostoevsky maintains, amounts merely to the spoliation of property-owners. It is devoid of any moral basis, and the very equality it struggles to achieve it would obtain by force. It is the equality of dictatorship. In this respect, atheistic socialism does not differ from Catholicism and may even be said to be in alliance with it. Although socialism repudiates the great bourgeois culture of Europe, it has no new cultural ideals of its own to offer. In a kind of apocalyptic vision, he sees Western Europe as a huge armed camp, doomed to self-annihilation in a struggle of unparalleled fierceness and bloodshed.

The fate of Europe, Dostoevsky affirms, belongs to Russia, for Russians only possess the capacity to be brothers to all peoples. Although he makes it clear in his articles that he is worried over the revolutionary tendencies of the younger generation, the incipient growth of capitalism, and the social evils that result, yet he is convinced that these conditions, borrowed from the dying West, will vanish. Russia has no English lords, no French bourgeoisie, and he is sure that it will have no proletariat. The real danger springs from the intellectuals and their contending theories. In his nationalistic fervour, however, he sees a way to reconcile the intellectuals, a notion that he had favoured ever since his youth. The extreme views of both Westerners and Slavophiles he believed to be wrong. Because of its deprivation of the great cultural heritage of the Renaissance, he felt it necessary for Russia to turn to Europe for advanced scientific knowledge and civilizing influences. Europe is a second fatherland for Russians, and only by knowing European thought will Russia be able to understand its own weaknesses and learn its world significance. In fact, he maintains that Europe has actually created the Russian intelligentsia and brought to it a clear comprehension of the country's popular beginnings and its mission of humble universal service. Westerners and Slavophiles are alike, then, in their intellectual beginnings. The Slavophiles err in believing that Russia must utterly eschew all European influence, and the Westerners make the mistake of thinking that Europe is a model for Russia. In reality, Dostoevsky claims, both parties have the same objective—the future world destiny of Russia— which demands that they should unite their forces. Their primary effort should be directed towards bridging the artificial chasm that exists between them and the Russian masses, for each is vitally necessary to the other. Without the intellectuals, the masses remain elemental and do not perceive their mission of renewing humanity, and by the same token the intellectuals, without the masses, are unable to achieve their ideal of uttering a new word to the world. The immediate task of the intellectuals is to raise the masses from their depths of unself-consciousness to national self-consciousness. Those socialists and liberals among the intellectuals who are filled with scorn for the masses and believe the Western European way of life is wise and beautiful are the real scourge of Russia. They have lost touch with the national sources and will be instinctively opposed by the masses for this betrayal of their birthright.

The manner in which the Russian people will win their foremost place in the sun is not made clear in *The Diary*. Practical details are not allowed to stand in the way of Dostoevsky's broad generalizations. His glowing pictures of Russia's destiny are the stuff of a seer's imagination. Behind them is his conception of the "Golden Age," the "living life," the blessed Utopia of happiness and brotherly love which his Meek characters ecstatically envision and towards which his passion-racked Doubles strive in vain. He keeps within the outer limits of reality only as a kind of concession to journalism. There is much that disturbs him in the national life, but all these immediate abuses fade to insignificance before the distant prospect of his imaginary "Golden Age."

Dostoevsky's whole hope is placed in the masses and in their faith in the Russian Christ, which has taught them self-perfection as individuals and as a nation. It is self-perfection alone, he maintains, that preserves the organism of nationality. The Eastern Church in its early stages, unlike the Roman Catholic Church, had separated itself from the government and hence has maintained its allegiance to the true Christ and to Christian self-perfection. The Russian government, which has endured so much suffering through the ages, has raised itself up to an acceptance of the social formula of Christ and is at one with the people and its religion. Dostoevsky was not uncritical of the government, but he deplored those forces which strove to alienate it from the people. If there were to be any democracy, he felt that it must start from the top rather than from the bottom, for he believed implicitly in the ancient Russian tradition of the oneness of the tsar and the people. "The tsar is their father," he declared. "For the people, the tsar is not some external power, not the power of some conqueror or other (as was so, for example, among the dynasties of the former kings of France), but an all-national, all-unifying power, which the people themselves have wished, which has grown in their own heart, and which they have loved . . . For the people, the tsar is the incarnation of themselves, of all their ideas, their hopes and beliefs." [2]

With fiery conviction Dostoevsky never wearies of repeating in *The Diary* his faith in the "God-bearing" Russian people. He sees in them the only possible solution, not only for Russia, but for Europe and for all humanity. In the togetherness and spiritual inseparability of the masses, and in their unity with the monarch, exists a great healing power for the ills of the world. In the masses, he declares, one finds true Russian socialism, which is not modern communism with its mechanical forms and materialistic way of life, but national universal unity in the name of Christ. This great national faith of the people will solve all things where the radicals and intellectuals will fail. Its moral socialism is not the socialism of darkness and horror, of the bitter class struggle of revolt and bloodshed. It is the socialism of love and meekness, of humanity and individual holiness. It will create a heavenly city on earth in which peasant and noble, merchant and landowner will forget their differences in a zealous union of brotherly love in the Russian Christ of suffering and forgiveness. All will embrace one another, and like the race of men in the "Golden Age," they will live on the bosom of the joyous earth and among the fields and woods; and by the running streams they will sing hymns to God in which they will worship the one salvation, the one eternal truth.

This mystical treatment of the messianic mission of Russia assumes a practical direction, in fact an imperialistic one, in Dostoevsky's later articles in *The Diary* on Pan-Slavism. His idea of pan-humanity was an active programme of Russian life and history which aimed at nothing less than the general peace of the world. Brotherly love that removes all contradictions he felt to be the peculiar genius of the Russian people, who were thus the only people capable of effecting the universal unity of mankind. In fulfilling this mission, he believed that Russia's thirst for universal service for the sake of mankind would enable it to become the servant of all in order to effect universal conciliation. The nation's true greatness derives from this unique aptitude for universal service; it is Russia's new message that will remake the world. When Russia declared war on the Turks in 1877, Dostoevsky combined the idea of universal service with what he believed to be Russia's mission to liberate the Slavs.

With something of the misdirected moral fervour with which Americans entered the Great War to save the world for democracy, Dostoevsky firmly pronounced that Russia fought the Turks in order to preserve the life and liberty of the oppressed Southern Slavs. He even endowed the conflict with a significance far beyond this. His country was fighting not only for the unity of its Slav brothers, but for a spiritual alliance of all those who believed that Russia, at the head of a united Slavdom, would bring by its self-sacrifice a message of universal service to mankind. He was aware that this glorification of a particular war was hardly in keeping with the Christ-like ethics he was accustomed to preach. His defence was curiously pragmatic, not unlike the present-day com-

munistic justification of violent means if the end makes
for the greater good of the greater number. War for an
idea, he insists, not a selfish war designed for the coer-
cion or conquest of others, raises the spirit of a nation
and contributes to an increase of brotherly love and to
the unity of man. Blood spilt in the resistance to evil
by violence is an antidote for the selfishness and
rank individualism encouraged by peaceful self-
satisfaction.

The greater good that would follow from the successful prosecution of this war Dostoevsky envisaged
in a prophetic and almost metaphysical manner. With
the defeat of Turkey would come the unification of all
Slavs, which would be an intermediate step towards
a higher aim. The Slavs, through the medium of the
Orthodox faith, which alone has preserved the image
of Christ in all its purity, would then be in a position
to fulfil their historic mission. This mission is essentially a religious one. Orthodoxy will be brought into
conflict with Catholicism and Protestantism; the Russian Eastern question will develop into a world-wide
question. The war will spread, and it will be better so,
for the victory of the East will undoubtedly save Europe from a tenfold greater spilling of blood. The face
of Europe will be changed, and much that is new and
progressive will begin in human relations. Russia's
mission of regenerating the world through universal
service and the Orthodox faith will finally be accomplished.

Dostoevsky was a nationalist and a patriot, but in
both he went beyond the limits of historic reality. It is
primarily as a religious thinker that his views on international affairs must be interpreted. The curious fact
is that if one substituted communism for his conception of the mission of the Orthodox faith, and world
revolution for his notion of a Pan-Slavic war against
Europe, the identity of his whole position with that of
modern Soviet Russia would be striking. Even more
startling as prophecy, in the light of the present world

situation, are certain of his statements regarding Russia's relations with other European countries and its future historic path. In one article he foretells the alliance of socialism and Catholicism in a defeated France, for both have a common enemy outside— Germany. Germany, which had been partial to Russia in its war against the Turks, will require Russian aid in opposing the united forces of Catholic France and socialism.

In any case [he remarks] one thing seems clear: *We are necessary* to Germany even more than we think. And she needs us not for a momentary political union, *but forever.* The idea of united Germany is broad and dignified, and peers into the depths of centuries. What will Germany share with us?—its object is all Western humanity. She has ordained for herself the Western world of Europe, and she shall bring to it her own principles in place of the Roman and the Romanic principles, and in the future will become its leader, but to Russia she will leave the East. Thus two great people are destined to change the face of this world . . . One must believe that the friendship of Russia with Germany is not hypocritical, but firm, and that it will be strengthened more and more, spreading and growing gradually in the national consciousness of both nations . . . But whether or not we shall come in time to the aid of Germany, in any case Germany will count on us not as a temporary ally, but as an eternal one.[3]

At the end of *The Diary*, in 1881, Dostoevsky appears to have altered his conviction concerning the intermediary state of Russia's historic mission in bringing the new word to Western Europe. He feels that the time has come for Russia to turn towards Asia, and he paints a vivid picture of Russia's pioneering activities and eventual conquest of the rich East. "In Europe we were toadies and slaves, but in Asia we will be Europeans."[4] Once Russia has asserted her control over Asia, Austria will unite with Germany and together they will make war on France. This will be the occasion for Russia, with her new might, to conquer Turkey, capture Constantinople, and begin her mission of

bringing Orthodoxy and salvation to Western Europe.
As for England, he declares: "Nothing new we could
do would upset her, for she is already upset by what
she fears we might do. On the contrary, now we hold
her in confusion and ignorance in appraising the future, and she expects the worst from us. When she understands the real character of all our actions in Asia,
then, perhaps, many of her own fears will be les-
sened." [5]

In Dostoevsky's conception of the world-mission of
Russia, it is not difficult to perceive a reflection of the
dualism that is projected in the characters of his novels.
That is, all humanity for him divides itself into the peoples of the West, whose pride and self-will lead them
to support an ideal of universal conquest by force, and
the people of the East, who fulfil their ideal of universal service through meekness and submissiveness. In
any event, his entire understanding of the historical
and social process is rooted in this conviction of a life-
and-death struggle between two mutually exclusive
moral elements. Any interpretation of his doctrine that
under-estimates the predominance of the moral element would be false to its spirit and intention. The
course of governments today, whether they be democratic, communistic, or totalitarian, he would severely
criticize for their lack of moral values. The only socialism that he accepted was based on the moral feeling
of man, on his spiritual thirst for humanity, and his
recognition of the human personality and its freedom.
He rejected any political theory that placed its emphasis upon social organization at the expense of the moral
worth of the individual. In an article in *The Diary*, he
declared that social and civil ideals cannot exist apart
from moral ideals. It is foolish to suppose, he maintains, that man can develop a rational formula to take
care of his social ideals. "At the birth of every people,
of every nationality, the moral idea always preceded
the birth of every nationality and actually created it.
This moral idea always proceeded from mystical ideas,

from the conviction that man is eternal, that he is not simply an earthly animal, but joined with other worlds and with eternity." [6] In no sense does he preach a levelling doctrine. Everyone should do his best according to his ability—the peasant as a peasant, the intellectual as an intellectual. Equality is achieved through love, not through despotism. An optimistic belief in the innate goodness and love in man provided the basis for all his moral values. A conviction that is fulfilled according to command or to reason leads only to pride. One must do only that which the heart commands. Most important, he insisted, is to do everything from active love. In the final dual struggle of the individual and of humanity, his heart went out to the meek and the humble. Who wishes to be higher than all in the Kingdom of God shall serve all. This was the mission of the Russian people—universal service to achieve universal peace.

Dostoevsky's solution of Russia's destiny, as revealed in *The Diary*, is not free from doubts and uncertainties. In an article on spiritualism, he set down an observation that faithfully reflected his own habit of mind: "How clear it was made to me then, precisely through experience . . . what strength disbelief may find and develop in and for itself, in a given moment, entirely apart from your will, although in agreement with your secret wish. And the same is probably true of faith." [7] He wished to believe in the Russian Christ as the only path to salvation for all humanity. It was a faith developed almost apart from his will. To an equal degree, he did not wish to believe in the socialist revolution as the path to salvation. Yet he could never ignore the facts of his age which constantly undermined his faith and fed the dual impulses ingrained in his mind. There can be no question about the declared conservative direction and essential religiosity of his position, but to accept this as unequivocal would falsify a psychological factor of his nature. His normal state of mind was between belief and disbelief, and a

careful reading of *The Diary* reveals that in the matter
of the salvation of humanity he fluctuated between the
path of Christ and that of the socialist revolution,
which he identified with atheism.

The information in *The Diary* on this score is not
plentiful, but it is sufficient to indicate a definite sympathy, if only a psychological one, with the revolutionary thought so inimical to Dostoevsky's avowed
tendencies. The publication of *A Raw Youth* in Nekrasov's radical journal, the favourable treatment of
the revolutionists in this novel, and Versilov's communistic "Golden Age" point to a modification at least
of his bitter feeling against the radical movement as
expressed in *The Possessed*. This line of thought continues in *The Diary*, beginning with the statement of
his liberalism in the foreword to the 1876 issue. In several succeeding articles, he displays an unusual ani-
mosity towards the abuses of capitalism and towards
the landowners for their harsh treatment of the peasantry, and he reflects a vague awareness of the class
struggle in criticisms of the past and present oppression of workers and peasants, and of the misery of poor
children sweated in factories. One of the most noticeable indications of his wavering, however, is to be
found in a series of articles on literary figures. His attitude towards Belinsky, during his middle period of
reaction, had been almost violent. He had literally
charged him with being the father of the hated radical
thought that had resulted in the enormities of Nechaev
and his followers. In his treatment of Belinsky in *The
Diary*, coloured perhaps by recollections of the inspiration which the great critic had afforded him in his
youth, he sees in him more of the Slavophile than the
Westerner, a lover of Russia and an espouser, in intention, of her world destiny. Nekrasov, too, another
friend of his youth, whose radical sympathies had
alienated him, he now praises as a great poet and the
champion of the downtrodden peasant. Even for the
scorned Turgenev, the Turgenev of the early Utopian

socialism, he finds words of praise; and in an article on George Sand, who had deeply influenced him, he lauds her revolutionary spirit and ideals. In all this writing there seems to be an undercurrent of new sympathy for the radical hopes and ideals of his own youth before he was sent to Siberia. It would be unwise to exaggerate the significance of these various manifestations of renewed esteem for individuals whom he had resolutely turned against and for their thoughts which he had severely attacked. This changed attitude, however, is in striking contrast to his pointed antagonism towards revolutionary socialism as evinced in many articles in *The Diary* devoted to the world-mission of Russia. Even contemporary readers observed his dual approach, and if nothing else, it indicates his own uncertainty about the path of Christian socialism that he preached.

Although *The Diary* is employed largely as a medium for expressing Dostoevsky's opinions on a variety of historical and current problems, its importance as a repository of purely literary material is not inconsiderable. Apart from the valuable articles containing his literary reminiscences, and an extensive critique of Tolstoy's *Anna Karenina*, there are several sketches and short stories of unequal artistic merit, and in one or two instances they throw further light on his creative methods.

In the columns of *The Diary* that Dostoevsky contributed to *The Citizen* in 1873 are two tales. One of them, "Vlas," is suggested to him by a reading of Nekrasov's well-known poem of the same title, in which he portrays the great sinner Vlas travelling the countryside in search of salvation for his misdeeds. The poem reminds Dostoevsky of the story of another Vlas, who appears before a holy man bewailing the fact that he is eternally damned. In his village he had accepted a dare to perform anything asked of him. He was commanded to go to communion and preserve the sacrament instead of swallowing it. Then he was ordered to place the wafer on a post and shoot it. As he took aim, he suddenly saw before him the cross with the crucified Christ on it. He dropped the gun and fell unconscious. Dostoevsky uses this anecdote as a basis for a penetrating psychological analysis of the motives behind the actions of Vlas. Some of his observations on the terror experienced by the culprit recall his analysis of the feelings of Raskolnikov before the murder of the old moneylender. The figure of the conscience-stricken and suffering Vlas leads Dostoevsky into generalizations on his favourite theme—the Russian people. Commenting on the motive that prompted Vlas to attempt the terrible sacrilege, he remarks: "This precipitancy is especially striking, this impetuosity with which a Russian sometimes hastens to assert himself, in certain characteristic moments of his own or of the national life, to assert himself in a splendid or a filthy manner. Sometimes there is simply no restraint. Whether it be love or wine, debauchery, pride, envy—here a Russian will surrender himself to a supreme degree, ready to break with everything, to renounce all,—family, custom, God." [8] But while violating the very things he holds most sacred, the Russian also has the infinite capacity to suffer for his misdeeds in a passionate longing for salvation. "I think," he concludes, "the chief, the most rooted spiritual need of the Russian people is the need of suffering, habitual and unquenchable, everywhere and in everything. With this thirst for suffering, so it seems, it has been afflicted from time immemorial. This stream of suffering runs through its whole history, not only from external unhappiness and disaster, but it wells up from the very heart of the people. Even in its happiness there is unfailingly a portion of suffering among the Russian people, otherwise happiness for it is not complete." [9]

In another early issue of *The Diary* appeared a short story, "Bobok," which is little more than a sketch. A hack writer attends a funeral, and, resting on a gravestone in the cemetery, he hears the voices of two corpses playing at cards. Soon all the buried people round about join in the conversation. It appears that they have the power of consciousness in the grave for a certain length of time. The rest of the story concerns the remarks of the dead, who come from various walks of life, and Dostoevsky indulges in a macabre kind of humour and vitriolic satire in reporting their talk. A plebeian, a general, a kept girl, an engineer, a shameless society lady, and others chatter with extreme frankness about their existence on earth, revealing the debauchery, thieving, and false morality of their lives. It is a brief, sordid exposé of the human frailties which these wretches had overlaid with sophistication and the pose of respectability. The sniggering indecency mounts to a crescendo when suddenly they agree with delight to cast off all shame and tell every intimate detail of their lives. There is an uproarious demand for the kept girl to begin the orgy with a recital of her own biography. Fortunately, at this point, the author on the gravestone sneezes and the voices cease at once.

In later numbers of *The Diary* appear two brief sketches. One of them, "The Peasant Marei," concerns an incident in Dostoevsky's childhood which was remembered while he was in prison, and now rises to the surface of his mind many years later. He recalls a rare holiday at Omsk when the drunken and quarrelling convicts filled him with revulsion. In a reverie his thoughts wander back to his childhood, when he roamed the fragrant woods round the family summer cottage. Suddenly he had imagined hearing the cry of "wolf!" In extreme terror he dashed into an open field to seek the protection of the peasant Marei. With fondness he dwells upon the gentle and almost motherly solicitude of the old serf who strove to quiet his childish fears. This recollection in prison, as by some miracle, banishes the hatred and anger from his heart, for he now imagines that any one of these unhappy criminals may be the very Marei, who with timid tenderness had touched his quivering lips with an earth-stained finger. His remembrance of things past, some twenty-five years after his imprisonment, is a curious confirmation of the turning to the masses which he began to experience at that time and which ultimately became the foundation of his faith in the world destiny of Russia.

The second sketch, "The Heavenly Christmas Tree," seems to have been inspired by a previous article in *The Diary* in which Dostoevsky tells of his meeting before Christmas a ragged and shivering boy who is begging on the streets. This reality is transposed into art in the brief story of a poor child who leaves the side of his dead mother to wander the bitter cold streets. His impressions of the gala Christmas festivities he encounters in his wanderings, in some of which he tries to join but is unfeelingly repulsed, are described with Dostoevsky's usual keen understanding of a child's reactions. The little boy finally hides in the dark corner of a courtyard and dreams of Christ's Christmas tree around which all the poor and unwanted children gather to make merry and receive their gifts. In this delightful vision of warmth and light he dies, frozen to death. The Dickensian atmosphere of the tale is relieved by a restraint and realism unusual even in Dostoevsky's sympathetic treatment of children.

The last two stories in *The Diary* are longer and more ambitious artistically. In an article Dostoevsky comments on a suicide that had been reported in the newspapers. An unhappy young girl, clasping an ikon to her bosom, had thrown herself out of a fourth-story window. The act stirred his imagination, and he pondered over the significance of the ikon. A month later appeared "A Gentle Creature," to which he gave the subtitle "A Fantastic Tale." Here one can observe Dostoevsky in the very process of transforming into art what he considered the "fantastic facts of reality," passing them through the alembic of his psychological analysis, and emerging with an idealism which he felt to be more real than the realism of contemporary novelists. He starts with the real suicide of the young girl who had leaped to her death with the ikon clasped in her arms, and he works backward in an effort to build up an imaginary frame of action which will be consistent with psychological realism. The girl had a husband. As she lies dead in the room, he tries desperately to clarify in his own mind the reasons for her act. Dostoevsky attempts to simulate the broken account of a man overwhelmed with grief and a sense of guilt. At first, in his efforts to remember, he contradicts himself in logic and in feelings. Gradually, however, the jerky narrative gains in coherency and convincingness, and in the end his recollections and self-analysis lead him irresistibly to what seems to be the truth of the tragedy.

The husband, before his marriage, had resigned from a distinguished regiment, because he had been accused of cowardice for not calling a man out to a duel. He had thought the reason for the duel silly, but later he admits to himself that he is a cheap egoist and insufferably proud. A small legacy enables him to start up in business. He deliberately elects to become a pawnbroker as a kind of scornful gesture against the society that repudiated him. A vague idea of accumulating wealth and revenging himself on the world motivates all his actions. He falls in love with a pretty, gentle girl who comes to his shop to pawn various objects, among them an ikon, and eventually he marries her. There now ensues an extraordinary psychological duel between the husband and his young wife. His good qualities have been poisoned by the experiences of his past, and he fancies himself an enigma. Although he deeply loves his wife, he treats her with severity and silence, expecting submissive adoration from her. His self-pity over his unhappy past, his stupid pride and affectation of suffering in silence lead him to believe that she will finally divine the nobility of his soul and worship him. The young wife at first is puzzled by his behaviour, and eventually her sincere love is frozen almost before it can find expression. She rebels, and learns from a would-be lover of the alleged cowardly act in her husband's past. At a rendezvous with the lover, the husband eavesdrops and becomes aware of her purity and devotion to him. Instead of melting him and bringing out his affection, this knowledge confirms his determination to make her submit. They cease to live together as man and wife, and in a moment of aberration she attempts to murder him. His courage, with the pistol at his head, convinces her that he is no coward, but the barrier to love that he has raised is too difficult for her to scale. She falls into a long period of illness, and when she recovers, her spirit is utterly broken. Finally, in a moment of illumination, he realizes that he has crushed all her natural love for him, and he falls at her feet, passionately desiring to give her the affection that he had hitherto been too proud to offer. It is too late. She is either afraid of his love or now realizes her inability to return it in an equal degree. Apparently, rather than deceive him, she commits suicide, jumping from the window with the very ikon that she had pawned in his shop clasped in her arms. The story is a finished example in miniature of Dostoevsky's acute psychological powers and suggests his own conviction that love should be freely given and freely received.

The last short story in *The Diary* contains an interesting restatement of Dostoevsky's faith in the "Golden Age." The hero of "The Dream of a Ridiculous Man" comes to the conclusion that nothing in the world matters. On the way home one evening, determined to carry out a plan to commit suicide, he brusquely repulses a little girl who appeals to him for aid. He sits down in his room with a revolver before him. Disturbing reflections over his treatment of the little girl crowd out the notions of suicide for the moment. He had refused to help her because he had felt that nothing mattered since he was soon to kill himself. Now, however, he feels ashamed of his actions, and the fact convinces him that he is still a human being and can suffer. In the midst of these reflections he falls asleep. He dreams that he has actually shot himself. After he had been buried for some time, he is suddenly whisked from the grave through space to earth as it existed ages before. He lands on one of the islands of the Greek Archipelago. Then ensues a description of the "Golden Age," very similar to those in "Stavrogin's Confession" and *A Raw Youth*, but many more details about the inhabitants are added. It is definitely a picture of earth before the Fall. The people know no sin. They instinctively love one another, have children in common, and death is a peaceful falling asleep. They have no creed, but they possess a sense of oneness with the whole universe. The newcomer, however, corrupts this sinless society. They learn to lie and become addicted to cruel sensuality, the worst of all sins. Dostoevsky's picture of their moral disintegration suspiciously resembles a description of modern society corrupted by rationalism and the radical movement. They grow wicked and begin talking about brotherhood and humanitarianism; science is introduced and they seek to explain life in order to teach others how to live; they become criminals and invent justice and the guillotine to preserve it. Knowledge is esteemed as higher than feeling, and the newcomer, in despair over these people whom he has learned to love, demands to suffer, to be crucified in order that he may atone for the corruption he has spread. They declare him dangerous and threaten to shut him up in a madhouse. At this point he wakes and is filled with a desire for life. The dream has taught him the truth that evil is not a normal condition of mankind and that people can be happy without losing the power of living on earth. The story ends with the Ridiculous Man repeating Dostoevsky's own convictions of the necessity to combat the idea that the consciousness of life is higher than life and that knowledge of the laws of happiness is higher than happiness. All that one must do is to love others like oneself.

During the years 1876 to 1877, while Dostoevsky was issuing *The Diary*, the idea for his last great novel was gradually and imperceptibly taking possession of his mind. The interrelation of art and reality, he believed, centred in the observation of the facts of everyday existence. The artist must have the power to perceive in these facts their profound significance, because from them comes the idea of his novel. *The Diary* is filled with the observation of such facts, and in some cases they are taken over directly into *The Brothers Karamazov;* in a few instances they have suggested an active development of ideas which also reappear in the novel. The relation of a father to his sons is the very core of *The Brothers Karamazov,* and children in general fill an unusually large place in the action. In *The Diary* he devotes several articles to children and evinces a deep concern over their treatment, education, and defenceless position in the lower strata of society. He writes of the children who command and those who hold aloof—a clear foreshadowing of the relative position of Kolya Krasotkin and Iliusha in the novel. The series of brutal crimes against children, which he recited in *The Diary*, are repeated almost literally by Ivan Karamazov. Perhaps more important is the fact that the central theme of the story of the Grand Inquisitor, the culminating point of the novel, is clearly suggested in *The Diary*. In fact, *The Diary* was a testing ground for a preliminary expression of key ideas—the argument for the immortality of the soul, purposeless suffering as an argument against the existence of God, the necessity of man's living in harmony with the universe—which are welded together in the artistic comprehensiveness of *The Brothers Karamazov*. Dostoevsky's thought and powers of observation over these two years were moving irresistibly in the direction of the conception of his masterpiece, and hence *The Diary of a Writer*, as a kind of preface to the novel, becomes a publication of special significance.

21

The
Karamazovs

In Russia *The Brothers Karamazov* is regarded as Dostoevsky's greatest novel. His most matured art, his wisdom, ideas, faith, and doubts find their fullest expression in this book. Nowhere else has he so successfully and so characteristically abstracted mind and will and passion from their background of names and clothes and exhibited them in such pure, disembodied states of being. Nowhere else has the white-hot intensity of his ideological world glowed so brightly or has he spiritualized ideas so arrestingly and so profoundly. All that life meant for him—its experiences, symbols, and vision—is reflected in these extraordinary characters. If the final test of a great novel is the enduring sense of having undergone a vital and lasting experience in the reading of it, then *The Brothers Karamazov* easily takes a place among the few supreme novels of world literature.

In a sense Dostoevsky had been preparing for this

task throughout most of his creative life. Certain ideas that went into the novel may well have flashed across his imagination while he was in prison in Siberia. The thematic continuity of his works, beginning with *Notes from the Underground,* and the character-types, starting with his earliest productions, achieve their fullest development in *The Brothers Karamazov.* That source of so much of his later fiction, the plan of "The Life of a Great Sinner," contributes its increment; and the boys' club, which figured so prominently and to no purpose in the various drafts of *The Idiot,* becomes an important feature. Finally, certain articles in *The Diary of a Writer* contain much material that has a direct bearing on the subject-matter and ideas of the novel.

On the evidence of a few jottings in his notebook, it has been inferred that Dostoevsky conceived the character of Smerdyakov in 1876,[1] which would suggest that the plan of the novel was surprisingly well advanced at a very early date. The most recent editor of the manuscript notes to the novel, however, convincingly establishes the fact that the reference to Smerdyakov really belongs to 1878.[2] In the last issue of *The Diary of a Writer* (December 1877), Dostoevsky frankly tells his readers that he is discontinuing the publication in order to devote himself to an artistic work that had been "imperceptibly and involuntarily composing itself" in his mind over the past two years. In the same month he writes to a friend: "There is a novel in my head and heart and it begs to be expressed."[3] As early as the summer of this same year, he had visited haunts of his childhood, the villages of Darovoe and Chermashnya, with the express intention of refreshing his memory on material for the novel. Clearly, then, the period of preliminary planning of *The Brothers Karamazov* belongs to the year 1877, although he very likely conceived the idea of the novel the year before.

With no other time-consuming occupation, the planning went forward rapidly in the early months of 1878. In March, Dostoevsky wrote to a pedagogical friend to request detailed information about the behaviour of school children, although these facts were not necessary until the second half of the book. In the spring, however, the sudden death of his young son interrupted the work. With the hope of assuaging his grief, his wife sent him on a trip to the monastery of Optina Pustyn, celebrated for the piousness of its elder, Father Amvrosi. He stopped off at Moscow and easily persuaded Katkov to give him an advance on the projected novel. Then he continued to the monastery in the company of his intimate friend, the philosopher Vladimir Soloviev, to whom he confided the plot of *The Brothers Karamazov.* At the monastery he talked with the elder who consoled him on the loss of his child in words which Dostoevsky recalled when writing the effective consolation of Zosima to the poor peasant woman bereaved of her child. Indeed, Optina Pustyn and Father Amvrosi provided special details for the monastic scenes and the characterization of Zosima in the novel.

Upon his return to Staraya Russa, Dostoevsky once more set to work. The first instalment was ready before the end of the year, and it appeared in the *Russian Messenger* in January 1879. The remainder, however, progressed very slowly. The immediate and enthusiastic public responses to the early sections supported his own conviction of the significance of the work and encouraged him to take the utmost care with the succeeding parts. It was his most deliberately and slowly written novel, as though he felt that his immortality depended upon this work alone. Only after three years of effort did he finish it—the last chapter was completed in November 1880—and his faith in the performance was amply justified, for *The Brothers Karamazov* raised him to the heights of national fame.

Despite the long period of deliberation over the various details, the plot of the novel seems to have occurred to Dostoevsky pretty much in its entirety. It is better constructed than most of his plots, and even includes carefully designed periods of relief from the intensity of the main theme. Although it is his longest novel, the bare outlines of the plot may be summed up in a few sentences. It is a story of crime in which Dmitri Karamazov and his father are rivals for the love of Grushenka. Smerdyakov, an illegitimate son, murders the father, and Dmitri is accused of the crime and convicted on circumstantial evidence. Into this sordid tale, however, Dostoevsky has introduced a titanic struggle of love and hate, with all its profound psychological and spiritual implications, and the whole is cast against the background of the life of a town and a monastery. The last two novels had reflected a steadily growing interest in religious problems. In *The Brothers Karamazov* the Church and God become the very foundation upon which he erects the huge superstructure of the work. Throughout, the whole novel is pervaded with a search for faith—for God. This search for God is the central "idea" of the novel.

It is surprising how often Dostoevsky draws upon actual happenings for the element of crime in his fiction. Behind the murders in *Crime and Punishment, The Idiot,* and *The Possessed* are real crimes which he had read about in newspapers. These are the "fantastic facts" of his theory of realism; from such realized facts come the ideas that take on flesh and blood when embodied in his characters. It is now fairly certain that the dominant theme of murder in the plot of *The Brothers Karamazov* was not an imaginary situation. In the manuscript notes to the novel, Dmitri, upon his first appearance, is referred to as "Ilinsky," and he is frequently indicated by this name in succeeding notes. Dostoevsky's use of the names of real people in the notes to designate characters who have been modelled on them was pointed out in the case of *The Possessed* in which the name Granovsky was often employed for Stepan Trofimovich, and Nechaev for Pyotr Verkhovensky. The name Ilinsky, it seems, was also that of a real person. In *The House of the Dead* Dos-

toevsky describes one of the convicts as "a certain parricide, formerly a nobleman and a public functionary.
He had given great grief to his father—a true prodigal
son. The old man endeavoured in vain to restrain him
by remonstrance on the fatal slope down which he was
sliding. As he was loaded with debts, and his father
was suspected of having, besides an estate, a sum of
ready money, he killed him in order to enter more
quickly into his inheritance." (Chapter II) Towards
the end of the book (Chapter VII) Dostoevsky takes
an occasion to remark that he has received news from
Siberia that this supposed parricide had been falsely
accused and unjustly condemned. From an account by
Dostoevsky's wife, it appears that the man's real name
was Ilinsky.[4] On the basis of this clue, a recent investigator made a detailed comparison and is able to offer
convincing evidence to the effect that Ilinsky in *The
House of the Dead* was unquestionably the immediate
inspiration for the characterization of Dmitri Karamazov.[5] From the account in *The House of the Dead*,
it is clear that Ilinsky made a deep impression on Dostoevsky, and the man's innocence no doubt fostered
his interest in the case. In appearance, background,
and behaviour Ilinsky has much in common with
Dmitri. More important, perhaps, is his reputed crime
of parricide and the judicial error that resulted in his
conviction, facts which are strikingly similar to those
in the plot of the novel. As a final bit of evidence in
support of this identification, it should be noted that
the town of Tobolsk, where Ilinsky was alleged to have
committed the crime, is the very town first mentioned
in the manuscript notes as the scene of the action of
the novel. (Dostoevsky finally changed the name in
the printed text.) Once again, then, Dostoevsky appears to have had recourse to the facts of real life instead of literary imaginings for the central theme of
the plot of a novel.

Although both the murder as the central theme and
the ideological direction seem to have been settled

upon at the outset, Dostoevsky experienced his usual difficulty with the events and their relation to the characters, which as yet were only vaguely imagined. On the very first page of the notes, definitely dated April 1878, and amid reminders to buy boots and tobacco, is the observation: "Memento (for a novel) —To find out whether it is possible to lie between the rails under a train when it is going at full speed." [6] This note, of course, refers to the episode of Kolya Krasotkin, which was not actually written up until two years later and appeared only in the tenth book of the novel. Further references to children in the early notes suggest that he had intended to introduce them at the beginning and had designed a more significant role for them than they have in the printed work. It is very likely that his unknown plan for a novel about "Fathers and Children," which he was contemplating even before he began to write *A Raw Youth* in 1874,[7] influenced this initial design for the opening of *The Brothers Karamazov*.

Once the actual writing began, however, Dostoevsky displayed a mastery over his rich material which was unusual in the early stages of his novels. With exceptional brevity, and representing something of a departure from his customary dramatic method of starting a work *in medias res*, nearly all the chief characters are presented in the first thirty-five pages, including the principal facts in their lives up to the point where their story begins. And within the brief scope of this concise exposition, the potential psychological development of each of these characters is at least suggested.

Like the great characters of previous masterpieces, the chief men and women of *The Brothers Karamazov* are cast in the form of embodied ideas. Nothing in human experience as we know it will satisfactorily explain the exaggerated motives and actions of old Karamazov, Dmitri, Ivan, Alyosha, Smerdyakov, Zosima, Grushenka, and Katerina Ivanovna. Nor is this exaggeration the kind that we expect in fiction or which is traditionally warranted in art. The ordinary meaning of realism is not broad enough to justify such creations. Yet these characters are real and vital. They win our sympathy, and we have little difficulty in identifying ourselves with this or that aspect of their natures. Many factors contribute to this realism in the apparently unreal. Like symbols in a modern allegory of life, the characters are personifications of ideas, but personifications treated so realistically that we effect a willing suspension of disbelief and accept them as living human beings. We never seem to think of Dostoevsky's characters absolutely in terms of themselves, in terms of their physical and surface characteristics. We think of them rather in terms of the ideas which they personify. They are not so much men and women as human souls, who live in a region of experience from which all the circumstances of ordinary life appear to have been eliminated, and in which only the soul survives. In this sense, artistic reality tends to approximate more and more closely to spiritual reality or to ideas of spiritual reality.

The father of this strange Karamazov brood has left his mark on each of his sons. Despite their striking individual differences, they are all Karamazovs by virtue of something deeper than the normal ties of kinship. The Karamazov taint is carnal sensuality, which in its less vicious manifestations Dostoevsky describes as a zest for living. It is the dominating characteristic of the father; it helps to wreck the life of Dmitri; it is always just below the surface in Ivan; and at odd moments it even rears its ugly head in the saint-like nature of Alyosha. Dostoevsky was interested in the subject of heredity, and this aspect of the novel may well have been influenced by Zola's *La Fortune des Rougon* which he had no doubt read. The children of the lust-loving father in Zola's novel also inherit the traits of their parent. Dostoevsky, however, would have little sympathy for the scientific materialism behind Zola's understanding of heredity. The inherited trait of the Karamazov sons does not lend itself to any physiological explanation. The moral transports of Dmitri, the questing rationalism of Ivan, and Alyosha's spiritual rapture defy scientific analysis. All of them are philosophers, as Dmitri remarks, and the animal instincts in them constantly struggle with the moral and spiritual side of their natures. They are all deeply imbued with a Schiller-like moral consciousness. Indeed, the ecstasy of love in Schiller's *Hymn of Joy* is one of the basic elements of the whole ideological conception of the novel, and the father and his two sons in *Die Räuber*, if we may judge from the frequent reference to them, were very much in Dostoevsky's mind in the characterizations of old Karamazov, Dmitri, and Ivan.

Although old Karamazov is a monster of lust and debauchery, it would be a mistake to regard him in this light only. He possesses a natural cunning and is by no means devoid of a subtle comprehension of the deeper motives of human behaviour, both in himself and in others. In his youth he made a living by playing the buffoon in the families of nobles, and he continues to play the buffoon with enjoyment but often with manifest design. Like Foma Fomich, in *The Village of Stepanchikovo*, who had also earned his keep as a hired jester, old Karamazov courts insult because he derives a pleasure from personal affront. On the other hand, he takes a cynical delight in baiting his real or imaginary enemies. By means of shady dealings, he has obtained some wealth, but his money makes him greedy for more. He is generous with himself, however, and his chief pleasure in life is to indulge his carnal appetites. Occasionally he is troubled by a stab of conscience, and at moments he reveals even a sentimental affection for his dead wives and his sons. In his cups, he may display the furtive spirituality of a repentant drunkard and go so far as to entertain the idea of the existence of God. None of his associates, however, is misled by these fugitive good impulses. The old cynic is utterly a sensualist, corrupt and immoral to the core. The dark Karamazov strain rules his life and finally leads him to his death.

Of the sons, the notes indicate that Alyosha took shape earliest in Dostoevsky's imagination. He describes him in the novel as "the future hero of my story," and various hints in the notes, as well as the evidence of Dostoevsky's wife, make it clear that he intended to continue the development of Alyosha in one or more sequels. Presumably he was to marry Liza, live through a period of sinning, during which he would come in contact with a variety of people, including revolutionary terrorists, and finally achieve salvation through suffering. Alyosha was obviously destined to undergo the holy pilgrimage of the hero in the plan of "The Life of a Great Sinner." In the end, however, Dostoevsky's death prevented the fulfilment of the vast design of his great unwritten masterpiece which had nurtured so much of his fiction.

These plans for the future development of Alyosha no doubt account for the sense of incompleteness of the characterization in the novel. However, the part he has to play is important and well sustained. His mother was a deeply religious, passive, and long-suffering woman, and these traits are inherited by Alyosha. The scene in which she holds him up as an infant before the ikon is a symbolic dedication of Alyosha to God. The "idea" he embodies is that of the religious spirit brought into contact with sin in which faith triumphs over unbelief. Although he represents the Christian ideal, there is nothing of the pale mystic about him, or of the seminarist engrossed in theological studies and smelling of the lamp. He is a novice at the local monastery, but his elder bids him take off his cassock and go out into the world and experience life. The red-cheeked, handsome Alyosha does not demur, for he believes that "everyone should love life above everything in the world." There is even latent in him the dark Karamazov strain. In this true son of

God, who carries in his heart the secret of renewal for all, Dostoevsky is clearly building a nature that will wrestle with the devil and not lose his soul.

In one of the early notes, not repeated in the novel in any form, Alyosha is referred to in a paraphrase of a line from the Second Part of *Faust:* "The highest beauty is not external but within." [8] Like Prince Myshkin, Alyosha possesses this "highest beauty," which is a moral beauty. There are striking resemblances between the two characters which are further supported by the fact that Dostoevsky often refers to Alyosha in the notes as "The Idiot." He has the intuitive wisdom of Myshkin and his selfless compassionate heart and radiant personality. Further, his part in the novel resembles somewhat that of Myshkin in *The Idiot.* He moves through the pages morally influencing the characters and events, without ever playing much of an active role. Like all the Meek characters, he is passive, submissive, ever ready to turn the other cheek, and Christ-like in his capacity for suffering. With his intuitive wisdom he understands the tempestuous passions around him, but his virginal soul is unscorched by their hot flame. His love for Liza recalls that of Myshkin for Aglaya Epanchina, for his feelings hardly transcend the emotion of pity and the desire to contribute to the spiritual and moral health of this strange young girl.

In Alyosha, however, one may detect slight deviations from the hitherto uniform pattern of the Meek characters. The variations, no doubt, were intended as a psychological basis for the greater change to come in his role of hero in the projected sequel. Thus, the dark Karamazov strain in him, which was to run its full course in the continuation, leads him to the edge of sin on several occasions. In his love for Liza, Alyosha at least once displays a feeling foreign to the Meek type. Even his religious faith is momentarily shaken by the incident of the stinking corpse and nearly overthrown by the arguments of Ivan. Such weaknesses in his moral armour, however, are quickly mended; his mission in the novel is to influence all by his sublime faith in life. He is the only one of the three brothers who is able to love life more than the meaning of life. For him alone is reserved the ecstasy of the "living life," mentioned by Versilov in *A Raw Youth*. In the famous scene which signalizes his recovery of faith, he experiences this higher synthesis of life as he leaves the monastery to go out into the night:

> The earth's silence seemed to melt into the silence of the heavens, the mystery of the earth was one with the mystery of the stars. Alyosha stood, gazed, and suddenly, as though his strength failed him, he threw himself down on the earth. He did not know why he embraced it. He could not have told why he longed so irresistibly to kiss it, to kiss it all. But he kissed it weeping, sobbing and bathing it with his tears, and vowing passionately to love it, to love it for ever and ever. . . . There seemed to be threads from all those innumerable worlds of God linking his soul to them, and it was trembling all over 'in contact with other worlds.' He longed to forgive everyone and for everything and to beg forgiveness, Oh, not for himself, but for all men, for all and for everything. (Part VII, Book III, IV)

Although incomplete, the picture of Alyosha is impressive. Had Dostoevsky lived to continue it in the sequel, the dream of most of his creative life—to portray a good man on his pilgrimage through sin and suffering to salvation—might have been fulfilled in a characterization of extraordinary grandeur.

Like his younger brother, Dmitri loves life, but the meaning of life continually puzzles him. He occupies the central position in the novel and perhaps ought to be considered the hero, for the story of *The Brothers Karamazov* is essentially the story of Dmitri. In him the Karamazov taint of carnal sensuality is most pronounced. There is a suggestion of dualism in his actions, but simplicity and deep feeling are the essence of his nature, qualities which make for a unified apprehension of life in Dostoevsky's scheme of things.

Dmitri acts on instinct, and his emotions provide always the clearest image of his nature. There is poetry in his soul which is reflected in his impulsive behaviour and colourful language. His whole life is like an epic in which the turbulent action is relieved by occasional lyric flights.

Dmitri can be introspective, but he thoroughly distrusts the rational approach to human experience. The only problem that seems to torment his generous mind is the struggle of the good and beautiful with the forces of evil in the heart of man. In those remarkable chapters, "The Confession of a Passionate Heart," he bares his soul to Alyosha in a self-revelation of love and hate. In telling of his strange adventure with Katerina Ivanovna, he is concerned solely with the state of his feelings over the way that proud woman humbled herself before him. He will have nothing of any rationalization of his actions. "To hell with all who pry into the human heart!" he exclaims. Yet he cannot evade the problem of the Karamazov vileness in his nature which contends with his yearning for the good and the beautiful. He deplores the thought that a man of lofty mind begins with the ideal of the Madonna and ends with the ideal of Sodom. What is still worse, he feels, is that both ideals coexist in the mind of man.

Yes, man is broad, even too broad. I'd have him narrower. The devil only knows what to make of it! What represents itself to the mind as shameful is beauty to the heart. Is there beauty in Sodom? Believe me, it is found in Sodom for the immense majority of people. Did you know that secret? The awful thing is that beauty is a mysterious as well as a terrible thing. God and the devil are fighting there and the battlefield is the heart of man. (Part I, Book III, iii)

The Karamazov devil conquers in the heart of Dmitri. He possesses those qualities, however, which Dostoevsky associated with the good man who can be saved. All the evil in him is ameliorated by his capacity to suffer and to repent. Like Zosima, who bows down before him as one condemned to suffer, he perceives, if only vaguely, that the individual must share the guilt and suffering of others. He does not offer any extenuation for the purely circumstantial part he played in the murder of his father, for he admits to a certain moral blame, to the feeling that he wanted to kill the old man. With Katerina Ivanovna he displays the same generous instinct. He had once loved her, but her proud nature and actions had turned his love into hate. After all, she lacked the very love which comes from the heart, the kind of love that Grushenka could give him and which he himself gave in return. Yet, after her most damaging evidence at the trial, he freely forgave her.

There is nothing in the novel comparable to the cumulative emotional effect and infinite pathos of the scene of Dmitri in the tavern. All the burning lust which had sent him on that wild ride to Grushenka is suddenly extinguished by the awful charge of parricide. The insistent cross-examination of the magistrate grips the attention as the soul of Dmitri is revealed with all its dross and all its innate nobility, the nobility of the natural man who acts from impulse and feeling. It is at this point, rather than at his trial, that he emerges as a great tragic figure.

Dmitri casts out the devil of evil by suffering and throws in his lot with God. With all his humility, however, he despairs of the fortitude he will require in Siberia, and his newly found faith wavers. Still, in the end, he is willing to take up his cross, for he is conscious of his baseness, of having sullied his own honour which he values above everything. As he is about to be committed to prison, he makes public testimony of his faults and admits that the tragedy which has befallen him is perhaps a necessary blow to arouse him to the need of reforming his ways. And he concludes: "I accept the torture of accusation, and my public shame. I want to suffer, and by suffering I shall purify myself. Perhaps I shall be purified, gentlemen? But listen, for

the last time, I am not guilty of my father's blood!"
(Part III, Book IX, ix)

Dmitri Karamazov is one of the greatest of all Dostoevsky's characters. He has that broadness, that wide heart which Dostoevsky admired so much in real life. Dmitri must have appealed to him as one of the most typical Russians that he ever created. For many readers, too, Dmitri has come to typify the Russian nature —its expansiveness, generosity, impulsiveness, innate nobility, and capacity for suffering, a man whose offences are inevitably the defects of his virtues.

Unlike either of his brothers, Ivan is more concerned with the meaning of life than with life itself. He puts life on the operating table, dissects it, and comes away disillusioned, without ever seeming to realize that life is to be lived. For many readers Ivan will always remain the most absorbing character in the novel; for many critics he is not only the most brilliant mouthpiece of Dostoevsky's ideas, but the very mental image of the man who created him. The "idea" that Ivan embodies is that of the purely rational being whose reason leads him into evil and to a denial of God. He is not, however, a mere allegorical personification of an abstract idea. The problem that tortures his soul is not apprehended in a cold, lifeless fashion. It is a live coal thrust into his heart, and the consequent sufferings of Ivan are dramatized against a background of pulsing life.

So different in many respects from the other members of the family, it might seem that Ivan has nothing in common with the Karamazovs. Even the father, who sees his own image in Dmitri, declares to Alyosha: "But I don't recognize Ivan, I don't know him at all. Where does he come from? He is not one of us in soul." (Part II, Book IV, ii) The father, however, is not correct. Ivan is a Karamazov, but an educated and rationalizing one. In him the Karamazov taint takes the form of intellectual evil. Dmitri admits that he was quite capable of murdering his father. In a sense, Ivan does murder him, for he deliberately plants the idea in Smerdyakov's head, knowing full well that his devotee will carry it out. In the notes, Dostoevsky actually designates Ivan as the murderer, indicating conclusively the full import of his moral guilt. No, Ivan is true Karamazov, and his theory that "all is permitted" is virtually an intellectual justification of the Karamazov lust for life.

Ivan is the last of Dostoevsky's remarkable series of Doubles, and in him is expressed most fully the philosophical development of the split personality. His ambivalence takes the highest form of the cosmic struggle of man with God, which had been foreshadowed by Terentev in *The Idiot* and Kirilov in *The Possessed*. In this struggle he is concerned precisely with those factors which were at the bottom of Dostoevsky's own search for faith—the problem of sin and suffering and their relation to the existence of God. Ivan passionately and obstinately searches for a way out of his dilemma, and with a seriousness that indicates that upon the results of his quest will rest his desire to live or not to live. The famous section "Pro and Contra," in which this philosophical and religious struggle is waged, is the true culmination of the novel, not only the greatest scene that Dostoevsky ever wrote, but certainly one of the most remarkable in literature. The whole ideological conception of the novel, as well as the resolution of Ivan's struggle, is centred in this section, and the subject deserves a separate chapter.

There is another Karamazov, although an illegitimate one—Smerdyakov. More in the spirit of a practical joke rather than of wanton lust, old Karamazov had begotten him of a vagrant idiot girl and brought him up as a servant in his own house. Smerdyakov is a macabre study in the psychology of human degeneracy. Although a bastard, he is tarred with the Karamazov brush. With his foppish manners, low cunning, and pretensions to learning, there can be little doubt that Dostoevsky designed him as a parody of Ivan.

The intellectual Ivan is his hero, and he poll-parrots his very arguments about the existence of God. In his smug bourgeois ambitions and offensively rebellious nature, Ivan considers him raw material for revolution —a bitter thrust against the radicals on Dostoevsky's part. The mere hint of his hero takes root in his shrewd mind; he murders old Karamazov and robs him of the money he had put aside to bribe Grushenka into submission. In those three unforgettable visits after the murder, Smerdyakov holds up to Ivan the mirror of his moral and intellectual depravity. Ivan is appalled at the image of himself, and it loses nothing of its verisimilitude as the revelation of this aping lackey. No villain of Dostoevsky is quite so repulsive as Smerdyakov, and none is described with such psychological mastery.

Although the Karamazov family holds the centre of the stage, there is a profusion of secondary characters who are nearly all sharply conceived and treated with a richness of detail unusual in the minor figures in Dostoevsky's novels. The three principal female characters are thoroughly in the tradition of the Doubles and among the best-drawn women in this group. Like previous female Doubles, their whole action in the novel centres in the emotion of love.

In the portrayal of Katerina Ivanovna, there is a considerable psychological advance over the other "infernal women" of Dostoevsky. Her dual nature becomes apparent from that day when Dmitri gallantly refused to take advantage of her voluntary submission after he had given her the money to save her peculating father from disgrace. Her love for the large-souled Dmitri takes the usual form of a struggle between pride and submissiveness. All her behaviour is dictated by this ambivalence. She desires to torture Dmitri and to be tortured by him. Her cruelty and denial had turned his love to hate. She has very much the same feeling for Ivan, but a Double himself, he fully appreciates her split personality. He clearly perceives

that she continually lacerates herself in welcoming
Dmitri's insults, and that her submissiveness and self-
abasement have their roots in her towering pride.
Even Alyosha understands perfectly that she must
ultimately dominate the man she loves. She might
have dominated Dmitri if it had not been for Grushenka; but she can never dominate Ivan; whose own
dualism comprehends this same incorrigible pride.
"She loved neither of them—neither Ivan nor Dmitri,"
Alyosha concludes. And in the absolute sense, this is
true. Subtly probing all the refined nuances of her ambivalent emotions, Dostoevsky reveals in Katerina
Ivanovna a woman caught between the grinding stones
of her dualism, between pride and submissiveness, between love and hate.

Grushenka is a more elementary type of the female
Double. In her appearance, background, and actions
she resembles Nastasya Filipovna in *The Idiot*. Like
her, Grushenka has suffered a deep moral hurt in her
youth and the fact has profoundly affected her outlook on life. It is difficult, however, to accept the violent change in her nature after she entices Alyosha to
her house. Apparently Dostoevsky was similarly troubled by this abrupt transformation. The seventh book,
which contains the attempted seduction, and is entitled "Alyosha" in the novel, he had called "Grushenka" in the notes. It is clear from this fact, and from
the notes themselves, that he had originally attached
much more significance to this turning point in Grushenka's life and had intended to devote considerably more space to the scene between her and Alyosha. Some of the themes in the notes are not worked
up in the novel, notably a few which suggest that
Alyosha was more sorely tempted by her charms than
appears to be the case in the final version. Compared
to the notes, this section in the novel is condensed,
the effects toned down, and the vital spiritual change
in Grushenka hinted rather than analysed in detail,
which seems to have been his initial intention. Of

course, the sudden softening of her nature, the emergence of an unexpected virtue and spirituality, may be psychologically justifiable on the basis of Alyosha's recognition of her true moral dignity—a situation comparable to that in *The Idiot* when Myshkin recognizes the moral dignity of Nastasya Filipovna. After this reformation in Grushenka, however, the further development of her character is quite consistent. Although the dual emotions of love and hate rule over her behaviour throughout most of the novel, like Dmitri, generosity, a wide soul, and a capacity to suffer seem to effect a synthesis in the contending forces of her nature. In the end, like Sonya Marmeladova, she is prepared to travel the prisoner's road to Siberia with the man she loves.

That strange girl, Liza Khokhlakova, whose mother provides the comic relief of the novel, reveals a nature in which emotional ambivalence dangerously approaches a pathological state. Self-abasement and the desire to suffer lead her to a point where she deliberately courts self-destruction. "I should like someone to torture me," she says to Alyosha, "to marry me and then torture me, deceive me and then go away. I don't want to be happy." Then she admits that she wishes to suffer, to kill herself. Finally, she tells Alyosha of her dream of the child crucified on the wall, and how pleasant this would be if she could see it and eat pineapple compote while listening to the groans. Such manifestations reveal the excessively morbid nature of Liza. She is capable at once of self-renunciation and mockery, of tenderness and torture, and of answering with ridicule a love self-affirmed. Her confused relations with Alyosha and Ivan indicate clearly the split nature of her personality. She likes Ivan because she imagines that she will suffer and be tortured in loving him; and she is attracted to Alyosha because she feels that she can tyrannize over him and make him suffer.

The notes show that a more important place in the novel was originally designed for Rakitin, that semina-

rist who seems as much out of place in the monastery
as the saint-like Alyosha would be in a brothel. His
ideological contrast to Alyosha and his scorn for the
Russian masses are more emphasized in the notes. It is
very likely that Dostoevsky was parodying a real figure in this characterization. Several have been suggested by critics, but the most plausible is the editor
of *National Notes*, A. A. Kraevsky, who had rejected
the first version of *Crime and Punishment*. Like
Kraevsky, Rakitin has essentially no concern with humanity or its morality. He is the type of liberal Westerner that Dostoevsky loathed. Like Alyosha and
Ivan, he occupies himself with higher questions of
religion and philosophy, but he has nothing of Alyosha's love for humanity and is incapable of the intellectual heights of Ivan. To his liberalism he adds a
touch of socialism, but only to a degree in which it
seems advantageous and not dangerous. Dostoevsky
no doubt intended him to represent the new democrat-
ically-minded youth of the day, who treated the
weighty problems of history, religion, and society so
superficially. Really all Rakitin wants is a career, and
he cavalierly contemplates one in the Church or in
journalism. He rather favours the idea of going up to
St. Petersburg and working on a fat periodical, and he
imagines that he will eventually become the editor
and supply it with liberal tendencies of slight socialist
leanings, because such a practice seems to be in vogue.
His place in the novel is as a contrast to the Karamazov
brothers; his shallow comprehension of life is opposed
to their intense and profoundly serious searchings into
the meaning of life. Ivan thoroughly understands
Rakitin and hates him as an enemy who adulterates
his own ideas.

As a kind of subplot, but artistically interwoven into
the fabric of the novel, is the theme of Captain Sneg-
irev and his family and the gang of boys under the
leadership of Kolya Krasotkin. The captain and his
family are surrounded with a halo of suffering, and

Dostoevsky spares no detail in his effort to lay bare the tragedy of their lives in all its senselessness. The contrast between this wretched family, whose misfortunes are beyond its control, and the Karamazovs, whose tragedy arises from their own folly, was an intentional part of the total design. Little Iliusha's behaviour over the beating of his father by Dmitri is infallibly true psychologically and emotionally, and the narrative at this point is wonderfully effective. The whole relationship between father and son is handled with delicateness and an uncanny understanding of a child's sense of dignity and of the fitness of things in a child's world.

Although Dostoevsky makes it amply clear that Kolya Krasotkin is a most unusual boy and a born leader among his comrades, this prodigy nevertheless strains the reader's credulity. To be sure, he is one of Dostoevsky's "thinking children," and his grave and mature language is quite in keeping with his mature actions. Yet, his trenchant observations on life and psychological wizardry exaggerate nature's most extravagant gifts to her fourteen-year-old sons. If disbelief is suspended and interest sustained, it is because of an unfailing human affection for the natural-born hero. Kolya is a boy-hero, and the extraordinary things he does seem to make little difference provided he does them heroically. In general, Dostoevsky's treatment of the whole group of children is remarkably effective. Another author might have lathered the beautiful death scene of Iliusha with mawkish sentimentality, but Dostoevsky never once goes beyond the limits of sheer human sentiment.

The swift tempo of the previous novels is deliberately toned down in *The Brothers Karamazov*. There are suggestions of the measured tone and epic sweep which Dostoevsky had formerly contemplated as the narrative method of his unwritten masterpiece, "The Life of a Great Sinner." Comic and digressive elements provide relief from the series of intense dramatic

scenes which are among the most brilliantly imagined
and artistically executed in the whole range of his
fiction. With impressive cumulative effect everything
leads up to the trial scene, which is handled in a consummate fashion. No novelist has ever surpassed Dostoevsky at this sort of thing. For years he had followed
court trials with almost a morbid curiosity, and he had
amassed a surprising amount of technical knowledge
on judicial procedure. In letters to the associate editor
of the *Russian Messenger,* N. A. Liubimov, we are informed of his infinite care about these technical matters. He seeks advice on legal points from lawyers and
expert medical opinion about the hallucinations of
Ivan. Not only does he fill in the background of Dmitri's trial with patient attention to all the details, but
the examination and testimony are contrived both to
advance the action and to bring out the further psychological development of the characters. The legal
evidence connected with the murder of old Karamazov
is complex, and Dostoevsky handles it with subtlety.
His ability to place himself in the position of all the
witnesses and the two lawyers, and in an entirely objective manner to present the conditioned reasoning of
each speaker, as this reasoning in every instance would
be limited by the speaker's imperfect knowledge of
the facts in the case, is little short of amazing. It is all
a triumph of the dramatic method in dealing with a
complexity of material over which a lesser artist would
have stumbled many times.

The novel ends on the glad note of resurrection,
when Alyosha informs Kolya and his young playmates
that the dead will rise again and joyfully tell over to
one another everything that has happened. Whether
he has in mind the resurrection of the fallen Dmitri to
a new life, it is hard to say. From the notes, one gathers
that Dostoevsky originally intended at the end to effect
a general reconciliation, at least between Dmitri, Grushenka, and Katerina Ivanovna. Such a denouement,
however, would have been quite unsuitable artistically,

and he wisely abandoned it. The novel concludes with the ultimate fate and future relations of Dmitri and Grushenka merely suggested, with the dualism of Ivan and Katerina Ivanovna unresolved, and with the future story of Alyosha still to be written.

22

Ivan Karamazov
versus
Pater Seraphicus

Dostoevsky considered the fifth and sixth books—"Pro and Contra" and "The Russian Monk"—the philosophic and artistic crown of *The Brothers Karamazov*. In an important letter to N. A. Liubimov, he wrote:

This book, 'Pro and Contra,' is in my view the culminating point of the novel; it must be finished with particular care. Its idea . . . is the presentation of extreme blasphemy and of the seeds of the idea of destruction at present in Russia among the young generation that has torn itself away from reality. Alongside with blasphemy and anarchism, there is the refutation of them, which is now being prepared by me and will be expressed in the last words of the dying Zosima . . . In the copy I have just sent you, I present only the character of one of the leading figures of the novel [i.e. Ivan], that character expressing his basic convictions. These convictions form what I consider the synthesis of contemporary Russian anarchism. The denial not of God, but of the meaning of His creation. The whole of socialism sprang up and started

with the denial of the meaning of historical actuality, and
arrived at a programme of destruction and anarchism. The
principal anarchists were, in many cases, sincerely convinced men. My hero takes a theme, in my view an
unassailable one: the senselessness of the suffering of
children, and from it deduces the absurdity of the whole of
historical actuality. I do not know if I have accomplished
this well, but I know that the figure of my hero is real in
the highest degree.[1]

Dostoevsky poses the question here but is careful, if
anything, to understate his intentions. There was some
danger that the associate editor of the *Russian Messenger* would question or even reject a part of the novel
devoted to a blasphemous theme. The hero will not
deny God, but the meaning of His creation; and to
calm the fears of the conservative head of the magazine, Dostoevsky hastens to add that he is already preparing the refutation of this blasphemy. However, in
the involved manuscript notes of "Pro and Contra,"
which reveal the mental struggle he underwent in
planning this section, there are frequent indications
that his real intention was precisely to deny the existence of God. In one note Ivan is made to say: "I
should wish to destroy the idea of God entirely." [2] In
succeeding notes the proof of God is dubbed as "all
nonsense," and Christ is described as suitable only "for
the elect, for the powerful and mighty; and even after
they have borne His cross, they will find nothing that
has been promised, as He found nothing after His
cross." [3] These and similar notations are not repeated
in the novel. Either Dostoevsky feared his editor or the
censor, or he was thinking ahead of the necessary unity
of an ethical plan in which Ivan's argument was to be
refuted. It is important to realize, however, that in the
initial design for "Pro and Contra," not merely a denial
of the meaning of God's creation, but a denial of God
was in Dostoevsky's mind; it is also the logical conclusion of Ivan's eloquent argument.

Nearly everything in this famous section of the novel

contributes to the further development of Ivan's dual nature and brings together all the facets of his thought in a pattern of compelling cogency. Like that other Double, Raskolnikov, Ivan has written an article about a favourite theory of his. The real point of the article, which is discussed in the early part of the novel, is the denial of virtue in the world because there is no immortality. If this be true, Ivan maintains, then everything, even crime, is permissible. His lack of faith and the first premise of his later argument for the denial of the meaning of God's creation are thus suggested at the very beginning of the novel.

Ivan resumes his argument much later in the chapter "The Brothers Make Friends," in the fifth book. Largely by way of disarming Alyosha, he starts out by remarking that he is not at all concerned with the futile question of whether man created God or God man. He is willing to believe that there is a God, but he cannot accept God's world. In the next chapter, "Rebellion," the high point of his argument, he elaborates this position. He first pictures to Alyosha what a worthless creature man is and the amount of suffering he has caused upon earth. If only the guilty suffered, he could forgive God and perhaps accept His world. This is only the prelude, however, to his attempt to convince Alyosha of the causeless cruelty of God-made man and of the religion of the cross.

Ivan then narrates the ghastly stories of the blameless sufferings of innocent little children. In another letter to Liubimov, in which he implores the editor not to change the word "excrement" in the tale of the child of five who was smeared all over with her own excrement by her parents, because she had failed to ask for the chamber-pot at night, Dostoevsky adds that all these accounts are absolutely true. He had taken them from newspapers or other authentic material, and a few of them he had already discussed in *The Diary of a Writer*. Ivan's narration of these horrible incidents in the lives of little children composes one of the most fearful sermons ever preached against the existence of an all-powerful, all compassionate God. And on a purely rational basis, as Dostoevsky recognized, Ivan's thesis is absolutely unanswerable. In *The Diary of a Writer* Dostoevsky had declared that the necessity of suffering on earth was at the very basis of religion; evil as well as good must exist in order that man may exercise his free will in the choice between them. Ivan insists, however, that the guiltless must not suffer, even for the sins of others. After he tells the story of the Russian general who had the little serf boy torn to pieces by hounds before his mother's eyes, he demands of Alyosha whether this tyrant ought not to be shot. Alyosha agrees that he should be, and Ivan triumphantly declares that he sees a little devil in his deeply religious brother.

Ivan demands justice for all these sins against innocent children, and not justice in heaven or hell, but on earth. If eternal harmony is to be paid for at the price of the causeless suffering of children, then he will renounce this harmony; if it is necessary to pay this price for truth, then truth is not worth such a price. The price is too high, says Ivan, and he hastens to give back his entrance ticket. "It's not God that I don't accept, Alyosha, only I most respectfully return Him the ticket."

"That's rebellion," Alyosha murmurs. He is forced to agree, however, that he cannot accept the fabric of human destiny or the future happiness of man if they are founded on the unavenged tears and unexpiated blood of even one little child tortured to death. Then suddenly Alyosha, in answer to a question of Ivan, insists that there is one Being who, because He has innocently suffered for the sake of mankind, has the right to forgive all this suffering of the innocent. It is on Christ, Alyosha hopefully maintains, that the edifice of the world is built.

This answer is exactly what the subtle Ivan had been expecting. As Dostoevsky remarks in his letter to Liubimov, Ivan's denial of the meaning of God's creation is closely joined in his mind with the denial of historical actuality. The saint-like Alyosha's forced admission that the general, who had the little serf boy torn to pieces, ought to be shot amounts to a surrender of the whole position of the world of Christianity and the social order founded upon it. It is revolution; it is the very argument of socialism that the world should be remade, and by force, if necessary. That this is the real import of Ivan's dialectic is clear in his account of "The Grand Inquisitor," which he offers up in the next chapter as a final refutation of Alyosha's last hope—the efficacy of Christ and His dictum that faith in Him involves man's free choice between good and evil.

In the figure of the Grand Inquisitor, Dostoevsky attempts to objectivize Ivan's plan of universal history from a teleological point of view. Ivan is the Grand Inquisitor and his story about him is a further confession of his atheism. The story is simple enough. Christ returns to earth during the Inquisition of Seville. He is welcome with joy by the populace, performs miracles, and is thrown into prison at the command of the Grand Inquisitor, who threatens to burn him on the morrow. There then takes place in the prison cell the well-known colloquy between the Grand Inquisitor and Christ. The Grand Inquisitor repudiates the whole course of His teaching. Christ's fatal mistake, he insists, began with His rejection of the temptations in the wilderness. Instead of happiness, He has offered man freedom, unmindful of the fact that man prefers peace, and even death, to freedom of choice in the knowledge of good and evil. The Roman Catholic Church, on the other hand, says the Grand Inquisitor, has allied itself with the devil and deprived man of his freedom. By giving them the bread which Christ had refused, the Church has enslaved the multitude and holds it in awe by miracle, mystery, and authority. He concludes that the Church has thus corrected the work of Christ who must leave them in peace, for only by utter submission to the will of the Church will man find happiness. In reply, Christ, who has remained silent, kisses the Grand Inquisitor who then releases Him. The meeting, however, in no respects alters the Grand Inquisitor's conviction of the true mission of the Roman Catholic Church.

One of Dostoevsky's main intentions in this story about the Grand Inquisitor was to aim a double-edged blow at the Roman Catholic Church and socialism. His identification of the two was pointed out in *The Idiot* and *The Possessed,* and it is asserted in articles in *The Diary of a Writer.* It is hard to understand why he persisted in this favourite idea. Even in his own day, although he was probably unacquainted with the evidence, the Catholic Church had taken a vigorous stand against socialism. And in the light of the bitter antagonism today, Dostoevsky in this instance seems to have been a poor prophet. He based his position on what he considered to be the mutual dependence of both on reason and authority, and on their negation of individual freedom in their efforts to achieve the ultimate happiness of man. It would almost seem that his deep hatred for both obliged him to combine them into a two-headed monster that everywhere seeks the universal destruction of mankind.

In Ivan's story the identification of Catholicism and socialism is not stated, but it is everywhere implicit. The Grand Inquisitor rebukes Christ for resisting the third temptation of the devil in the wilderness—the kingdoms of the world and the glory of them. "Hadst Thou accepted that last counsel of the mighty spirit," he declares, "Thou wouldst have accomplished all that man seeks on earth—that is, some one to worship, some one to keep his conscience, and some means of uniting all in one unanimous and harmonious ant-heap, for the craving for universal unity is the third and last anguish of men." Anyone acquainted with Dostoevsky's descriptive epithets for socialism and its aims will recognize the allusions to them in this passage, and a number of similar ones in the chapter could be quoted. In the manuscript notes several observations which are excluded from the novel expressly deal with socialism. In still another letter to Liubimov, after he had dispatched the chapter, "The Grand Inquisitor," Dostoevsky's intention is made perfectly clear. He writes:

It is finished what *the lips have spoken proudly and blasphemously*. The modern denier, the most vehement one, straightway supports the advice of the devil, and asserts that that is a surer way of bringing happiness to mankind than Christ is. For our Russian socialism, stupid but terrible (for the young are with it)—there is here a *warning*, and I think a forcible one. Bread, the tower of Babel (i.e. the future kingdom of socialism), and the completest overthrow of freedom of conscience—that is what the desperate denier and atheist arrive at. The difference only being that our socialists (and they are not only the underground nihilists—you are aware of that) are conscious Jesuits and liars, who will not confess that their ideal is the ideal of the violation of man's conscience and of the reduction of mankind to the level of a herd of cattle. But my socialist (Ivan Karamazov) is a sincere man who frankly confesses that he agrees with the Grand Inquisitor's view of mankind, and that Christ's religion (as it were) has raised man much higher than man actually stands. The question is forced home: 'Do you despise or respect mankind, you, its coming saviours?' And they do all this in the name of the love of mankind, as if to say: 'Christ's law is difficult and abstract, and for weak people intolerable;' and instead of the law of liberty and enlightenment, they bring to mankind the law of chains and of subjection by means of bread.[4]

The negative aspects of Ivan's story about the Grand Inquisitor, however, must be regarded as a reaffirmation, within the artistic limits of the argument, of Dostoevsky's own religious position. If this be true, his position reflects a degree of doubt, quite in keeping with everything that has been said about his faith up to this point, and yet not at all reflected in the positive statement of his faith in the next, the sixth book of the novel. Ivan's repudiation of the meaning of God's world on the basis of the causeless suffering of the innocent and on the Grand Inquisitor's condemnation of Christ for preaching man's freedom of choice in the knowledge of good and evil are joined in Dostoevsky's mind as the central problem of religious faith. Suffering becomes part of the answer to the problem of sin. He was a firm believer in the spiritualizing role of suffering; it was not caused by sin but was a necessary condition to the forgiveness of sin. That is, the sinner was not forgiven by others, but by his suffering he earned the right to forgive himself, and both sin and suffering were predicated on the free operation of man's will.

This position, however, is not an answer to Ivan's argument of the blameless suffering of innocent children. Dostoevsky had admitted that it was unanswerable. Like Alyosha, he would have joined Ivan's rebellion on this score. Then the strange silence of Christ and still stranger kiss in answer to the denunciation of His doctrine of man's freedom and to the Grand Inquisitor's own principle of authoritative and compulsive Christianity is hard to understand. The artistic requirements of the scene, no doubt, obliged Dostoevsky to portray a purely human Christ, not the Christ of dogmatic religion. Christ's actions in the face of the Grand Inquisitor's argument, however, may well symbolize that Dostoevsky acknowledged the historical necessity of both freedom and authority, despite the fact that they contradict each other.

The only solution of this contradiction is the voluntary submission of the individual to Christ which in turn involves the submission of one man to another. Ivan Karamazov is not prepared to submit either to Christ or to man, and the final resolution of his nature centres in this dilemma. Like most of Dostoevsky's Doubles, Ivan is unable to understand the higher harmony between man and the world of God. For him, their relation is one of rule and obedience, and he searches for a way out of this endless antagonism. The contradiction tortures him because it is rooted in his own nature in the form of pride and submissiveness. His colossal pride involves him in a kind of cosmic struggle with God, for if God exists, Ivan feels himself a wretched, insignificant person, a plaything in the hands of some all-powerful force. His struggle, however, is not waged on an arid, intellectual battlefield. To be sure, he is a thinking Double, like the underground man and Raskolnikov, but he is also a prey to all manner of human emotions. His relations with his father and brothers and with Smerdyakov and Katerina Ivanovna play their part in the final resolution of the contending forces of his soul. Indeed, the realization that he is the moral, if not the actual, murderer of his father contributes to the eventual disintegration of his theories of life and religion.

It is towards the end of the novel (Book XI, Chapter IX) that his future destiny is worked out. His mental struggle has fretted him into a state of nervous illness, during which he has hallucinations and is confronted by his Double, who effectively dramatizes his ambivalence. Unlike Golyadkin's *alter ego* in Dostoevsky's early tale, the Double takes the form of a devil and represents Ivan's troubled conscience. The apparition is shabbily dressed and affects an air of false gentility. In reality, he has the manners of a flunkey and reflects all the cynicism and nastiness that belong to one side of Ivan's nature.

The Double exposes Ivan to himself, raking up his past, and ridiculing his youthful ideas. He reminds him of the story of the Grand Inquisitor and of another work, the "Geological Cataclysm." In this poem, which the Double summarizes, Ivan betrays his own solution of the fierce struggle that goes on within him. Like Terentev in *The Idiot* and Kirilov in *The Possessed*, Ivan declares that the only thing necessary is to destroy the idea of God in man. When this comes about—and he believes the period analogous with the geological periods—then the old conception of the world and the old morality will pass. "Man will be lifted up with a spirit of divine titanic pride and the man-god will appear." This period, however, may never come because of the inveterate stupidity of man; but in the meantime, the Double continues—paraphrasing from Ivan's poem—anyone who still believes that there is no God and no immortality may become a man-god, and for him all is permitted.

Here is Ivan's hoped-for solution of his dualism. In his egotistic pride, Raskolnikov had reasoned that by murdering the old money-lender he could assert his power and become a Napoleon. Ivan thinks, in his titanic pride, that by removing God and the meaning of His world he will become a man-god. The difficulty, however, as his Double points out, is that he requires a moral sanction to remove God. Ivan does not possess the single-minded determination of the Self-Willed character or the fearful logic of action of a Kirilov. He is a Double, and hence the problem of the world is not resolved by his idea of a human divinity, because such a solution does not appeal to him as reasonable. Another way out of the conflict is to admit the illimitable power of God and His world over him, that is, to become submissive, like Raskolnikov at the end of *Crime and Punishment*. Such a solution, however, means submission to a God that permits irrational unhappiness and the suffering of innocent children. Both paths are unacceptable, and Ivan is forced to remain a helpless victim of his own indignation.

The insolent Double had ridiculed Ivan's intention of confessing at the trial that Smerdyakov had killed old Karamazov. Such an act, the Double sneers, would simply be lip-service to that very virtue among men which Ivan scorns. In this respect, Ivan is like Stavrogin, who believed it silly to commit suicide since the act would suppose a magnanimity of soul which was mere hypocrisy. At the trial, however, the submissive side of Ivan's nature predominates and he confesses Smerdyakov's deed and his own moral guilt. The next moment, however, he qualifies his confession by the ambiguous statement: "Who doesn't desire his father's death?" Psychologists have interpreted this as an indication of a parricide complex that Dostoevsky laboured under. That is, he felt a moral guilt for the death of his own father, which he had subconsciously wished for. Ivan's statement, however, is entirely in keeping with the proud, self-willed aspect of his dual nature, and it perhaps carries no meaning other than a reflection of this.

After his confession, Ivan suffers a physical and mental breakdown. Dostoevsky hints that he will recover, but it was evidently his intention that Ivan, a rebel against God, should stand forth at the end as a complete spiritual bankrupt. His Double had revealed everything servile in Ivan's nature, and morally he rots. Dostoevsky seems to have realized his artistic failure in attempting to resolve the ambivalence of Raskolnikov and Versilov, for he refuses to indicate whether or not Ivan will solve his dualistic contradictions and achieve salvation by discovering the higher synthesis of life. No doubt, Alyosha's prayer is to be regarded as the final word on Ivan: "As he fell asleep he prayed for Mitya and Ivan. He had begun to understand Ivan's illness: 'The anguish of a proud determination, a profound conscience!' God, in whom he does not believe, and truth were gaining mastery over his heart, which still did not wish to submit . . . 'God will conquer!' he thought. 'He [Ivan] will either rise up in the light of truth or . . . he will perish in hate, revenging on himself and on everything his having served that which he does not believe,' Alyosha bitterly added, and again he prayed for Ivan." (Book XI, Chapter X) The prayers of Alyosha, however, could not save the tortured soul of this greatest of all Dostoevsky's Doubles.

After his arraignment of Christianity in "Pro and

Contra," Dostoevsky took fright at the convincingness of Ivan's devastating argument for the overthrow of God. It is a unique case of an author's artistic integrity triumphing over his personal belief, or perhaps it would be more correct to say, over what he wanted to believe. Throughout the course of this study, sufficient evidence has been presented to indicate that one side of Dostoevsky's dual nature must have been strongly attracted to the atheistic and radical convictions of Ivan. As indicated in previous chapters, there is even much to support this point of view in his writings after the reactionary period of *The Possessed*. However that may be, once "Pro and Contra" was finished, he felt an urgent necessity to refute Ivan. In his anxious concern that prized readers, such as his publisher Katkov and his important conservative friend Pobedonostsev, might not imagine that he intended to leave Ivan's crushing argument unanswered, he hastened to send them letters to reassure them. Indeed, when Pobedonostsev, now Procurator of the Most Holy Synod, read the blasphemy of "Pro and Contra," he sternly and impatiently awaited the answer.

Dostoevsky had written to Liubimov that the refutation would be expressed in the last words of the dying Zosima in the very next book (Book VI). While he was still working on this book, "The Russian Monk," he wrote of it to Liubimov:

It is not a sermon, but a story, an account of his own [Zosima's] life. If I succeed, I shall achieve a good work: *I will compel people to admit* that a pure, ideal Christian is not an abstraction, but a vivid reality, possible, clearly near at hand, and that Christianity is the sole refuge of the Russian land from all its evils. I pray God that I may succeed, for the part will be a pathetic one. If only I can get sufficient inspiration! And the main theme is such, that it does not even occur to contemporary writers and poets, therefore it is quite *original*. For its sake the whole novel is being written. If only I can succeed: that is what troubles me now.[5]

On the fifty pages of "The Russian Monk" Dostoevsky expended more effort—two full months—than on any other of the twelve books of the novel. The care with which he worked is evident in the manuscript notes which are full, clear, and often in a form that required little elaboration in the finished version. Artistically, however, he seemed to realize that this prolix and rather boring section had little of the power and vigour of the book that it was intended to refute. He felt impelled to defend it to Liubimov:

All the critics who do not like us will cry out: 'Is the Russian Monk like that; how dared he put him on such a pedestal' . . . I think I have not sinned against reality: it is true not only as an ideal, but it is true as reality. I only wonder if I have succeeded. I myself think that I have not expressed even a tenth part of what I wanted. Yet I regard Book VI as a culminating point of the novel. You will understand that a great deal in the precepts of my Zosima (or rather the manner of their expression) belongs to his character, that is, to the artistic presentation of his character. Although I myself hold the same opinions which he expresses, yet if I expressed them personally *from myself*, I should express them in a different form and in a different style. But he could not speak in a different style, nor *express himself in a different spirit* than the one which I have given him.[6]

The character of a Russian monk had been fixed in Dostoevsky's imagination for many years. Such a figure was briefly sketched in the plan of "The Life of a Great Sinner"; it took more definite form in Tikhon, the monk in "The Confession of Stavrogin," the excluded chapter of *The Possessed;* Makar Ivanovich in *A Raw Youth* is to a certain extent a variation of the character; and finally, we have the fully-drawn figure of Zosima. Behind all these conceptions, no doubt, was the real eighteenth-century Russian monk, Tikhon Zadonsky, a celebrated elder, whose sermons Dostoevsky greatly admired. In fact, not a little of the material of the sixth book is modelled on the sermons of Tikhon

Zadonsky. Dostoevsky deliberately attempted to reproduce the naïve spirit of the expository style of these old sermons; they even influenced the consciously contrived simplicity and wise *naïveté* in the language and thoughts of Zosima. Against the modern background of the novel, however, this antique flavour does not contribute to the realism of the portrait, and the prolixity of the whole section makes it artistically one of the least successful books.

As an ideological answer to the powerful reasoning of Ivan, Dostoevsky had even greater cause to worry over the success of his efforts. He frankly wrote to Pobedonostsev that he was dissatisfied with his refutation and feared that it was insufficient, and that he had not achieved one fraction of his purpose. Nevertheless, if we make due allowance for the demands of the artistic framework, "The Russian Monk" must stand as the most formal and the final presentation of Dostoevsky's religious and political views, if we except his Pushkin speech, which came later.

The emotional atmosphere so necessary for the proper reception of the material in "The Russian Monk" had been created by the preceding book, "Pro and Contra." Ivan and Zosima, who have a mutual esteem for each other, are mighty, well-matched antagonists. The aesthetics of the novel required that in their struggle the diametrically opposed ideological systems of each be expressed with equal force of spirit and thought. Dostoevsky has instilled in Zosima the essence of his Meek characters, but there is much in his nature which distinguishes him from the previous representatives of this type. Unlike Myshkin, his is a meekness acquired from experience with life. In a sense, he is the fulfilment of a type of character development that Dostoevsky had long since projected. Zosima resembles the hero of the plan of "The Life of a Great Sinner" after he has pursued a path of sin on his holy pilgrimage to salvation. Or to take another parallel, Zosima's career has much in common with the suggested one of Alyosha in the proposed sequel to *The Brothers Karamazov* in which he was to "sin his way to Jesus." The brief sketch of Zosima's contact with the world, however, hardly justifies the psychological change in his nature from the strong, almost dual personality into the meek exponent of saintliness. The artistically successful achievement of such a transition seemed to be beyond Dostoevsky's powers. Zosima is a highly intelligent man. He has subdued his nature more completely than the other Meek characters, and unlike all of them, he is a philosopher who has a definite ethical and social ideal. This ideal contains the answer to Ivan's denial of God, and it is essentially Dostoevsky's answer.

It is important to observe that Zosima does not attempt to refute directly Ivan's impeccably logical argument in "Pro and Contra." Rather Zosima presents a picture of world harmony in the nature of a sentimental lyrical effusion which is entirely different from Ivan's realistic picture of world disharmony. Here are two separate worlds, two systems of ideas going along on parallel planes which never collide. For example, Zosima is not allowed to face the terrible question which Ivan put to Alyosha: What should be done with the general who had his serf boy torn to pieces by dogs? The religious Alyosha had agreed with Ivan— "Shoot him." This answer, with all its implications, would have undermined the whole position of Zosima, who simply regards the world otherwise; his resolution of social and religious questions takes him along another path.

The positive ideal of Zosima rests on the foundation of true orthodoxy as the only salvation of humanity, the only creative and free force making for harmony in the world. The Book of Job is his favourite one in the Bible, as it was Dostoevsky's. Zosima accepts implicitly Job's justification of suffering, which amounts to an optimistic belief in the essential goodness of Divine providence and to the conviction that all is for the best in this best of possible worlds. His is an un-historical, rosy Christianity which enables him to separate himself from its realistic basis and draw a seductive picture of God's world.

Zosima does not deny the importance and acuteness of the social problems pointed out by Ivan. Unlike Ivan, however, he accepts the world with all its evil and suffering, for he loves the world as the creation of God. The world is beautiful, he declares, despite the groans and suffering which do not at all destroy the harmony of life, and, in fact, are a necessary element in it. Suffering is not a violation but a fulfilment, an act of Godly justice, which corrects transgression for the sake of the whole and for our own good. That is, the secret of universal harmony is not achieved by the mind, as the rationalizing Ivan imagined, but by the heart, by feeling and faith. If one loves all living things in the world, this love will justify suffering and all will share each other's guilt. Suffering for the sins of others will then become the moral duty of every true Christian.

If Zosima's ethical ideal is difficult to accept, his social ideal is a direct contradiction of the pragmatic world in which we live. Many of the points in his argument, which is an answer to Ivan's advocacy of socialism implied in his story of the Grand Inquisitor, had been stated in Dostoevsky's previous fiction and especially in *The Diary of a Writer*. Zosima deliberately parallels Ivan's presentation of evidence, but the conclusions he draws from it are utterly different. He accepts Ivan's thesis that "all is permitted," but he qualifies its conclusion with the dictum: "Do not oppose evil with force." He agrees with Ivan's ironic argument that Church and State are incompatible. However, instead of the government absorbing the Church, he envisions the time when the Church will swallow the government as an institution of the powerful of this world. Even the abuses of bourgeois capitalism, the suffering of little children in sweat shops, win the concern of Zosima, but for these realistic social miseries he offers an unrealistic solution.

His solution of the material problems of man and nations is based on the same premises as his solution of man's problem of religious faith—submissiveness and self-perfectibility, the perennial traits of the Meek character. He feels that there is no need for Ivan's protest and indignation over social inequalities and suffering, since everything in the world is for the best and tends towards the general good. That the world is divided into the rich and the poor, he frankly admits. The socialism of the West, however, is no cure for this, and least of all in Russia. There the peasantry has a seemly dignity and no envy for the rich. It is impossible, he says, that there should not be servant and ruler in the world, but the time will come when all shall serve each other and brotherly unity will exist. Each is at fault before all.

I dream of seeing [he explains] and already see clearly our future: It will be so, that even the most corrupt of our rich will end by being ashamed of his riches before the poor, and the poor, seeing his humility, will understand and give way before him, and with joy and kindness will respond to his honourable shame. Believe me, that it will end in that; things are moving to that. Equality is to be found only in the spiritual dignity of man, and that will be understood only among us. If we were brothers, there would be brotherhood, but until then, there will never be any division of wealth. We preserve the image of Christ, and it will shine forth like a precious diamond to the whole world. So may it be, so may it be! (Book VI, Chapter III).

The ultimate destiny of Russia is disposed of with the same prophetic detachment from reality and in words with which Dostoevsky had long since familiarized his readers. Russia will escape the godless socialism of the West and become its saviour. The Russian people are not isolated. They are moving towards universal brotherly love and self-perfection, and in the end, salvation will come from the people, from their faith and their meekness. While the peasants have God in their hearts, no atheistic or socialistic reformers can seduce them from their mission of bringing salvation to the world.

The precepts of Zosima, in brief, teach man not to rebel against suffering and poverty, but to seek them out, for he will learn from them meekness and tolerance. Instead of becoming indignant over man's inhumanity, he counsels reconciliation with it. In place of anger over injustice, he advises prayer. Poverty, humility, suffering, and prayer are the foundations of his practical philosophy of life, and constitute the highest degree of human existence in which man will achieve complete freedom and happiness.

It is little wonder Dostoevsky feared that the continuous catechism of this sixth book was not a convincing answer to the crushing argument of Ivan in "Pro and Contra." Even the majestic figure of the Russian monk, which he hoped to portray in Zosima, fails in majesty because the image and Zosima's reasoning are bereft of all realism. Zosima's philosophy of optimism is one of stagnation, of failing power, of idleness and beggary which amounts to the debasing of life. In reconciling man with all the evil and suffering in the world, Zosima condemns him to a philosophy of the futility of both body and spirit. It is a negation of the whole ideal of progress.

In this tremendous battle of religious and social ideologies which marks the culminating point of *The Brothers Karamazov*, there is something tragic in Dostoevsky's failure to acquit himself successfully of the "civic deed" he had undertaken in trying to refute the position of Ivan, the arch rebel against God. The liberals and radicals of the time exposed the conservative ideology of the novel and berated the author as a reactionary, and conservative critics condemned him for atheistic tendencies. In the search for God—the "idea" of the novel—it is ironic that one aspect of Dostoevsky's dual nature gave strength and convincingness, almost against his will, to the atheistic and socialistic beliefs of Ivan. An implied recognition of this fact, as well as a peculiar artistic satisfaction in the unobserved reasons for his failure to answer Ivan effectively, are to be found in his private reactions to the critics in his notebook:

Ivan Fedorovich is profound, not one of your contemporary atheists, demonstrating in his disbelief merely the narrowness of his conception of the world and the obtuseness of his own stupid abilities . . . The villains teased me for my ignorance and a retrograde faith in God. These thickheads did not dream of such a powerful negation of God as that put in the ['Grand] Inquisitor' and in the preceding chapter, to which the *whole novel* serves as an answer. I do not believe in God like a fool (a fanatic). And they wished to teach me, and laughed over my backwardness! But their stupid natures did not dream of such a powerful negation as I have lived through. It is for them to teach me!

And in another place, he writes: "Even in Europe there have never been atheistic expressions of such power. Consequently, I do not believe in Christ and His confession as a child, but my hosanna has come through a great *furnace of doubt*." [7]

In truth, *The Brothers Karamazov* itself is a "great furnace of doubt," and in it Dostoevsky never succeeded in forging his hosanna. None of his novels so faithfully mirrored the dual struggle that went on within him. Although he would not admit it to himself, the search for God had no ending. His mind was with the reasoning of Ivan, his heart with the precepts of Zosima. This mighty struggle of mind and heart, however, seems to add an element to *The Brothers Karamazov* that transcends the mortal experiences which the characters and scenes in a novel ordinarily reflect. There is a sense of infinity in the book which reaches out beyond the mundane passions of its sordid tale of crime to an unseen and unknown translucent globe where exist the ultimate, universalized reasons for all human behaviour. Perhaps it is the prophetic quality that pervades the novel; perhaps it is the constant reference of effects to causes beyond the scope of man's immediate experiences that conveys this feeling of the infinite which these extraordinary characters embrace and which embraces them. Whatever it may be, this awareness of an intimate contact with a world outside the realm of human consciousness profoundly intensifies our aesthetic pleasure and significantly contributes to the supreme art of *The Brothers Karamazov*.

CONCLUSION

In a letter that accompanied the manuscript of the Epilogue to *The Brothers Karamazov*, Dostoevsky hopefully remarked to his publisher that he intended to live another twenty years and to go on writing. Less than three months later (28 January 1881), he was dead. The continuation of his masterpiece and the writing of several projected works, the titles of which he jotted down in his notebook—a Russian *Candide*, a book about Christ, an epic on *The Commemoration of the Dead*, and his reminiscences—were literary hopes that were buried with him. His toil, however, had not been without great honour, even before he died. In June 1880, on the occasion of the dedication of the Pushkin statue in Moscow, he had delivered a speech that had electrified a distinguished audience and aroused the people to a recognition of him as a national literary hero. Taking the famous poet and his works as a prophetic symbol of Russia's destiny, he pronounced a ringing message on the world-mission of his country that inspired his enraptured listeners to shout "genius!" "saint!" "prophet!" Both Westerners and Slavophiles, and even the young generation of radicals in the audience, found something in his speech which they could accept with enthusiasm. In reality, he had simply repeated, in a more effective manner, the deeply felt convictions that he had uttered in his novels and journalism for many years. His praise of European culture and Russia's indebtedness to it satisfied the Westerners; the Slavophiles were pleased with his glorification of native genius; and the young radicals saw a hint of the coming revolution in his insistence that for the Russian sufferer universal happiness is necessary if he is to find peace. Throughout the whole performance, however, ran his own special message of meekness and faith in Christ, whose precepts of suffering and love will enable the Russian people to bring about the brotherhood of man.

The fact that adherents of opposing schools of thought could take comfort in Dostoevsky's speech must be regarded as a final reflection of his dualism. In truth, the evidence of the present study seems to justify the conclusion that the dual impulses of his nature were the most significant factor in the development of his creative art and profoundly influenced his opinions on religious, social, and political questions. Herein lies a certain consistency which explains his creative process and defines his thinking.

It is necessary, however, to resist the tyranny of labels and refuse to designate Dostoevsky by any of the commonly accepted names which we apply to the literary artist and thinker. His divided soul rendered him incapable of unbroken allegiance to any credo of art or philosophy. Tolstoy said of him that his whole life was a struggle between good and evil, which is as true for the great characters of his novels as for their creator. Out of this struggle came his lifelong search for freedom—moral and spiritual freedom. He accepted the most autocratic government in the world, because he believed that it did not interfere with the equality that is to be found only in the spiritual dignity of man. Authority became repulsive to him when it attempted to organize man's existence on a purely rational basis and thus deprive him of the free choice between good and evil, so essential to his self-perfection. It was not disillusionment with the hopes of socialism to remedy abuses in Russia that turned him to a mystical and religious panacea—a reaction painfully common today among intellectuals who have lost their faith, perhaps prematurely, in the efficacy of man's rational schemes for political and social betterment. From the very beginning of his creative life, Dostoevsky had profoundly distrusted the capacity of the intellect to establish those principles by which men may live in universal peace and happiness. He felt that hate, not love, was the medium through which the socialists would attempt to achieve the unification of man. They did not understand that love, like God, was apprehended by the heart, not by the reason. This conviction led him to God, and to His religion, for he perceived that without religion, morality was impossible. In the sense that he was intensely dissatisfied with the world in which he lived, Dostoevsky was perhaps more radical than the revolutionists of his day. Like Christ, however, his vision of a purer and finer world was founded on the love and innate goodness that dwell in the hearts of men. Equality did not mean for him an equal distribution of property and work, or an equal share in power and subjugation. Rather equality existed in a union of people through love and meekness, and in a lofty expression of moral feeling through service to each other.

Often the famous works of an artist seem infinitely nobler than their creator; in the same sense, the novels of Dostoevsky are more noble than the man himself and will outlive his religious and social thinking. Intellectuality can never be the sole measure of a great novelist; he achieves immortality, as it were, in spite of it. It is no mere accident or paradox that Dostoevsky, a powerful if sometimes inconsistent thinker, should have been so deeply sceptical of reason as a key to the understanding of the individual and of life itself. His personal dualism continually led him into an impasse between the head and the heart. If God seemed to be the ultimate irrationality of man's mind, an unreasoning faith in Him appeared to be absolutely essential to assure the harmony of man's relation to the world in which he lived. Although Dostoevsky's finest characters, the Doubles, reflect the mental struggle of his own split personality, his heart went out to his Meek creations, whose spirituality and goodness are expressed not through ratiocination, but through an outpouring of moral feeling.

Feeling, however, is not confined to the Meek characters, for the whole intellectual climate of Dostoevsky's fiction is pervaded by it in the sense that he *felt* his thoughts. All the ordinary surface features of the consummate novelist he possessed to an extraordinary degree, but this quality of *feeling* suffuses them and gives to his best productions a high seriousness and a sense of vital experience. Unlike the rationalist, Ivan Karamazov, Dostoevsky was more concerned with life than with the meaning of life. If he regarded life as a mystery, he did not seek to explain by reason what reason is powerless to explain. Life never became an abstraction, void of sense and value. Although he is commonly accepted as one of the most eminent precursors of the so-called psychological novelists, unlike many modern writers, he did not allow psychological analysis to become an end in itself. He emphatically believed that the novelist's business was not simply to explain life, but to see that life was lived in his books. Despite his almost excessive emphasis upon dialogue, his conversation is not pervaded by a desiccated intellection, which provides us with infinite talk about life, characters, emotions, sex, and about political, economic, and social theories. In his own life, he was never afraid of expressing his genuine feelings, sentiments, and emotions, nor did he ever deny these profoundly human attributes to the creatures of his imagination. If he is ever happy, he tells us, it is during the long nights when he sits with these men and women of his fancy as he would with real individuals. He loves them, rejoices and grows sad with them, and at times he even weeps sincere tears over their misfortunes. This is what is meant by *feeling*. He imaginatively and emotionally identifies himself with his characters, with all their experiences and actions. Even their political, religious, and social theories he apprehends passionately and sensitively so that they never seem like cold, artificial products of the mind. This quality of *feeling*, which we never fail to identify with life itself, contributes perhaps more than anything else to the deep and abiding experience we enjoy in reading his great novels.

NOTES

NOTES FOR CHAPTER 1

1. *Pisma*, ed. A. S. Dolinin (Moscow-Leningrad, 1928), I, No. 26, p. 73.
2. Ibid., I, No. 27, pp. 74-5.
3. Ibid., I, No. 28, p. 77.
4. Ibid., I, No. 27, p. 75.
5. N. A. Nekrasov eventually became one of the foremost publishers and literary figures in Russia.
6. Nekrasov was a follower of Belinsky, the leader of the intellectual "Westerners," who believed that the salvation of Russia depended upon its remodelling itself on the lines of the civilization of Western Europe. *National Notes* was one of the principal journalistic organs of this group.
7. *Dnevnik Pisatelya*, gosudarstvennoe izdatelstvo (Moscow-Leningrad, 1929), XII, 29-31.
8. Ibid., XII, 31-3.

NOTES FOR CHAPTER 2

1. *Pisma*, I, No. 32, pp. 86-7.
2. *Tvorchestvo Dostoevskogo*, 3rd ed. (Moscow, 1928). I am indebted to this book for certain ideas concerning the subject of dualism and its relation to Dostoevsky's characters.

NOTES FOR CHAPTER 3

1. *Pisma*, I, No. 31, p. 84.
2. Ibid., I, No. 31, p. 85.
3. Ibid., I, No. 32, p. 87.
4. Ibid., I, No. 33, p. 89.
5. *Dnevnik Pisatelya*, XII, 297-8.
6. Cf. J. Neufeld, *Dostojewski: Skizze zu seiner Psychoanalyse* (Wien, 1923).
7. Cf. "Der Doppelgänger," *Imago*, Zeitschrift für Anwendung der Psychoanalyse auf die Geisteswissenschaften, vol. III (1914), p. 133.
8. Cf. W. Stekel, *Peculiarities of Behaviour* (New York, 1924), II, 242 ff.
9. *Pisma*, I, No. 40, p. 100.
10. N. N. Strakhov, *Biografiya, pisma i zametki iz zapisnoi knizhki F. M. Dostoevskogo* (St. Petersburg, 1883), p. 373.

NOTES FOR CHAPTER 4

1. See especially A. S. Dolinin, "Dostoevsky sredi Petrashevtsev," *Zvenya*, No. 6 (1936), pp. 514-45.
2. N. N. Strakhov, *Biografiya*, p. 83.
3. Cf. E. Pokrovskaya, "Dostoevsky i Petrashevtsy," *Dostoevsky, stati i materialy*, ed. A. S. Dolinin (Petersburg, 1922), I, 266 ff.
4. V. Belinsky, *Pisma* (St. Petersburg, 1914), III, 235.
5. *Dnevnik Pisatelya*, XI, 133-4.
6. *Pisma*, I, No. 58, pp. 129, 131.
7. Ibid., I, No. 61, p. 142.
8. Ibid., I, No. 58, p. 129.
9. Ibid., I, No. 60, p. 139.

NOTES FOR CHAPTER 5

1. *Pisma*, I, No. 62, p. 145.
2. Ibid., I, No. 63, p. 146.
3. Cf. S. Stephenson Smith and Andrei Isotoff, "The Abnormal from Within: Dostoevsky," *The Psychoanalytic Review*, No. 4 (Oct. 1935), XXII, 361-91.
4. *Pisma*, I, No. 75, pp. 166-7.
5. "The Little Hero," which he had written in the Peter-Paul prison in 1849, was published only in 1857. Its appearance signified that the government had withdrawn its ban on Dostoevsky in print.
6. *Pisma*, I, No. 117, p. 246.
7. Ibid., I, No. 109, p. 236.
8. Ibid., I, No. 117, pp. 246-7.
9. Ibid., I, No. 75, p. 165.

NOTES FOR CHAPTER 6

1. *Stati, gosudarstvennoe izdatelstvo* (Moscow-Leningrad, 1930), XIII, 45-6.
2. Ibid., XIII, 91.
3. Cf. V. F. Pereverzev, *Tvorchestvo Dostoevskogo*, pp. 128-63.

NOTES FOR CHAPTER 7

1. *Pisma*, I, No. 109, p. 236.
2. Ibid., I, No. 110, p. 239.
3. Ibid., I, No. 120, p. 256.

NOTES FOR CHAPTER 8

1. *Zimnie zametki o letnikh vpechatleniyakh*, III, 83.
2. Ibid., III, 84-5.
3. Ibid., III, 86-7.
4. *Pisma*, I, No. 194, p. 355.
5. Ibid., I, No. 196, p. 362.
6. Cf. A. S. Dolinin, "Dostoevsky i Suslova," *F. M. Dostoevsky stati i materialy* (Leningrad, 1925), II, 156.

NOTES FOR CHAPTER 9

1. *Pisma*, I, No. 226, p. 407.
2. Ibid., I, No. 222, p. 408.
3. Ibid., I, No. 234, pp. 418-19.
4. *Iz arkhiva F. M. Dostoevskogo, Prestuplenie i Naka-zanie*, ed., I. I. Glivenko (Moscow-Leningrad, 1931).
5. *Pisma*, I, No. 234, p. 420.
6. Ibid.
7. Ibid., I, No. 238, p. 429.
8. *Iz arkhiva F. M. Dostoevskogo, Prestuplenie i Naka-zanie*, p. 68.
9. *Pisma*, II, No. 292, p. 59.
10. *Dnevnik Pisatelya*, XII, 342-3.
11. *Pisma*, I, No. 234, p. 419.
12. *Iz arkhiva F. M. Dostoevskogo, Prestuplenie i Naka-zanie*, p. 62.
13. Ibid., p. 167.

NOTES FOR CHAPTER 10

1. *Pisma*, II, No. 318, p. 150.
2. Ibid., II, No. 323, pp. 169-70.
3. Cf. *Dnevnik Pisatelya*, XII, 33-6.
4. *Iz arkhiva F. M. Dostoevskogo, Prestuplenie i Naka-zanie*, p. 168.
5. Ibid., p. 60.
6. Ibid., p. 66.
7. *Iz arkhiva F. M. Dostoevskogo, Prestuplenie i Naka-zanie*, p. 66.
8. Ibid., p. 60.
9. Cf. ibid., p. 65.
10. Ibid., p. 216.
11. Ibid., p. 216.
12. Ibid., p. 73.
13. Ibid., p. 173.
14. Ibid., p. 212.

NOTES FOR CHAPTER 11

1. *Iz arkhiva F. M. Dostoevskogo, Prestuplenie i Naka-zanie*, p. 58.

2. Ibid., p. 56.
3. Ibid., p. 67.
4. Ibid., p. 86.
5. Ibid., p. 176.
6. Ibid., p. 73.
7. Ibid., p. 168.
8. Ibid., p. 187.
9. Ibid., p. 173.

NOTES FOR CHAPTER 12

1. The miser in a verse play of Pushkin, *The Covetous Knight*, which is a psychological study of greed.
2. *Pisma*, I, No. 178, pp. 333-4.
3. Ibid., I, No. 222, p. 403.

NOTES FOR CHAPTER 13

1. *Pisma*, II, No. 333, p. 220.
2. *Iz arkhiva F. M. Dostoevskogo, Idiot*, ed. P. N. Sakulin and N. F. Belchikov (Moscow-Leningrad, 1931). The excellent analysis of the material in this volume by the late Professor Sakulin has been very helpful.
3. *Pisma*, II, No. 279, p. 33.
4. Cf. V. S. Dorovatovskaya-Liubimov, "*Idiot* Dostoevskogo i ugolovnaya khronika ego vremeni," *Pechet i revoliutsiya* (1928), III, 31-53.
5. A. G. Dostoevskaya, *Vospominaniya* (Moscow, 1925), p. 115.
6. *Iz arkhiva F. M. Dostoevskogo, Idiot*, p. 13.
7. Ibid., p. 38.
8. Ibid., p. 28.
9. Ibid., p. 39.
10. Ibid., p. 43.
11. Ibid., p. 44.
12. Ibid., p. 47.
13. Ibid., p. 59.
14. Ibid., p. 72.
15. Ibid., p. 76.
16. *Pisma*, II, No. 292, p. 60.
17. Ibid., II, No. 294, p. 71.
18. Ibid., II, No. 292, p. 61.

19. *Dnevnik Pisatelya*, XI, p. 235.
20. *Iz arkhiva F. M. Dostoevskogo, Idiot*, p.120.

NOTES FOR CHAPTER 14

1. *Iz arkhiva F. M. Dostoevskogo, Idiot*, p. 98.
2. Ibid., p. 155.
3. Ibid., p. 137.
4. Ibid., p. 130.
5. Cf. V. S. Dorovatovskaya-Liubimov, "*Idiot* Dostoevskogo i ugolovnaya khronika ego vremeni," pp. 35-8.
6. *Iz arkhiva F. M. Dostoevskogo, Idiot*, p. 163.
7. Ibid., p. 158.
8. Ibid., p. 160.
9. *Pisma*, II, No. 321, p. 160.
10. Ibid., II, No. 323, p. 170.

NOTES FOR CHAPTER 16

1. *Pisma*, II, No. 318, p. 150.
2. Ibid., II, No. 339, pp. 244-5.
3. Cf. *Plan* "Zhiti velikogo greshnika," ed., N. L. Brodski, in *Dokumenty po istorii literatury i obshchestvennosti* (Moscow, 1922); "Plan of the Novel 'The Life of a Great Sinner,'" *Criterion*, No. 10 (London, 1922), I, 336, 345-6; *Zapisnye tetradi F. M. Dostoevskogo* (Moscow-Leningrad, 1935), see in *Ukazatel* under "Zhitie velikogo greshnika."
4. *Pisma*, II, No. 332, p. 213.
5. K. stands for *Knyaz*, i.e., "Prince" A. B.
6. This line is unclear in the manuscript.
7. *Zapisnye tetradi F. M. Dostoevskogo*, pp. 46-7.
8. Ibid., p. 48.
9. *Pisma*, II, No. 343, pp. 252-3.
10. *Zapisnye tetradi F. M. Dostoevskogo*, p. 57.
11. *Pisma*, II, No. 353, p. 283.
12. Ibid., II, No. 358, p. 294.
13. Ibid., II, No. 353, p. 283.

NOTES FOR CHAPTER 17

1. *Zapisnye tetradi F. M. Dostoevskogo*, p. 199.
2. *Pisma*, II, No. 356, pp. 288-9.

3. *Zapisnye tetradi F. M. Dostoevskogo*, p. 244.

4. Ibid., p. 142.

5. Ibid., p. 87.

6. Ibid., p. 271.

7. Ibid., p. 91.

8. This chapter has been recovered and is printed in F. M. Dostoevsky, *Polnoe sobranie khudozhestvennykh proizvedeni*, gosudarstvennoe izdatelstvo (Moscow-Leningrad, 1927), VII, 555-86; it has been translated into English by Avrahm Yarmolinsky in *The Possessed* (Modern Library, N. Y., 1936), pp. 691-736.

9. *Zapisnye tetradi F. M. Dostoevskogo*, p. 184.

10. This letter was written in October 1870, from Dresden. When he returned to Russia he had fuller information at his command which he made use of in the novel.

11. *Pisma*, II, No. 356, p. 288.

12. *Zapisnye tetradi F. M. Dostoevskogo*, p. 92.

13. Ibid., p. 45.

14. See p. 60.

15. *Zapisnye tetradi F. M. Dostoevskogo*, p. 242.

16. Ibid., p. 100.

NOTES FOR CHAPTER 18

1. *Dnevnik Pisatelya*, XI, 147.

2. *Zapisnye tetradi F. M. Dostoevskogo*, pp. 231-2.

3. Ibid., p. 92.

4. Ibid., p. 341.

NOTES FOR CHAPTER 19

1. *Dnevnik Pisatelya*, XI, 147-8.

2. See *Pisma*, III, 333.

3. *Letters of F. M. Dostoevsky to his Family and Friends*, translated by Ethel C. Mayne (London, 1914), p. 249.

NOTES FOR CHAPTER 20

1. *Dnevnik Pisatelya*, XI, 500.

2. Ibid., XII, 438-9.

3. Ibid., XII, 325-6.

4. Ibid., XII, 454.

5. Ibid., XII, 457.
6. Ibid., XII, 408.
7. Ibid., XI, 273.
8. Ibid., XI, 35.
9. Ibid.

NOTES FOR CHAPTER 21

1. Cf. *Die Urgestalt der Brüder Karamasoff: Dostojewskis Quellen, Entwürfe und Fragmente, erläutert* von W. Komarowitsch (München, 1928), pp. 492 ff.
2. Cf. *F. M. Dostoevsky, materialy i issledovaniya*, ed. A. S. Dolinin (Leningrad, 1935), p. 362.
3. *Pisma*, III, No. 612, p. 284.
4. Cf. L. P. Grossman, *Tvorchestvo Dostoevskogo* (Odessa, 1921), p. 36.
5. Cf. V. G. Reizov, "K istorii zamysla *Bratyev Karamazovykh*," *Zvenya*, No. 6 (1936), pp. 545-59.
6. *F. M. Dostoevsky, materialy i issledovaniya*, p. 81.
7. See p. 288.
8. *F. M. Dostoevsky, materialy i issledovaniya*, p. 87.

NOTES FOR CHAPTER 22

1. "Dostoevsky on *The Brothers Karamasov*," translated by S. S. Koteliansky, *The New Criterion*, No. 3 (1926), III, 552-3.
2. *F. M. Dostoevsky, materialy i issledovaniya*, p. 126.
3. Ibid., pp. 129, 138.
4. "Dostoevsky on *The Brothers Karamasov*," pp. 554-5.
5. Ibid., p. 555.
6. Ibid., p. 557-8.
7. N. N. Strakhov, *Biografiya* (quoted by A. S. Dolinin in *F. M. Dostoevsky, materialy i issledovaniya*, pp. 79-80).

BIBLIOGRAPHY

Systematic bibliographical studies of Dostoevsky's productions in Russia and of all works about him, from 1846 to 1929, have been published. A list of these studies, as well as the bibliography from 1923 to 1929, may be found in the last volume of Dostoevsky's complete works—*Stati, gosudarstvennoe izdatelstvo* (Moscow-Leningrad, 1930), XIII, 617-25. A bibliography of Western European works on Dostoevsky up to 1923 has been made by Jan M. Romein—*Dostojewskij in der Westersche kritiek* (Haarlem, 1924). The list added below, culled from the mass of Dostoevsky bibliography, is highly selective. It consists mostly of critical books and articles which have some pertinency to the various problems considered in the present study, and special emphasis is placed on recent material.

I SOURCE MATERIAL

Dostoevski, F. M., *Polnoe sobranie khudozhestvennykh proizvedeni,* gosudarstvennoe izdatelstvo (Moscow-

Leningrad, 1926-30), vols. I-XIII. Vols. XI-XII contain *Dnevnik Pisatelya,* and the last volume the miscellaneous articles. With the exception of the journalistic articles and *The Diary of a Writer,* Dostoevsky's works have been translated by Constance Garnett: *The Novels of Fyodor Dostoevsky* (London, 1912-20), vols. I-XII. *The Diary of a Writer* has been translated in full by Boris Brasol (Scribner's, New York, 1949, 2 vols.).

Pisma, ed., A. S. Dolinin (Moscow-Leningrad, 1928-34), vols. I-III. The last volume of this set has not yet been published. Some of the same letters have been translated from the German by Ethel C. Mayne: *Letters of F. M. Dostoevsky to his Family and Friends* (London, 1914).

Pisma Dostoevskogo k zhene, ed., V. F. Pereverzev (Moscow-Leningrad, 1926). Translated by Elizabeth Hill and Doris Mudie: *The Letters of Dostoevsky to his Wife* (New York, 1930).

Chetyre stati, 1847, iz neizdannykh proizvedeni, ed., V. S. Nechaeva (Petrograd, 1922).

Dostoevskaya, A. G., *Dnevnik,* 1867 g. (Moscow, 1922). Translated from the German edition of René Fülöp-Miller and Fr. Eckstein by Madge Pemberton: *The Diary of Dostoyevsky's Wife* (New York, 1928).

Vospominaniya, ed., L. P. Grossman (Moscow, 1925). Some material not included in these reminiscences of Dostoevsky's wife was later published in *F. M. Dostoevski, stati i materialy,* ed., A. S. Dolinin (Petersburg, 1922), I, 477-504. A large part of the volume was translated by S. S. Koteliansky and J. M. Murry: *Dostoevsky: Letters and Reminiscences* (New York, 1923), and in *Dostoevsky Portrayed by his Wife: the Diary and Reminiscences of Mme Dostoevsky,* translated and edited by S. S. Koteliansky (New York, 1926).

Strakhov, N. N., *Biografiya, pisma i zametki iz zapisnoi knizhki Dostoevskogo* (St. Petersburg, 1883).

Cheshikhin-Vetrinski, V. E., editor, *F. M. Dostoevski v vospominaniyakh sovremennikov, pismakh i zametkakh* (Moscow, 1912).

Brodski, N. L., editor, *Dokumenty po istorii literatury i obshchestvennosti* (Moscow, 1912).

Grossman, L. P., editor, *Dostoevski na zhiznennom puti* (Moscow, 1928).

Komarowitsch, W. L., editor, *Die Urgestalt der Brüder Karamasoff: Dostojewskis Quellen, Entwürfe und Fragmente* (München, 1928).

Sakulin, P. N., and Belchikov, N. F., editors, *Iz arkhiva F. M. Dostoevskogo, Idiot* (Moscow-Leningrad, 1931).

Glivenko, I. I., editor, *Iz arkhiva F. M. Dostoevskogo, Prestuplenie i Nakazanie* (Moscow-Leningrad, 1931).

Dolinin, A. S., editor, *F. M. Dostoevski, materialy i issledovaniya* (Leningrad, 1935).

Konshina, E. N., editor, *Zapisnye tetradi F. M. Dostoevskogo* (Moscow-Leningrad, 1935).

Grossman, L. P., editor, "Pervaya zapisnaya knizhka," *Zvenya*, No. 6 (1936), pp. 413-38.

Dolinin, A. S., *V tvorcheskoi laboratorii Dostoevskogo* (Moscow, 1947).

II CRITICAL LITERATURE

Abraham, Gerald, *Dostoevsky* (London, 1936).

Ashevsky, S., "Dostoevski i Belinski," *Mir Bozhi*, No. 1 (1904), pp. 197-239.

Avanesov, P. I., "Dostoevski v rabote nad *Dvoinikom*," *Tvorcheskaya istoriya*, ed., N. K. Piksanov (Moscow, 1927), pp. 154-91.

Bakhtin, M. M., *Problemy tvorchestva Dostoevskogo* (Leningrad, 1929).

Belchikov, N. F., "Dostoevski i Pobedonostsev," *Krasny arkhiv*, No. 2 (1922), pp. 240-55.

"Kak pisal romany Dostoevskogo," *Pechat i revoliutsiya* (1928), II, 88-93.

"Chernyshevski i Dostoevski," *Pechat i revoliutsiya* (1928), V, 35-53.

Dostoevski v protsesse petrashevtsev (Leningrad, 1936).

Beletsky, A. I., "Dostoevski i naturalnaya shkola v 1846 g.," *Nauka na Ukraine* (Kharkov, 1922), IV, 332-42.

Bem, A. L., editor, *O Dostoevskom, sbornik statei* (Prague, 1929-33), vols. I-II.

editor, *Dostojevskij, sbornik statí* (Prague, 1931).

Berdyaev, N. A., *Dostoievsky: an Interpretation* (London, 1934).

Borshchevski, S., "Shchedrin i Dostoevski," *Literaturny kritik,* (1939), v-vi, 66-102; viii-ix, 85-108.

Brodski, N. L., editor, *Tvorcheski put Dostoevskogo* (Leningrad, 1924).

Carr, E. H., *Dostoevsky* (London, 1931).

Chulkov, G. I., "Dostoevski i pleyada Belinskogo," *Nekrasov* (Leningrad, 1926).

Chulkov, G. I., "Dostoevski i utopicheski sotsializm," *Katorga i ssylka,* Nos. 2-3 (Moscow, 1929), pp. 9-36, 134-51.

   Kak rabotal Dostoevski (Moscow, 1939).

Coleman, S. M., "Phantom Double," *British Journal of Medical Psychology* No. 14 (1934), pp. 254-73.

Cyževskyi, Dmitri, editor, *Dostojewskij-Studien* (Reichenberg, 1931).

Dobroliubov, N. A., *Zabitye liudi* (Moscow, 1923).

Dolinin, A. S., editor, *Dostoevski, stati i materialy* (Leningrad, 1922-5), vols. i-ii.

   "Ispoved Stavrogina," *Literaturnaya mysl* (1923), i, 138-62.

   "Dostoevski sredi petrashevtsev," *Zvenya,* No. 6 (1936), pp. 512-45.

Dorovatovskaya-Liubimova, V. S., "*Idiot* Dostoevskogo i ugolovnaya khronika ego vremeni," *Pechat i revoliutsiya* (1928), iii, 31-53.

F. M. Dostoevski, Trudy gosudarstvennoi akademii khudozhestvennykh nauk (Moscow, 1928).

   Klassiki v marksistskom osveshchenii, sbornik statei (Moscow, 1929).

Freud, S., "Dostoevsky and Parricide," *The Realist* (London, 1929), ii, 18-33.

Fülöp-Miller, René, *Der unbekannte Dostojewski,* (München, 1926).

Gide, André, *Dostoevsky,* translated from the French, with an introduction by Arnold Bennett (New York, 1926).

Glivenko, I. I., "*Prestuplnie i Nakazanie,* materialy k romanu," *Krasny arkhiv,* No. 7 (1924), pp. 145-200.

   "Raskolnikov i Dostoevski," *Pechat i revoliutsiya* (1926), iv, 70-82.

Gorbachev, G. E., "Sotsialnye korni propovedi Dostoevskogo," *Borba klassov,* Nos. 1-2 (Moscow, 1924), pp. 172-207.

Gorki, M. *Stati* (Petrograd, 1918).

Grigorovich, D. V., *Literaturnye vospominaniya,* ed., V. L. Komarovich (Leningrad, 1928).

Grossman, L. P., "Gofman, Balzak i Dostoevski," *Sofiya* (1914), No. 5.

"Problema realizma Dostoevskogo," *Vestnik Evropy,* No. 2 (1917), pp. 65-99.

Tvorchestvo Dostoevskogo (Odessa, 1921).

Seminari po Dostoevskomu (Moscow, 1923).

Put Dostoevskogo (Leningrad, 1924).

Poetika Dostoevskogo (Moscow, 1924).

Spor o Bakunine i Dostoevskom (Leningrad, 1926).

Istomin, K. K., *Nachala i kontsy tvorchestva* Dostoevskogo (Moscow, 1922).

Ivanov, V., "Dostoevski i roman-tragediya" in *Borozdy i mezhi* (Moscow, 1916).

Kampmann, T., *Dostojewski in Deutschland* (München, 1931).

Kappen, Richard, *Die Idee des Volkes bei Dostojewski* (Würzburg, 1936).

Kashina-Evreinova, A. A., *Podpole geniya* (Petrograd, 1923).

Kaus, Otto, *Dostojewski und sein Schicksal* (Berlin, 1923).

Kirpotin, V. Ya., *Molodoi Dostoevski* (Moscow, 1947).

Kirpotin, V. Ya., *F. M. Dostoevski* (Moscow, 1947).

Komarovich, V. L., "Neizdannaya glava romana *Besy* F. M. Dostoevskogo," *Byloe,* No. 18 (1922), pp. 219-26.

"Mirovaya garmoniya Dostoevskogo," *Atenei* (Leningrad, 1924), I-II, 112-42.

"Genezis romana *Podrostok*," *Literaturnaya mysl* (Leningrad, 1925), IV, 366-86.

Dostoevski, sovremennye problemy istoriko-literaturnogo izucheniya (Leningrad, 1925).

Koni, A. F., *Vospominaniya* (St. Petersburg, 1906), pp. 73-90.

Lavrin, Janko, *Dostoevsky, A Study* (London, 1943).

Leontiev, K. N., *Sobranie sochineni* (St. Petersburg, 1912), VII, 438-48; VIII, 151-216.

Lloyd, J. A. T., *Fyodor Dostoevsky* (London, 1947).

Losini, F., *Eine Studie uber Dostojevskij* (Rome, 1932).

Loygue, G., *Un homme de génie—Th. M. Dostojewsky*.
  Étude médico-psychologique (Lyon, 1904).

McDowall, Arthur, *"The Possessed* and Bolshevism," London Mercury, No. 97 (Nov. 1927), xvii, 53-61.

Meier-Gräfe, Julius, *Dostojewski der Dichter* (Berlin, 1926).

Merezhkovsky, D. S., *Tolstoi as Man and Artist, with an Essay on Dostoevsky* (New York, 1902).
  Prorok russkoi revoliutsii (St. Petersburg, 1906).

Mikhailovsky, N. K., *Poslednie sochineniya* (St. Petersburg, 1905), ii, 254-308.

Modzalevsky, B. L., "Dostoevsky o *Bratyakh Karamazovykh," Byloe*, No. 15 (1920), pp. 99-134.

Murry, J. M., *Fyodor Dostoevsky, a Critical Study* (London, 1924).

Neufeld, J., *Dostojewski. Skizze zu einer Psychoanalyse* (Wien, 1923).

Pereverzev, V. F., *Tvorchestvo Dostoevskogo* (Moscow, 1912, 3rd, ed., 1928).

Pisarev, D. I., *Polnoe sobraine sochineni* (St. Petersburg, 1911), v, 247-305.

Pogozheva, L., "Kompozitsiya romana *Prestuplenie i Nakazanie," Literaturnaya ucheba*, Nos. 8-9 (Aug.-Sept. 1939), pp. 110-20.
  "Masterstvo kolorita u Dostoevskogo," *Literaturnaya ucheba*, No. 4 (April 1939), pp. 51-61.

Pokrovsky, G. A., *Muchenik bogoiskatelstva* (Moscow, 1929).

Polyakova, M., "Dostoevski v otrazhenii sovremennosti," *Literatura i marksizm*, No. 6 (Moscow, 1929), pp. 117-45.
  "Sotsialnaya priroda geroev Dostoevskogo," *Novy Mir* (1931), iv, 145-54.

Rahv, Philip, "Dostoevski and Politics: Notes on *The Possessed," Partisan Review* (July 1938), pp. 25-36.

Rank, Otto, "Der Doppelgänger," *Imago* (1914), vol. iii.

Reizov, V. G., "K istorii zamysla *Bratev Karamazovykh," Zvenya*, No. 6 (1936), pp. 545-73.

Rozanov, V. V., *Legenda o velikom inkvizitore* F. M. Dostoevskogo, 3rd. ed. (St. Petersburg, 1906).

Rozanova, A. P., *Gody blyzosti s Dostoevskim* (Moscow, 1928).

Shchegolev, P., *Petrashevtsy*, sbornik materialov (Moscow, 1926-8), vols. I-III.

Shestov, L., *Dostojewski und Nietzsche*, Philosophie der tragödie, aus dem Russischen übertragen von R. von Walter (Berlin, 1931).

Skabichevsky, A. M., *Sochineniya*, 3rd. ed. (St. Petersburg, 1903), II, 685-746.

Skobtsova, E. I., *Dostoevski i sovremennost* (Paris, 1929).

Smith, S. Stephenson, Isotoff, Andrei, "The Abnormal from Within: Dostoevsky," *The Psychoanalytic Review*. No. 4 (Oct. 1935), XXII, 361-91.

Soloviev, V. S., *Sobranie sochineni*, 2nd. ed. (St. Petersburg, 1912), III, 186-223.

Squires, P. C., "Fyodor Dostoevsky. A Psychopathographical Sketch," *The Psychoanalytic Review*, No. 4 (Oct. 1937), XXIV, 365-87.

Suarès, André, *Trois hommes: Pascal, Ibsen, Dostoevski* (Paris, 1919).

Troyat, Henri, *Firebrand. The Life of Dostoevsky* (London, 1947).

Tseitlin, A., *Povesti o bednom chinovnike Dostoevskogo* (Moscow, 1923).

"Prestuplenie i Nakazanie i Les Misérables," *Literatura i marksizm* (1928), V, 20-58.

Tynyanov, Iu., *Dostoevski i Gogol* (Moscow, 1921).

Uspenski, G. I., *Polnoe sobranie sochineni* (Kiev, 1903), IX, 250-84.

Verner, I., "Tip Kirillova," *Novy Put* (1903), X-XII.

Vinogradov, V. V., *Evoliutsiya russkogo naturalizma: Gogol i Dostoevski* (Moscow, 1929).

Volynski, A. L., *Dostoevski* (St. Petersburg, 1906).

Yarmolinsky, Avrahm, *Dostoevsky, a Life* (New York, 1934).

Zamotin, I. I., *F. M. Dostoevski v. russkoi kritike 1846-81* (Warsaw, 1913).

Zhukov, L. A., "Kritika kapitalizma u Dostoevskogo," *Trudy instituta* (Moscow, 1938), pp. 138-58.

Zweig, Stefan, *Three Masters, Balzac, Dickens, Dostoevsky*, translated from the German by Eden and Cedar Paul (London, 1930).

Index

ERNEST J. SIMMONS, after thirty years of teaching at Harvard, Cornell, and Columbia, where he was Chairman of the Department of Slavic Languages and Professor of Russian literature at the Russian Institute, resigned in 1959 to devote his time to writing. As a member of learned organizations, he pioneered in developing Russian Area Studies in America, edited *The American Slavic and East European Review*, and founded and edited Columbia Slavic Studies. He made various research trips to Russia and in 1947 went there on a cultural mission for the American Council of Learned Societies. Professor Simmons has lectured widely in the United States as Phi Beta Kappa Visiting Scholar and Danforth Lecturer, and also in many European universities. Known as an outstanding critic of Russian literature, he has edited scholarly volumes and contributed frequently to learned journals and literary periodicals here and abroad. Of the books which he himself has written, the best known are *Pushkin* (1937), *Leo Tolstoy* (1946), and *Russian Fiction and Soviet Ideology* (1958). *Dostoevsky, the Making of a Novelist* was originally published in 1940. His most recent book is *Chekhov, a Biography* (1962). Professor Simmons is married, has one son, and lives in Dublin, New Hampshire.

THE TEXT of this book is set in Caledonia, a Linotype face designed by W. A. Dwiggins. Caledonia belongs to the family of printing types called "modern face" by printers—a term used to mark the change in style of type-letters that occurred about 1800. Caledonia borders on the general design of Scotch Modern, but is more freely drawn than that letter. Composed, printed, and bound by H. Wolff Book Manufacturing Co., New York, N. Y.